SUSTAINING DEVELOPMENT

NEW HORIZONS IN ENVIRONMENTAL ECONOMICS

This important series is designed to make a significant contribution to the development of the principles and practices of environmental economics. It includes both theoretical and empirical work. International in scope, it addresses issues of current and future concern in both East and West and in developed and developing countries.

The main purpose of the series is to create a forum for the publication of high quality work and to show how economic analysis can make a contribution to understanding and resolving the environmental problems confronting the world in the twenty-first century.

Recent titles in the series include:

Biodiversity, Conservation and Sustainable Development
Principles and Practices with Asian Examples
Clem Tisdell

Green Taxes
Economic Theory and Empirical Evidence from Scandinavia
Edited by Runar Brännlund and Ing-Marie Gren

Global Environmental Change and Agriculture
Assessing the Impacts
Edited by George Frisvold and Betsey Kuhn

The Political Economy of Environmental Policy
A Public Choice Approach to Market Instruments
Bouwe R. Dijkstra

The Economic Valuation of Landscape Change
Theory and Policies for Land Use and Conservation
José Manuel L. Santos

Sustaining Development
Environmental Resources in Developing Countries
Daniel W. Bromley

Valuing Recreation and the Environment
Revealed Preference Methods in Theory and Practice
Edited by Joseph A. Herriges and Catherine L. Kling

Designing Effective Environmental Regimes
The Key Conditions
Jørgen Wettestad

Environmental Networks
A Framework for Economic Decision-Making and Policy Analysis
Kanwalroop Kathy Dhanda, Anna Nagurney and Padma Ramanujam

The International Yearbook of Environmental and Resource Economics 1999/2000
Edited by Henk Folmer and Tom Tietenberg

Sustaining Development

Environmental Resources in Developing Countries

Daniel W. Bromley

Anderson-Bascom Professor of Applied Economics, University of Wisconsin-Madison, USA

NEW HORIZONS IN ENVIRONMENTAL ECONOMICS

Edward Elgar

Cheltenham, UK • Northampton, MA, USA

Published by
Edward Elgar Publishing Limited
Glensanda House
Montpellier Parade
Cheltenham
Glos GL50 1UA
UK

Edward Elgar Publishing, Inc.
6 Market Street
Northampton
Massachusetts 01060
USA

A catalogue record for this book
is available from the British Library

Library of Congress Cataloguing in Publication Data

Bromley, Daniel W., 1940–
Sustaining development : environmental resources in developing countries / Daniel W. Bromley.
(New horizons in environmental economics)
Includes index.
1. Sustainable development—Developing countries. 2. Natural resources—Developing countries—Management. 3. Right of property–
–Developing countries. 4. Environmental policy—Developing countries. 5. Developing countries—Economic policy.
6. Deforestation—Developing countries—Case studies. I. Title.
II. Series.
HC59.72.E5B76 1999
333.7′09172′4—dc21 98–45767
CIP

ISBN 1 85898 888 8

Printed and bound in Great Britain by Bookcraft (Bath) Ltd.

Contents

PART III EMPIRICAL ISSUES

Acknowledgements

The publishers wish to thank the following who have kindly given permission for the use of copyright material.

American Journal of Agricultural Economics for article: 'The Village Against the Center: Resource Depletion in South Asia', with Devendra P. Chapagain, **66**(5), December 1984, 868–73.

Blackwell Publishers for article: 'Reconstituting Economic Systems: Institutions in National Economic Development', *Development Policy Review*, **11**(2), 1993, 131–51, reset.

Carfax Publishing Ltd for articles: 'Co-Management or No Management: The Prospects for Internal Governance of Common Property Regimes through Dynamic Contracts', with Brent M. Swallow, *Oxford Agrarian Studies*, **22**(1), 1994, 3–16; and 'Necessity and Purpose in Chinese Agriculture: 1949–95', with Zhiqun Xue-Lascoux, *Oxford Development Studies*, **24**(3), 1996, 261–80.

Elsevier Science for articles: 'Development Reconsidered: The African Challenge', *Food Policy*, **20**(5), 1995, 425–38; 'Property Relations and Economic Development: The Other Land Reform', *World Development*, **17**(6), 1989, 867–77; 'Indigenous Land Rights in Sub-Saharan Africa: Appropriation, Security and Investment Demand', with Espen Sjaastad, *World Development*, **25**(4), 1997, 549–62; 'Property Rights, Externalities and Resource Degradation: Locating the Tragedy', with Bruce A. Larson, *Journal of Development Economics*, **33**(2), 1990, 235–62, reset; 'Extensification of Agriculture and Deforestation: Empirical Evidence from Sudan', with Abdelmoneim H. Elnagheeb, *Agricultural Economics*, **10**, 1994, 193–200; and 'Natural Resource Prices, Export Policies, and Deforestation: The Case of Sudan', with Bruce A. Larson, *World Development*, **19**(10), 1991, 1289–97.

Frank Cass Ltd for article: 'The Economics of Cain and Abel: Agro-Pastoral Property Rights in the Sahel' with Rogier van den Brink and Jean-Paul Chavas, *Journal of Development Studies*, **31**(3), February1995, 373–99.

Island Press for excerpt: 'Economic Dimensions of Community-Based Conservation', in David Western, R. Michael Wright and Shirley C. Strum (eds), *Natural Connections: Perspectives in Community-Based Conservation*, 1994, 428–47, reset.

Journal of Economic Issues and Association for Evolutionary Economics for article: 'The Enclosure Movement Revisited: The South African Commons', **XXVIII**(2), June 1994, 357–65.

Kluwer Academic Publishers for articles and excerpt: 'The Commons, Common Property, and Environmental Policy', *Environmental and Resource Economics*, **2**, 1992, 1–17; 'Institutions, Governance and Incentives in Common Property Regimes for African Rangelands', with Brent M. Swallow, *Environmental and Resource Economics*, **6**, 1995, 99–118; 'Rainfed Mechanized Farming and Deforestation in Central Sudan', with Abdelmoneim Hashim Elnagheeb, *Environmental and Resource Economics*, **2**, 1992, 359–71; and 'Deforestation: Institutional Causes and Solutions', in Matti Palo and Jussi Uusivuori (eds), *World Forests, Society and Environment*, forthcoming 1998.

The University of Chicago for article: 'On Risk, Transactions, and Economic Development in the Semiarid Tropics', with Jean-Paul Chavas, *Economic Development and Cultural Change*, **37**(4), July 1989, 719–36.

Every effort has been made to trace all the copyright holders but if any have been inadvertently overlooked the publishers will be pleased to make the necessary arrangements at the first opportunity.

PART I

THE DEVELOPMENT PROBLEM

[1]

Sustaining development

The enduring economic problem concerns how to organize human action such that 'making a living' today is not destructive of the prospects that future persons will also be able to 'make a living'. This approach, I admit, sounds like yet another definition of 'sustainable development'. I have chosen a title for this collection that is equally suggestive. My use of 'sustaining' is purposefully in the indefinite form because the economic problem is not to discover *the* 'sustainable path' and stick to it, but rather to keep working on the institutional arrangements of the economy so that human action is guided in propitious directions. Sustaining development is not something we get right once – it is something that we must work on every day.

This idea of a continual reworking of the institutional arrangements in a developing economy may strike some readers as odd. Most of economic analysis posits some maximization problem and then sets out to derive the necessary and sufficient conditions for an efficient allocation of resources. In many development studies the institutional structure is considered exogenous and the problem becomes one of 'getting prices right' so that atomistic agents will behave in the 'correct' (that is, efficient) manner. From this presumption of right behaviour human action will conduce to bounteous agricultural production, the generation of an economic surplus in rural areas, the creation of new jobs in urban manufacturing, the proper use of the natural environment, and the realization of a modern economy in which agriculture is but a minor part of total economic activity.

Of course 'getting prices right' follows logically from the prior problem of getting the *institutional arrangements right*. However, institutional arrangements (the working rules of an economy) are rarely 'right' and that is the fundamental policy problem in the developing world. And, as I cautioned above, getting the rules right is not something that happens once – it is a process that is forever under way.

The articles collected together here represent conceptual and empirical work on the economic development problem in general, and on the environmental dimensions of economic development in particular. The empirical work is drawn largely from the doctoral dissertations of my former graduate students who appear here as my co-authors. Throughout, I have tried to pull together material that addresses both the conceptual and the practical aspects of the development problem.

The thread running through these chapters is that economics, properly understood, is the study of *how individuals and groups organize themselves for their provisioning*. And the essence of that organization is the institutional arrangements laid down both to liberate and to constrain individual behaviours. There is a tendency in much of the economics literature to imagine that these institutional arrangements can be picked for their efficiency properties and implications. That is, some suppose that there are efficient and inefficient institutional arrangements. However, it is a mistake to suppose that this is so – or that it is logically possible to be so (Field, 1979, 1984; Hodgson, 1998).

To be sure there are institutional arrangements that lead to greater *productivity* than other kinds, and it is precisely these institutional arrangements that we would like to identify and advocate provided, of course, that future productivity is not sacrificed for the sake of present productivity. But 'efficiency' is another matter altogether.

This problem with efficiency as a truth rule for institutional arrangements arises from the very concept of efficiency and Pareto optimality. Recall that every competitive equilibrium is Pareto optimal. From this it follows that every Pareto optimal outcome is a competitive equilibrium *with respect to some particular institutional set-up and resulting distribution of income* that constitutes the necessary starting point for any jockeying towards Pareto optimality. The problem, of course, is that public policy is precisely concerned with new institutional arrangements and economic agendas that will then hold profound implications for future relative endowments and incomes across the population. And these changes will then lead to yet a different constellation of Pareto optimal outcomes. If we imagine that policy is the quest for efficient institutions then we are seeking guidance on changes in the structural parameters of an economy when it is those very structural attributes that underpin the concept of Pareto optimality. If those structural attributes change then the Pareto optimal state will change. In other words we are invited to adopt a decision rule for institutional change (public policy) that is itself a function of changes in the system that the decision rule pretends to judge. The incoherence of this approach to public policy is comprehensive (Bromley, 1990).

This logical flaw arises from the failure in much of applied economics – and the policy advice it brings forth – to maintain a clear separation between the context of explanation of particular institutional arrangements, and the context of justification for those institutional arrangements. Recall that a theory with empirical content is a combination of a few core assumptions and postulates, together with auxiliary assumptions about the world the theory purports to explain. These auxiliary assumptions are often called 'applicability theorems' because they are plausible explanations of how the core model connects with the world we seek to understand. These assumptions make the model 'applicable' to the real world by transforming it from a story of human action into a testable theory about events in the real world. From this conjunction of the core model and the applicability theorems we can derive testable hypotheses about some economic phenomena of interest.

We build such theories with the presumption that human action is best explained by rational modes of thought and action. We then append some applicability theorems to that starting point and this gives us a theory that sees the world in terms of rational (and maximizing) modes of thought and action.

But then our explanation of economic phenomena based on this theory is used to offer theoretical justification for particular outcomes and modes of human behaviour. For example, the core model from economics predicts that *if* individuals are rational *then* they will respond to economic incentives and this will result in 'efficient' behaviour. This 'if–then' chain concerns the context of explanation. But the necessary barrier between explanation and justification is breached when the conclusion from the context of explanation (the 'then' part about responses leading to efficient choices) becomes the antecedent condition for a new 'if–then' chain that presumes the consequent of the prior chain (efficiency) to be the desired state.

The logical flaw here is that this new 'if–then' chain concerns not the context of explanation but rather the context of justification. If people are efficient then they will respond to relative prices as our model predicts. And if they do not so respond, then they should. Suddenly, economists – always reluctant to pronounce on what ought to be – are pleased to declare that efficiency ought to be the goal of public policy. And, in a related vein, social institutions (the working rules) should be selected on the basis of their efficiency-producing properties. Then human behaviour that does not seem consistent with efficiency – behaviour predicated on habit, custom, collective action motivated by a particular vision of the future – is labelled irrational and inefficient.

Notice that the desired consequence (efficiency) does not acquire its legitimacy and authority from any expression of the collective will (Mishan's 'ethical consensus'), but rather from the core model out of which it is derived. So economic theory – whose purpose is to explain and to predict – becomes, via the above logical twist, a vehicle to *justify* certain processes (markets) and outcomes (choices that are efficient). Economic theory becomes transformed from a mode of explanation into a mode of justifying particular social arrangements (institutions). This is where economics in the service of public policy goes off the rails (Bromley, 1990, 1997; Mishan, 1980).

We see this approach at work in several forms. We are told that property rights evolve in the interest of efficiency (and it is optimal that they should so evolve), that firms are efficient responses to transaction costs in markets (and markets are efficient responses to transaction costs in firms), and that the growth of the western world was made possible by the adoption of new efficient institutions that replaced the bad old kind that merely served to redistribute income (North and Thomas, 1971). We see here a quest for the explanation and *justification* of institutional arrangements using the choice-theoretic metaphor of economics. In logical terms, these are models of mechanical cause. The doctrine of mechanical cause sees events in the present *causing* outcomes in the future; events in time $t = 0$ *cause* an outcome in $t = 1$.

We see mechanical cause at work in policy analysis when we allege that deforestation in the tropics is *caused* by landlessness or by the construction of roads into wilderness areas, or by non-existent property rights, or by population growth. Mechanical cause suggests that underinvestment in natural resources or agricultural production in the tropics is *caused* by lack of secure property rights, and that pollution is *caused* by the wrong incentives on the firm. Mechanical cause is prevalent in economic analysis because it represents how we tend to think about economic processes. That is, we tend to regard present outcomes as the result of (as being caused by) prior events, and we regard future outcomes as the result of (as being caused by) present events.

Mechanical cause is at work in benefit–cost analysis when we compute future benefits and costs predicated upon changes undertaken today; then the present value is computed so that alternative actions might be considered and compared. Mechanical cause is prevalent in research that seeks to assess the economic value of various aspects of the environment using contingent valuation methods. These monetized values then become the justification for future actions. Mechanical cause lies behind regulatory impact assessment (actually a subset of benefit–cost analysis) when assessments are made of how changes in the status quo will impose 'regulatory costs' (called 'losses') for the sake of some future uncertain benefits. These alleged 'costs' of regulations are then seen as causing the 'inflationary' impacts of particular regulations. The flaw here, of course, is that regulations *must be inflationary* or they are not doing their job. Finally mechanical cause is at work when we imagine that we can determine efficient legal rules (institutional arrangements) for the economy.

But of course an approach that seeks to explain institutional arrangements by appeal to economic causes and consequences is conceptually incoherent. As Schumpeter notes:

> when we succeed in finding a definite causal relation between two phenomena, our problem is solved if the one which plays the 'causal' role is non-economic. We have then accomplished what we, as economists, are capable of in the case in question and we must give place to other disciplines. If, on the other hand, the causal factor is itself economic in nature, we must continue our explanatory efforts until we ground upon a non-economic bottom (Schumpeter, 1961, pp. 4–5).

To Schumpeter this 'non-economic bottom' is the socio-cultural aspect of a polity that does not acquire its nature or content from economistic modes of thought and action. Such structures are predicated on habits, customs, beliefs, religion, and the shared commitments of the members of a particular community (or a nation-state). The cultural materialist would refer to these aspects as the 'superstructure' (Harris, 1979). The Schumpeterian imperative serves as a warning that the fundamental dimensions of our social existence cannot be reduced to the consequentialist effect of atomistic maximizing behaviour. That is, the institutional structures of an economy must be explained in other terms because these arrangements arise from other necessities, and they are sustained on other grounds.

To locate this other 'non-economic bottom' requires that we understand the critical role of a different version of causality. In essence, the doctrine of mechanical cause means that the *future is assessed in terms of the present*. A correct understanding of what it means to 'get the rules right' requires that the *present must be understood in terms of the future*. Public policy is the conjunction of new intentions, new working rules (new institutions), and compliance with those new working rules by atomistic economic agents. That is, policy – human volition at work – starts with an implicit conversation about the *purposes of the future*.

The political community contemplates the future and asks questions such as: what is the preferred configuration of land use in forested uplands? How clean should the water in streams and lakes be (or how much of certain diseases arising from polluted water is acceptable)? Or the political community may ask what sort of working conditions are considered acceptable for those who work in the nation's factories? Or the questions might concern housing and health care for the elderly. Finally, the political community may discuss whether schooling should be mandatory for children up to a certain age. From the answers to those questions an emerging consensus will ultimately prevail that advocates new parameters for land use, water quality, or new rules for safety in factories, new rules for housing policy and health care for the elderly, or new rules on school attendance for children. We might think of this as the 'future speaking to the present'.

The essential fallacy in much traditional policy analysis is that the analysis conflates two distinct *realms of reason*. It is not in doubt that economics is the application of reason to choice. The problem, however, concerns *whose* reason is relevant to collective choice. In conventional analysis, a proposed action – say a dam or some other type of project – is said to be justified if the NPV (Net Present Value) is non-negative (or if its Internal Rate of Return exceeds the current opportunity cost of funding). And, if the applied economist feels particularly pleased with the analysis, a claim might then be advanced to insist that the preferred policy is that which maximizes social welfare over time. In this formulation, the utility of future persons (as a time-period class) is discounted. The practical effect of this approach to public policy is that the *realm of reason of future persons* is pre-empted by the truth rule pertinent not to the future but to those of us now living. *Our* realm of reason (the present) becomes *their* realm of reason.

Is there an alternative to this epistemology? Can we find other grounds to provide justification for particular development policies? If so, the alternative paradigm must be grounded in an epistemology that sees causality and justification running *from the future back to the present*. This conceptualization of the policy problem requires a different vision of causation. It requires a metaphor that allows the purposes of the future to inform choice in the present. In other words, this vision of the policy problem requires the concept of *final cause*. Bertrand Russell had this to say about the idea of final cause:

> the 'final cause' of an occurrence is an event in the future for the sake of which the occurrence takes place... things are explained by the purposes they serve. When we ask 'why?'...we may mean either of two things. We may mean: 'What purpose did this event serve?' or we may mean: 'What earlier circumstances caused this event?' The answer to the former question is a teleological explanation or an explanation by final causes; the answer to the latter question is a mechanistic explanation (Russell, 1945, p. 67).[1]

When we understand final cause, it permits us to think about halting deforestation not because it is suddenly economically efficient to do so, but because of our commitment to how we wish the future to be constituted. A consideration of final cause might easily reveal that children should be required to attend school until some particular age (say 17 years), not because of any efficiency properties emanating therefrom, but because the future seems better than the present (and the past) if this rule were to be adopted. Of course, mandatory schooling deprives the labour force of cheap malleable labour. It is costly to establish a school system to accommodate all children; many families might suffer from the loss of their children's meagre earnings potential, and the present monetized value of the benefit stream arising from mandatory schooling is quite uncertain. But because public policy forces us to think of the present in terms of the future, mandatory schooling becomes an obvious thing to endorse. Not on utilitarian grounds, mind you, but on the grounds of the purposes of the future.

The problem with traditional policy analysis is that it has us explain and justify *future economic circumstance in terms of the present*. However, explanations and justifications of economic phenomena can only be logically coherent when they offer ways to *understand the present in terms of the future*. This, after all, is how humans choose. The human will in action – prospective volition – assesses the present in terms of the future. Indeed we are pleased to differentiate ourselves from the lower orders of life by our ability to 'reason backwards', as it were. Reasoning backwards is precisely the act of understanding the present in terms of the future, and deciding how we wish the future to unfold for us. When we approach public policy in this way, we are asking about the future purposes to be served by current choices. And when economists ask about the purposes of the future, we are able to assist in the formulation of development policies on the same terms as those whose task it is to move a nation-state (or a particular community within a nation-state) into the future.

If we would abandon models of mechanical cause in favour of models of final cause, we would be able to participate in the development process not as arbiters of ultimate truth (by advocating the circular concept of efficiency), but as advocates for clarity in problem formulation, the careful development of feasible solutions, the discussion of the advantages and disadvantages of various solutions, and then assistance in the difficult matter of programme implementation. In essence, the material in this book seeks to address the development problem from the perspective of final cause rather than mechanical cause.

Overview

The book is divided into three parts. In Part I, I address the institutional underpinnings of an economy. Chapter 2 concerns the essential role of law and the legal system in allowing the transition from a centrally planned economy to a market economy. This paper originally appeared in 1993, several years after the demise of the Soviet Union, while euphoria about the political and economic transition was strong. Having got rid of the oppressive hand of the Soviet state, the presumption was that a full-blown market economy would suddenly appear.

Now, some eight years after the collapse of the Soviet Union, the Belarus and Ukrainian economies remain in chaos, and the Russian economy is only slightly better off. In essence we see in the former Soviet Union attempts to build a market economy before there is a coherent state. In these circumstances, a number of individuals are getting rich from selling natural resources and other assets they probably do not own. Compounding this, the absence of the legal foundations of capitalism means that most transactions are, of necessity, enforced by what we call 'private ordering'. In less polite terms, contracts are enforced by brute force (thugs) with the cost of non-compliance often high and irreversible. Of course there are 'markets', but such markets have little to recommend them on efficiency grounds.

The point here is that a well-functioning economy consists of a set of ordered relations (institutional arrangements) that give structure to the realms of behaviour (opportunity sets) of atomistic economic agents. These institutions, by structuring opportunity sets, both liberate and constrain individuals, and they channel self-interest in generally useful directions. That is the purpose of such institutions.

In Chapter 3, Jean-Paul Chavas and I offer a related explanation of the role of institutions in guiding behaviour in highly uncertain environments. We offer tentative explanations for observed economic behaviours in the semi-arid tropics. In these settings, where institutional arrangements tend to be weak, one sees a preponderance of transactions restricted to the domains over which trust exists. Such behaviours constitute feasible survival strategies in highly variable settings. We argue, however, that economic development in such settings will not occur until transactions can transcend these realms of localized trust among transactors. The institutional under-pinnings of a market economy provide the collective good that can reduce transaction costs across time and space. When that happens, the spatial and temporal domain of transactions expands and the economic system becomes more integrated and more productive.

In Chapter 4 I address the traditional presumptions of economic development in Africa. This paper was first presented at a conference at the Rockefeller Foundation's Villa Serbelloni in Bellagio, Italy, where a small number of us gathered in 1993 to ponder the development prospects in sub-Saharan Africa. Here I explore two central problems in economic development. The first, and one that concerned Chapters 2 and 3, is that sub-Saharan Africa is a place where the idea of a transcendent nation-state is still being worked out. To the extent that economic development as that idea is generally understood is something that occurs in – and with the acquiescence and support of – a nation-state, the problem of an inchoate state is not a minor inconvenience. The second point of Chapter 4 is more metaphysical. Specifically, I ask whether the prevailing doctrine of 'development' that has occupied our mind since the end of the Second World War is still compelling and all-encompassing. In particular I question whether the implicit teleology in the development literature is still appropriate to Africa.

As we move to Part II of the book, the emphasis shifts from the development problem in general to the conceptual issues in the use and management of environmental resources in the developing countries. I start with a conceptual piece (Chapter 5) that seeks to establish clarity in terminology about property regimes over environmental resources. Beginning with early work in ocean fisheries that referred to such fisheries as 'common property', and continuing on to Garrett Hardin's misnamed 'tragedy of the commons', coherence in understanding property regimes has been in scarce supply. There is now an emerging consensus that the earth's atmosphere and the high seas are not 'common property' at all but open access resources over which no property rights exist. That is, true common property exists in those regimes in which multiple owners are clearly identified, their rights to something valuable are not in doubt – and those rights are, in fact, protected by some authority structure – and the group of co-owners has some management structure and process in place to mediate use of the resource. This chapter is concerned with clarifying and standardizing language and concepts about environmental property regimes.

In Chapter 6 I come to the first of several chapters that concern land ownership and land use in the developing world. In this particular chapter I was motivated by the common perception in the 1980s that the development prospects in many countries were impeded by the absence of private land. The point in this paper is that one must be careful not to confuse cause and effect in such matters. The 1980s was the time when the development assistance agencies seem to have discovered 'land titling' as an instrument of so-called 'tenure security'. This interest derived from – and reinforced – prevailing economic doctrine that the only 'efficient' (there is that word again) structure of assets is that which is as atomized as decision units are thought to be. Since western economies reify the atomistic decision-maker, it follows that land and other assets must also – if 'efficiency' is to prevail – be equally atomized.

But of course this imposition of atomism on other cultures is just that. This chapter seeks to explain that the degree of individualization of land control is a social artefact of a number of parameters – prominent of which is the inherent 'productivity' of the land resources. It is not necessarily the case that individual ownership and control *causes* increased productivity. To assume so is to fall victim to the dogma of mechanical cause. Rather, one must look at the *purposes* to be served by land and inquire as to the appropriate institutional arrangements in light of those purposes. If land is seen as playing an essential integrative role in an economy, then collective ownership and control may well be more 'productive' than individualized control. We must always be careful of imposing our values – and our analytical metaphors – about land ownership on those who might have a number of reasons to see the issue in a quite different light.

In Chapter 7, Espen Sjaastad and I carry the argument a step further. With the use of a more formal model of incentives and pay-offs, we show the conditions under which investment in higher productivity actually increases tenure security in land. This formulation turns conventional wisdom on its head and serves as a reminder that simple culture-bound explanations of complex phenomena are often simple and culture bound.

In Chapter 8, Bruce Larson and I explore a related point, again in very formal language. The problem we address here concerns the extent to which property relations can be said to *cause* different patterns of resource use (and misuse). This paper, as with the previous chapters, is a response to much received wisdom in the 1980s that common property resources must, of necessity, be overexploited in comparison to private property resources. As with most sweeping generalizations, we show that verity is in the details. We show in this chapter that collective ownership and management of renewable natural resources are not at all foredoomed to the bleak prospect of abuse and dissolution.

Continuing this theme, in Chapters 9 and 10 – both co-authored with Brent Swallow – we address the specific problem of grazing regimes in sub-Saharan Africa. In Chapter 9 we continue the discussion of the previous chapter by investigating the possibilities for coherent managerial regimes of common property resources. The discrete-time dynamic model illustrates the feasibility of common property regimes *if*: (1) the external boundaries of the regime receive official protection from some authority structure; (2) the number of users is 'small'; (3) the range resource is reasonably resilient with respect to current rates of use; and (4) the users share a somewhat long time horizon.

In Chapter 10 we extend this work by showing that there is considerable institutional richness embodied in what is usually called 'common property' regimes. We argue here that given this locally induced variability, and the fragile and detached nature of many African governments, group management regimes – under one of several variations of common property – may well be the most efficacious management structure of highly stochastic range resources.

In Chapter 11, I explore the incentives at the local level to manage biological resources. The issues being discussed here concern various institutional arrangements for assisting local people to enhance the sustainable management of environmental resources on which they are dependent. Often pressure for conservation originates at the international level, yet resource use must be altered in villages and remote forest locations far from the locus of concern for biodiversity. Mediating between these two distinct realms is often difficult.

Chapter 12 concerns itself with the process of land reform in a newly democratic

South Africa. The most obvious problem is one of the transference, as it were, of property regimes across political regimes. The issue here is that property rights are creatures of the political system in which they are given legitimacy. When a revolution occurs, as it certainly has in South Africa, of what continued legitimacy under the new structures and constitution are property regimes created under the old apartheid regime? In South Africa the first problem is to deal with land restitution claims of those who were dispossessed under apartheid. While there is interest in undertaking land reform, that must necessarily wait until the new government is sure about who actually owns the land. After all, the government cannot very well undertake a land reform programme regarding land of uncertain provenance.

The final chapter in Part II (Chapter 13) concerns institutional arrangements in Chinese agriculture between 1949 and 1995. Our concern here is to investigate the changing nature of various institutional arrangements in China across both time and space. We see considerable regional variability in these working rules, and we also see evidence that the Chinese are intent on experimenting with different arrangements over time. The Production Responsibility System was introduced first, soon to be followed by the Household Responsibility System. Finally, in the 1980s, we see an illustration of 'institutional dispersion' as the authorities continued to search for situation-specific incentive regimes.

In Part III the material turns towards more empirical work, with the emphasis being on incentives for those who use and depend upon environmental resources in the developing world. Devendra Chapagain and I undertook one of the early studies to explore how villagers say they would behave in several hypothetical situations (Chapter 14). This work in experimental economics follows that carried out in laboratories but our setting was Belkot Panchayat in Nepal. Our work challenges conventional wisdom that the dominant strategy in such settings is for villagers to free-ride on the good behaviour of others. The evidence finds support of a shared commitment to the well-being of nearby forest resources, regardless of how others behave with respect to the forest. To return to a theme discussed earlier in this chapter, beliefs and norms (super-structure) are found to be important factors in individual choice. The 'rational calculation of individual gain and loss' is – as we ought to expect – always mediated by the larger institutional background within which choice is exercised.

The enduring debate over the appropriate property regimes for environmental resources (discussed in Chapters 5, 6, 7 and 8) takes on an added dimension in Chapter 15 where we show the effects of climatic variability on the classic struggle between the sedentary farmer and the nomadic pastoralist. A dynamic programming model is used to illustrate the emergence of a dual economy where climate plays a decisive role in the somewhat fluid boundary between these two production systems in the West African Sahel.

The next three chapters continue our research in the Sahel, this time shifting to the Sudan. In Chapter 16 we focus attention on the implications of extensification of agriculture for forests. The price of charcoal, a byproduct of deforestation, was found to be an important explanatory variable in the areal expansion of agricultural production. We see in this work the important linkages between energy policies, agricultural policies, and forestry policies. In Chapter 17 a related issue is explored – the use of shelter-belts in new irrigated agriculture schemes. The Sudan Mechanized

Farming Corporation requires its farmers to devote at least 10 per cent of the total area to shelter-belts. Again we see the relation between agricultural policies and larger economic forces at work. Attitudes about the value of shelter-belts are important, but so is the price of gum arabic. If the price of gum arabic falls, or is expected to be low in the future, there is little interest in preserving shelter-belts, despite the official rule. If the Sudanese government would allow the producer price of gum arabic to rise then the incentive to preserve shelter-belts in agricultural areas increases to an important degree.

In Chapter 18 we continue our work on forestry-related issues in the Sudan, showing how government pricing policies contributed to the decline of the *Acacia senegal* forests and the eventual decline of the international market for gum arabic. The soil-conserving qualities of *Acacia* forests in the Sahel illustrate the delicate balance between the *commodity value* of certain natural resources and the *environmental value* of those same resources. We also see the critical nature of government pricing policies towards these multi-purpose natural assets.

Finally, in Chapter 19, I develop in greater detail the issue of final cause discussed in the early parts of this chapter. The setting is deforestation, and the epistemological issue is *why* deforestation exists – on the scale that it does – in the developing world. The empirical work in Chapters 16, 17 and 18 follows conventional economic analysis to suggest that deforestation *is caused by* low prices for gum arabic, high prices for charcoal, high agricultural prices, and so on. These empirical models employ the doctrine of mechanical cause, and the structure of the models – and their results – conform to our intuition and to economic theory. But, as explained at the outset, the notion of *why* in science has two meanings. The first meaning is one of prior cause, while the second meaning is one of purpose.

Is deforestation really *caused* by population growth or higher timber prices? Or is deforestation caused by the fact that governments find the export earnings from timber sales too compelling to resist? The answer, I suggest, is that both mechanical cause and final cause require consideration in our conceptual and empirical work. If we seek to *explain* deforestation only in terms of mechanical cause we will seriously miss a full explanation of why deforestation occurs in the first place. That is, our mechanical models can illustrate second-order effects on deforestation, but they cannot really explain *why* deforestation occurs. Put another way, given that there is (and will be) deforestation, we may be able to show why it increases or decreases as a function of the usual explanatory variables. But we will not answer the question of *why* until we build models that incorporate *purpose*.

Note

1. The idea of final cause is developed in greater detail in Chapter 19.

References

Bromley, Daniel W. (1990), 'The ideology of efficiency: searching for a theory of policy analysis', *Journal of Environmental Economics and Management*, **19** (1), 86–107.

Bromley, Daniel W. (1997), 'Rethinking markets', *American Journal of Agricultural Economics*, **79** (5), 1383–93.

Field, Alexander J. (1979), 'On the explanation of rules using rational choice models', *Journal of Economic Issues*, **13** (1), 49–72.

Field, Alexander J. (1984), 'Microeconomics, norms, and rationality', *Economic Development and Cultural Change*, **32** (4), 683–711.

Harris, Marvin (1979), *Cultural Materialism*, New York: Random House.

Hodgson, Geoffrey M. (1998), 'The approach of institutional economics', *Journal of Economic Literature*, **36**, 166–92.

Mishan, E.J. (1980), 'How valid are economic evaluations of allocative changes?', *Journal of Economic Issues*, **14**, 143–61.

North, Douglass and Robert P. Thomas (1971), 'The rise and fall of the manorial system: a theoretical model', *Journal of Economic History*, **31**, 777–803.

Russell, Bertrand (1945), *A History of Western Philosophy*, New York: Simon & Schuster.

Schumpeter, Joseph (1961), *The Theory of Economic Development*, New York: Oxford University Press.

[2]

Reconstituting economic systems: institutions in national economic development

The problem of economic transformation

The major economic transformations now under way in Eastern Europe and the former Soviet Union provide a convenient and compelling opportunity to assess the presumptions of economic development. Such rethinking is important not only for how academics regard the process of national economic transformation, but for policy guidance as well. Indeed the term economic 'transformation' may be more useful than the ambiguous and loaded term 'development'. But while the conventional discourse on development policy has focused on the agrarian nations of the tropics, difficult times in Eastern Europe[1] serve to remind us of the need to think more broadly – as well as more creatively – about what might be called the 'development problem'.

Stories in the popular press about Eastern Europe suggest that the challenges there are of a fundamentally different nature from those in, say, Asia or sub-Saharan Africa. In the tropics, the tradition has been to invest in infrastructure and in agricultural projects; only in the last decade or so have macroeconomic conditions received much attention. The policy response to these considerations – structural adjustment – is now standard fare. In certain settings these imposed efforts at getting 'prices right' have led to political unrest.

If early evidence from Eastern Europe is any indication, the primary concern there is to get capital and private titles into the hands of creative entrepreneurs freed from the heavy hand of the state. Markets will then evolve, goods and services will materialize, and economic conditions will improve. Macroeconomic policy is central to this transformation as well. Attention is paid, therefore, to the exchange rate of dubious currencies. While these changes are being debated, economic and social conditions continue to deteriorate at an alarming pace. Inflation is severe, and undermines not only current incomes but the value of assets recently distributed to citizens in the form of shares in private firms. Crime is increasing and we are witnessing the rise of a small class of entrepreneurs who may, if nothing else, affirm the worst propaganda of the Lenin–Stalin era.

Unfortunately most attention these days focuses on the standard macroeconomic conditions and prescriptions, while the essential ingredient in the transformation to a market economy remains undiscussed. That central idea in economic transformation is the *institutional preconditions for decentralized and autonomous markets* (see Chapter 3 and Schmid, 1992, for a treatment of related themes). It will be argued here that these institutional preconditions have been ignored in conventional development programmes in the agrarian tropics, and that they now run the risk of being overlooked as Western advisers consider the economic transformation problems of Eastern Europe.

This article starts with a few observations on the standard economic approach to the development problem. It then presents the essential institutional challenge to the conventional view of economic transformation, which will lay the foundation for a discussion suggesting a necessary reconsideration of the economics of development – one that recognizes the centrality of institutional arrangements as a necessary underpinning for any economic system.

The scope of economics in the face of development problems

Since Lionel Robbins, most economists see their subject as being concerned with constrained choice. In other words individuals and firms, faced with myriad wants and limited means, allocate scarce resources so as to maximize an objective (or utility) function. Most economists believe, as did Robbins, that the discipline of economics is 'neutral between ends'. With the incorporation of mathematics and statistics into the mainstream of economic theory, formal models – and hypothesis testing – have become the hallmark of real and 'rigorous science'. This formalism has helped contribute to the conviction that contemporary economics is more objective (more value-free), and hence more scientific, than that brand of economics practised by earlier economists. Finally most economists believe that efficiency is the *truth rule* by which all decisions should be evaluated (Bromley, 1990).

With an emphasis on resource allocation and efficiency, economics is at its most powerful when a number of other conditions can be regarded as exogenous. Tastes and preferences are best regarded as both exogenous and stable. The endowments that each market participant brings to the process of exchange are usually regarded as fixed. And, of course, the institutional set-up of the economy is beyond 'scientific' analysis. Given stable tastes and preferences, given fixed endowments, and given fixed institutional arrangements, maximization algorithms can be employed to great benefit. The insights derived from constrained maximization exercises are legendary and are not at issue here.

But an economist interested in broader questions – one interested in the political economy of development – would find these constrained maximization exercises unduly sterile. To liberate economics from the Robbins-inspired box of constrained choice, economics must be considered as the *study of how individuals and groups organize themselves for their material and social provisioning*. Resource allocation is certainly important in this broader conception of economics. However, on the basis of this more expansive notion, there is seen to be more to economics than mere maximization subject to a number of constraints. A meaningful economics of development cannot limit itself to the study of constrained choice problems. Nor can it only be concerned with aggregate indicators such as savings and investment, per capita income, and trade balances.

Under a broader notion of economics, one would feel free to undertake a study of the nature of the institutional arrangements in an economy, as well as the allocation of scarce resources undertaken *within* those institutional arrangements. Institutional arrangements of interest would include the conventions, rules, and entitlements that define domains of choice for economic agents. There are two levels of important economic transactions in a society. The first is concerned with negotiations and bargains over the structure of *choice sets*; it is here that transactions (*Ordnungspolitik*) take place about the 'rules of the game'. The second level of transactions, more familiar in conventional economics, concerns market transactions from within choice sets (Bromley, 1989a).

This article refers to the first kind of choices as entailing *institutional transactions*, and the second kind of choices as entailing *commodity transactions*. Institutional transactions can be about rules and conventions, or about entitlements such as property rights. As observed by Dahlman (1980: 85):

> In the process of defining property rights, the economic system must make two interrelated decisions ... The first is to decide on the distribution of wealth; who shall have the rights to ownership of the scarce economic resources even before, as it were, trading and contracting begin. The second refers to the allocative function of property rights; they confer incentives on the decision makers within the economic system ... one set of decisions must be treated as endogenous for the system, and constitute the exogenous conditions for each trading agent in the resulting set of trades; the second set of decisions is made in the context of the making of these trades.

When we start with this broader view of economics – one that admits the institutional set-up as a legitimate subject of scientific enquiry – we become concerned with the economic transactions that are endogenous to the economic system, yet *exogenous to any economic agent within the system*. Those economists who confine their work to constrained maximization algorithms, or those who believe that efficiency analysis is both necessary and sufficient to ensure objectivity in science, will avoid analysis of the endogenous dimension. They will, instead, show much more interest in maximizing models that take institutions, preferences, and endowments as exogenous.

However this partial approach is inadequate when the subject of interest is that of national economic development. Similarly the partial approach will fail to offer a coherent understanding of economies in transition, as in Eastern Europe. Imagine a serious discussion about national economic development in which the economist must avoid analytical consideration of: (1) changing tastes and preferences; (2) changing endowments; and (3) changing institutional arrangements. Indeed, national economic development (or economic transformation) in the absence of change in tastes and preferences, in the absence of change in endowments,[2] and in the absence of changes in institutional arrangements is a logical contradiction. To a certain extent, then, economics that is preoccupied with constrained choice is incomplete and often badly suited to a serious discussion of national economic development.

This is reflected in the fact that most economists address economic development through *growth* models. There, in the neoclassical version, factor and product prices respond to scarcity so that the economy tends towards full employment equilibrium. In the Keynesian variant, prices are less flexible and hence equilibria are possible in which unemployment persists and not all markets clear. However, national economic development is a process in which institutional arrangements – the rules of the economy – are the conscious variables of choice. Choices with respect to rules are driven by a collective determination of the performance indicators deemed appropriate for the society under study. For example, should the nation's natural resources be owned by the state and managed by a branch of the government, or should they be sold to individuals in the private sector? If the former course is followed, how will the extraction of certain natural resources be organized? If the latter course is followed, what share of the economic rents from the sale of natural resources will be expropriated through taxation?

Answers to these logically prior questions about the nature of the institutional set-up in an economy will be dominated by considerations of who is able to define the terms under which commodity transactions will occur. Let us turn to a discussion of that issue.

The institutional perspective

The institutional set-up of an economy is concerned, in the final analysis, with the nature of incentives that inform – and constrain – individual maximizing behaviour. These incentives are not independent of the perceived role of the state in that economy.

The incentive problem

An economy is a set of ordered relations among self-interested agents. The essential problem of economic organization is to design a set of signalling devices and hence signals that will guide these self-interested agents to act in the interest of the larger community. In this, the aggregate of individual actions will be larger than the mere sum of their parts. The problem for any nation-state is to create an institutional structure that comprises a signalling mechanism for atomistic agents. Markets provide that signalling mechanism. But markets cannot function in a state of nature. Markets, if they are to represent legitimate signalling, must function with low transaction costs. Transaction costs entail the costs of: (1) obtaining information about possible market opportunities; (2) negotiating contracts or bargains; and (3) enforcing bargains or contracts that have been achieved.

The nation-state, if it is to flourish, requires a low-cost economic signalling mechanism, and it must always strive to keep transaction costs low. The fragmented and autarchic economies in Africa are stifled by high transaction costs. Similarly, the command economies of Eastern Europe were burdened with very high information, contracting, and enforcement costs. In such circumstances bad signals result in poor economic performance. Indeed, in a command economy, prices are not meaningful information, but rather disinformation or propaganda. The transition to a market economy in Eastern Europe – and the improvement of the market economy in many agrarian nations – requires the greatest attention to be devoted to the nature and extent of signalling.

From all the press coverage and discussion about Russia's efforts at economic transformation, one would think privatization was both necessary and sufficient for the market to appear. However, there is nothing inherently good about privatization which justifies it as an end in and of itself. Rather, privatization is a means to some end, namely better signalling and hence better incentives transmitted to economic agents.

Even in the face of bad or missing signals, command economies were reasonably good at the 'bundling of resources' to provide those goods and services deemed to be important: science, education, health care, housing, and transportation. Even in a market economy the state will often play an important role in this process – either through the budget or through the law-giving activity of the legislature and the courts. In these circumstances, the state provides a 'public' good or a 'collective consumption' good. The legal foundations of exchange are a collective good in the sense that, once available, these institutional arrangements are available to all participants in the economy, and their use is not subject to rationing by congestion. They constitute the 'law' that reduces transaction costs and allows markets both to arise and to emit meaningful signals which reflect marginal values with some social significance. Not all prices are of equal normative significance; those from distorted or imperfect markets claim scant normative attention.

For the most part, conventional economics – and conventional approaches to economic transformation – fail to address the problem of the sequential nature of institutional innovation. Because institutions represent the rules and conventions of a nation-state, it is essential to recognize that collective values are the necessary building blocks of these institutions. Whose interests are to count? How will these interests be articulated through the political system? In a word, we cannot establish a meaningful and functioning economic system unless and until we have the coherent political entity we call the nation-state.

The sequential primacy of a nation-state suggests that we must start with some sense of an ethical consensus – what an economist would call the social welfare function – across the polity. This then leads to some sense of the purposes of the state and therefore its pertinent policy interests. We then get what we may call operating institutions – rules – that will frame individual domains of choice.

Law is the empirical manifestation of the transformation from a state of nature to a civil society – civil in the Kantian sense of *bürgerliche Gesellschaft* where we find the triumph of reason over emotion and brute force. A civil society requires the recognition of an authority system. Property rights mean nothing without the authority to enforce duties on non-owners. And here lies the fundamental dilemma confronting a Russia that wants to become a market economy. The Russian citizen, having just been liberated from one authority system, is understandably reluctant to create and empower another. However, it is impossible for the nations of Eastern Europe to have a market economy without an authority system that creates and legitimizes that market. That authority system can only come from a meaningful state; there is no middle ground. Unfortunately, in many agrarian nations of the tropics, the current state and its accompanying authority system are seen to squander scarce financial resources on military equipment and personnel, ostentatious lifestyles, and political friends who can offer the necessary support and legitimization.

The authority system will be manifest in terms of the legal relations it defines and enforces. As a start, we may regard the necessary characteristics of a meaningful and coherent legal system to be: (1) clear lines of authority and the division of responsibility among governmental units; (2) clarity and precision in legal rules; (3) mechanisms and processes for the protection of property rights; (4) procedures that offer stability and predictability; (5) a sense of fairness focused on law as process rather than outcome; and (6) accessibility of laws and regulations to the public (Dean, 1992).

As already noted, the central problem for any nation-state is to create an institutional structure that will channel self-interest into socially useful directions. This requires more than having government 'get out of the way'; it requires a new and prominent role for government as the agent of the political entity we know as the state. Without that there is a state of nature in which aggressive individuals can become very rich by selling what they probably do not own.

The economies of Eastern Europe and the agrarian tropics will not flourish until the existing political system reveals what sort of institutional structure it wishes to put in place. In the meantime, low-level anarchy prevails. The command economies of Eastern Europe were characterized by a legal system that entailed the *presumption of prohibition*. In other words, if it was not expressly written down it was presumed to be prohibited. As can be imagined, this presumption of prohibition stifled all manner of otherwise useful activity. In contrast, a viable economy requires a legal system that entails a *presumption of permission*; if it is not expressly forbidden, it is permitted. This profound shift in the burden of proof and liability for action stands as the basic issue in legal structures for a nation-state. With the presumption of prohibition, we end up with the fear of a powerful state and an oppressive government; in such circumstances there cannot be a viable economy. This situation describes the command economies of Eastern Europe. But the converse, a presumption of permission, must be seen as part of a larger consensus about which actions are impermissible. In other words, a system predicated upon a presumption of permission still needs to be embedded in a social fabric that sets general parameters for acceptable commercial behaviour.

Evidence to date would seem to suggest that the naive acceptance of the notion of the 'magic of the market' has beguiled the Russians into the pernicious idea that a market economy is one without laws. They seem to imagine that *laissez-faire* translates into 'anything goes'. On this tack, yet more chaos is to be feared. If this low-level anarchy is allowed to continue, can a new authoritarianism be far behind? But what is the nation-state to do?

The role of the state

Summing up his long experience in economic development work, Peter Bauer noted that a few principles determined the success of development effort (Bauer, 1991: 190–91):

> This historical experience...was not the result of conscription of people or the forced mobilization of their resources...Nor was it the result of forced modernization of attitudes and behavior, of large-scale state-sponsored industrialization...it was not brought about by the achievement of political independence, by the inculcation in the minds of the local people of the notion of national identity, by the stirring-up of mass enthusiasm for the abstract notion of economic development, or by any other form of political or cultural revolution. It was not the result of conscious efforts at nation building...or of the adoption by governments of economic development as a formal policy goal or commitment. What happened was in very large measure the result of the individual voluntary responses of millions of people to emerging or expanding opportunities created largely by external contacts and brought to their notice in a variety of ways, primarily through the operation of the market. These developments were made possible by firm but limited government, without large expenditures of public funds and without the receipt of large external subventions.

From Bauer's observations on development experiences, we can conclude that there are two fundamental roles for the state: (1) to establish an institutional structure (a collective good) that will encourage industry on the part of atomistic economic agents; and (2) to create the means and opportunities for that institutional structure to be modified through time as social and economic conditions warrant. Social efficiency is determined by the extent to which institutional arrangements can be fashioned to preclude equilibria at inefficient outcomes. Game theory demonstrates that the isolation problem (the classic prisoner's dilemma) results in stable outcomes at Pareto inefficient points. What is missing in the isolation problem is the institutional structure external to the group which creates the conditions whereby binding agreements can be established and enforced. It is these binding agreements that convert the isolation problem into the coordination game that we know as an assurance problem. In coordination games the equilibrium point (or points) are Pareto efficient (Bromley, 1989a).

Economic transformation and development are promoted to the extent that the state can foster institutional arrangements that will establish a *coordination problem* among its separate citizens; acting as independent economic agents. Rural or urban élites can have an inordinate influence on the design of the particular institutional structure chosen, and also on the transfer mechanisms that give rise to information, as well as to benefits and costs.

To think of the state as an *authority system* may serve to remind us that there must be a coercive force in any social setting, in the sense that entitlements – rights and duties – cannot exist, indeed can have no meaning, in the absence of an enforcement structure to which one can turn for protection of one's claims. The nation-state is an authority system whose purpose is to give meaning to all transactions. When one has rights it means that the state will come to one's defence in a dispute. To have clear contractual rights in exchange means that the state stands ready to enforce agreements surrounding that exchange. In this way the state is a party to every transaction.

The compelling question then becomes, how shall the state act in its capacity to influence the nature and content of market transactions? To address that question, we must turn to a more specific discussion of institutions and institutional change.

The institutional underpinnings of economic development

It has been suggested above that conventional economics has a tendency to model economic development as if fully articulated markets already exist. In the case of the transition to market economies in Eastern Europe, the tendency seems to be to suggest that widespread privatization will create its own market *de novo*. Under this assumption, the transformation problem is taken to be one of simply reallocating factors of production to their most productive use.[3] On this tack, the economist is modelling economic growth, with development regarded as the result of prior 'growth'. For instance, as incomes rise, as primary schooling rates increase, as infant mortality falls, and as diets improve, one would conclude that 'development' has occurred.

However, economic development – if it is to have a meaning in its own right – must be regarded as a far more comprehensive undertaking, one in which a wide range of *structural* aspects of the economy are purposefully modified as new circumstances warrant. On this approach, one undertakes explicit institutional change, the clear purpose of which is to 'get the rules right'. If we adopt this alternative view, economic transformation (or economic development) is a conscious act that causes economic growth as well as future economic development (and transformation). It should be noted that development is a *causal factor* rather than being a final product of a process of economic growth. Reference was made above to *getting the rules right*. The rules in this model are the institutional arrangements encompassing two related dimensions. The first of these reflects a regularity in human behaviour based on shared preferences and shared expectations of the actions of others, while the second is based on a socially sanctioned and enforced set of expectations of the actions of others. In other words institutions are capable of being demarcated into two classes: conventions and entitlements. A convention is a regularity in human behaviour which brings order and predictability to human relationships. An entitlement is a socially recognized and sanctioned set of expectations in a society with regard to *de jure* or *de facto* relations that define the opportunity sets of individuals with respect to the opportunity sets of others (Bromley, 1989a). Institutions permit us to carry on our daily lives with a minimum of repetitive and costly negotiation. *Institutions reduce transaction costs.*

John R. Commons defined an institution as: 'collective action in restraint, liberation, and expansion of individual action' (Commons, 1990: 73). To Commons institutions were the 'working rules of going concerns'. Such working rules indicate (Commons, 1968: 6):

> what individuals *must* or *must not* do (a duty), what they *may* do without interference from other individuals (privilege), what they *can* do with the aid of collective power (right), and what they *cannot* expect the collective power to do in their behalf (incapacity or exposure).

It is through the establishment of institutions that societies create markets. Indeed, markets can *only* exist within a legal system that has consciously set out to create ordered domains of exchange. A market is a process whereby ownership of, and control over, future income streams is transferred among participants. Markets are concerned with changes in ownership and control of future streams of benefits and costs. The essence of a market is the exchange of both information and ownership with an eye to the future. Markets are arenas of information about the terms of trade, about future expectations, and about future control over income streams. A market without rules *about* transactions is a contradiction in terms.

Realistic notions of markets, therefore, require that we imagine the existence of a large number of buyers and sellers separated across time and space, all acting to exchange items which, upon completion of the transaction, will leave both parties better off. Such notions of exchange require a legal environment in which willing buyers and sellers can negotiate trades. The requirements of any market are therefore, at minimum, ownership of the things to be exchanged and information about exchange opportunities. The essence of the legal foundation of an economy is to provide a predictable structure within which exchange activity can flourish. This legal foundation is required whether the economy is organized along lines that give the government a dominant role, or so that the private sector is the dominant active agent.

The difficulty comes with the realization that no economic system, whether market-oriented or command-oriented, can thrive if locked into an inflexible structure that does not recognize the exigencies of new technology, new scarcities, or new preferences on the part of buyers. Indeed, such flexibility is said to represent one of the main benefits of market as opposed to command processes. It is, however, a mistake to attribute this flexibility to the existence of markets rather than to the real cause, which is a legal environment that recognizes new opportunities and that functions to capitalize on those opportunities. Markets do not *cause* adaptation to new conditions. Rather, markets *allow* responses to those situations as permitted by the legal foundations of the economy.

The social problem, therefore, is to create a legal structure that offers both predictability and flexibility; a structure that establishes order, yet allows for change. We are concerned, therefore, with rules about transactions as well as with rules for *changing* rules about transactions. It is important to understand that predictability of institutional arrangements is not the same thing as inflexibility.

In the transactions referred to here as institutional transactions we encounter the domain in which the institutional preconditions of exchange are determined – with markets being but one special arena of exchange. The obvious interest here in institutional transactions lies in the fact that institutional change to encourage greater market activity in the developing countries will occur at the level of conventions and entitlements. In other words, the existing structure of rights and duties which defines current economic (commodity) transactions will be modified through institutional transactions to bring about a different structure of entitlements.

It is institutions that: (1) define the choice sets of independent economic sectors; (2) define the relationships among individuals; and (3) indicate who may do what to whom – and how much it will cost. It is the aggregate of institutional arrangements that determine, at a particular moment, economic conditions. In other words, there is a prevailing structure of norms, conventions, rules, practices, and laws that shape or define the choice sets of individuals and groups in an economy. In a centrally planned economy these are the input quotas, the production plans, the accounting prices, the shipping schedules, the housing supply, the availability of jobs, and the like. These institutional arrangements define the space within which individuals and groups are free to exercise decision-making discretion.

In a market economy, institutional arrangements consist of a different constellation of constraints and opportunities: tax laws, wage rates, contractual obligations for workers, products liability for commodities, health insurance premiums and coverage, working conditions in factories, farms and mines, and the like. This set of norms, conventions, habits, practices, customs, laws, and administrative rules defines choice domains: I can change jobs, I cannot drive at 90 miles per hour; I can build a house on a particular piece of land, I cannot build a cement factory; I can hire workers for my factory, I cannot refuse to hire them on religious or racial grounds.

So the institutional environment defines the choice domain – the opportunity set – within which members of the society may operate. But economic conditions also influence the structure of institutional arrangements. Patent and copyright laws create a particular environment within which intellectual innovation flourishes or suffers, and therefore technological change occurs or is stifled. When new technological and economic opportunities arise, it is necessary for new institutional arrangements to emerge to foster development of those opportunities. New economic conditions – for instance a new technical possibility – create the demand for a new law (an institution) which in turn makes the economic environment conducive to large investments in the development of that particular technology. New economic conditions create a need for a new institutional form, and that new institutional form then creates the new economic environment.

Let us now consider the different ways in which new institutional arrangements might come about, and the economic implications of these different sources of change in the choice domain of individuals (these are spelled out in more detail in Bromley, 1989a, 1989b).

New relative prices

Changes in relative prices – and so income opportunities – induce institutional change that will permit the attainment of greater income flows within the larger economy. This class of institutional change is familiar. New relative prices bring about increased economic activity in an arena in which existing institutional arrangements are not well suited to this new level of economic activity. The new prices create new income possibilities that require institutional innovation. Institutional change of this sort finds its origin in the notion of conventions and the coordination problem (Lewis, 1986; Ullmann-Margalit, 1977).

In this situation of institutional change, social attitudes about the economic activity under consideration are not important. The issue of paramount importance is the productive capacity of the economy.

New technical opportunities

Sometimes changes in technological opportunities induce institutional change to permit capture of new income streams. When this happens, factor and product mixes adjust to reflect new conditions of technical and price efficiency. Here, institutional change is driven by new technological opportunities that can increase the total production of goods and services and also increase economic efficiency.

In this instance, we would expect to see collective action undertaken by the manufacturers of the new technology and those inclined to purchase it. Social attitudes may have changed to the extent that the new technology may be regarded as superior in some sense: say, solar collectors that will allow shifts away from depletable fossil fuels. But there are other examples where the dominant motivation is less high-minded. What drives institutional change in this case are the prospects for new income streams among the manufacturers of the new technology, and the prospects for those using the new technology to save on costs.

New collective attitudes about relative income shares

Changes in collective attitudes about income shares across segments of the population sometimes induce institutional change to modify income distribution directly. Relative prices and hence factor and product mixes change accordingly, but as *effects* rather than *causes* of institutional change.

There are instances in which collective attitudes about the income shares of different segments of society change over time, resulting in new institutional arrangements to modify those relative shares directly. The Tudor poor relief efforts of the 1530s in England – and especially the subsequent Poor Law of Elizabeth's reign – signal early efforts at institutional reform of this type. The War on Poverty in the United States, and progressive marginal income tax rates, are other examples of institutional arrangements aimed at altering the income position of various segments of the population.

New collective attitudes about the full consumption set

Institutional change arises from yet another situation in which changes in collective attitudes about the nature and content of a nation's full consumption set induce institutional change to modify that set. Relative prices and hence factor and produce mixes will change accordingly, but again as *effects* rather than *causes* of institutional change.

The early nineteenth century saw a profusion of institutional changes in Britain as the undesirable human effects of the Industrial Revolution became both more apparent and less accepted. About this same time (1824) the Combination Acts were repealed with the purpose of allowing workers to collaborate for their mutual defence against the powerful factory owners. The Combinations of Workmen Act (1859) made explicit the right of workers to engage in peaceful picketing. These institutional changes, and many more, reflected changing attitudes about broad social welfare considerations. They were manifestations of the changing weight of social authority as between the owners of capital, including land, and the owners of labour. Admittedly, efforts to restrict the length of the work day were opposed by capitalists on economic grounds and some notion of their 'right' to an income.[4]

When social attitudes concerning child labour, slavery, or general safety conditions in the workplace are such that these situations do not give ground for much concern, then the economist would have one family of social indifference curves to consider. On the other hand, as attitudes change about these matters, then preferences for safety and humane working conditions will change. Both outcomes are, by definition, Pareto-optimal points since they lie on society's production possibilities frontier; both are productively efficient output combinations as are all possible points along the frontier. Moreover, both points are socially efficient, given particular social objectives as reflected in the two possible families of social indifference curves. Once institutional change had been carried out in response to new social attitudes, the price of manufactures would respond to these new institutional realities and the new top-level optimum would ultimately be attained. It should be noted that relative prices *follow* this type of institutional change rather than *drive* it.

The social utility function (U) is a 'collectivized' set of preferences based on the expression of choices through current collective mechanisms. Arguments in this function, and the weights attached thereto, are a reflection of the goods and services deemed pertinent by the citizenry. The mapping of two possible social indifference curves reflects a combination of two forces: changing preferences about worker safety in the social 'consumption bundle', and different weights assigned to workers *vis-à-vis* others in the social welfare function. With respect to this second factor, at any moment the social utility function (U) reflects in commodity space what the social welfare function (W) reflects in utility space.

It follows that judgements about the economic efficiency implications of institutional change require some general knowledge of the relevant social welfare function. The social indifference curves derive from the social utility function which is specified in terms of the bundle of goods and services (including public and/or collective goods). The social welfare function is specified in terms of the utilities of the members of society:

$$W = W(U_a, U_b, U_c, \ldots, U_i) \qquad (1)$$

The social welfare function is a collective choice rule which aggregates the preferences of members in society, and is understood to have a very special role in the problem of collective choice. Sen (1982) specifies four types of issues that are relevant to social choice: (1) the aggregation of individual *interests* to arrive at collective *decisions*; (2) the aggregation of individual *judgements* to arrive at collective *decisions*; (3) the aggregation of individual *interests* to arrive at *welfare judgements*; and (4) the aggregation of individual *judgements* to arrive at *welfare judgements*. The use of a social welfare function here is concerned with the fourth issue: the aggregation of individual judgements to arrive at a collective welfare judgement. In other words, the nature of the social welfare function is a matter of deciding how to aggregate individuals' judgements of welfare into some collective rule. This requires that collective judgements be made on the strength and relevance of judgements made by individuals in society. To put it somewhat differently, the problem is to determine whose interests will count as the economist attempts to aggregate their respective judgements about welfare.

The institutional change being considered here, where the driving force is one of new social attitudes rather than new relative prices or new technology, is concerned with *the reallocation of economic opportunity*. This is an ongoing process of modifying institutional arrangements (and thus redefining individual and group choice sets) in response to the changing nature of attitudes and preferences in society as a whole. It is not something driven by the relentless pursuit of productive efficiency, for the simple reason that for any given structure of institutions there are infinitely many productively efficient points along production possibilities' frontiers; and there are infinitely many institutional possibilities as well. Judgements about whether a particular institutional change is socially preferred (let alone socially optimal) cannot be made without knowledge of the relevant social welfare function.

From the foregoing, it should be obvious that the problem of economic transformations – or of economic development – is primarily concerned with what is called here 'reallocating economic opportunity'. To the extent that new institutional arrangements will provide the foundation for this reallocation of economic opportunity, we see that traditional approaches to development, operating as they do from within a given institutional set-up, necessarily miss the essence of development. But some institutional change in the name of 'economic development' may not necessarily accord with shared perceptions of desired future states. Two examples can be given.

Gaining new economic advantage

Opportunities arise in which some economic agents, because of their capacity to influence institutional arrangements, can obtain a new economic advantage. In such circumstances, institutional change is accomplished in the absence of new collective attitudes and/or new relative prices. The basic argument can be best presented as part of a general model of rent-seeking (Krueger, 1974).

The standard rent-seeking model can be discussed by considering an example in which less costly imported shoes are restricted from the market as a result of actions taken by domestic shoe manufacturers. I call this type of institutional change a *redistribution of economic advantage* (Bromley, 1989a). The difference between institutional change that redistributes economic advantage and that which reallocates economic opportunity, is to be found in the nature of the social utility function – and indirectly in the social welfare function. In the worker safety problem there existed a family of social indifference curves that revealed social efficiency to be consistent with an emerging preference for greater safety conditions. In the matter of import restrictions on shoes there is no social utility function that reveals such restrictions to be socially desired and therefore social efficiency is not achieved by the restrictions.

The redistribution of economic advantage consists in the creation of institutional arrangements that find no support in the social welfare function nor in the social utility function. In other words, certain economic interests are able to use their special position to secure selective institutional arrangements that will redound to their particular benefit as against the harm inflicted on others. *Rent-seeking* then becomes a description of the activity whereby economic agents compete for the rents created through the prior redistribution of economic advantage. Put somewhat differently, individual economic agents engage in political activities to redistribute economic advantage in their favour. Regulatory agencies ostensibly concerned with protecting others against just such behaviour will often exacerbate the situation by enhancing the flow of rents to the regulated sectors.

But seeking new economic advantage may be less prevalent in the development problem than efforts to preserve existing economic advantage. After all, economic development (or economic transformation) is, by definition, threatening to those reasonably well served by the status quo. Finally, let us consider situations in which existing advantages are preserved.

Maintaining existing economic advantage

In this instance, existing institutional arrangements are regarded as inviolate by those who will be harmed by institutional change, and these latter interests are able to use the legislature and the courts – or simply the 'informal' avenues of influence – to insulate themselves from the costs of change, without any collective consensus that they should be so protected. The existing institutional set-up yields income streams to the current owners of productive assets, and these income streams are predominantly determined by the existing institutional structure, including property rights. Such an institutional set-up – which largely determines the benefit streams accruing to those fortunate enough to have the protection of the state for a particular set of productive assets – is taken as the norm against which all institutional change is judged.

Under certain circumstances, those well served by the status quo will be able to resist all efforts at institutional change. Alternatively, when new institutional arrangements arise and are given effect through the law, the payment of compensation will often be demanded by those who claim to be harmed by the new institutional structure. We might think of this as an example of compensation as extortion.

A clear example of this final category of preserving current economic advantage is that of land reform in the former Spanish colonies of Latin America and the Philippines. In some places, all efforts at land reform have been averted by a small number of individuals with the capacity to influence the authorities. In other places, land reform proceeds only in the presence of compensation. Under either situation, we see an important form of rent-seeking. When a new institutional set-up is introduced, it is the manifestation of a new set of community values, and therefore those able to demand compensation to forgo violating these new norms are able to extort economic gain from what is no longer deemed to be acceptable behaviour.

Getting prices right by getting rules right

> Exchange, the most obvious manifestation of the network of relationships, reflects the internal organization of society, but it is the result of the organization of production rather than its cause (Coquery-Vidrovitch, 1985: 99).

The development community has belatedly come to recognize the importance of institutions – the legal foundations of exchange – through its interest in structural adjustment policies. Because prices are merely reflections of a willingness to exchange ownership of future benefit streams – which are themselves defined by the underlying institutional set-up – the preoccupation with 'getting prices right' leads, logically, to the problem of 'getting the *rules* right'. There are two aspects to the latter issue. One dimension of rules in a market economy is that concerned with the *agency problem*. Agency problems are concerned with incentive alignment within firms (between owners and employees) in order that the firm may reach its objective(s) efficiently. But agency problems are also concerned with incentive alignment between policy decisions at the national level and the behaviour of atomistic agents within the national economy – whether those agents be firms or consumers. In this domain the 'right' rules ensure that firms are efficient and that the total economy is also efficient in attaining its policy objectives. Welfare economics is concerned, to a certain degree, with these two agency problems when it addresses productive efficiency and when it addresses what we call *top-level* efficiency.

There is, however, another critical aspect to getting the rules right which is of greater interest here. The straightforward analytics of welfare economics assume that all transactions are (nearly) costless. In fact, as noted earlier, certain transactions in a market economy are very costly in terms of gaining information about transacting opportunities and formalizing and enforcing contracts struck. Viable market economies require rules in this second domain as well, for it is these that hold down the transaction costs of market processes. An economy with vague and misunderstood property rights, with no contract law and with no uniform commercial code, is one with very high transaction costs. It is not enough to get one set of rules 'right' if the absence of the second set of rules keeps transaction costs high.

Rules in the first domain might be seen as rules *of* transactions which provide 'correct' incentives. In the second domain, they might be seen as rules *about* transactions which allow the 'correct' incentives to provide decisive signals to atomistic agents. Inadequate rules *about* transactions result in high transaction costs. Eliminating the explicit role of government as a producer, as a buyer, and/or as a seller will have minimal impact on overall economic performance so long as high transaction costs prevent independent entrepreneurs from stepping in to replace the state. In addition, improved technical inputs, in the absence of approved contractual infrastructure, will mean that the new income streams derived from these inputs will be concentrated in the hands of a few. In the absence of accompanying institutional arrangements necessary to economic development, these new income streams will not work their way through the economy to induce other changes and improvements.

The allocation of economic resources, and the exchange of goods among individuals, can take place within an informal framework (for example, family and friends), or within a more formal framework (the 'market') (Ben-Porath, 1980). In either case it is necessary that implicit or explicit contracts exist: these contracts are the rules *about* transactions – what I call the *legal foundations of exchange*. In any economy, exchange is the essence of a contractual arrangement, and it is contracting over the future that gives vibrancy to an economy. The parties to a transaction exchange ownership of a future stream of benefits promised by the respective objects of exchange – money and the commodity in question. This is a contract precisely because specific performance is implied.

The legal foundations of exchange concern the fundamental issue of securing contractual behaviour such that individual transactors need not undertake the task of enforcing their own exchange (enforcing their own contracts). This *private ordering* becomes necessary when the legal foundations of exchange are absent. When they are missing or underdeveloped, the rules *about* transactions are deficient. In an economy without the necessary legal foundations, where private resources have to be devoted to the tasks of collecting information about contracting possibilities and arranging and enforcing contracts, market opportunities are artificially attenuated. When market opportunities are attenuated, economic development is inhibited.

Markets function not because of the absence of law, but only with the explicit presence of law. Markets are 'efficient' only when the legal foundations exist to hold down the costs of transacting across time and space. To those who imagined that markets would automatically appear if only government would get out of the way, recent difficulties in Eastern Europe must have come as a surprise.

The lessons of American economic growth are dominated by the instrumental use of the law to encourage enterprise – whether the land acts, the creation of new mining law, or the writing of a new water law to fit new ecological and economic conditions in the arid western part of the country (Horwitz, 1977; Hurst, 1956, 1982). Economic development requires the instrumental use of the law – contract law, property law, bankruptcy law, administrative law, and tort law. The disappointing results observed in Eastern Europe – and in much of the tropics – are the logical outcome of societies which lack the legal foundations of exchange. It is not enough to legitimize private property rights. The economy must possess a meaningful set of institutions about transactions, as well as a coherent set of institutions of transactions.

Conclusions

Several points have been made in this article. First, the economy is a set of ordered relations that indicate arenas of choice for atomistic economic agents. Second, the arenas of choice given by the set of ordered relations are defined or determined by convention, by habit, and by rules and entitlements represented by the legal system. These are the institutional arrangements of an economy, and they have been too long ignored in traditional treatments of development. Exchange cannot exist without a structure of elaborate rules *about* transactions. Third, rules, in the absence of an authority system to give meaning to them, are not rules at all but mere suggestions.

Many nations, both agrarian and those in Eastern Europe, have yet to constitute themselves as meaningful authority systems with respect to the economy as a set of ordered relations. They may be 'authority systems' in one unhappy sense of the term, but the coercive powers of the state are not yet applied constructively to the economy as a going concern. Fourth, a viable economy is one in which the set of ordered relations provides predictability without rigidity and flexibility without chaos. To say that the economy is a set of ordered relations is in no way to imply a *dirigiste* approach. But economics and the economy are about futurity, and a system in which the future is not only unknown but unpredictable is an economy with no hope. The use of the word 'unpredictable' does not mean that one can predict with perfection. But the essential condition in any economy is to provide a climate for independent actions with intertemporal implications. Chaos is the antithesis of this condition.

Finally, there is the fact that the problem of economic development is *not* one of getting prices right. Rather, the problem is to get the rules right. Prices are mere artefacts of the momentary convergence of technology, ecology, human needs or wants, disposable income, and the institutional arrangements that indicate who can exchange what with whom and how much it will cost. Only by focusing on the right rules – the institutional arrangements – will sustainable economic development occur.

Notes

1. In this article 'Eastern Europe' will be used as a shorthand term for the nations in Central and Eastern Europe, as well as the newly independent republics which were formerly part of the Soviet empire.
2. Endowments represent control over income and wealth, the nature and extent of which are determined by property rights – one class of institutional arrangements.
3. But the determination of which uses are most 'productive' is, of course, itself a function of the underlying institutional set-up that indicates important information about relative values at any moment. We begin to see something of the circularity in pronouncements about 'efficiency'.
4. The Oxford economist Nassau Senior gained a certain notoriety by using flawed economic logic to suggest that the shortened work day would take all profits from manufacturers. In other words, he argued that the first ten or so hours of each work day were needed for the capitalist to cover all other costs. It was only beyond the tenth hour of daily work per labourer that the capitalist could finally obtain a return on *his* efforts in the enterprise.

References

Bauer, Peter (1991), *The Development Frontier*, Cambridge, MA: Harvard University Press.

Ben-Porath, Yoram (1980), 'The F-connection: families, friends, and firms and the organisation of exchange', *Population and Development Review*, **6**, 1–30.

Bromley, Daniel W. (1989a), *Economic Interests and Institutions: The Conceptual Foundations of Public Policy*, Oxford: Basil Blackwell.

Bromley, Daniel W. (1989b), 'Institutional change and economic efficiency', *Journal of Economic Issues*, **23** (3), 735–59.

Bromley, Daniel W. (1990), 'The ideology of efficiency: searching for a theory of policy analysis', *Journal of Environmental Economics and Management*, **19**, 86–107.

Commons, John R. (1968), *Legal Foundations of Capitalism*, Madison, WI: University of Wisconsin Press.

Commons, John R. (1990), *Institutional Economics: Its Place in Political Economy*, New Brunswick, NJ: Transaction Publishers.

Coquery-Vidrovitch, Catherine (1985), 'The political economy of the African peasantry and modes of production', in Peter Gutkind and Immanuel Wallerstein (eds), *Political Economy of Contemporary Africa*, London: Sage.

Dahlman, Carl J. (1980), *The Open Field System and Beyond*, Cambridge: Cambridge University Press.

Dean, Richard (1992), 'Law and economic reform in Russia: a status report', paper presented at a conference on Transitions to the Market Economy in Russia, University of Wisconsin, Madison, 9 October.

Horwitz, Morton J. (1977), *The Transformation of American Law, 1780–1860*, Cambridge, MA: Harvard University Press.

Hurst, James Willard (1956), *Law and the Conditions of Freedom in the Nineteenth-Century United States*, Madison, WI: University of Wisconsin Press.
Hurst, James Willard (1982), *Law and Markets in United States History*, Madison, WI: University of Wisconsin Press.
Krueger, Anne (1974), 'The political economy of the rent-seeking society', *American Economic Review*, **64**, 291–303.
Lewis, David (1986), *Convention: A Philosophical Study*, Oxford: Basil Blackwell.
Schmid, A. Allan (1992), 'Legal foundations of the market: implications for the formerly socialist countries of Europe and Africa', *Journal of Economic Issues*, **26** (3), 707–32.
Sen, A.K. (1982), *Choice, Welfare, and Measurement*, Oxford: Basil Blackwell.
Ullmann-Margalit, Edna (1977), *The Emergence of Norms*, Oxford: Clarendon Press.

[3]

On Risk, Transactions, and Economic Development in the Semiarid Tropics*

Daniel W. Bromley and Jean-Paul Chavas
University of Wisconsin—Madison

Recent interest in the institutions and production relations of tropical agriculture seem to hold promise for increased collaboration between economists and anthropologists in efforts to explain existing patterns of production and socioeconomic interaction. This focus on customs, and on the more formal institutional arrangements, is encouraging given the continuing concern for food production in much of the semiarid tropics. Two recent papers are particularly germane to this growing literature. H. P. Binswanger and M. R. Rosenzweig have offered a foundation for addressing the production relations in agriculture, with a general focus on conditions in South Asia.[1] More recently, Binswanger and J. McIntire provide an explanation for "the major institutions and customary features of production relations in three agroclimatic subzones of the land-abundant tropics that have simple technology and high transport costs."[2] They also offer predictions of how these institutions and features might change in response to the opening-up of subsistence economies and to population growth.

Our approach here is consistent with this recent work in several respects. First, it is explanatory, in that we offer possible explanations for observed behavior in the land-abundant tropics where agriculture is a mixture of cropping and livestock management. Second, it is predictive, in that we draw on economic theory to hypothesize likely changes in behavior in the face of institutional change. Finally, it is offered in the interest of stimulating a concern for the institutional preconditions of economic development. By such preconditions we have in mind the institutional arrangements that can stimulate the economic development process. In particular, we focus on the role of transactions in the economy. We do not believe that there is anything intrinsically undesirable about transactions that are restricted to a circle of family and acquaintances. On the contrary, such transactions play an important

0013-0079/89/3704-0043$01.00

role in the implementation of survival strategies allowing economic agents to deal with their uncertain environment. However, we argue that the development process can be heavily influenced by the array of transaction opportunities. Moreover, we suggest that the current agricultural problems of the semiarid tropics are at least partially attributable to a restricted domain for transacting.

It is our fundamental premise that sustained agricultural development in the agro-ecosystem here being discussed is likely to occur only when economic agents have the opportunity to engage in a variety of economic transactions that transcend the traditional transactions among family and clan. Such expansion of their transactions portfolio will be possible only when there has been a reduction in the current costs of transacting among independent economic agents in nontraditional arenas. Those transaction costs, which are high because of the absence of a shared system of contracting with others outside of the family/tribe, will fall only when a collective good has been established that can be referred to as the "legal foundations of the economy."[3]

Much attention has been devoted to the explicit role of governments in stimulating or possibly retarding the development of productive agriculture.[4] One of our concerns here is with the ability of private or public initiatives to help develop the legal foundations of the economy. For example, the distortions of agricultural incentives associated with government policy have provided the basis for frequent criticism of governments as explicit economic agents—as marketing boards, as input suppliers, or as sources of credit. We are concerned, however, that a retreat in these activities would seem to offer little promise for economic development in the absence of alternative mechanisms that would help to expand transaction opportunities. This proposition should not be taken as a defense of the current explicit role played by many governments (in the form of parastatals and otherwise).[5] But we are concerned that advocacy for less explicit governmental activity in the economy has not been matched by an equal concern for the legal foundations of the economy that will permit and facilitate more reliance on new transacting opportunities.

We submit that the essence of a productive agriculture is not just fancy inputs, nor simply getting government out of the way but, rather, the existence of implicit or explicit contracts among economic agents that would facilitate exchange opportunities beyond the traditional confines. In the absence of those opportunities, economic activity tends to be autarkic and confined to that level at which trust among agents is known to exist. In the African context this means the family, kin group, tribe, or village. In India, this includes the caste system, which provides a form of implicit contract among economic agents.[6] It is from this foundation of trust and expectations that new initiatives are energized. The allocation of economic resources and the exchange of goods and services among individuals can take place within an informal framework (e.g., family and friends) or within a more formal framework (e.g., the market).[7] In either case it is necessary that implicit or explicit contracts exist, such contracts playing a crucial role in resource allocation and thus in the process of economic development. It is our contention here that sustained agricultural development in the land-abundant arid tropics awaits the development of a more elaborate structure of implicit or explicit contracts across both space and time. We argue that nationwide agricultural economic development requires that such an infrastructure be created so that localized trust and commitments are eventually transcended by trust and commitment over the geographic scope of the nation-state. Also, we distinguish between contingent contracts that are conditional on the uncertain state of the world and unconditional contracts in which the terms of exchange are certain at the time of the transaction. In the semiarid tropics, we argue that survival issues make risk allocation an important aspect of economic decisions. This indicates a need for contingent contracts that will help to improve the handling of risky outcomes across individuals. The design and implementation of contingent contracts is thus an integral part of the development process. As such, we emphasize the role of contingent contracts in risk allocation. By reducing the need for farm enterprise diversification, these contracts can stimulate specialization. This specialization can increase productivity by facilitating the division of labor and improving the effectiveness of agricultural research adapted to local agroclimatic conditions. Finally, by improving risk allocation, contingent (conditional) contracts can make unconditional contracts appear more attractive to individual agents. This would facilitate market exchange and allow regions or nations a greater opportunity to benefit from trade through their respective comparative advantages.

We now turn to a conceptual view of the transaction problems faced by independent economic agents in the semiarid tropics. This model will illustrate the formal side of our argument about risk and the role to be played by a collective good whose purpose is to reduce transaction costs among economic agents. While we believe that the model will be accessible to a wide range of readers, those less interested in the formal model may quite easily skim this section and then move directly to Section II.

I. A Conceptual View of the Problem

Consider an economy consisting of n individuals. The ith individual makes private decisions, denoted by a vector z_i, while facing an uncertain state of the world represented by the random vector e_i, $i = s, \ldots, n$. Also, all n individuals face a vector of collective goods, denoted by

x.[8] We assume that each individual has preferences represented by the Von Neumann-Morgenstern utility function.

$$U_i(w_i, z_i, x, e_i), i = 1, \ldots, n, \tag{1}$$

where w_i is the ith individual's initial wealth, the utility function (1) being strictly increasing in w_i. Under the expected utility maximization hypothesis, (1) will provide the basis for an analysis of the allocation of private goods (z), collective goods (x), and risk (e) in the economy.

Although the model presented here is general, we will focus our attention on economic issues in the semiarid tropics. In this context, we will consider that the individuals in (1) include farmers for whom the e's represent drought, pestilence, famine, or other stochastic events beyond the control of farmers. Also, we will emphasize the role of the collective goods (x). In particular, we will consider that the collective goods include contractual arrangements concerning transactions among the n individuals in the economy, and we will then analyze the implications for development policy.

The economic problem for the farmer is, therefore, seen to have two dimensions, the first of which is familiar. He makes economizing decisions about the factors under his control (z) so as to maximize expected utility. But he also is interested in the provision of collective goods that will influence the nature and scope of economic transactions. Here the concern is for the boundary of his economic activities in both a spatial and a temporal dimension. The spatial dimension addresses whether he will transact with those beyond local acquaintances. Will he transact with an unknown herder? Will he trust a buyer of grain whom he has just met for the first time? Will he agree to deliver a product to someone with uncertain credit rating? The intertemporal dimension concerns his willingness to participate in transactions in which benefits and costs are separated in time. These transactions may be with someone he knows or with a stranger.

When the farmer contemplates expanding the nature and scope of his usual transacting domain, he understands that there are benefits to such new transactions (greater possible economic gains, the spreading of risk), but there are also costs (unreliable trading partner, enforcement difficulties); the farmer views these prospects in a cost-benefit framework. In particular, he has a willingness to pay for the collective goods as they influence his own welfare. The collective goods include what we call here the "legal foundations of the economy." For example, such collective goods can lower information, contracting, and enforcement costs of transactions beyond the family/clan and so permit the farmer to expand both the nature and scope of private economic transactions. The collective goods can also facilitate the implementation and design of risk-sharing schemes in the economy. Finally, collective goods can help in the provision of physical and human capital when economies of scale make such capital unattractive for individuals acting independently.

The individual's willingness to pay for the collective goods can be cast in terms of his desire to be part of a group that will provide x at an acceptable cost. In other words, the individual contemplates engaging in a collective economic activity that will improve his welfare. This collective economic activity will require scarce resources devoted to the dissemination of information and the perfection of mechanisms whereby contracts might be better enforced. Members of the group make an investment decision regarding the amount of the collective good to be made available and the way in which the benefits and costs of the collective good are distributed among members of the group. These benefits and costs can be conceptualized as a system of transfers (that can be positive or negative) to the members of the group. We define the vector of transfers $T = (t_1, \ldots t_n)$, where t_i denotes the transfer received (or paid if negative) by the ith individual as a member of the group. Collective (or group) behavior is associated with the design and implementation of these transfer mechanisms as well as with the establishment of x.

The implementation of the transfers (T) requires information on the situation of all individuals in the group. However, each individual has imperfect information about the situation and the actions of other individuals in the group. We account for it here by assuming that each individual observes messages sent by other members of the economy.[9] These messages are realizations of random variables that are correlated with other random variables characterizing the uncertain state and/or actions of the n individuals. This correlation with the other random variables of interest reflects the quality of the information conveyed by the messages: the messages would provide perfect information if they are perfectly correlated, while they would be uninformative if they were independently distributed.

Denote by m_i the vector of messages sent by the ith individual and observed by the other members of the group. Let M_{-i} represent the information consisting of all messages in the economy except the message from the ith individual

$$M_{-i} = (m_1, \ldots, m_{-1}, m_{i+1}, \ldots, m_n).$$

Hence, for the ith individual, M_{-i} is treated as a random vector with a given subjective probability distribution.

The information available to the group is denoted by the vector $M = (m_1, \ldots, {}_n) = (M_{-i}, m_i)$, representing all messages in the economy.

In general, the transfer mechanism can then be characterized as

$$T(M) = [t_1(M), \ldots, t_n(M)],$$

where each transfer is conditional on the information available to the group. Given these transfers, the *i*th individual's utility function (1) can then be expressed as

$$U_i[w_i + t_i(M), z_i, x, e_i], \tag{2}$$

where $t_i(M)$ is a wealth transfer resulting from group behavior.

The utility function (2) distinguishes between two kinds of uncertainty. The uncertainty represented by e_i—weather or other stochastic events beyond the control of the individual—is exogenous. The second type of uncertainty is represented by M_{-i}. It is a strategic uncertainty associated with imperfect knowledge of the situation of other members of the economy and, hence, of their propensity to engage in collective action affecting both the collective goods (x) and the transfers (T). For example, a farmer may consider turning his animals over to another for herding at some distance. However, the owner may never be certain that the herder will not sell an animal and yet claim that it had perished. Contractual arrangements and their enforcement can then be negotiated to attempt to make this strategic uncertainty acceptable to the parties involved.

The objective function of the *i*th individual is then taken to be the maximization of the expected value of (2), or

$$\max_{z_i} E_i \, U_i[w_i + t_i(M_{-i},m_i), z_i, x, e_i],$$

where E_i is the expectation operator over the random variables e_i and M_i, given the information available to the *i*th individual. Note that, if the *i*th individual is averse to income uncertainty (with $U_i[\cdot]$ being a strictly concave function of w_i), then the existence of strategic uncertainty will tend to make the individual worse off. In particular, the transfer $t_i(M_{-i}, m_i)$ is regarded as uncertain whenever the messages M_{-i} provide imperfect information about the other members of the economy. And a risk-averse individual would always prefer receiving $E_i[t_i(M)]$ for certain rather than receiving the uncertain transfer $t_i(M)$. This indicates that the nature and extent of strategic uncertainty is expected to influence collective behavior.

In order to formalize collective choices, we denote by $C(x,M)$ the cost of aggregate collective actions for the group. Since the cost of the group choice mechanism must be paid out of the private wealth of the members of the group, the following budget constraint must be satisfied:

$$C(x,M) + \sum_{i=1}^{n} t_i(M) = 0. \tag{3}$$

The cost $C(x,M)$ in (3) represents the cost of establishing the collective goods (x) as well as the cost of obtaining information about other agents, the cost of contracting and bargaining with other agents, and the cost of enforcing the agreements that have been struck. The cost $C(x,M)$ would therefore include conventional transaction costs related to the establishment of the collective goods (x) and the transfer mechanism $T(M)$. This reflects the fact that the members of the group must incur costs to observe the messages M, to act on those messages, to ensure that the actions agreed on are in fact carried out, and in general to support the legal foundations of the economy.

Note that one aspect of the collective goods (x) may be the production of information. This can be done by establishing (at a cost) a communication scheme among agents of the group so that information is improved. In this context, the amount of strategic uncertainty (as reflected by the quality of the messages M) would be endogenous. It would depend on the willingness of individuals to provide truthful information about their socioeconomic situation and intention; on the communication schemes established within the group; and on the incentive structure implied by the transfer mechanism $T(M)$.

The above discussion provides a basis for a welfare analysis of collective behavior. To see that, define the willingness to pay of the ith individual for the collective goods (x) and the transfer mechanism $T(M)$ as the amount of wealth P_i that satisfies

$$\underset{z_i}{\text{Max}}\ E_iU_i[w_i + t_i(M) - P_i,z_i,x,e_i] = \underset{z_i}{\text{Max}}\ E_iU_i[w_i,z_i,0,e_i]. \tag{4}$$

Using the absence of collective action (i.e., $T = 0$, $x = 0$) as the reference point, expression (4) defines P_i as the mechanism payment that the ith individual is willing to make in order to be included in the group and benefit from some collective good x and transfer T. In this context, collective (or group) action is feasible if there exists a particular group size and composition ($n > 1$), a transfer mechanism $T(M)$, a vector of collective goods x, and a cost situation $C(x,M)$ such that the budget constraint (3) is satisfied and $P_i \geq 0$, $i = 1, \ldots, n$. In other words, group behavior to establish and sustain the collective good can be expected to occur if and only if each member of the group receives nonnegative benefits from participating in the group.

Note that under risk aversion a positive risk premium is associated with strategic risk. This suggests that, ceteris paribus, strategic uncertainty would dampen the willingness of individuals to engage in collective action. In other words, collective action would be more lively to take place in situations where strategic uncertainty is relatively small. Conversely, when strategic uncertainty is large and the possible net benefits from collective action are significant, high transaction costs may inhibit the very collective action necessary to reduce strategic uncertainty.

If we assume that collective behavior is feasible, then a group will have incentives to become organized with respect to particular collective goods x and transfers T as follows:

$$\operatorname*{Max}_{n,T,x} \sum_{i=1}^{n} p_i, \text{ subject to (3) and (4).} \tag{5}$$

That is, group size and composition, the transfer mechanism, and the collective goods would be chosen such that aggregate welfare is maximized, subject to the group budget constraint. Such group behavior is designed to provide benefits to its members.

Expression (5) formalizes the process of public decision making. Through the choice of x and T, expression (5) establishes a basis for the analysis of implicit or explicit contracts involving transactions among the members of the economy. For example, by generating appropriate messages, collective actions can reduce information costs to individuals concerning market prices, weather, or any other pertinent subject. Also, contracting costs can be reduced by the creation of somewhat standardized contracts for similar transactions (e.g., the use of standard weights and measures or the clear assignment of liabilities). Another example is a system with accessible and reliable processes for dispute settlement, which would lower the enforcement costs of contracts that have been abrogated.

This analysis suggests that the transfers $T = (t_1, \ldots, t_n)$ have two roles to play in the economy. First, such transfers can be used to pay for the cost of the chosen mechanism, that is, for the cost of group action. Second, they can be used to redistribute wealth among members of the group. In an uncertain world, this redistribution can be motivated as an insurance contract. For instance, risk-sharing strategies among members of the group can be attractive if each agent faces different and imperfectly correlated risks. Or, risk-sharing strategies are beneficial if different members of the group are differentially risk averse or if they have access to different qualities of information.

II. Some Agricultural Development Issues in the Semiarid Tropics

The above discussion suggests that the economic well-being of an agricultural producer in the semiarid tropics is related to the conditions under which transactions may occur. Put another way, when opportunities for economic transactions are restricted to family or close acquaintances, there are limitations on the farmer's ability to spread risk, augment consumption choices, and specialize in enterprises in which he may have a comparative advantage. The corollary of this is that economic development will be inhibited by the limited opportunity for economic agents to transact with other members of the economy.

The extent to which development prospects are retarded by limited opportunities for transacting appears to be more severe in the semiarid tropics than in the more intensive agricultural zones of the developing world. One reason is the relatively high cost of transacting in the semiarid tropics, a condition arising from the extreme diversification of agriculture and its spatial (extensive) nature. When the costs of obtaining information, negotiating, and enforcing contracts are high, certain transactions will simply not occur because the costs exceed the potential gain to the various parties. In this situation, economic activity tends to remain autarkic. Thus, a reduction in transaction costs would increase the incentive to transact to the benefit of the parties involved. This would stimulate the design and implementation of implicit or explicit contracts that constitute the legal foundation of the economy. The spread of mutually beneficial transaction opportunities over space and time would then play a crucial role in sustained agricultural development.

In this section, we will discuss current transaction opportunities typical of farmers in the semiarid tropics. This will provide an illustration of the arguments presented in Section I, as well as offering an assessment of the role and motivations of current rural institutions in the semiarid tropics.

It will be convenient to regard transaction opportunities as falling within three possible arenas. At the simplest level, the family provides an arena of exchange and transaction. The second arena within which transactions may occur will be referred to here as the "network." By a network, we have in mind a circle of friends/acquaintances with whom transactions are reasonably frequent. A third transaction opportunity for the agricultural producer arises from what we will term "trading." By trading, we mean the opportunity to engage in occasional transactions with strangers.

Each of these transaction opportunities can be defined by a set of attributes. One of these attributes concerns the possible conditionality of the transaction. Here, we define a transaction to be unconditional if the nature and terms of exchange are completely determined at the time of the transaction and carry no condition for repeat transactions between the parties involved. Alternatively, a transaction is said to be conditional (or contingent) if the nature and terms of exchange depend on some states of the world that are unknown at the time the transaction is agreed on. Note that we see the distinction between unconditional and conditional transactions not as a bipolar opposition but, rather, at possible extreme points of a continuum. Both family and network transactions are typically considered to be conditional in the sense that current transactions are influenced by previous transactions and/or are entered into knowing what specific future transactions will be expected. On the contrary, trading transactions are often impersonal one-shot affairs that carry no obligation or expectation for repeat transactions; they are unconditional transactions.

Economists are familiar with the benefits to be obtained from unconditional transactions: the benefits are the gains from trade due to different technologies and/or preferences for the parties involved. This provides an incentive for individuals to trade and to specialize in the production of those products for which they have a comparative advantage.[10]

The efficiency of market exchange with low transaction costs has been studied extensively in the economics literature. For example, in the context of competitive markets without uncertainty, it is well known that Pareto efficiency is obtained under fairly general conditions.[11] Even in the presence of uncertainty, Pareto efficiency can still be obtained if there exist complete contingent-claim markets.[12] These contingent-claim markets involve transactions that are conditional on uncertain states of the world. This suggests that, in the absence of uncertainty, appropriate unconditional transactions can be efficient. However, conditional (or contingent) transactions are required to obtain efficient exchange under uncertainty. A typical example is an insurance contract where a current payment (the premium) is made in exchange for future receipts that are conditional on realized future states of the world. As discussed in Section I, the benefits from an insurance contract among individuals facing different types and distributions of risk can be derived from risk-sharing schemes in which individuals are compensated only when they face certain unfavorable situations.

Although these arguments are very general and could be made in any situation, they are particularly relevant for farmers in the semiarid tropics. First, almost by definition, the semiarid tropics cover geographical areas of the world where rainfall uncertainty is significant, thereby making food production a risky activity. Second, in many parts of the semiarid tropics, the prospects for technological interventions to reduce the effects of rainfall uncertainty through irrigation appear to be limited.[13] Third, given high population growth and often deteriorating economic conditions, survival issues have become critical. With declining agricultural production per capita, many people live near the minimum subsistence level.[14] In this context, unfavorable events (such as the recent drought in parts of Africa) can easily threaten the lives of many individuals. This makes the existence of risk-management schemes crucial for survival. Thus, it is our hypothesis that risk-management schemes provide an important motivation for transactions between individuals in the semiarid tropics. As argued above, such schemes can only be implemented in the context of conditional (or contingent) contracts. Since risk allocation affects the efficiency of transactions, it follows that the design and implementation of conditional contracts is an integral part of the economic development process.

As noted by Binswanger and McIntire, explicit insurance contracts typically do not exist in the semiarid tropics. This implies that risk allocation must be handled either privately or through implicit insurance schemes. Risk can be managed privately by attempting to reduce the severity of the effects of unfavorable events. In practice, this may include the use of locally adapted cereal varieties or a reliance on intercropping and various diversification strategies. Alternatively, risk can be managed privately through capital accumulation. For example, in years of crop failure, households can consume their accumulated capital to insure their survival. Thus, there is an incentive for farmers in the semiarid tropics to accumulate wealth for insurance reasons. As discussed by Binswanger and McIntire, food stocks and livestock are the two most common forms of capital accumulation.[15] In particular, livestock has the advantage of growing in size and number (thus providing possibly positive expected returns) while involving relatively low (compared to crops) production risks.[16]

Although the private strategies just mentioned can reduce the effects of environmental risks, they do not eliminate them. In particular, the fact that weather risk is high—and that yield risks tend to be highly covariant within small geographical areas—makes diversification strategies less effective as a risk-management tool. Also, the existence of recurring droughts along with the current population explosion and slow technological progress have made long-term capital accumulation difficult for many farmers of the semiarid tropics. These conditions suggest that private means of managing risk have severe limitations and, in general, are likely not sufficient to provide a reasonable guarantee of survival. In this context, the incentive for developing implicit insurance schemes among various individuals is strong.

As argued above, implicit insurance schemes necessarily involve conditional contracts and transactions. Many aspects of the socioeconomic organization of farmers in the semiarid tropics involve implicit contracts that appear to play a crucial role in risk management. Here, we will focus on two of these aspects: the structure of property rights in land and the role of the family and network in risk sharing schemes.

The Structure of Property Rights in Land

While Western property rights often emphasize the right to exclude others, exclusion rights are typically unconditional and cannot, therefore, play a role in insurance schemes. In order to help improve risk allocation, there is an incentive to develop nonexclusive conditional property rights. Certain property arrangements in Africa can then be seen as an integral part of risk-sharing strategies.

The typical African land tenure finds land ownership to be collective (land is owned by the village or tribe), but rights to the fruits of the land are individual.[17] The absence of private ownership as known in the Western world carries with it the absence of a land market, a subject of some concern to Western economists. But, the absence of a right to exclude someone desperately in need of the means of life means that risks are more effectively pooled. This institutional structure has precluded the rise of a small landlord class in Africa and the attendant landlessness so common in Latin America. In other words, land entitlements in Africa contribute to the general redistribution of both wealth and risk. The fact that private land ownership and a land market have been very slow to develop in Africa can be interpreted as indirect evidence that the insurance benefits from current land rights are significant.

A clear advantage of the absence of exclusive land rights concerns animal husbandry. The seasonal migration of cattle is motivated by the variability of rainfall and the necessity of following the rains. This can lead to transhumance (if the cattle migration is seasonal) or pastoralism (if the migration is permanent). Such systems can thus be efficient institutions for the use of resources that are highly variable both temporally and spatially. In particular, these systems provide the ability to manage locally covariant risks. Moreover, since humans cannot directly use most of the plants that grow in arid regions, any use of the land through the intermediation of livestock may be an efficient use of a natural resource that would otherwise remain unused. However, transhumance or pastoralism is feasible only if land rights are nonexclusive.

The Role of Families or Networks

Transactions involving families or networks are conditional in the sense that transactions typically bear implicit mutual obligations to both parties. Family members have strong obligations to engage in future transactions with other family members. Obligations with the members of a network of friends or acquaintances also exist, although they are typically weaker. These obligations can often be interpreted as implicit insurance contracts that act as risk-sharing schemes. It is not uncommon in Africa to find these mechanisms at work when a family or an individual is adversely affected by a stochastic event of some magnitude. Thus, when economic agents bear differential exposure to risk, or are differentially equipped to deal with risk, risk-pooling strategies among individuals can be beneficial. However, any insurance contract is typically implemented in the face of imperfect information about the actual situation of individuals, thus implying the existence of strategic uncertainty (see Sec. I). Strategic uncertainty may create a problem of adverse selection in that the individual least (most) able to contribute to the insurance scheme is also the person most (least) likely to need indemnification. In addition, there is the moral hazard problem in which an insurance contract may lead individuals to be more careless than they would otherwise be.

Strategic uncertainty is expected to be of a limited nature among family members. The family is typically a domain of low information cost, low contracting cost, and low strategic uncertainty among its members. The family can, therefore, be an efficient institutional mechanism for the sharing of noncovariant risks (e.g., the risk of noncontagious diseases). The benefits from risk sharing are expected to depend on the size of the family: the larger the family, the easier it will be to pool noncovariant risks among family members. In other words, insurance benefits provide an incentive for the existence of large extended families, as typically found in Africa.[18] Unfortunately, as pointed out by Binswanger and McIntire, some of the uncertainty facing farmers in the semiarid tropics tends to be locally highly covariant. For example, a crop failure will likely affect simultaneously all members of a family living in the same location. In this context, temporary migrations of some family members can be an efficient risk management scheme to the extent that it exposes the migrants to different uncertainties.

Given the existence of locally covariant risk, there is an incentive for individuals (or families) to share risks with other individuals facing uncertainties that are less covariant. Network transactions can provide the means for such insurance schemes. However, conditional transactions with members of the network as opposed to the family typically involve somewhat higher information, contracting, and enforcement costs, as well as some strategic uncertainty. Thus, there is an incentive to establish social groups with good communication among its members. Such groups would help to reduce transaction costs and strategic uncertainty within the group and would facilitate the design and implementation of conditional contracts. These (implicit) contracts would be motivated by the benefits associated with risk sharing between the members of the group. In general, one would expect that the smaller the group, the lower the transaction costs but also the lower the insurance benefits. Given these trade-offs, there is a potential for many forms of contracts for different groups, each playing a role in the allocation of particular risks. For example, the presence of village-level mutual work agreements in Africa can be seen as a form of risk pooling and wealth redistribution within a village. Also, through gift exchange and reciprocal transactions, the tribe or the clan may pool risk across families. The importance of reciprocal exchange in various societies has been emphasized by anthropologists for many years.[19] Here we emphasize the role of such exchange as collective risk management strategies. First, there is evidence that such strategies are fairly effective in managing environmental risks and are crucial for the survival of many farmers in the semiarid tropics.[20] Second, the fact that, even today, reciprocal transactions within the village or the clan are still commonly made by African farmers suggests that their insurance benefits are significant.

So far we have emphasized the role of conditional transactions in environmental risk management in the semiarid tropics. It is now appropriate to discuss briefly the role of unconditional transactions. We have argued earlier that trading transactions in the semiarid tropics typically involve unconditional contracts. Such contracts generate benefits from trade if the parties involved have a different comparative advantage with respect to the item traded.[21] However, such contracts cannot play a direct role in risk management in the sense that, being unconditional, they cannot provide compensation in the event of unexpected adverse situations. This indicates that trading transactions by themselves would likely not be able to generate an efficient risk allocation in the semiarid tropics. For example, it has been argued that the development of markets can have a detrimental impact on the ability of farmers to handle climatic uncertainty.[22] The fact that—for many farmers in the tropics—the grain transactions involving family and network often dominate (in volume) the grain trading transactions suggests that insurance motives are relatively strong. In other words, the insurance benefits of conditional contracts may sometimes be larger than the gain from trade associated with unconditional transactions. If this is the case, then the fuller development of markets could have a negative influence on economic development if appropriate risk-sharing schemes are not a part of the economic development policy. Alternatively, given the presence of appropriate risk-management institutions, markets can help in the development process. Some of these issues are explored further below.

III. Some Implications for Agricultural Development Policy

Poor agricultural performance in the semiarid tropics has often been attributed to the combined impact of inadequate incentives—output prices, input costs, and the supply of education and health services—and inefficient systems of marketing, transport, extension, and other support services.[23] In this context, it is then argued that a development policy should include the improvement of all the institutional supports—marketing, transportation, and finance—needed to generate a large supply response to improved prices. Although these arguments are clearly valid in general, we are concerned that they fail to emphasize the influence of development policy on risk allocation. Like D.

Newbery and J. Stiglitz, we would like to focus attention on the role of risk-management schemes in the economic development process.[24]

To make the point, consider a particular policy that does not attempt to improve risk allocation and does not stimulate in any way the development of conditional transactions within the economy. In the semiarid tropics, this would imply that risk would be managed either privately or through implicit contracts within the family or network (see Sec. II). Such contracts can be quite useful to handle noncovariant risks. However, yield risks are often locally covariant, implying that these contracts would not perform well as insurance schemes for yield risks unless they cover extensive geographic areas.[25] And without subsidies that would reduce transaction costs and strategic uncertainty, the geographic coverage of such schemes would likely be limited. As a result, a significant part of the yield risk would have to be borne privately, implying a strong incentive for private diversification strategies (see Sec. II). If the benefits of reduced risk exposure from such strategies are large, then farmers may be willing to forgo some of the possible gains from trade; they would diversify enterprise selection rather than specialize in the activities in which they have a comparative advantage. Although such a risk management strategy may be optimal from the point of view of the farmer, it has serious implications for national economic development.

First, it makes agricultural research more difficult in the sense that researchers would need to be concerned with many production activities. From past experience, it is generally understood that agricultural research has been most effective when focusing on monocultures grown over extended geographic areas (e.g., corn or rice). This suggests that there are benefits in research specialization that would not be obtained in the context of a diversified agriculture.

Second, farm diversification strategies likely increase the transaction costs of trade. By a spatial spreading of various farm outputs, transportation costs are increased. Spatial diversification also increases information costs concerning spatial supply-demand conditions and thus makes market transactions more difficult. In this context, it would become difficult for farmers to benefit from trade.

Third, by definition, farm diversification would not allow much specialization in production activities. This would not facilitate the division of labor and therefore could make productivity gains more difficult to attain. Also, it would slow down the spread of communication and education related to the production activities (e.g., extension services) because of economies of scale in providing the corresponding infrastructure.

These arguments suggest that, in the absence of insurance schemes over extensive geographic areas, the incentive for private diversification can have some adverse effects on economic development in the semiarid tropics. In particular, the absence of insurance schemes may slow down productivity growth and technological progress and may therefore reduce the possible gains from trade. This indicates that the investment in collective goods supporting the development of risk-sharing schemes may play an important role in the development process. Our argument is that such schemes should be considered and evaluated more seriously in the design of development policies.

For example, consider a policy that would lower transaction costs and strategic uncertainty concerning a particular risk-sharing scheme involving a group of individuals. By shifting some of the risk from individuals to the group, this would decrease the incentive for private diversification.[26] As a result, farmers would tend to specialize in activities where they have a comparative advantage. Productivity of labor would likely increase. Also, agricultural research could focus on fewer products and thereby increase its effectiveness in developing new technologies. Moreover, transportation costs and other market transaction costs would be lowered, thus stimulating trade and increasing the gains from trade. Finally, in the case of regional (or national) specialization, this would facilitate the development of infrastructure related to production activities.

This suggests that the allocation of risk is an integral part of the development process and should be an explicit part of agricultural development policies. Together with proper incentives and the improvement of all the institutional support (e.g., for research or marketing), the design and implementation of efficient conditional redistribution schemes can be crucial in the effectiveness of agricultural development policies in the semiarid tropics. By placing the issue of redistribution and conditional transactions in a broader context, it may help to integrate the views of economists and anthropologists. Also, by allowing a better evaluation of various agricultural programs, a conscious concern for conditional transactions and risk spreading may help to improve economic development policy.

Notes

* We are grateful to two anonymous reviewers for helpful comments on an earlier version of the paper. In addition, seminar participants at the Harvard Institute for International Development provided useful suggestions during a presentation by Daniel Bromley.

1. H. P. Binswanger and M. R. Rosenzweig, "Behavioral and Material Determinants of Production Relations in Agriculture," *Journal of Development Studies* 22, no. 3 (April 1986): 503–39.

2. H. P. Binswanger and John McIntire, "Behavioral and Material Determinants of Production Relations in Land-abundant Tropical Agriculture," *Eco-*

nomic Development and Cultural Change 36, no. 1 (October 1987): 73–99, quote on 73.

3. See, for instance, Daniel W. Bromley, *Markets and Agricultural Development: The Promise and the Challenge* (Binghamton, N.Y.: Institute for Development Anthropology, July 1986). For a more thorough treatment of economic institutions, see Daniel W. Bromley, *Economic Interests and Institutions: The Conceptual Foundations of Public Policy* (Oxford: Blackwell, 1989).

4. Robert Bates, *Markets and States in Tropical Africa: The Political Basis of Agricultural Policies* (Berkeley and Los Angeles: University of California Press, 1981); T. W. Schultz, ed., *Distortions of Agricultural Incentives* (Bloomington: Indiana University Press, 1978); C. Peter Timmer, *Getting Prices Right* (Ithaca, N.Y.: Cornell University Press, 1986).

5. Indeed we share the common concern about the deleterious effects of much of this activity (see Bates; Schultz, ed.; Timmer).

6. "Caste solidarity partly explains how they [Marwaris] established themselves initially; they used to provide each other with credit on easy terms anywhere in India at any time of the day or night" (*Economist* [September 6–12, 1986], p. 40).

7. Yoram Ben-Porath, "The F-Connection: Families, Friends, and Firms and the Organization of Exchange," *Population and Development Review* 6 (March 1980): 1–30.

8. We use the term "collective good" to denote those activities that are undertaken by a group of individuals for their collective benefit. The term "public good" is often used, but we avoid that terminology here since "public" may cause some to believe that all collective goods must be provided by the public sector (government). While we do not deny that there is a role for the state (the public sector) in providing a level of the collective good (x), it should not be assumed that this is the only possible mechanism.

9. See J. C. Harsanyi, "Games with Incomplete Information Played by Bayesian Players," *Management Science* 14 (1967–68): 159–82, 320–34, 486–502; or James W. Friedman, *Game Theory with Applications to Economics* (Oxford: Oxford University Press, 1986).

10. The concept of comparative advantage was first proposed in David Ricardo, *On the Principles of Political Economy and Taxation* (London: John Murray, 1817). The concept has since then been refined to constitute the basis of trade theory (see Akira Takayama, *International Trade* [New York: Holt, Rinehart & Winston, 1972]).

11. An allocation is Pareto efficient if there is no feasible allocation where everyone is at least as well off and at least one agent is better off. For example, see Hal R. Varian, *Microeconomic Analysis* (New York: Norton, 1978).

12. See Gerard Debreu, *Theory of Value,* Cowles Foundation Monograph 17 (New Haven, Conn.: Yale University Press, 1959); or D. N. G. Newbery and J. E. Stiglitz, *The Theory of Commodity Price Stabilization: A Study in the Economics of Risk* (Oxford: Clarendon, 1981).

13. For example, see Peter J. Matlon and D. S. Spenser, "Increasing Food Production in Sub-Saharan Africa: Environmental Problems and Inadequate Technological Solutions," *American Journal of Agricultural Economics* 66 (1984): 671–76.

14. In the context of Africa, see World Bank, *Toward Sustained Development in Sub-Saharan Africa: A Joint Program of Action* (Washington, D.C.: World Bank, 1984). In the context of India, see Richard H. Day and I. J. Singh, *Economic Development as an Adaptive Process: The Green Revolution in the Punjab* (Cambridge: Cambridge University Press, 1977).

15. Binswanger and McIntire (n. 2 above) note the difficulties of food stock accumulation in the face of storage cost, storage losses, and limited durability of food grain. This suggests that livestock is likely to be the major form of wealth accumulation.

16. This corresponds to statement S-4 in Binswanger and McIntire: "(a) The cheapest way of producing cattle usually involves transhumance, the seasonal migration of cattle among different geographic subzones. (b) Animal husbandry has lower production risks than cropping for two primary reasons. First, during minor droughts crops may fail to produce a harvest, but vegetative growth may still provide some fodder for animals. Second, in the case of local droughts, animals may be shifted to other areas unaffected by drought. (c) The same reasons imply that covariance between animal husbandry and crop production is lower than the covariance of yields among different crops or fields in the same area. Secular droughts imply failure of both crop and animal husbandry enterprises" (pp. 75–76).

17. For example, see J. C. DeWilde, *Experiences of Agricultural Development in Tropical Africa* (Baltimore: Johns Hopkins University Press, 1967). See also Ester Boserup, *The Conditions of Agricultural Growth* (Chicago: Aldine, 1965).

18. See Claude Meillassoux, *Maidens, Meal and Money* (Cambridge: Cambridge University Press, 1981).

19. For example, see Claude Lévi-Strauss, *The Elementary Structures of Kinship* (Boston: Beacon, 1969); or Frederic L. Pryor, *The Origins of the Economy* (New York: Academic Press, 1977).

20. For example, see Michael J. Watts, "The Political Economy of Climatic Hazards: A Village Perspective on Drought and Peasant Economy in a Semi-Arid Region of West Africa," *Cahiers d'Etudes Africaines* 23 (1983): 37–72.

21. In the African context, see Claude Meillassoux, *The Development of Indigenous Trade and Markets in West Africa* (Oxford: Oxford University Press, 1971).

22. See Watts.

23. For example, see World Bank (n. 14 above).

24. Newbery and Stiglitz (n. 12 above).

25. See Binswanger and McIntire (n. 2 above), proposition 8, p. 79.

26. This assumes that private diversification and group insurance are substitutes. See Isaac Ehrlich and Gary S. Becker, "Market Insurance, Self-Insurance and Self-Protection," *Journal of Political Economy* 80 (1972): 623–48.

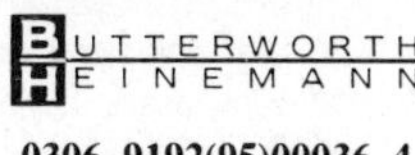

0306–9192(95)00036–4

Food Policy, Vol. 20, No. 5, pp. 425–438, 1995

0306–9192/95 $10.00 + 0.00

Development reconsidered: The African challenge

Daniel W. Bromley
Department of Agricultural Economics, University of Wisconsin, 427 Lorch Street, Madison, WI 53706, USA

The theory of economic development, when applied to much of sub-Saharan Africa, is found to be mis-specified both empirically and teleologically. The prevailing theory of economic development, fashioned out of the experience of economic transition towards industrialisation in the temperate climates, is alleged to fail to be empirically relevant to conditions in sub-Saharan Africa. Of equal importance, the normative precepts of the prevailing theory of economic development render it of dubious pertinence to societies in which the superiority of an urbanised and industrialised existence remains an open question. The more agrarian nations of Africa offer their own economic and physical reality that challenges the applicability of the conventional theory of economic development. External development assistance to these nations must be reconsidered in light of the conditions and purposes inherent in these agrarian states.

Keywords: economic development, sub-Saharan Africa, reconsiderations

Since the mid-1970s, the development community has paid special attention to the prospects for sustained development on the African continent, particularly in sub-Saharan Africa. Much serious thought has been devoted to the question of why many African countries were unable to make a successful transition to a modern economy in the way many countries of South and Southeast Asia already had (World Bank, 1981, 1983, 1984). Comparisons between Asia and Africa were frequent and often unflattering. Since the fall of the Berlin Wall in November 1989, and the attendant rush to assist the foundering economies of the former Soviet empire, there is fear that development assistance to sub-Saharan Africa will become the victim of not only donor fatigue but also crowding out.

The received wisdom of economic development in general, and agricultural development in particular, persists in the academic and donor communities. This traditional view of economic development envisions four stages (see Timmer, 1990). During the first stage, the emphasis is on institutional change, investments in new technology, the development of markets and the incentives they offer, and a major commitment to the improvement of rural infrastructure.

In the second phase, the agricultural sector is more closely linked with the industrial sector, there is continuing pressure to improve technology and incentives, and policy makers seek to improve factor markets to mobilise rural resources.

In the third phase, agriculture is successfully integrated into the nascent industrial economy. Urban consumers spend a smaller share of their incomes on food, agriculture is under pressure to be more efficient, and rural labourers start to move out of agriculture into urban jobs. Productivity of rural factors of production often lags behind that of urbanised factors, and so political problems associated with income distribution may arise.

Finally, in the fourth phase, the journey is almost complete. Agriculture becomes a small and often insignificant share of the national economy, consumer expenditures for food fall further as a share of household budgets, urban unemployment creates pressure to retain labour in agriculture, and governments are likely to begin protecting agriculture as a way of life.

Two things about this sequence of events stand out. First, the theory is informed by the historical experience in Europe, especially that of England, dating from the late 18th century. This story is, above all, Anglo-Saxon history in the temperate climates of Western Europe and, to a lesser extent, North America.

Second, this received wisdom is aggressively teleological. Progress is, by definition, industrial in nature, and it is good and proper that the agricultural labour force – and the share of national income contributed by agriculture – continue to shrink as development occurs. Even the terminology, 'development', leaves little doubt as to the desired outcome. Few favour the opposite of development: stagnation, backwardness and 'underdeveloped'.

The point here is not to challenge the received wisdom of development, for the reigning theory seems quite able to describe and explain recent history in many places. Rather, this paper explores whether this particular teleological construct is quite the universal theory we imagine it to be when it is applied to conditions in sub-Saharan Africa. While the theory may have been appropriate for Western Europe, North America and parts of the Pacific Rim, it is still an open question as to whether it is the pertinent theory for sub-Saharan Africa. The received wisdom of development may well have brought success to much of the currently developed world, but is it an appropriate construct for regions that have remained agrarian, poor and 'underdeveloped'?

To ask the question in a different way, is it possible that the developed economies, which dominate so much of the world's industry and trade, might block the path for others who seek a similar passage? If so, the received wisdom of development is a historically particularistic theory that cannot offer a coherent explanation of the current state of economic conditions in much of sub-Saharan Africa.

When the prevailing theory of development is transported from the countries in which it evolved to countries of sub-Saharan Africa, then the transferability of that theory ought to be given some thought. If the theory itself could become the focus for discussion, less time might be spent puzzling over the failure of countries in sub-Saharan Africa to follow the received wisdom. Instead, rather more time might be devoted to constructing a new theory of development.

What might this epistemological enquiry suggest about the development problem? In essence, it is inevitable that this enquiry would lead to a consideration of the very nature and structure of development theory. This would lead, then, to a careful assessment of the role of the core economic model, and of the auxiliary assumptions necessary to render that economic model empirically pertinent to sub-Saharan Africa. I turn to a brief exposition of this matter.

On models, applicability theorems and development theory

When considering the nature of development theory it is important to recall that the economist's empirical task is to construct abstract representations of human processes that offer tentative but plausible explanations of observed behaviours. That process usually starts by making reference to an axiomatic structure of premises (or assumptions) and postulates (or propositions). Indeed, the core model of a particular discipline is what differentiates that discipline from others. Economists usually start with human behaviour under conditions of scarcity. We further assume rationality, self-interest (which is not the same as greed), and the desire for improvement in one's personal circumstances. There are other aspects which might be appended, but this description is a reasonable statement of the minimal set of assumptions thought pertinent to human behaviour.

This core model can, of course, be used to generate testable hypotheses. The pertinence of these derived hypotheses will often be improved if other characteristics are appended to the core model. For instance, self-interest can be expanded, that is elaborated, to encompass the interests of others for whom one feels particularly close. We see that self-interest in the expanded version of the model extends to one's children, one's spouse, one's cousins, or the members of one's village.

The core model that speaks only to self-interest in the narrowest sense, once it is augmented with other conditions, has an improved chance of fitting a particular empirical situation. While the core model of self-interest may be quite applicable to the recluse living on a South Pacific isle, it will not be particularly apposite to an individual enmeshed in a South Pacific village. The core model is not wrong for this more social setting; it is simply incomplete. The very act of annexing several other conditions can then render the basic model both more reasonable, and more plausible. We then know that the elaborated model will be better able to generate tentative and testable hypotheses about behaviour.

A full theory of human behaviour therefore consists of two parts: a core model that is tautological in nature (axiomatic); and a set of applicability theorems that allow for the mapping of the core model into the particular empirical setting of interest to the researcher. We refer to this augmented model – with its applicability theorems (auxiliary assumptions) – as an economic theory. This theory is then capable of rendering empirically pertinent hypotheses about observable phenomena of interest to the economist. We can think of it as:

Economic model + applicability theorems <=> economic theory

The agricultural transformation referred to earlier, with its four stages, constitutes a theory of development. It is a constellation of if–then propositions that link particular actions (or policies) to particular human behaviours, and ultimately to certain outcomes. If the right institutional change is introduced, and if new technology is introduced, and if markets are structured in particular ways, and if certain investments are made in rural infrastructure, then agriculture will 'get moving'.

Once this happens, if agriculture can be properly linked with industry, if the proper incentives are introduced to stimulate a healthy agricultural sector, and if factor markets can be improved to mobilise rural resources, then agriculture can become a 'contributor to growth' in the larger economy. The full integration of agriculture into the macroeconomy will happen if there is a decline in the share of consumers' budgets spent on food, if agriculture is exposed to the same competitive pressures operating in the urban sector, and if lagging rural labour productivity can be avoided.

Development reconsidered: D.W. Bromley

This theory of development is thus dependent upon the axioms from the core of economics (the model), but it is substantially augmented by a set of applicability theorems derived from the empirical conditions that were necessary to create the theory in the first instance. The theory of economic development was built up over time by the careful identification of the empirical conditions present as agriculture developed in Western Europe and North America since the mid-19th century. It became a theory precisely because it contains logical if–then propositions with some empirical legitimacy.

Although the theory of economic development is grounded on the core model from economics, it is dominated by the applicability theorems that append that minimal set of axioms and postulates in the model. To say that the accepted theory of agricultural and economic development may not fit the conditions in sub-Saharan Africa says nothing about the core model at the heart of neoclassical economics. Rather, agnosticism about the theory of economic development speaks simply to the appropriateness of the set of applicability theorems that have been appended to the core model in the process of building up the currently accepted theory of development. The core neoclassical model is not a theory of development. We do not have a theory until the necessary applicability theorems have been appended to the core. Development of a theory is a continual process of selective accretion to the core tautological model.

The critical role of applicability theorems to the full articulation of a theory of development becomes obvious when the empirical conditions so vital to that complete theory – those empirical conditions underlying its essential structure – differ markedly from the new empirical reality into which the theory is to be projected. Clear explanation of cause and effect is impossible if the empirical manifestation of the reigning theory of economic development is seriously at odds with some new empirical setting. That is the problem to be addressed next.

Does the theory fit the circumstances?

The enigma about development in Africa arises, in part, because of the fallacy of composition inherent in discussions of Africa as a single entity. This observation is certainly not new, but it is pertinent to the previous discussion of models and applicability theorems. There are, in fact, five Africas of interest to the development community.

First is the region of North Africa with its Arab and Muslim influence. Second, West Africa is characterised by abundant rainfall and smallholder cultivation. Third, Sahelian Africa features extreme aridity and is largely inhabited by pastoralists. Fourth is the region of Central Africa with thick jungles and bounteous minerals. Finally, the countries of East and Southern Africa have the common features of wild animals, nature parks and mixed agriculture. These distinctions are, of themselves, somewhat arbitrary but it is clear that the prospects for African development cannot be comprehended if this large and varied landmass is treated as some undifferentiated whole.

We must also look carefully at the received theory of development in locations other than Africa that seem, at first glance, to be more homogeneous. There is mounting evidence that the theory may not even fit those circumstances. For instance, Timmer writes:

> The failure of agricultural productivity per worker to rise as fast as national productivity in these three countries [Italy, Japan, the USSR] might thus be seen as an

Table 1 Regional groupings of 18 agrarian countries in Africa

Central Africa	Eastern/Southern Africa	Sahelian Africa	West Africa
Burundi	Ethiopia	Burkina Faso	Benin
Central African Republic	Madagascar	Chad	Ghana
Rwanda	Malawi	Gambia	Guinea-Bissau
Uganda	Mozambique	Mali	
	Tanzania	Niger	
		Senegal	

> early signal that the patterns in the less developed countries seeking to start down the path of modern economic growth might be significantly different from the historical path followed by the Western countries (Timmer, 1990, p. 55).

Citing research by Bairoch, Timmer notes that:

> Only Italy in 1840 had a lower productivity level than that of Africa and Asia in modern times. The gap in agricultural productivity on average between European countries beginning their industrial revolutions and Africa and Asia is . . . about 45% (Timmer, 1990, pp. 55–56).

Then, quoting Bairoch (1975, pp. 40–41), Timmer further observes:

> A gap of about 45% is sufficiently wide for us to be able to assert that agricultural conditions in the currently developed countries before the beginning of the industrial revolution must have been very different from those of the underdeveloped countries of Asia and Africa today (Timmer, 1990, p. 56).

The received theory of development might thus be quite inappropriate to problems of development outside the areas of the world whose empirical conditions gave the theory its applicability theorems, its structure and thus its empirical propositions. To consider this possibility is to inquire into the nature of the applicability theorems that gave the conventional theory its empirical relevance. How does one begin to think about a theory's applicability theorems? We might start by differentiating the 48 African countries by those traits that seem pertinent to a more coherent theory of economic development. That is, we identify those countries that might be called agrarian in nature. For present purposes, a country that in 1991 had more than 20% of its GNP arising in agriculture and, at the same time, less than 20% of its GNP arising in industry would be considered 'agrarian'. Eighteen African nations fit this profile (see Table 1).

These 18 nations are spread rather evenly among the regions of Sahelian Africa, Eastern/Southern Africa and Central Africa. Three countries are drawn from West Africa. None of the North African countries is considered agrarian by this definition. In what ways do these 18 agrarian African countries differ from the remaining 30 African countries that we might regard as mixed economies? Data for the agrarian and mixed African countries, along with selected agrarian countries from Asia and Latin America, can be compared (see Table 2).[1] These latter

[1]In these latter two regions, the definition of agrarian does not depend on the fraction of GNP arising from agriculture and industry. Rather, these countries were chosen on the basis of the acknowledged importance of agriculture in their economy, regardless of the industrial share of GNP. The Asian countries are Bangladesh, China, India, Indonesia, Nepal, Pakistan, Philippines and Sri Lanka. The Latin American countries are Colombia, Costa Rica, Dominican Republic, Ecuador, El Salvador, Guatemala, Honduras, Nicaragua, Paraguay and Uruguay.

Development reconsidered: D.W. Bromley

Table 2 Sample of economic data for selected countries of Africa, Asia and Latin America

Attribute	Agrarian Africa	Mixed Africa	Agrarian Asia*	Agrarian Latin America[†]
GNP per capita, US dollars, 1991	274	1 142	408	1207
Official development assistance per capita, US dollars, 1989–91	55.3	63.1	14.6	45.9
Official development assistance as per cent of GNP, 1989–91	25.0	8.4	4.8	6.8
Debt service as per cent of exports, 1989–91	26.7	23.3	24.9	32.1
Debt service as per cent of borrowing, 1989–91	60.5	117.6	93.4	149.1
Current borrowing per capita, US dollars, 1989–91	12.3	69.5	21.3	88.6
Average annual per cent GNP growth, 1980–91	2.5	3.0	5.2	1.6
Food production index per capita (1979–81=100)	94.1	90.6	111.5	97.9
Cropland per capita, ha, 1991	0.3	0.3	0.1	0.3
Per cent of cropland irrigated, 1989–91	4.5	10.0	38.6	11.2
Average annual fertilizer use, kg per ha of cropland, 1989–91	18.0	37.0	105.8	68.9
Food aid in kg of cereals per capita, 1988–90	7.9	11.3	4.9	18.1
Agricultural labour force as per cent of total labour force, 1991	77.3	55.4	61.4	35.7

* The agrarian Asian countries are: Bangladesh, China, India, Indonesia, Nepal, Pakistan, Philippines and Sri Lanka.

[†] The agrarian Latin American countries are: Colombia, Costa Rica, Dominican Republic, Ecuador, El Salvador, Guatemala, Honduras, Nicaragua, Paraguay and Uruguay.

Source: *World Resources: 1994–95: A Guide to the Global Environment*; World Resources Institute, Washington, DC. Published by Oxford University Press, Oxford (1994). Data gathered from various tables.

countries are included here to give the reader unfamiliar with African conditions a somewhat better perspective on the agrarian and mixed African economies.

From the data in Table 2, it is apparent that agrarian African nations have very low GNP per capita and a high level of official development assistance per capita. Development assistance is also a high percentage of GNP. Debt service as a per cent of exports is rather modest but, as a per cent of total borrowing, debt service is very low. These agrarian states thus seem to be avoiding the trap of devoting much of their new credit to the service of existing debt.

The agrarian African nations are not big borrowers per capita and, compared with the other 48 nations in Table 2, they enjoy a rate of growth in GNP that is quite consistent with the others in Table 2. The index of growth in food production is about average, compared with other countries, as is the case for cropland area per capita. The agrarian nations of Africa differ in these respects: they have a high percentage of total labour force engaged in agriculture; irrigation is not prevalent compared to their cohort in Africa or elsewhere; and fertilizer use is very low. They are somewhat modest recipients of food aid.

Directly compared with their African neighbours, these 18 agrarian nations are somewhat poorer in terms of GNP, they are three times more dependent on development assistance (as a per cent of GNP), they are positively frugal in terms of debt service as a per cent of borrowing (as well as in total borrowing per capita), and they use half of the fertilizer on lands that are only half as likely to be irrigated. These conditions aside, the data suggest that these 18 nations are not drastically different from many of their neighbours.

Does the received theory of development pertain to them? Does it even pertain to their African neighbours? Will these African agrarian nations, not to mention many of their continental neighbours, become highly urbanised and industrial? Do their leaders and citizens aspire to this sort of future? More important, if they aspire to a somewhat more agrarian future, are they thereby destined to be classified under the sobriquet 'underdeveloped'?

This question is pertinent because, their relative poverty aside, these nations do not seem seriously deficient in other economic indicators. The mixed African economies (the other 30 African nations) receive more official development assistance per capita, their debt service is almost 120% of current borrowing (twice that of the agrarian nations), their current borrowing per capita is almost six times that found in the agrarian nations, and their index of food production lags behind that of the agrarian nations in Africa (see Table 2). Most telling, the mixed African economies irrigate twice the proportion of their cropland and use twice the fertilizer per unit of cropland as do the agrarian nations, but they still do not appear to have an enviable level of performance in the agricultural sector.

The point of these comparisons is to suggest that we are considering two quite different African economies here. One of the economies is agrarian, and it is certainly poor. But is it performing all that badly, given its technological and ecological conditions? The other economy is more industrial, with higher GNP, but it clearly has some lingering economic problems. The implication here is that the development prescription for the one group of countries must be quite different from that which is appropriate for the other. There is a different set of applicability theorems and hence a different development path appropriate to these two groups of countries. The received theory of development must be differentiated to account for the very different empirical realities of sub-Saharan Africa.

That the empirical conditions in sub-Saharan Africa call into question the relevance of the traditional theory of economic development still leaves open the more fundamental aspects of that theory, namely its teleology. To that I now turn.

Is the teleology tenable?

> Economic development is a process by which an economy is transformed from one that is dominantly rural and agricultural to one that is dominantly urban, industrial and service-oriented in composition. The objectives of the process can be usefully categorised as increased social wealth, equity and stability. But because these objectives require a diversification of the economy away from agriculture (no high-income, equitable, stable nations have agriculture as their dominant activity), the process is one of major structural transformation (Mellor, 1990, p. 70).

Following the prevailing view, expressed so well here by Mellor, practically all African economies are seriously underdeveloped. While the agrarian nations are almost exclusively agricultural – and hence, by the common definition, more underdeveloped than their moderately industrialised neighbours – it is less clear that the agrarian nations are any less stable and egalitarian than the remaining 30 nations of Africa, or the 18 Asian and Latin American economies listed in Table 2. Indeed, political difficulties in Nigeria, Côte d'Ivoire, Sierra Leone and Kenya in the 1990s suggest that stability may have little to do with the usual economic indicators of development.

The fundamental question remains paramount for policy guidance: does the 'end state' of development – that is, a highly industrialised and highly urbanised economy in which agriculture is virtually unnoticed and economically insignificant –

serve as the sole compelling and pertinent teleology for most of Africa? Is there but one possible outcome? Are all countries to wind up urbanised and industrialised? Is it possible that there are paths other than that followed in Western Europe? Can the term 'developed' be applied only to economies that are urbanised and industrialised? By tradition, in the academic and donor community, this is the case.

If a country with less than 10% of its labour force engaged in agriculture is regarded as developed, most nations of Africa will remain underdeveloped into the 21st century.[2] The share of the labour force in agriculture is not likely to fall from the average of 63% for Africa as a whole, in the mid-1990s, to less than 10%. Will they be regarded as developed if that percentage falls to, say, 40%? Does development require that it drop to 20%, which was the European and Japanese average in 1970?

There is an obvious problem. As long as the definition of development is structural in nature, that very definition, that concept of economic development, is driven by the metaphor of the Industrial Revolution in Western Europe at the turn of the 19th century.

Economists, perhaps inadvertently, have come to regard a developed economy as superior to an undeveloped one. That judgment is couched in seemingly objective statistical evidence of higher income, increased urbanisation, more industrial workers as a share of the total and a better investment climate.

We may insist that it is the leaders of these nations who seek the Holy Grail of development and that economists are really quite neutral and scientific about it. But this does not obviate the reality that the theoretical construct we use to prescribe and describe development is fraught with its own ideological components. Higher per capita income might not be a true measure of individual well-being. A highly urbanised setting might not be superior to one that is rural.

We may remain silent as to whether or not societies should develop. But, having done so, we are not free thereafter to call them underdeveloped or backwards if they should choose to follow a different path. There is no scientific basis to pronounce a developed economy as superior, or Pareto-preferred, to one that is not developed. The mere fact that the prevailing view of development is widely shared among Western-trained economists and political leaders does not, in any way, remove that teleology from the domain of value judgements.

There are two aspects of the so-called development problem in Africa: (1) the institutional problem; and (2) the existential problem. The institutional problem speaks to the role that a nation's legal and social infrastructure play in determining feasible courses of action in particular situations. The existential problem speaks to the empirical reality in which a particular nation state finds itself in terms of location, climate and natural resource base.

The institutional problem

If we consider the development problem in rather stark terms, it is possible to envision a production possibilities frontier (PPF) showing the technically feasible boundary for the production of industrial goods and agricultural commodities (see Fig. 1). The location of this frontier is a combination of at least two factors: (1) the physical endowment of a particular nation-state; and (2) the technological artefacts

[2] In Europe, between 1970 and 1990, the share of the total labour force in agriculture fell by more than half (from 20 to 9%). In the USA it fell exactly by half (from 4 to 2%). In Japan the drop was more precipitious, falling from 20 to 6% over this same period.

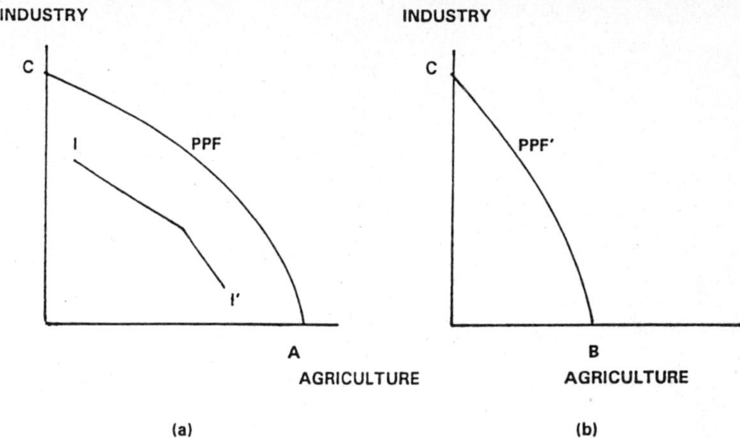

Figure 1 Two production possibilities settings

that are brought to bear on that physical endowment. For instance, panel (a) of Fig. 1 shows a PPF for a nation that is reasonably well situated for industrial pursuits; it has good access to sea routes and a long tradition of entrepreneurial activity. A major river produces adequate water for agricultural production.

However, imagine a situation in which irrigated agriculture were not prevalent in this hypothetical country. If that were the case, panel (b) rather than panel (a) in Fig. 1 might more accurately depict the situation. The difference between points A and B in the two panels is a reflection of the investment in irrigated agriculture, as well as the other infrastructural developments that are part of its modernising agricultural sector.

The location of the PPF in Fig. 1 is also dependent on something else. The nation's institutional set-up has a profound impact on its production possibilities. If crime, sloth and other detrimental forces were widespread, then the locus I–I′ would be relevant. In essence, the PPF represents the production possibilities frontier, assuming institutional arrangements are not seriously deleterious to the general economic condition.[3] In welfare theory, the PPF is usually abstracted from the institutional domain in which the economy must function. In consequence, we too often forget about the fundamental role that institutions, a collective good, play in defining the nation's production set (Bromley, 1989, 1993; Bromley and Chavas, 1989).

Figure 1 reminds us that ecological conditions and technology are but a part of the story of the economy. In one sense, the process of development is often concerned with 'getting the rules right' such that the economy moves from the locus I–I′ to the production possibilities frontier C–A (Bromley, 1993). Notice that 'getting the rules right' also plays a profound role in shifting the PPF to the northeast, which indicates better technology and better infrastructure.

Efforts to address the development challenge for the mixed African economies

[3]The difficulties created by civil turmoil pose a serious threat to any economy. In panel (a), such actions tend to render the locus I–I′ more pertinent than the PPF given by C–A. The locus I–I′ is itself a production possibility frontier if the current institutional structure is taken into account. In that sense, it (I–I′) is no less relevant to economic analysis than is the PPF (C–A) in panel (a).

must start by recognising the important role of the locus I–I′, which is referred to here as the institutional feasibility locus (IFL). One might think of the IFL as the institutionally pertinent PPF.

The relevance of the IFL serves to remind us that the process of development as traditionally conceived is not a natural state of affairs, but is rather something that must be purposefully set in motion and sustained with vigilance and collective commitment. It is hard work to create the circumstances in which a nation-state might move closer to its largely hypothetical production possibilities frontier. Indeed, development, as we have come to understand that idea, must often be imposed on countries. What else can one conclude from the experience with structural adjustment programmes in many countries?

Structural adjustment programmes are precisely concerned with moving nations closer to the imagined PPF through the expedient of eliminating the institutional impediments that keep it on the IFL. More correctly, structural adjustment programmes move the IFL to the northeast until, when the rules are finally right, the IFL becomes precisely coincidental with the PPF.

The existential problem

So far we have considered countries that might be regarded as reasonably well endowed in terms of their physical and locational aspects, of their existential situation. For agriculture, this can be taken to mean that they have favourable rainfall patterns or irrigation is feasible. This notion of endowment can be extended to physical attributes, such as access to ocean shipping, fertile soils, etc. These nations have a moderate chance at economic progress if they can but get their institutional climate conducive to entrepreneurial activity. But are there countries for which this is not the case?

The 18 agrarian nations in Africa have a setting (a 'situational endowment') that is much less favourable to the activities that are central to the traditional idea of development. Twelve nations in Africa are landlocked and nine of them are agrarian states as defined here. Only Botswana, Zambia and Zimbabwe are landlocked nations that fall in the mixed economies group. Of the 18 agrarian nations, nine are landlocked, seven are arid or semi-arid, and 10 are 'small'.[4] Nine countries have two of these three traits. Burkina Faso has all three; it is arid, small and landlocked.

Being small, landlocked and arid (or semi-arid) cannot but have profound impacts on the nature and position of a nation's production possibilities frontier. Being landlocked and arid, but large, opens up economic possibilities that are not there when constrained by national boundaries. Being arid and small, but having access to oceans, opens up prospects for development not available to an arid and small landlocked nation. And being small and landlocked, but well endowed in rainfall, would relax the constraint of extreme aridity.

In Fig. 2, a stylised PPF is drawn for a hypothetical agrarian African nation that is arid, small, and perhaps without access to oceans for trade. This PPF is labelled 'AE' for agrarian economies, which is in contrast to the PPF for the mixed economies of Africa ('ME'). The institutional feasibility locus (IFL) is superimposed from Fig. 1 to illustrate something implicit in Table 2. Even if the agrarian nations did everything right in an institutional and technical sense, it would perhaps

[4]Being a 'small' nation is, of course, arbitrary. I have simply regarded as small those that are less than half the size of Kenya, itself a rather small African nation.

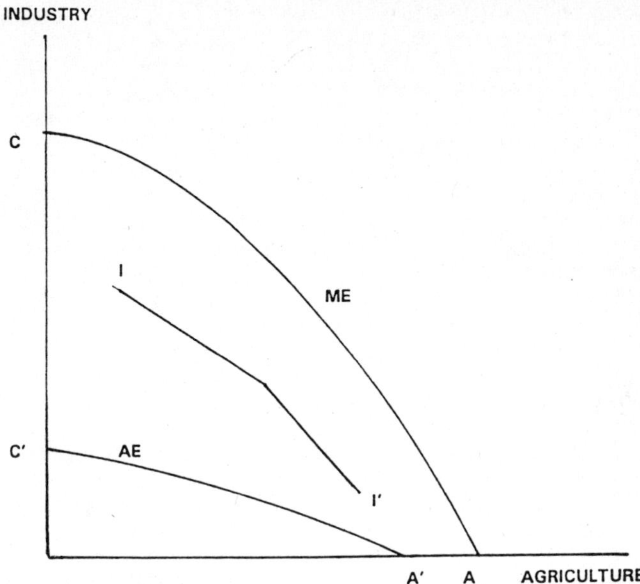

Figure 2 Production possibilities frontiers

be difficult to move out in production space to the vicinity of the IFL for the mixed economies.

The development 'problem' for Africa looks different if the status quo is found to be institutionally determined (as in some of the mixed economies), rather than existentially determined. Even this distinction is somewhat arbitrary. For instance, if Senegal, the Gambia, Guinea-Bissau, Mali, Burkina Faso, Ghana and Benin were one nation rather than seven, it would have profound implications for a new production possibilities frontier.

The development challenge is very different when one is working on an institutional feasibility locus that offers room for material improvement. On the other hand, when a nation-state is boxed in by a PPF such as AE in Fig. 2, the future of development is probably bleak.

Whither African 'development'?

The accepted idea of economic development has operated with something like Fig. 1 in mind. There is a PPF that is rather generous in terms of the status quo, and the development problem is two-fold: to augment that production possibilities frontier through technical change; and to undertake structural adjustment programmes that will move the IFL outwards towards the PPF.

For parts of agrarian Africa, however, the PPF is both unforgiving in its position, and extremely difficult to move very far to the northeast (see PPF labelled AE in Fig. 2). More critical perhaps, the movement along the axes in Fig. 2 is likely to be asymmetrical. Thus, while it may be possible to extend the horizontal intercept out, by means of careful investments in agriculture, it seems improbable that the PPF (AE) can be moved up the vertical axis very far, if at all.

By Western standards, some nations in Africa face the prospect of continued relative poverty. These nations perhaps face a future of being called 'under-developed' in terms of a teleology that is not of their choosing, and that is loaded with normative connotations from alien cultural precepts.

It remains to be proven that pastoralists and simple cultivators are somehow deprived in their essential existence in comparison with the urban apartment dweller of Lagos. Nothing in economic theory can prove that assertion. To equate level of income with happiness is simply to make a value judgement. To equate 'range of choice' with happiness is equally loaded.

This is not uncontroversial ground I am traversing. Who, it might be insisted, would deign to defend life in dirt-floored huts? There are two answers, one metaphysical and one empirical. The empirical response, based on earlier arguments, is that one need not be forced into the defensive role by explaining that which is largely ineluctable. Guilt is not the inevitable companion of those who would describe reality and necessity.

As for the metaphysical side, where is it written that all of humankind must, in order to be happy, reside in concrete jungles called cities? Where do we go for proof that wage labourers, performing at whatever task the market has given them, are better off than the African pastoralist sitting under a baobab tree contemplating the wind?

It is arguable that the idea of the coherent nation-state is still to take hold in some parts of sub-Saharan Africa. It follows, therefore, that the purposes of the future are not considered as collective concerns. And so it also follows that the idea of economic development as we understand that term has yet to take hold.

The long-run, sustainable success of economic assistance programmes still requires, as a precondition, the existence of a coherent nation-state. Until the relatively young nations of Africa structure themselves internally so that discourse about the purposes of the future is possible, sustained economic progress will be most difficult to achieve. In the absence of this structure, many economies will remain stuck on the institutional feasibility locus well inside the technically feasible PPF.

Nation-states must create institutional arrangements (incentives and sanctions) that will redefine the domains of choice for atomistic economic agents. Some of these incentives and sanctions will come from the arena of volitional choice, that is markets. Others will necessarily come from the arena of compulsion, whereby the nation-state has to create the legal foundations of capitalism. Both will constitute a new behavioural arena for economic agents, which has the purpose of improving the human condition (Bromley, 1993). Until these institutional preconditions for a vibrant economy are in place, much potential economic surplus will simply be dissipated in high transaction costs (Bromley and Chavas, 1989).

Past efforts to provide assistance in Asia have largely focused on coherent nation-states that had made some minimal commitment to the idea of development as an industrialising process. Most of these nation-states were mature survivors of colonial interventions. Some of them had mounted national armies to repel external aggressors (as opposed to regional armies engaged in civil war). Most of these nations depended upon the careful management of scarce water to cultivate a food grain that was the basis of the food supply. These sedentary societies had highly elaborated institutional arrangements for influencing and controlling the actions of its citizens.

Sub-Saharan Africa presents a picture differing from almost all the attributes described above. In essence, the very idea of economic development has to be redefined so that it fits the empirical circumstances found in sub-Saharan Africa.

The necessary first step is to abandon the automatic presumption of economic development. As outsiders, our purpose in collaboration with the nations of sub-Saharan Africa needs to be redefined so that it occurs under different presumptions. Are we there to cause economic development, or are we there to assist with particular problems for which we have special expertise? If the latter, we need not undertake these activities only on the condition that particular nations will someday choose a path that we have defined as economic development. We will be under no illusions as to why we as donors are there, thus making it easier to focus attention on the real problem of the moment. Is groundwater being depleted? Are pesticides getting into drinking water? Are children exposed to unnecessary hazards? Are crop diseases ravaging fields? Are post-harvest losses larger than they might be? Is land ownership an impediment to productivity or equity?

The foreign assistance community abounds with expertise to assist with each of these problems and many more. That assistance is part of a long-run commitment to technical co-operation with a number of nations and their citizens in most parts of Africa. Such assistance need not presume development, nor should it be justified on those grounds. It is quite enough to justify such assistance on the grounds that it helps individuals deal with their difficult circumstances.

As this technical co-operation progresses, some nations will seem to embrace the traditional idea of development, while others will not. When the idea of development is endogenised and acted upon by a few nations, we will begin to see some of the changes now familiar in Asia and Latin America. Prior technical assistance will provide an enhanced plateau from which further development might proceed.

For those nations that fail to embrace the prevailing doctrine of economic development, technical and financial assistance will not have been in vain. Certain conditions, and certain lives, will have been improved. Beyond that, little else may have happened. But it is not for us as outsiders to denounce this outcome, or to despair that we have been unsuccessful in our economic development assistance. For we were never really giving development assistance. We were simply helping to solve particular problems, in particular places, that affected particular people.

The history of the idea of economic development suggests that we will certainly fail if we persist in believing that we can bring 'development' to much of sub-Saharan Africa. Our idea of economic development must be reconsidered and augmented with the companion idea of gradual economic transitions. Each nation-state will adopt its own particular version of what it regards as development. Since the mid-1960s, outsiders have told African nations what constitutes economic development, and what they must do to achieve it. Perhaps the time has come to experiment with programmes in which African nations figure out what they want and when they want it. Perhaps it is time for them to determine the purpose of their future. We should be ready when they call us. Indeed, we might even help them in that determination. But we should go quietly and with much humility about the alleged benefits of modernity and the 'development' that caused it.

References

Bairoch, P. (1975). *The Economic Development of the Third World Since 1900.* University of California Press, Berkeley, CA.

Bromley, D.W. (1989). *Economic Interests and Institutions: The Conceptual Foundations of Public Policy.* Blackwell, Oxford.

Development reconsidered: D.W. Bromley

Bromley, D.W. (1993), Reconstituting economic systems: institutions in national economic development, *Development Policy Review* **11** (2), 131–151.

Bromley, D.W. and Chavas, J.-P. (1989), On risk, transactions, and economic development in the semi-arid tropics, *Economic Development and Cultural Change* **37**, 719–736.

Mellor, J.W. (1990), Agriculture on the road to industrialization, in (C.K. Eicher and J.M. Staatz, eds), *Agricultural Development in the Third World.* Johns Hopkins University Press, Baltimore, pp 70–88.

Timmer, C.P. (1990), The agricultural transformation, in (C.K. Eicher and J.M. Staatz, eds), *Agricultural Development in the Third World.* Johns Hopkins University Press, Baltimore, pp. 47–69.

World Bank (1981), *Accelerated Development in Sub-Saharan Africa: An Agenda for Action.* Washington, DC.

World Bank (1983), *Sub-Saharan Africa: Progress Report on Development Prospects and Programs.* Washington, DC.

World Bank (1984), *Toward Sustained Development in Sub-Saharan Africa.* Washington, DC.

World Resources Institute (1994), *World Resources 1994–95: A Guide to the Global Environment.* Oxford University Press for the World Resources Institute, New York, NY.

PART II

PROPERTY REGIMES IN DEVELOPMENT POLICY

[5]

The Commons, Common Property, and Environmental Policy

DANIEL W. BROMLEY
Anderson-Bascom Professor and Acting Director, Institute for Environmental Studies, University of Wisconsin, Madison, U.S.A.

Abstract. The conceptual confusion among property, common property, open access resources, and the "tragedy of the commons" is identified and rectified. Property rights are defined and clarified. From that it is possible to understand the traditional confusion between open access resources and common property resources. It is urged that common property *regimes* be used in place of common property *resources*. This will emphasize that institutional arrangements are human creations and that natural resources can be managed as private property, as common property, or as state property. It is the property regime — an authority system — that indicates the rules of use of a variety of natural resources.

Key words. Commons, common property, property rights.

I. Introduction

There can be no more important aspect of scholarship than that of concepts and language. If scholars use the same words or terms to describe fundamentally different fact situations, ideas, or phenomena, then progress in understanding is impeded rather than advanced. In the literature on natural resources and environmental policy, it would be difficult to find an *idea* (a concept) that is as misunderstood as that of the *commons* and *common property*. The mischief to arise from the continuing failure to understand common property is perverse in both scholarly discussions, and in public policy formulation. On the former front, scholars will show no hesitancy to expound on the problems inherent in common property without the benefit of first defining *property*, and without betraying any understanding of the historical and contemporary facts surrounding common property regimes. On the practical side, scholars will show equal confidence in advising all who will listen about how to "solve" the so-called *tragedy of the commons*. This mischief is then perpetuated among politicians who, as Keynes put it, are under the thrall of some now defunct economist. While this may be a bit strong, there is cause for serious concern when policy recommendations are predicated upon false problem definitions.

The literature is full of casual references to *common property resources* as if this were a universal and immutable classification — almost as if the prevailing institutional form were somehow inherent in a natural resource. Never mind that in one place trees and fish and range forage are controlled and managed as private property, in another setting they are controlled and managed as state property, in another setting they are controlled and

Environmental and Resource Economics **2**: 1—17, 1992.

managed as common property, and in other settings they are not controlled or managed at all but are instead used by anyone who so desires to use them. I would submit that there is no such thing as a common property *resource* – there are only resources controlled and managed as common property, or as state property, or as private property. Or, and this is where confusion persists in the literature, there are resources over which *no property rights* have been recognized. We call these latter resources *open access resources* (*res nullius*).[1]

The key concept here is *property*. Property is a benefit (or income) stream, and a property right is a claim to a benefit stream that some higher body – usually the state – will agree to protect through the assignment of duty to others who may covet, or somehow interfere with, the benefit stream. Rights have no meaning without correlated duties and the management problem with open access resources is that there are no duties on aspiring users to refrain from use (Bromley 1989a, 1989b). Property *is not* an object but is rather a social relation that defines the property holder with respect to something of value (the benefit stream) against all others. Property is a triadic social relation involving benefit streams, right holders, and duty bearers (Hallowell 1943). It is for this reason that I urge us to consider the concept of *property regimes*. Regimes, after all, are human artifacts reflecting instrumental origins, and a property regime is fundamentally instrumental in nature. That is, property regimes take on their special character by virtue of collective perceptions regarding what is scarce (and hence *possibly* worth protecting with rights), and what is valuable (and hence *certainly* worth protecting with rights). Property is a social instrument, and particular property regimes are chosen for particular purposes.

The fallacy in traditional approaches to the commons is that writers have failed to understand the concept of property, they have very often treated a particular natural resource as if it had inherent characteristics that suggested it would everywhere be controlled under a particular type of property regime, and they have often failed to note that the world is replete with reasonably successful common property regimes.[2] By successful I mean that the natural resource has not been squandered, that some level of investment in the natural resource has occurred, and that the co-owners of the resource are not in a perpetual state of anarchy. In short, common property regimes exist and function very much like private property regimes and state property regimes. That is, some are not working very well, while others work very well indeed.

It is important to determine if there are reasonably successful common property regimes operating in the world. Recent literature confirms the existence of such regimes, some of which appear to work very well indeed (Berkes, 1989; Berkes *et al.* 1989; Bromley and Cernea, 1989; McCay and Acheson, 1987; National Academy of Sciences, 1986). It is also of interest to note a renewed interest in institutional arrangements over natural resources.[3] In the remainder of this paper, I will focus on property regimes as authority systems. This emphasis is necessary for the simple reason that the essence of property rights is a structure of duties that will give any particular benefit stream protection against adverse claims. And where does that protection come from if not from the "state"? By this I do not necessarily mean some remote central government. I mean simply a *unit of coercion* that has the legitimate sanction to enforce structures of rights and duties. The authority system can either be a central government, or it can be a local village council. The important issue here is that individuals feel compelled to comply with the institutions in effect. With any property regime there are two levels at which this unit of coercion must operate. At the boundary of the regime, it is essential that the property rights of the regime itself possess legitimacy *vis-à-vis* the larger political and economic environment. This dimension assures that non-owners will not be able to benefit with impunity from the resource under a common property regime.

Inside the regime, coercion operates to hold members in check in their use of the natural resource. With common property regimes this authority will operate on the group of co-owners, while in private property regimes this authority defines accepted norms of behavior for the individual owner.[4] Recall that in a common property regime one individual co-owner has no rights unless one also has duties; it is the reciprocal nature of rights and duties among co-owners that defines the authority system. Some may regard common property regimes as essentially "cooperative" in nature and hence the idea of coercion *within* the group may appear incongruous. But of course the problem here is with the idea of "cooperation." Farmers on an irrigation system — a classic case of a common property regime — certainly compete for scarce water and in this sense cooperation may seem irrelevant. But on closer inspection the idea of cooperation can be seen as similar to compliance in that each irrigator cooperates by complying with the internal rules of water allocation among competing interests. Farmers cooperate for the simple reason that in the absence of this shared structure of rights and duties there would be anarchy.

To discuss coercion in this sense may call for some clarification. Nozick's minimal state — characterized by autonomously developed institutional arrangements — may seem coercion free. But of course any set of rules, whether autonomous or imposed, have as their purpose a modification in individual behaviors. This redefinition of individual choice sets, regardless of the source of institutions, comprises "coercion" in that individuals agree to be bound by new choice domains. Rousseau insisted that humans were born "free," while Thomas Paine argued that humans did not willingly enter into civil society — and thereby relinquish some "natural" rights — only to be made worse off. He argued that they did so only because such structures promised to comprise (a Pareto) improvement from the Hobbesian anarchy of the status quo ante. The assurance provided by mutual coercion, mutually agreed upon, was a necessary evil. Civil society (a *burgerliche gesellschaft*) was the only way to secure the "natural rights" which all humans were born to. Left unspecified was the exact content of these natural rights that were to be protected by civil society.

Kant challenged the "natural" dimension of property rights. His position was that Locke had confused empirical possession with *de jure* or intelligible possession (Williams, 1977).[5] That is, while physical appropriation is necessary for something to become mine — that is, for me to be able to control its benefit stream — such appropriation is not sufficient. Put somewhat differently, Kant argued that empirical possession cannot establish meaningful ownership. Kant further maintained that this confusion in Locke led him (Locke) to fail to see that a social convention — a social contract — is logically prior to meaningful ownership; only *intelligible possession* constitutes property.[6] Ownership is a concept in the mind of non-owners as much, if not more, than it is in the mind of owners. It is this recognition *on the part of others* that distinguishes intelligible possession from empirical possession.

Such recognition is the essence of a meaningful authority system that gives operational content to the idea of property rights. As suggested above, such authority systems can arise autonomously from within a group, or they may arise by imposition from without. I have elsewhere devoted considerable discussion to the difference in these two paths (Bromley, 1989b). Schotter (1981) has likewise discussed both forms of institutional innovation. Regardless of the origins of such institutional arrangements, their purpose is precisely to define an authority system which can give meaning to the notion of property rights.

Let me now turn to a discussion of authority systems and property regimes.

II. The Decline of Authority Systems: An Historical Overview

Much of early human history was characterized by self-conscious natural resource use, in which people would move, or they would take extreme actions (infanticide, imposed "family planning") to control their total demands on the natural resources on which they depended. A major break in this pattern of self-conscious resource management appeared with the gradual breakdown of internalized social mechanisms for controlling resource demands, a process that was greatly abetted by the rise of powerful leaders presiding over large territories that transcended traditional "villages." Natural resources came to be regarded as sources of revenue instead of merely sources of sustenance for the local population. Many such rulers sought to create quasi-military states, an exercise that required the generation of considerable revenue. These accumulators of wealth relied on two general sources for their income — the agricultural produce of their subjects, and the export of whatever natural resources were available. And this brings us to the second aspect explaining the break with the past.

Colonial powers were beginning to explore the tropics for a variety of products, not least of which was wood. The revenue desires of the new territorial rulers fit nicely with the material needs of European nations. When supply uncertainties — or higher prices — were not to the satisfaction of the more powerful nations it became expedient to impose more direct rule. Colonial adminstration is not inexpensive and in many instances it was required to pay for itself out of locally generated revenues. This brought colonial administrators directly into the business of resource exploitation to cover the costs of their presence. These two force — first the rise of powerful territorial rulers, and then the appearance of colonial administrators — both accelerated the deterioration of village-level social conventions that had previously acted to control resource use. It was necessary for alien (whether regional or European) sources of power and authority to undermine and destroy local systems of power and authority; otherwise, the legitimacy and authority of the alien power would be compromised and challenged. These changes — territorial governments replacing local-level administration, and in its turn colonialism, largely destroyed any vestiges of real authority residing at the local (or village) level.

My point here is that villages have, over time, lost their ability to be the locus of control and authority over the actions of their residents with respect to natural resource use and management. Not only were villages undermined by remote centers of political and economic power, but forces also led life at the village level to become individualistic. As the village became more atomized — more individualized — it became increasingly difficult to take the necessary, and customary, collective actions to address natural resource shortages. As populations grew, aided by new medical technologies that reduced infant mortality, many collectively managed "village" lands were invaded and illegally appropriated by families — a process that was facilitated by the powerlessness of the village management regime to prevent such incursions. The poorest segments of the village, afraid or unable to privately appropriate the village "commons", were left behind and forced to rely, increasingly, on the poorest lands that remained in the shrinking commons. With the collective area shrinking because of illegal "privatization", a rapidly increasing population was forced to rely on an ever-smaller area.[7]

What do I mean by the village as an "authority system"? In India, for example, the village had been a territorial concept, not necessarily identified with any particular group of households or families. Households had a common and customary obligation to one another in both social and economic matters. The essence of village life was a structure of both permission and restraint, within which all human endeavor operated. Prevailing status and authority systems left few in doubt as to their domain of choice in a number of private and public affairs. Indeed, one could argue that the very purpose of a village was to serve as a unit of control and cooperation such that the welfare of the group would be enhanced. The village served as an economic and social unit of great significance to the use and management of land and related natural resources.

This significance can be understood by considering the relationship of rights in land to the political structure of the Indian village; those who owned no land were socially and economically subordinate to landholding interests. Within this stratified structure the village community still enjoyed an effective system of self-government. The secret of its success lay in the nature of property in land and the various other allied institutions that subsisted in the village. As long as rights in land were governed by rules and customs which prevented the emergence of great disparities in wealth and income the system of self-government remained efficient. But a change in the institutions of landed property led almost immediately to the decay of this self-governance (Gupta, 1964).

The effectiveness of the village as an authority system was dependent upon the exercise of influence and control over actions of individual members of the community. Prior to colonialism, ruling monarchs/leaders exercised control over the political and economic life of villages. The villages were not only suppliers of necessities for such leaders, but local outposts of control and authority over scattered peoples in the hinterland. The political legitimacy of the ruling entity was secured through the extension of representatives down through the political structure of regional town, and ultimately, rural village. There was always the need for revenue to support the activities of the ruling class. During that time the question of who actually owned land was not as important as it was to become. The availability of surplus agricultural land served to relieve population pressure against the land. To be sure, population growth has diminished the feasibility of this option.

In India, the disintegration of the important role played by villages can be traced to the introduction of new land laws, the related intrusion of urban interests into the rural village, the opening up to external trade and markets, and the centralization of revenue and judicial administration leaving the village councils with little or no formal role. With the full spread of colonialism, much of this political and economic structure — already under stress — was finally destroyed. The essence of colonial adminstration was to harness the political power of the villages to secure legitimacy for the alien power. It became necessary to undermine existing authority systems responsive to the pre-colonial rulers, and to supplant them with authority systems that would be responsive to the interests and imperatives of the colonial administration.

The individualization of village life, fostered by the privatization of the better village lands, left the peasant increasingly dependent on the market, and on the moneylender. It would not be correct to assume that all of these forces leading to the disintegration of the village were the direct result of colonial rule; many changes were underway prior to colonial administration.

One obvious component of such change was the increased importance of markets for local natural resources quite in advance of any colonial administration. The British East India Company, for instance, was founded in 1600 but direct British colonial administration in India was not in full flower until after the Sepoy Rebellion of 1857.

In Africa, the French were particularly contemptuous of indigenous structures and institutions. In northwest Africa (what we now know as Algeria, Tunisia, and Morocco) the French encountered a thinly settled nomadic (or pastoral) peoples in the dry mountainous regions of the hinterland. The French claimed a portion of the lands unclaimed by the tribes or claimed only on the basis of custom, while the tribes were given firm title to what remained to them. This process restricted tribal territories and led to increased crowding of the nomads, and also insufficient space for settlements. As with other colonial administrations, the French wanted to individualize titles to land, and this structure eventually evolved into a form of both government and private colonization. The government side of it entailed the establishment of entire new villages in barren areas, but the private colonization was the more important. In 1873 the French sought to break up collectively owned lands by decreeing that individual plots must be established to become the private property of individuals under French law. If only a single collective holder desired individualization, then it was required to occur, regardless of the wishes of the other collective owners. The result was a plundering of tribal properties, and an increase in lawsuits. In the process, Frenchmen, but also urban Algerians and other notables, acquired large estates. French land holdings doubled in the twenty years between 1870 and 1890 – from 800,000 ha to 1.6 million ha. By 1930, 26,153 Europeans owned 2.3 million ha, compared to 7.7 million ha owned by only 617,543 Algerians (von Albertini, 1982, p. 268).

The British in West Africa were not markedly different. In the far west of Africa – the Gold Coast – cocoa production expanded rapidly because it fits in well with the traditional economic and social structure. Lots of land "belonged" to the tribes, villages, and clans, but the produce from it went to the individual farming family. Immigrant families "rented" land, cleared the jungle, and planted both foodstuffs and cocoa seedlings, which bore fruit in 4–6 years. But erosion and a retreat of the forest began. Additionally, more profound changes were underway. Food production declined and the production for export began. Cash became prevalent, and the individualization of land holdings was not far behind.

The story of colonial administration of village political and economic life was similar – impose European institutional arrangements so as to: (1) encourage the cultivation of those crops of interest to the colonial administration; (2) provide tax revenues to support that same administration; and (3) undermine indigenous political structures and processes to further strengthen the position of that colonial administration. These transformations essentially destroyed the village as an autonomous decision-making unit, which was, of course, the very reason for those imposed institutional changes.

Once colonialism gave way to national independence — largely in the two decades following World War II — prevailing systems of authority at the village level were once again in need of modification and realignment with the new imperatives and interests of a national government. The disruptions destroyed, yet again, evolved relationships of power, influence, and authority. During these eras of creation and modification of local-level systems of authority and control over daily life, populations were expanding rapidly, and technology was altering the way in which people used — and interacted with — their environment. At the very time when the ability to control individual behavior at the village level was at its lowest, populations were expanding and the pressure on the natural resource base was accelerating. Degradation of forested areas was the predictable outcome.

The new independent nation-states that arose following World War II have shown little interest in revitalizing local-level systems of authority. As with previous rulers and colonial administrators, the governments of these nation-states do not relish the thought of local political forces that might challenge the legitimacy and authority of the national government. This means that many forested areas have become the "property" of the national government — an act of expropriation when viewed from the perspective of the residents of millions of villages. This expropriation is all the more damaging when the national governments lack the rudiments of a management capability. These new governments are struggling with the problems of governance, economic development, self-sufficiency, and political stability. In this setting, we see resource destruction continuing — and even accelerating.[8]

In the Ivory Coast, commercial loggers have long engaged in wanton high-grading of timber stocks, leaving the lesser-valued timber for others to poach and burn so as to provide agricultural plots. As the better stocks have disappeared the value of recent timber marketings has fallen, putting yet more pressure on the remaining stands so as to sustain export earnings. These practices have — in a familiar pattern — been legislated against, but only indifferently enforced. In fact, since independence the Government of the Ivory Coast has pursued an extremely destructive course of action toward its forests so as to earn foreign exchange and tax revenues. As a result:

> . . . loggers continue to exploit the remaining forests, more or less uncontrolled, and farmers have followed roads developed for logging operations, establishing cocoa, coffee and food crops, with the widespread practice of "slash and burn" farming. Such intrusions have also begun in the classified forest reserves and national parks. Government now estimates that this process transforms about 0.4 million ha of unspoiled high forest per year. Were these trends to continue, Ivory Coast could become a net importer of timber before the end of the century [World Bank, 1985, p. 2].

The World Bank Report continues by pointing to a persistent practice in renewable resource management — showing more interest in the symptoms of problems than in the root cause of those problems. Specificially, we are told that the continued degradation of forests poses scant ecological threat. However, it is reported that the subsequent invasion by land-hungry farmers imposes severe damage on the remaining forest cover causing increased soil erosion, reduced rainfall, and lower water tables. Hence, the "Government is becoming more conservation-minded in its approach to forestry in particular, and to natural resources in general (World Bank, 1985, p. 3)." Notice that while the government is unwilling to threaten the political power of the commercial loggers who savage the forest, the entrance of small farmers into the cleared space is viewed as an important ecological crisis that motivates the Government to become "conservation minded." Is it easier to get "conservation minded" against farmers than against loggers who generate foreign exchange and commercial timber? There seems little interest in dealing with the conditions that cause farmers to invade the cleared forest. But it is clear in the Government's mind that the farmers are the "enemy" of the forest. "Conservation" then becomes an *anti-farmer* activity, doing little to endear it (conservation) to the masses in the villages upon whose shoulders the success of such programs will ultimately fall. It would seem more reasonable to undertake development interventions to deal with the land-use problems of the farmers than to blame them for degradation and set them against conservation. Successful forest management programs in the developing countries *must* be coincident with farmers' interests, not opposed to them.

III. Property Rights as Systems of Authority[9]

I am concerned with authority systems precisely because a natural resource regime is an explicit (or implicit) structure of rights and duties characterizing the relationship of individuals to one another with respect to that particular resource (Bromley 1989b). New institutional arrangements are continually established to define the property regime over land and related natural resources — whether that regime be one we would call state property, private (individual) property, or one of common property. These institutional arrangements define (or locate) one individual *vis-à-vis* others, both within the group (if there is one), and with individuals outside of the group. By thus defining one individual's choice domain *vis-à-vis* that of others, property rights indicate who has the *legitimate authority* to act in a predetermined manner. This authority, coming as it does through officially recognized property relations, carries the implicit backing of the state. Officially sanctioned property rights mean, at bottom, the willingness of the state to step in to protect the interests of those holding the property rights under discussion. Without effective (or credible) enforcement one has anarchy; small wonder that the relentless theme of the propertied classes down through history has been to insist that the *primary* function of the state is to protect private property. One can search in vain for the dispossessed making a similar argument.

We can define property relations between two or more individuals (or groups) by stating that one party has an interest that is protected by a *right* only when all others have a *duty*. It is essential to understand that *property* is not an object such as land, but is, rather *a benefit stream that is only as secure as the duty of all others to respect the conditions that protect that stream.* When one has a right one has the expectation in both the law and in practice that their claims will be respected by those with duty. For most purposes it is sufficient to consider four possible resource regimes: (1) state property regimes; (2) individual property regimes; (3) common property regimes; (4) non-property regimes (open access).

A. STATE PROPERTY REGIMES

In a state property regime, ownership and control over use rests in the hands of the state. Individuals and groups may be able to make use of the resources, but only at the forbearance of the state. National (or state) forests, national (or state) parks, and military reservations are examples of state property regimes. Shifts from state property to other types, or vice versa, are possible. For instance, the 1957 nationalization of Nepal's village forests by the government converted a common property regime at the village level into a state property regime.[10] The state may either directly manage the use of state-owned natural resources through government agencies or lease them to groups or individuals who are thus given usufruct rights over such resources for a specified period of time. The "tree growing associations" created experimentally in West Bengal (and elsewhere in India) consist of groups of landless or marginal farmers who are given a block of marginal public land for tree planting are examples. The members are not granted land titles, but the group is given usufruct rights on the land and ownership rights of its produce (Cernea, 1985).

State property regimes are characterized by the separation of ownership and control (management) from actual use. That is, "ownership" resides with the citizenry at large, management and control resides with a class of bureaucrats, while use resides with a subset of the citizenry.

B. INDIVIDUAL PROPERTY REGIMES

Individual property regimes are the most familiar to many of us, though of course much "individual" property is, in fact, co-owned by spouses. Those who see ultimate wisdom in private property must answer for several phenomena. First, much of the world's landlessness is not attributable to an absolute physical scarcity of land but rather to its ownership concentrated in the hands of a few powerful families. This is especially prevalent in large parts of Latin America. Second, we are often told that private property leads to the "highest and best use of land." With large segments of Latin America's best agricultural land devoted to cattle ranching, skeptics may be excused if they challenge that particular truth. Notice that individual property is not necessarily — as Proudhon put it — "theft", but a good deal of theft has ended up as individual property — especially in the western world where European colonizers appropriated vast terrain inhabited by tribal peoples.

The best land in most settings has already been privatized and the worst has been left in the "public domain" — either as state property, as common property (*res communes*), or as open access (*res nullius*). It is not legitimate to ask of common property regimes that they manage highly variable and low-productivity resources, and also to adapt and adjust to severe internal and external pressures when conditions beyond the bounds of that common property regime preclude the adaptation to those internal and external pressures. That is, the "internal pressure" of population growth may be impossible to resolve if traditional adaptation mechanism — hiving off for instance — are now precluded by increased population growth *beyond the confines of the common property regime under study*. Likewise, if private property and associated fences prevent the traditional movements of a people and their livestock it is hardly legitimate to blame them and their property regime. Private property regimes *appear* to be stable and adaptive because they have the social and legal sanction to exclude excess population, and effectively to resist — through the power of the state — unwanted intrusions. These powers have been eroded for common property regimes. To see the exclusionary aspect of private property, recall the effects of primogeniture. The dispossession of younger sons (to say nothing of *all* daughters) is regarded as a *costless* social process and therefore it looks as though private property is robust and adaptable; it "works." Private property in such a setting may "work" for the oldest son; but those with no rights in the estate may be harder to convince.

C. COMMON PROPERTY REGIMES

The third regime is the common property regime (*res communes*). First, note that common property represents private property for the group (since all others are excluded from use and decision making), and that individuals have rights (*and duties*) in a common property regime (Ciriacy-Wantrup and Bishop, 1975). In one important sense then, common property has something very much in common with private (individual) property — exclusion of non-owners; common property is corporate group property. The property-owning groups vary in nature, size, and internal structure across a broad spectrum, but they are social units with definite membership and boundaries, with certain common interests, with at least some interaction among members, with common cultural norms, and often their own endogenous authority systems. Tribal groups or subgroups, villages or subvillages, neighborhoods, transhumant groups, kin systems or extended families are all examples. These groupings hold customary ownership of certain resources such as farm land, grazing land, and water sources.

Corporate group property regimes are not incompatible with private, individual use of one or another segment of the resources held under common property. For instance, the ownership of certain farmland may be vested in a group, and the group's leaders may then allocate portions of the land to various individuals or families. As long as those individuals cultivate "their" plot, no other person has the right to use it or to benefit from its produce. But notice that the cultivator holds use rights only (usufruct) and is unable to alienate or transfer either the ownership or the use of that land to another individual. Once the current user ceases to put it to good use the land reverts to the jurisdiction of the corporte ownership of the group.

The essence of any property regime is an authority system that can assure that the expectations of rights holders are met. The presence of compliance through the expedient of an authority system is a necessary condition for the viability of any property regime. Private property would be nothing without the requisite authority system that makes certain the rights and duties are adhered to. This same situation exists for common property. When the authority system breaks down — for whatever reason — then common property (*res communes*) degenerates into open access (*res nullius*). It is not the property regime that explains compliance and "wise" natural resource use. It is, instead, the authority system that insures that the particular property regime is adhered to. In private property regimes the owner can always call on the coercive power of the state to assure compliance and to prevent intrusion by non-owners. In common property regimes two problems may arise. The first is that a breakdown in compliance by co-owners may be difficult to prevent because of the loss of opportunity arising from changes elsewhere in the economy. If spreading privatization precludes seasonal adaptation to fluctuating resource conditions then overuse of a local resource may be necessary by members of the group. Secondly, if the state holds common property in low esteem — that is, if the state disregards the interests of those segments of the population totally dependent upon common property resources — then external threats to common property will not receive the same governmental response as would a threat to private property. The willingness of the state to legitimize and protect different property regimes is partly explained by the state's perception of the importance of the citizens holding different types of property rights. If pastoralists are regarded as politically marginal — a reasonable hypothesis in many parts of the world — then the property regimes central to pastoralism will be only indifferently protected against threat from others. If those threatening pastoralist property regimes happen to have more favor from the state then protection of common property will be haphazard at best. The natural resources important to pastoralism have a relatively low value in exchange and hence it is easy for national governments to discount the economic and political importance of pastoral peoples. However, there is no other economic use of many of these resources at the extensive margin and hence their use in pastoral economies is rational both individually, as well as collectively. It is, in essence, the principle of comparative advantage at work (Bromley, 1989a).

D. OPEN ACCESS REGIMES

Finally we have the open access situation in which there is no property (*res nullius*). Because there are no property rights in an open access situation, it is logically inconsistent to assert — as many often do — that "everybody's property is nobody's property." It can only be said that "everybody's access is nobody's property." Whether it is a lake fishery, grazing forage, or fuelwood, a resource under an open access regime will belong to the party to first exercise control over it. The investment in (or improvement of) open access regimes must first focus on this institutional dimension. If property and management arrangements are not determined, and if the investment is in the form of a capital asset such as improved tree species or range revegetation, the institutional vacuum of open access insures that use rates will eventually deplete the asset.

Open access results from the absence — or the breakdown — of an authority system whose very purpose was to assure compliance with a set of behavioral conditions with respect to the natural resource. Valuable natural resources that are available to the first party to effect capture have become open access resources through a series of institutional failures that have undermined former collective management regimes. There is no authority in an open-access regime. Governments who have appropriated forests from local-level management bodies — primarily villages — and have failed to manage them in an effective manner have created *de jure* state property, but *de facto* open access; the absence of effective management and enforcement has simply turned the forest into a resource that can be exploited on a first-come-first-served basis.

IV. Concluding Observations

There is a critical difference between *open access resources* and *common property resources*, and the difference turns on the very concept of *property*. Property is a future benefit stream, and hence there is no *property* in an open access situation, there is only the opportunity to use something. Many of us see situations of open access and improperly regard them as situations of common property. At the same time, most of us have seen common property regimes at work without recognizing them as such. Irrigation systems represent the essence of a common property regime. There is a well-defined group whose membership is restricted, there is an asset to be managed (the physical distribution system), there is an annual stream of benefits (the water which constitutes a valuable agricultural input), and there is a need for group management of both the capital stock and the annual flow (necessary maintenance of the system and a process for allocating the water among members of the group of irrigators) to make sure that the system continues to yield benefits to the group. There could not be a clearer illustration of a common property regime than irrigation systems, despite the fact that they do not always work as well as they ought to. Having said that, there is a growing literature that documents the extent to which common property regimes — given proper external legitimacy by the state, and given technical assistance within the range — function better than many state property regimes (Chopra *et al.* 1990).

Most often when we observe resource problems in the developing countries these situations arise under open access, not under true common property. An equally serious mistake is made in identifying the specific problem to be addressed. We will usually suggest that the problem is one of poor range condition, or a lack of water, or undernourished livestock, or a lack of fuelwood for cooking. Unfortunately, these are not problems but are rather symptoms of problems. Development assistance projects to fix symptoms do not fix problems.

The real problem is, in many of these instances, the absence of effective group management regimes necessary to allow the sustained use of the resource base over time. That is, an earlier situation of common property has deteriorated into one of open access. These resource regimes must bear the brunt of their own indigenous population growth, but often must also absorb those individuals displaced from other areas who can freely migrate. Because these migrants cannot, by definition, settle on private lands, there is no other option open to them. Even if the migrants go to urban areas they must be supplied with fuelwood and/or charcoal which comes from the public domain.

An important question remains: why don't common property regimes always adapt to changing conditions in a way that will protect the natural resource? A corollary question, therefore, is why should such management regimes be supported through project interventions? The answer is quite obvious. To install or to support a particular property regime on the basis of its ability to resist external pressure is the wrong approach — especially when that pressure arises in a manner that is quite unrelated to the nature of the property regime itself. Collectives select property regimes on the basis of their suitability for the resource in question — its variability, its productivity, and so on. If we have learned anything over the past several years about property regimes it is that the choice of regimes *must* be based on the characteristics of the natural resource under consideration, and the characteristics and objectives of the human associations that interact with these natural resources. To think that there are universal truths about suitable property regimes – that is, to imagine that individual (private) property, or state property, or common property are always appropriate for specific natural resources – is to commit a most serious form of sophistry.

Development interventions will be successful only if we approach the choice of particular property regimes with the idea in mind that such regimes are policy instruments rather than policy goals. We must, therefore, have a clear idea as to what the dependent population wishes to accomplish with respect to the particular natural resource under consideration. We must also understand the dynamics of the resource, and be certain how various degrees of use will affect its long-run viability. Any property regime is the legally and socially sanctioned ability to exclude certain users, and so the fortunate owner(s) can force others to go elsewhere. Common property regimes, because they are predicated on groups, are less successful at excluding individuals in order to keep total resource demands in line with sustainable use. Private property regimes, on the other hand, have a longer history – and a social expectation – of excluding individuals. If exclusion of excess population is thought to be unacceptable, private property regimes *appear* to avoid the problem of exclusion through partible inheritance where plots are successively divided among heirs. The outcome of this process, however, is an ownership structure in which individual plots are too small to be viable economic units. Common property regimes, unlike individual property regimes, do not result in atomization, but rather seek ways to accommodate the increased population. Where this accommodation is successful the long-run viability of the resource is secured.

The challenge to the social sciences is to comprehend the interplay of human and biotic communities in such a way that we might better suggest property regimes that are propitious for both.

Notes

1 It is encouraging that some textbooks now recognize the important distinction between open access resources and common property resources. See, especially, Pearce and Turner (1990).

2 Though it would take us beyond the domain of natural resources, it must be understood that a private club is a common property regime. Such clubs, whether "country clubs" or more restricted collectives, are joint management regimes controlling assets, and allocating use rights among co-owners or members.

3 There is now an International Association for the Study of Common Property.

4 Recall that it is illegal to grow, for instance, marijuanna on land that one may own in fee simple (freehold). This tends to remind us that private ownership of land does not imply complete autonomy for the owner.

5 By "intelligible possession" Kant meant the social recognition of the property claim of the "owner." In my terms this is the *triadic* aspect of rights that recognizes the owner and the claim against all others.

16 *Daniel W. Bromley*

[6] See Sugden (1986) for an argument along Lockean lines that empirical possession constitutes property rights.
[7] See Jodha (1986) for an account of the degree of privatization of common lands in India.
[8] For a discussion of the role of commercial logging in resource degradation in India see (Guha, 1990).
[9] Portions of this section are taken from Bromley and Cernea (1989).
[10] However, in the absence of effective enforcement of the new property regime, coupled with the villagers' perception that "their" forests had been expropriated by the government, the resource became — for all practical purposes — an open-access resource which villagers felt free to squander.

Bibliography

Berkes, Fikret (ed.) (1989), *Common Property Resources; Ecology and Community-Based Sustainable Development*, London: Belhaven Press.

Berkes, Fikret, David Feeny, Bonnie McCay, and James M. Acheson (1989), 'The Benefits of the Commons', *Nature* **340**(6229), 91—93, July 13.

Bromley, Daniel W. (1989a), 'Property Relations and Economic Development: The Other Land Reform', *World Development* **17**(6), 867—77.

Bromley, Daniel W. (1989b), *Economic Interests and Institutions: The Conceptual Foundations of Public Policy*, Oxford: Basil Blackwell.

Bromley, Daniel W. (1991), *Environment and Economy: Property Rights and Public Policy*, Oxford: Basil Blackwell.

Bromley, Daniel W. and Michael M. Cernea (1989), *The Management of Common Property Natural Resources: Some Conceptual and Operational Fallacies*, Washington, D.C., World Bank Discussion Paper 57.

Bromley, Daniel W. and Devendra P. Chapagain (1984), 'The Village Against the Center: Resource Depletion in South Asia', *American Journal of Agricultural Economics* **66**, 868—73.

Cernea, Michael M. (ed.) (1985), *Putting People First: Sociological Variables in Rural Development*, Oxford: Oxford University Press.

Chopra, K., G. K. Kandekedi, and M. N. Murty (1990), *Participatory Development and Common Property Resources*, New Delhi: Sage.

Ciriacy-Wantrup, S. V. and Richard C. Bishop, (1975), 'Common Property as a Concept in Natural Resource Policy', *Natural Resources Journal* **15**, 713—27.

Guha, R. (1990), *The Unquiet Woods*, Oxford: Oxford University Press.

Gupta, Sulekh Chandra (1960), 'The Village Community and Its Disintegration in Uttar Pradesh in the Early Nineteenth Century', in: *Readings in Indian Economic History*, ed. by B. N. Ganguli, London: Asia Publ. House.

Hallowell, A. Irving (1943), 'The Nature and Function of Property as a Social Institution', *Journal of Legal and Political Sociology* **1**, 115—138.

Hardin, Garrett (1968), 'The Tragedy of the Commons', *Science* **162**, 1243—1248.

Jodha, N. S. (1986), 'Common Property Resources and Rural Poor in Dry Regions of India', *Economic and Political Weekly* **21**, 1169—81, July 5.

McCay, Bonnie and James M. Acheson (1987), *The Question of the Commons: The Culture and Ecology of Communal Resources*, Tucson: University of Arizona Press.

National Academy of Sciences, Panel on Common Property Resource Management (1986), *Common Property Resource Management*, Washington, D. C.: National Academy Press.

Netting, Robert (1977), *Cultural Ecology*, Menlo Park, Ca.: Cummings Publ. Co.

Nozick, Robert (1975), *Anarchy, State and Utopia*, New York: Basic Books.

Pearce, D. W. and R. K. Turner (1990), *The Economics of Natural Resources and the Environment*, Hemel Hempstead, UK: Harvester Wheatsheaf.

Pinkerton, E. (ed.) (1989), *Cooperative Management of Local Fisheries*, Vancouver: University of British Columbia Press.

Runge, Carlisle F. (1981), 'Common Property Externalities: Isolation, Assurance, and Resource Depletion in a Traditional Grazing Context', *American Journal of Agricultural Economics* **63**, 595–607.

Runge, Carlisle F. (1984), 'Institutions and the Free Rider: The Assurance Problem in Collective Action', *Journal of Politics* **46**, 154–81.

Schotter, Andrew (1981), *The Economic Theory of Institutions*, Cambridge: Cambridge University Press.

Sen, A. K. (1982), *Choice, Welfare, and Measurement*, Oxford: Basil Blackwell.

Steward, Julian (1955), *Theory of Culture Change*, Urbana: University of Illinois Press.

Sugden, Robert (1986), *The Economics of Rights, Cooperation, and Welfare*, Oxford: Basil Blackwell.

von Albertini, Rudolf (1982), *European Colonial Rule, 1880–1940: The Impact of the West on India, Southeast Asia, and Africa*, Westport, CT: Greenwood Press.

Wade, Robert (1987), *Village Republics*, Cambridge University Press.

Williams, Howard (1977), 'Kant's Concept of Property', *Philosophical Quarterly* **27**, 32–40.

World Bank (1985), *Ivory Coast: Second Forestry Project, Staff Appraisal Report*, Washington, D.C.

[6]

World Development, Vol. 17, No. 6, pp. 867–877, 1989.
Printed in Great Britain.

0305–750X/89 $3.00 + 0.00

Property Relations and Economic Development: The Other Land Reform

DANIEL W. BROMLEY
University of Wisconsin, Madison

Summary. — Continued concern for development has led to the suggestion that private property rights should be created to stimulate economic development. This suggestion derives from an incomplete understanding of the property relations on the public domain lands in the arid tropics, and from a confusion of cause and effect between property and economic productivity. A model of the private-public boundary in land is developed that challenges the view that wealth would increase if land at the extensive margin were privatized. The various types of property regimes in land are defined and explained.

1. INTRODUCTION

The history of development assistance has been one of concentrated efforts to stimulate the sort of agricultural plant that exists in the donor countries — private-land based, intensive cultivation, some emphasis on mechanization, and much emphasis on the social infrastructure necessary to support that system. Where large tracts of land are under the control of a few individuals, the conventional precondition is to redistribute land to the landless so that this smallholder agriculture might be established. I will not speak to the advantages and disadvantages of this programmatic focus, nor to its record of success (or failure, for some are quite critical).

My concern here is with "the other land reform." Specifically, I am concerned with that vast domain of nonprivate land at the extensive economic margin on which millions of persons in Africa and South Asia depend for the bulk of their daily sustenance. I call it the "other land reform" to emphasize that the institutional arrangements on these lands are so little understood (and, quite often, misunderstood) that only by a careful assessment will we be able to deal properly with economic development on these lands that time, and the development community, seem to have forgotten. To consider the other land reform is to focus the mind on the institutional arrangements that may account for the current degradation of these lands, but may also — under the proper programmatic focus — hold the hope for their future.

We are not talking about trivial land areas, nor about livelihoods for the few. Recent official estimates place the standing forest cover of India at 72 million hectares (22% of the total land area), but the actual figure is said to be closer to 23 million hectares — or 7%. Whichever figure is the correct one, lands that were formerly forested are part of the public domain of interest here.[1] Degradation over the past century has reduced forest cover from an estimated 40% of what was British India (Commander, 1986). Other stories from sub-Saharan Africa tell a similar tale.

The pastoralists/nomads of sub-Saharan Africa are well-known users of lands at the extensive economic margin. But others are equally dependent upon the public domain. Recent work by Jodha in India indicates that for 21 (dry tropical) districts over seven states, between 84 and 100% of the poor households relied on public domain lands for ". . . food, fuel, fodder, and fibre items" (Jodha, 1986, p. 1172). Between 10 and 24% of the richer households in his study areas made use of the public domain for pond silt to enrich their fields, and for timber.

This vast domain in the arid tropics, on which so many individuals must depend — and usually the poorest ones at that — is the subject of a renewed interest among economists and development agencies. Drawing on the writings of biologists such as Hardin (1968) regarding the so-called tragedy of the commons, and the more ideological tracts by conservative commentators (Smith, 1981), one sees increasing belief that the way to solve resource degradation in the arid tropics is to create private property rights in land. This interest in privatization proceeds from an incomplete understanding of the full gamut of property regimes, from a refusal to acknowledge the obvious destruction of privately-owned lands the world over (e.g., soil erosion), and from naiveté regarding who would ultimately benefit from such privatization efforts. Indeed, Jodha's research indicates that public domain lands in India have shrunk by 26–63% over the past 30 years, and that 49–86% of these privatized lands ended up under the control of the better-off segments of society. Moreover, the process of privatization was often the impetus for the destruction of the native vegetation (Jodha, 1986).

The often passionate interest in privatization of public domain lands requires careful consideration within the development community for the obvious reason that the idea of atomistic control of economic resources is so embedded in Western economic and social thought; it is so much a part of our logic and culture that to demur is to be thought blasphemous. Often, it is our most fundamental truths that warrant close scrutiny. Such is the case with development programs that emphasize privatization of the public domain in the arid tropics.

In this paper, I will discuss the notion of property rights and their role in the management of natural resources such as grazing forage, fuelwood, fodder, or timber. In Section 2, I will present a model of property rights and economic productivity that challenges the conventional wisdom that private property in land will *cause* an increase in the production from land. I will then turn to a discussion of the various types of property regimes of relevance in the arid tropics. Finally, I will close with a discussion of the relative merits of development assistance programs focused on private land versus development programs focused on the vast public domain of the arid tropics.

2. PROPERTY RIGHTS AS CAUSE OR EFFECT?

The conventional wisdom is that private property rights are a necessary condition for the generation of economic wealth; in land this means that private ownership of land is a precursor to the realization of an economic surplus. A recent interest within economics in property rights has led to the recognition of the so-called property rights school of thought, best represented by Demsetz (1967), Cheung (1970), Alchian and Demsetz (1973), and Furubotn and Pejovich (1972). This view has been reflected in recent attempts to explain the origins of agriculture (North and Thomas, 1977). The North and Thomas position is that prior to the development of the property rights paradigm there was no theory that could be used to explain the Neolithic Revolution. The property rights paradigm provided them with the foundation to suggest that it was the development of exclusive property rights over the resource base that provided a change in incentives sufficient to encourage the rise of cultivation and domestication. The view is elaborated in the following quote:

> When common property rights over resources exist, there is little incentive for the acquisition of superior technology and learning. In contrast, exclusive property rights which reward the owners provide a direct incentive to improve efficiency and productivity, or, in more fundamental terms, to acquire more knowledge and new techniques. It is this change in incentive that explains the rapid progress made by mankind in the last 10,000 years in contrast to his slow development during the era as a primitive hunter/gatherer (North and Thomas, 1977, p. 241).

This view of the origins of agriculture, both its confusion over concepts of property as well as its selective reading of history, has been challenged elsewhere (Runge and Bromley, 1979). The current task is to address the more general problem of the contemporary analogue of early hunter/gatherers — that is, those who graze animals and collect food and fiber from the vast tracts of public domain lands in the arid tropics. They are, after all, still *hunters and gatherers* — hunting for forage for their livestock, and for other food and fiber products that are collected and carried back to a home base. Our problem is to compare this ranging activity with that of sedentary agriculture of such interest to contemporary development programs.

Consider a village with a fixed population, some of whom must rely on hunting/gathering for sustenance, while the remainder can rely upon cultivated agriculture. In this model, labor is the fixed factor of production — the total hours of labor available per unit of time — while land is the variable factor. That is, the fixed labor force will range over an ever-increasing land area in search of food and fiber (or, forage for its stock). The only way in which total production of food and fiber can be increased is to range over more land, or to augment the labor force (L_2 or L_3 in Figure 1). As the necessary distances increase, notice that the production increases at a decreasing rate, reflecting the fact that the extra distances being traveled reduce the productivity of the hunter/gatherers. The binding constraint on the production system from hunting/gathering is the spatial distribution of flora and fauna.

Now imagine that we introduce sedentary agriculture into the village economy; the question becomes one of a mix of land uses between cultivation and hunting/gathering. Continuing to hold labor constant, and letting land vary, we would obtain Figure 2; the net value of production reflects the net increment to the village over and above the necessary costs of production from the two sectors. Here, assume that the labor force (L^*) of the village is divided so that one portion works in agriculture ($L^* - L_1$), while the remainder (L_1) works in the hunting/gathering sector. The production function A reflects total net value of production from cultivation, while H/G_1 reflects total net value of production from hunting/gathering. The function A turns down because good quality agricultural land at the disposal of the village is in limited supply. Had the relationship been drawn in conventional terms, the productivity of workers in the two sectors would cross, indicating the proper allocation of labor between the two. This formulation simply shows the proper land allocation between the two sectors. At point B the net profitability of agriculture falls below that obtainable from hunting and gathering, even

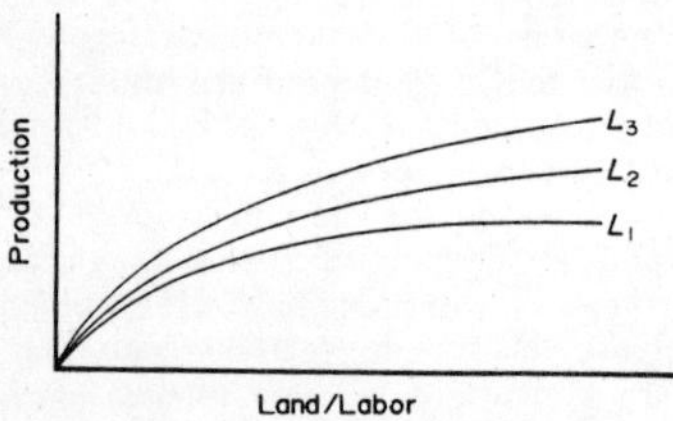

Figure 1. *Production from hunting/gathering.*

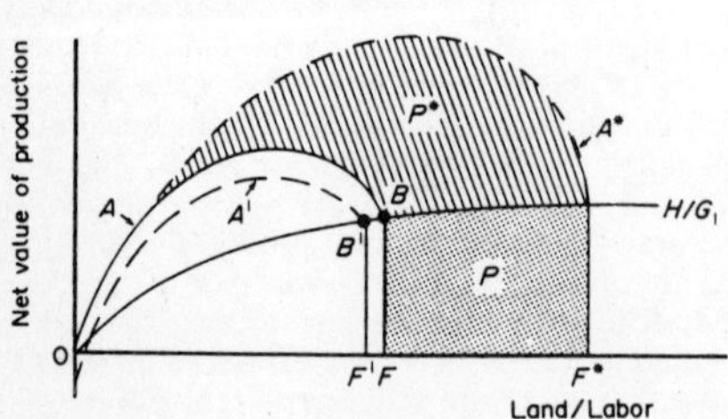

Figure 2. *The private/public frontier.*

though the net profitability of hunting/gathering is barely increasing as more land is combed for sustenance. We assume that the land in the cultivated sector is under private ownership, and that the land on which hunting/gathering occurs is in the public domain.

Those who suggest that privatization of land will bring forth new production have in mind this public domain land beyond point F — the frontier between private land the the public domain. That is, they ask us to believe that if the land out to F^* could be converted to private ownership, then A would become A^*, and the incremental net production (P^*) would exceed that now obtainable from the public domain (P). It is said to be the collective management of this public domain land between F and F^* that accounts for its low net production.

The model so far has ignored a consideration that must be reckoned with if we are to obtain a complete picture of the problem of institutional choice (type of property regime); that consideration being the costs of the particular property regime pertinent for each type of land. On the cultivated private land, we know that there must be a system of boundary surveys to demarcate the various plots of the respective owners. Additionally, there must be a process in place to record transfers of plots among new owners; this would include the measurement of the plots, the verification of a clear title to the plot, and the costs of the record keeping system in which the transaction would be recorded. Add to these official administrative costs those associated with the actions of the private owners; foremost here would be the possibility of fencing.

The administration of the public domain is not costless either. There must be meetings among the members of the village to determine the specific locations of use, to discuss rates of harvesting, and so forth. There is a reasonable case to be made that the costs of privatization (fences, measurement, title insurance, record keeping) are greater than those of the collectively-managed public domain of the village. When these hidden costs of land administration and use are incorporated into the model, we get a somewhat modified picture. Letting the costs of the public domain be a numeraire, we can depict the differential impact on the net production of the private lands by a reduction in net profit equal in magnitude to the higher infrastructure costs on the private lands. This is shown in Figure 2 with function A^1. Notice that these costs must be paid whether or not there is any production forthcoming from the private lands; A^1 is negative in the early stages. Also note that this incorporation of differential overhead costs of private land shifts the ideal boundary point to the left (F^1).

This recognition of differential costs in two different property regimes does not really address the implicit hypothesis of those advocating extension of the private boundary into the extensive economic zone. That assumption is that privatization will *cause* production to rise by enough over and above the administrative costs that it would be wise (profitable) to extend the private/public boundary to the right. In this view, the collective management of the public domain *impedes* its natural productivity.

This is, of course, an empirical question that cannot be answered by assertions from economic theory; the mere fact that high productivity is correlated with private land does not prove that private land *causes* high productivity. Indeed, it is maintained here that the current boundary observed in the arid tropics between private land and the public domain represents the economically appropriate boundary — point F^1 in Figure 2. Beyond F^1 the net profitability from private cultivation of that land (along function A^1) would be less than that enjoyed along H/G_1 in the figure.[2]

To this point, the public domain has been treated as a single institutional entity, when in fact there are several types of property regimes that must be considered. Indeed, the confusion in the conventional literature over the "tragedy of the commons" arises from a failure to understand the concept of property, and therefore to fail to understand common property regimes.

3. ALTERNATIVE PROPERTY REGIMES

The resources of the public domain on which most villagers depend are renewable resources, capable of yielding a sustainable offtake over an indefinite time horizon. The sustainability of that use-regime is directly related to the annual harvest vis-á-vis the stock that is left behind. Humans enter these systems and take particular products that have value to them, and leave the rest. The harvesting of wood and the grazing of animals not only changes the biomass that is available for the future, but the composition of the biomass is altered as well. Indeed, the very intent of human interaction with the ecosystem is to alter the composition of that natural system to more closely conform to the products considered useful or valuable by humans.[3]

Our understanding will be enhanced if we start with the recognition that land and related resources in the rural sector are characterized by a whole complex of institutional arrangements that will vary across resources, and through seasons of the year. In some locations, or at certain times of the year, these resources may be under the control of only one individual, or one household. When this is the case, their management resembles that which is pertinent to a variety of individual (or private) resources. In other locations, or at other times of the year, however, the management of some of these resources may transcend the nominal individual or household and involve instead a number of individuals or households. Those development advisors unfamiliar with local institutional arrangements will often confuse this situation with an absence of property rights, and will then suggest that the solution is to be found in the establishment of such rights. In point of fact, as will be elaborated below, successful common-property regimes are characterized precisely by the existence of individual rights. What changes between different types of property regimes is the *scope* of the primary decision-making unit (Ciriacy-Wantrup and Bishop, 1975; Dasgupta and Heal, 1979; Netting, 1976; Rhoades and Thompson, 1975; Wade, 1987).

The essence of control over resources is that there exist socially recognized and sanctioned rules and conventions that make it clear who is the "owner" of the resource in question; call these *resource decision units*. Each decision unit will have certain interests in the management of the resource, and those interests will find expression in claims made by the decision unit (Bromley, 1989). When various claims are adjudicated and given formal protection, we say that rules and conventions are established that bestow entitlements on each decision unit. Entitlements entail a socially recognized structure of *institutional arrangements* that both constrain and liberate individuals in their behaviors with respect to other individuals; as such, institutions are at the core of group management regimes over agricultural resources. It is the institutional arrangements that comprise the binding agreement that transforms the isolation problem of a prisoners' dilemma into a cooperative game.[4] Because *property* represents a secure claim or expectation over a future stream of benefits arising from a thing or a situation (a resource, if you will), we can regard such collective management systems as *common-property regimes*. It is this failure to understand property rights that attach to resource decision units that has led to the persistent confusion between *common-property resources* and *open-access resources*, and therefore to the "inevitability of the tragedy of the commons."

A common-property regime will consist of a

well-defined group of authorized users, a well-defined resource that the group will manage and use, and a set of institutional arrangements that define each of the above, as well as the rules of use for the resource in question. In addition to the rules of use there will be rules for changing the rules of use. While it is common to refer to "common-property resources," this terminology suggests that there are certain resources that are *always* managed as common property. There are, however, no "common-property resources," just as there are no "private-property resources." There are, instead, resources that are managed as private property in one place, and as common property in another.

A resource regime derives its meaning from the structure of rights that characterize the relationship of individuals (or, as suggested earlier, primary decision units such as households or kin groups) to one another, and to the object(s) of value. The nature of these institutional arrangements defines the extant property regime over land and related resources — whether that regime be one we would call private property, or one of common property. That is, the institutional arrangements define one individual vis-á-vis others — either within the group or outside of the group. We can characterize these relations between two (or more) individuals (or groups) by stating that one party has an interest that is protected by a *right* only when all others have a *duty*. Property is a right to a benefit stream that is only as secure as the duty of all others to respect the conditions that protect that stream. When one has a *right*, one has the expectation in both the law and in practice that one's claims will be respected by those with *duty*. There are other situations in which an individual does not have a right to undertake certain actions, but instead has only *privilege*. With a right I am protected against the claim of another by their duty. With privilege I am free to do as I wish, since the other party has no rights. Put differently, an individual with privilege is free to ignore the interests or claims of those with no rights (Bromley, 1978, 1989).

The difference between a common-property regime and an open-access regime can now be made clear. In a situation of open access, I have privilege with respect to use of the resource, since no one else has the legal ability to keep me out — they have no rights. But since I have no ability to prevent them from using the resource, I have no rights, and they have privilege. It follows, therefore, that an open-access situation is one of mutual privilege and no rights. Contrast this with a common-property regime, in which there are rules defining who is in the resource management group and who is out. That is, some have a right to be in, while others have a duty to stay out. Of those recognized as being in, each has a duty to obey the rules of the group (compliance) and each has the right to expect others also to obey the rules. Here there are mutual duties and rights. It is the rights of the members limiting group size (and hence total use), along with the rights of the members proscribing the use that each will make (the stint), that together constitute property. Hence the term *common-property regime*.

Invoking the concepts of entitlements and property, it should be clear that those who confuse open-access regimes with common-property regimes, or who write of the "tragedy of the commons," have an imperfect understanding of the concept of property. If property regimes were properly understood, much mischief in the literature would never have occurred.

Before elaborating the various types of regimes for the management of agricultural resources, we should pause and mention the dynamic aspect of these legal relations. Rights and duties, as well as privilege and no rights, define individuals and groups at a particular moment in time. When an individual or a group has the legal ability to alter the status-quo structure of legal entitlements, then we say that individual (or group) has *power*, while the party who is put in a new legally binding situation has *exposure*. If a party is not able to change the legal entitlements that define it with respect to others, then that party has *no power* and the other party has *immunity* (Bromley, 1989).

When economic conditions change, or when tastes and preferences change, or when a new technique appears on the horizon, then it becomes necessary to reevaluate existing structures of entitlements (institutions) to make sure that they are not counterproductive; if these entitlements change by mutual consent we assume that both parties have been made better off, or at least one of the parties is no worse off. If, however, one party was excluded in the deliberations, or if that party was ignored or overridden, then power has been exercised.

With an understanding of right and duty, privilege and no right, it is now possible to provide a general classification of possible resource regimes, and to thereby place the common-property regime into context. I propose that, for most purposes, it is sufficient to consider four possible resource regimes: (1) state-property regimes; (2) private-property regimes; (3) common-property regimes; and (4) nonproperty regimes (or open access). Let us consider each in turn.

In a state-property regime, the control over use rests in the hands of the state. Individuals and groups may be able to make use of the resources, but only at the forbearance of the state. National forests, national parks, and military reservations are examples of state-property regimes. The nationalization of Nepal's village forests by the government in 1957 converted a common-property regime into a state-property regime.[5]

The most familiar property regime is that of private property. While most think of private property as individual property, we must remember that all corporate property is private property, yet it is administered by a group.[6] It is also essential that we be reminded of the pervasive duties that attend the private control of land and related resources; few owners are entirely free to do as they wish with such assets.

The third regime is the common-property regime. Notice that common property represents private property for the group (since all others are excluded from use and decision making), and that individuals have rights (and duties) in a common-property regime (Ciriacy-Wantrup and Bishop, 1975).

Finally we have the open-access situation in which there is no property. While the aphorism "everybody's property is nobody's property" has gained wide acclaim in the confused literature on the tragedy of the commons, this is logically inconsistent. It can only be said that everybody's access is nobody's property. The fallacy of the tragedy of the commons allegory is that by failing to understand property, and thus to see the world as dichotomous between open access (which is bad) and private property (which is claimed to be good), the commentators could leap from the presumption of destruction to the presumption of wise management, with one quick sleight of hand. The four different property regimes, and their characteristics, are summarized in Table 1. Note that it is difficult to blame the degradation of natural resources on the problem of common property since the preconditions of common-property regimes (restricted membership and use) are missing. Degradation is not the fault of the property regime, but rather of the breakdown in the incentive mechanisms necessary for the concept of property to have any meaning.

Table 1. *Four types of property regimes*

State property	Individuals have *duty* to observe use/access rules determined by controlling/managing agency. Agencies have *right* to determine use/access rules.
Private property	Individuals have *right* to undertake socially acceptable uses, and have *duty* to refrain from socially unacceptable uses. Others (called "non-owners") have *duty* to refrain from preventing socially acceptable uses, and have a *right* to expect only socially acceptable uses will occur.
Common property	The management group (the "owners") has *right* to exclude non-members, and nonmembers have *duty* to abide by exclusion. Individual members of the management group (the "co-owners") have both *rights* and *duties* with respect to use rates and maintenance of the thing owned.
Nonproperty	No defined group of users or "owners" and so the benefit stream is available to anyone. Individuals have both *privilege* and *no right* with respect to use rates and maintenance of the asset. The asset is an "open-access resource."

4. TOWARD IMPROVEMENT OF PROPERTY REGIMES AND RESOURCES

The recognition of three types of property regimes, and one regime that is not a property regime at all (open access), then provides a structure within which to discuss the kinds of development assistance that are most likely to succeed in the arid tropics. I will not dwell on the private land resources, since that is the subject of most development assistance programs at the current time.

Consider first the open-access regime. By definition this is a situation of mutual privilege and no right; no one user has the right (ability) to preclude use by any other party. Here the natural resource is subject to the rule of capture and belongs to no one until it is in someone's possession; whether grazing forage or fuelwood, a resource under an open-access regime belongs to the party to first exercise control over it. The investment in (or improvement of) open-access regimes must first focus on the institutional dimension. In the absence of that, and if the investment is in the form of a capital asset such as improved tree species or range revegetation, the institutional vacuum assures that use rates will eventually rise to the point of depleting the asset.

Hence with open-access resources, the necessary precondition is to convert the open-access regime to one of common property. That is, to convert mutual privilege and no-right into a situation of mutual right and duty. Once the regime is converted to common property for the group — say all of the members of the village — then unauthorized use by outsiders will have been brought under control. An example would be if the migration patterns of herders were changed to prevent their use of village lands. The village lands would be converted from an open-access regime to one of common property for the members of the village.

With this institutional change complete, one could then begin to address the question of use rates of those within the relevant decision unit (the village). A great deal of resource degradation arises from population growth within the relevant decision unit. This use, though exceeding the ability of the renewable resource to sustain its annual yield, cannot be stopped because of the nominal right of every villager to take what he or she needs to survive. The breakdown of the common-property regime arises because of the failure of the decision-making process within the decision group. There is a failure to deal with the obvious reality that as a village grows, and therefore as the number of rights holders grows apace, the total demands on the resource will ultimately exceed its rate of regeneration. If the village believes that all of this larger population has a right to take whatever it wishes, then it becomes obvious that no villager has a right to anything other than what he or she can capture by being there first. A common-property regime for the group becomes an open-access regime for the individuals within the group.

To improve the situation requires a reduction in total offtake until the resource base can generate sufficient annual yield to meet the needs of the new (lower) harvesting, plus allow for some continued regeneration. The obvious problem is to meet the reduced needs of those deemed to be excessive claimants on the resource base until that regenerative capacity is restored. Or, if it is determined that the resource will never be able to sustain the level of demands to be placed on it, then there must be some capital investment to augment it. But capital investment in the absence of a prior institutional fix will simply assure that the new asset is squandered as the old one was.

The final resource regime upon which improvements might be concentrated is the state-property regime. The record of management here has been very disappointing (Bromley, 1986). The appearance of management by the establishment of governmental agencies, and the appearance of a coherent policy by issuance of decrees prohibiting entry to — and harvesting from — state property, has led to continued degradation of resources under the management of government agencies. When, in 1957, the government of Nepal nationalized village-level forested areas in order to bring them under more controlled management, their destruction was accelerated (Bromley and Chapagain, 1984).

If degradation of state lands is to be arrested, current practices of indifferent enforcement must be stopped (Thomson, 1977), and staffing levels and incentives must be sufficient to administer and manage that domain which the government has taken unto itself. The record to date is not encouraging.

The final issue to be addressed concerns the *economic feasibility* of investing scarce development resources and time in public domain lands vis-á-vis those lands under private control. It is obvious that, on a per acre basis, the private lands in the arid tropics are often extremely productive. Would it not make more sense to continue to invest there rather than to invest in the public domain? Or, would it not make more sense to continue to expand the irrigated area so as to convert lands out of the public domain and into the private domain?

To answer the question properly requires a number of complex considerations. But, as a brief response, several factors stand out. The conversion of land from the public to the private domain will usually require major investments in irrigation works in the face of a shadow price for foreign debt that is high and rising. Given the dismal record of production from irrigation projects in the arid tropics, the burden of expanded irrigation is further compounded (Bromley, 1982; Easter, 1977; Wade, 1975).

Second, a few considerations regarding economic feasibility seem in order. First, public domain projects must be evaluated, keeping in mind that many of the benefits will appear in the rather distant future. Under the conventional practice of discounting future benefits and costs, such projects will automatically appear to be less favorable (or less productive) than investments whose benefits appear in the nearer term. That is, most investments imply large immediate expenditures (costs) and then a stream of benefits into the future. Projects with identical net benefits over their respective lifetimes will rank differently depending upon the time stream of benefits received; those with the bulk of their benefits in the future will be discriminated against.

It is incorrect to assume that they are less productive or offer fewer benefits than projects with a different time stream of benefits; we must simply conclude that the *present value of the benefits* is different. If one adheres strictly to conventional benefit-cost protocol, then all projects with more distant benefits will be discriminated against. It should be obvious that slavish adherence to an investment criterion that selects only those projects with the highest present-valued net benefits will result in few, if any, resource protection projects winning acceptance.

The irony of this cannot be overstated; we fail to take proper care of the livelihood and habitat of future generations because *our* valuation of the benefits is less than our valuation of projects which will take care of the present generation. The fact that we are in a position to dictate the nature of the resource endowment with which those in the future must live has not been lost on philosophers and those concerned with intergenerational ethics. It can be thought of as the tyranny of discounting. One sensible solution is to use one discount rate for project costs, and another for project benefits. The rate at which project costs would be discounted would represent the social opportunity cost of funds diverted from the private sector to the public sector. The rate at which project benefits would be discounted would be the social marginal rate of time preference. There is no reason why these two rates should be equal, and it is usually accepted that the former will exceed the latter. Marglin (1967) has suggested this approach.

Second, we must remember that benefit-cost analysis is not a dogma but is simply an evaluation tool. But being an evaluation tool does not also make it an inviolate decision rule. We must be careful to keep these two functions distinct. One can undertake a very conventional (and narrow) benefit-cost evaluation, and then employ several decision rules regarding which projects to undertake. Or, one can employ a broader and more inclusive benefit-cost evaluation and then follow a quite restrictive decision rule regarding which projects to undertake.

Third, the very concept of feasibility is a product of the economic environment within which alternative investment activities are evaluated; the context will dominate the outcome. When an evaluation of the benefits and costs of a project on private lands is undertaken, the benefit stream is largely defined by the existing infrastructure that will allow those investments to appear favorable vis-á-vis a public domain project. Marketing channels, transportation systems, agricultural extension workers, and input supply networks are usually in place and the new project is not "billed" for any of those costs; the benefit-cost analysis will usually include only the direct project costs, allowing the project a free ride on the existing infrastructure.

By way of contrast, a project on public domain lands will be less likely to benefit from such infrastructure and hence the project will necessarily reflect all of the costs related to its full realization. That this distorts the evaluation process against public domain endeavors should be obvious.

The maintained hypothesis here is that a broad-gauged evaluation of development assistance projects in the public domain would reveal that a number of endeavors are indeed economically feasible. When proper shadow pricing is undertaken on both classes of development assistance projects — that is, those on the private domain and those on the public domain — it is my view that the public domain projects will prove to be feasible locations for the concentration of institutional development and technological change. If those lands could be improved in terms of their productivity, notice that the curve H/G_1 in Figure 2 would shift up and suggest that the optimal boundary between private and public land might shift back to the left.

5. CONCLUSIONS

A fuller understanding of the institutional arrangements that define property seems necessary to a more careful assessment of the resource regimes in the developing countries. A large proportion of the population in these countries obtains a substantial fraction of their daily sustenance from lands that are *not* held in fee simple (freehold). Of particular relevance to current development concerns, those most dependent upon such lands tend to be the least advantaged members of society. The history of development assistance has been one of almost exclusive focus on private property — either in the form of more scientific agricultural practices for these lands, or in the form of land reform programs to redistribute large private estates to the landless. Few comparable efforts exist to understand the nature of economic activity on other types of lands (that is, lands under other property regimes).

The large literature on the so-called tragedy of the commons contains a fundamental asymmetry. There is ample evidence, and it is growing, of the destructive land-use practices undertaken by private (freehold) owners of many land and related natural resources. Soil erosion and deforestation are but two prominent examples.[7] In the face of this evidence, few observers challenge the ultimate social wisdom of freehold land. We are told, rather, that there must be economic incentives (bribes, tax breaks) to induce the private owner to behave in socially acceptable ways; such bribes are often justified on the ground that the public is, somehow, "interfering" with the owner's "right" to do as he or she desires.

But when evidence of resource degradation on nonprivate land is observed, the fault is immediately said to lie with a quaint property regime that fails to assign clear ownership and, by implication, stewardship. Indeed there is almost universal agreement among development experts that the solution is to create private property for individuals, or to create state property so that the destructive users might be displaced or properly controlled by some remote government agency. We see few serious recommendations that the resource regime be studied carefully to understand the structure of rights, duties, privileges, and no rights. We see little recognition that resource regimes in the developing countries might be revitalized by efforts to understand their systemic problems, as opposed to expropriation of the resource by the state. In short, there seems little recognition of the rich array of institutional alternatives whereby land and related resources might be managed.

This continuum of choice and control — ranging between complete individualization and total collectivization — is the subject of great intellectual and popular debate. Indeed, the debate goes back to the Greek philosophers (Schlatter, 1951). The essence of contemporary economics is to celebrate the individual as the proper decision maker, and from that it follows that the individual must have full control over the necessary productive inputs (of which land and related natural resources are central). In conventional economic theory we start with the assumption that all valuable resources are individually owned, fully mobile, and exchangeable in small increments in well-functioning markets. We then conclude that these conditions will assure an efficiently operating system. Notice that the paradigm demands the very premises that allow us to reach such happy conclusions regarding efficiency. That is, we say that *if* the right conditions exist — divisibility, mobility, full ownership of all valuable resources, full information, and well-functioning markets — then the allocation of all factors of production will be efficient. As a definition this is fine; as policy prescription in a world where not all valuable resorces are fully divisible and capable of individual ownership, where all resources are not fully mobile, where information is imperfect, where many markets — but especially contingent-claims markets — are not present, and where the future is unrepresented, then our standard advice is suspect. These conditions that render facile privatization recommendations so misguided are precisely the conditions that characterize natural resource use in the developing countries.

The mischief to arise from such policy pronouncements can be attributed to the fact that those giving advice do not always understand the critical distinction between open-access resources (*res nullius*) and common-property resources (*res communis*). Open access is a free-for-all, common property represents a well-defined set of institutional arrangements concerning who may make use of a resource, who may *not* make use of a resource, and the rules for how the accepted users shall conduct themselves. By failing to understand this essential difference, many then commit an equally serious mistake. That is, institutional arrangements over natural resources (property arrangements) are thought to be at two polar extremes; one either has individual (or private) property, or one has a free-for-all.

By failing to understand that property arrangements are not bimodal but in fact are to be found along a continuum, observers are led to embrace one pole on the evidence of imminent disaster at the other. Moreover, such reasoning ignores centuries of wise use of commonly-controlled resources in the Swiss Alps (Netting, 1976), in the Andes (Rhoades and Thompson, 1975), and in other locations where exogenous technology and market processes have not disrupted the human-ecosystem interaction. Third, such reasoning invites incredulity in the developing world when various cultures are told that their salvation lies in the extreme individualization of all resource decisions. Finally, and possibly most damaging, the record of resource use in countries where individualization is present and revered would lead the neutral observer to ponder the ultimate wisdom of unconstrained atomization of control.

Development assistance programs that begin to address *the other land reform* would open up a range of meaningful endeavors that would seem to hold considerable promise for the natural resources of the arid tropics, and for the millions of poor people who must now depend upon these lands.

NOTES

1. I will use the term "public domain" here as shorthand for all of those lands held in *other than* freehold (fee simple). I will classify types of ownership regimes later in the paper. The conventional view is that

approximately one-half of India is uncultivated — and hence public domain land (Bentley, 1984).

2. The presence of irrigation is one obvious way in which the optimal boundary can be adjusted in the arid tropics. In the absence of irrigation however, the presumption must be that the village has located the efficient boundary between private and public land.

3. See the work on coevolutionary development by Norgaard (1981).

4. The prisoners' dilemma is a situation in which each of the participants has a consistent tendency to defect from an agreement and to seek to better her or his own situation at the ultimate expense of the others in the group. This tendency to defect means that the aggregate of all participants is less well off than if the individuals had stuck together. See Friedman (1986); Guttman (1978); Schotter (1981); or Shubik (1982).

5. Although, as will be suggested below, in the absence of consistent administration and enforcement the forests became open-access regimes.

6. The important difference between corporate property and common property, even though both are "private property" for the group, is that in common-property regimes the owners are actively engaged in use and control of the asset. Corporate property usually has intervening parties (management) that control use and decision making.

7. It is common in the United States for state laws to require the reforestation of private lands following the harvest of timber; laws which would presumably not be necessary if private owners had not been prone to clear-cut lands and then leave them to erode.

REFERENCES

Alchian, Armen, and Harold, Demsetz, "The property rights paradigm," *Journal of Economic History*, Vol. 13 (1973), pp. 16–27.

Bentley, William, *The Uncultivated Half of India: Problems and Possible Solutions* (New Delhi, India: Ford Foundation, 1984).

Bromley, Daniel W., *Economic Interests and Institutions* (Oxford: Basil Blackwell, 1989).

Bromley, Daniel W., "Natural resources and agricultural development in the tropics: Is conflict inevitable?" in Allen Maunder and Ulf Renborg (Eds.), *Agriculture in a Turbulent World Economy* (Oxford: Gower, 1986), pp. 319–327.

Bromley, Daniel W., *Improving Irrigated Agriculture: Institutional Reform and the Small Farmer*, World Bank Staff Working Paper, No. 531 (Washington, DC: World Bank, 1982).

Bromley, Daniel W., "Property rules, liability rules, and environmental economics," *Journal of Economic Issues*, Vol. 12 (March 1978), pp. 43–60.

Bromley, Daniel W., and Devendra P. Chapagain, "The village against the center: Resource depletion in South Asia," *American Journal of Agricultural Economics*, Vol. 66 (December 1984), pp. 868–873.

Cheung, Steven N. S., "The structure of a contract and the theory of a non-exclusive resource," *Journal of Law and Economics*, vol. 13 (April 1970), pp. 49–70.

Ciriacy-Wantrup, S. V., and Richard C. Bishop, "Common property as a concept in natural resources policy," *Natural Resources Journal*, Vol. 15 (October 1975), pp. 713–727.

Commander, Simon, "Managing Indian forests: A case for the reform of property rights," *Development Policy Review*, Vol. 4 (1986), pp. 325–344.

Dasgupta, P. S., and G. M. Heal, *Economic Theory and Exhaustible Resources* (Cambridge, Cambridge University Press, 1979).

Demsetz, Harold, "Toward a theory of property rights," *American Economic Review*, Vol. 57 (May 1967), pp. 347–359.

Easter, K. W., "Improving village irrigation systems: An example from India," *Land Economics*, Vol. 53 (February 1977), pp. 56–66.

Friedman, James W., *Game Theory with Applications to Economics* (Oxford: Oxford University Press, 1986).

Furubotn, Eirik, and Svetozar Pejovich, "Property rights and economic theory: A survey of recent literature," *Journal of Economic Literature*, Vol. 10, No. 4 (December 1972), pp. 1137–1162.

Guttman, Joel M., "Understanding collective action: Matching behavior," *American Economic Review*, Vol. 68 (May 1978), pp. 251–255.

Hardin, Garrett, "The tragedy of the commons," *Science*, Vol. 162 (1968), pp. 1243–1248.

Jodha, N. S., "Common property resources and rural poor in dry regions of India," *Economic and Political Weekly*, Vol. 21 (July 5, 1986), pp. 1169–1181.

Marglin, Stephen, *Public Investment Criteria* (London: Allen and Unwin, 1967).

National Research Council, *Common Property Resource Management*, Conference Proceedings, Panel on Common Property Resource Management (Washington, DC: National Academy Press, 1986).

Netting, Robert, "What Alpine peasants have in common: Observations on communal tenure in a Swiss village," *Human Ecology*, Vol. 4 (April 1976), pp. 135–146.

Norgaard, Richard B., "Sociosystem and ecosystem coevolution in the Amazon," *Journal of Environmental Economics and Management*, Vol. 8 (September 1981), pp. 238–254.

North, Douglass C., and Robert P. Thomas, "The first economic revolution," *The Economic History Review*, Vol. 30 (1977), pp. 229–241.

Rhoades, Robert E., and Stephen J. Thompson, "Adaptive strategies in Alpine environments: Beyond ecological particularism," *American Ethnologist*, Vol. 2 (1975), pp. 535–551.

Runge, Carlisle F., "Institutions and the free rider: The

assurance problem in collective action," *Journal of Politics*, Vol. 46 (1984), pp. 154–181.

Runge, Carlisle F., and Daniel W. Bromley, *Property Rights and the First Economic Revolution: The Origins of Agriculture Reconsidered*, Center for Resource Policy Studies, Working Paper No. 13 (Madison, WI: University of Wisconsin, January 1979).

Schlatter, Richard, *Private Property: the History of an Idea* (London: George Allen and Unwin, 1951).

Schotter, Andrew, *The Economic Theory of Social Institutions* (Cambridge: Cambridge University Press, 1981).

Shubik, Martin, *Game Theory in the Social Sciences* (Cambridge, MA: MIT Press, 1982).

Smith, R., "Resolving the Tragedy of the commons by creating private property rights in wildlife," *Cato Journal*, Vol. 1 (Fall 1981), pp. 439–468.

Thompson, James T., "Ecological deterioration: Local-level rule making and enforcement problems in Niger," in Michael Glantz (Ed.), *Desertification: Environmental Degradation in and Around Arid Lands* (Boulder, CO: Westview Press, 1977), Chapter 4.

Wade, Robert, "The management of common property resources: Collective action as an alternative to privatisation or state regulation," *Cambridge Journal of Economics*, Vol. 11 (1987), pp. 95–106.

Wade, Robert, "Administration and the distribution of irrigation benefits," *Economic and Political Weekly*, Vol. 6 (November 1975), pp. 743–747.

[7]

Pergamon

World Development, Vol. 25, No. 4, pp. 549–562, 1997

0305–750X/97 $17.00 + 0.00

PII: S0305-750X(96)00120-9

Indigenous Land Rights in Sub-Saharan Africa: Appropriation, Security and Investment Demand

ESPEN SJAASTAD
University of Norway, Oslo

and

DANIEL W. BROMLEY*
University of Wisconsin, Madison, U.S.A.

Summary. — We discuss the links between rights appropriation, tenure security, and investment demand in sub-Saharan Africa. Common assertions regarding indigenous tenure are: (a) insecurity of tenure leads to suboptimal investment incentives; and (b) appropriation of land rights in the public domain is rent-dissipating. We argue that land use and investment decisions among African farmers often have two motives — productivity and rights appropriation. The usual assertions thus seem contradictory. We offer a conceptual model to show that indigenous tenure may provide equal or higher investment incentives than private rights, and may promote modes of rights appropriation that are productive rather than wasteful. © 1997 Elsevier Science Ltd

Key words — property rights, indigenous tenure, investment, productivity

1. INTRODUCTION

Many economists have argued that indigenous land rights in the Third World lead to inefficient resource allocation. Inefficiencies are thought to arise because indigenous land rights are ambiguous, are communal, and are afforded insufficient protection in legislatures — resulting in tenure insecurity which in turn leads to inferior investment incentives, undersupply of credit, and constraints on efficiency-enhancing market exchanges (see, e.g., Dorner, 1972; Johnson, 1972; World Bank, 1974). These arguments have been advanced as a justification for government action in land administration matters, and especially conversion to freehold titles in the Western strain. Recently, these views have been challenged on the grounds that: (a) indigenous land rights are often neither communal nor ambiguous; (b) indigenous tenures are flexible enough to cope with increasing land scarcity and to permit a gradual, "autonomous" individualization of rights, and; (c) state intervention in land matters often is more harmful than beneficial (Ault and Rutman, 1979; Bates, 1984; Bruce, 1986, 1993; LTC, 1990; Migot-Adholla *et al.*, 1991; Bassett, 1993; Platteau, 1996). A recent empirical study by Besley adds to this literature in an important way. Besley writes that:

> The results in this paper reinforce the need for careful empirical studies of land rights and investment in low-income environments. They also reinforce the importance of understanding the determinants of rights as well as their consequences. Given the importance of investment to long-term poverty alleviation, it is important to understand what, if anything, governments can do. Developing land rights is often offered as a feasible intervention, especially in Africa. It would be premature to say that this does not work. However, the analysis of this paper warns against viewing it as a panacea for problems of low growth and investment before the process determining the evolution of rights is properly understood (Besley, 1995, p. 936).

In this paper we address the question of tenure security and its effects on investment demands as land becomes scarce and prices (implicit or explicit) rise. The issues are discussed within the context of sub-Saharan Africa; specifically where land initially is abundant and shifting cultivation practices dominate,

*The research was funded by the Norwegian Research Council. We would like to thank Ole Hofstad for his helpful comments. Final revision accepted: October 26, 1996.

although the main points of this paper have application beyond this relatively narrow scope.

In the next section we briefly present how these issues have been viewed in mainstream property rights theory, as well as offer some common misgivings. In section 3 we describe how land rights and land use develop in a typical rural sub-Saharan African community as land becomes scarce. We also develop a conceptual model which compares investment incentives of indigenous tenure and freehold. In section 4, we present a discussion of the central issues, and some concluding remarks.

2. PROPERTY RIGHTS THEORY, TENURE SECURITY, AND INVESTMENT

The property rights school (roughly equivalent to what Bardhan (1989) calls the "transaction cost" approach) can be traced back to, among others Gordon (1954) and Coase (1960). Using the fishery as an example, and in much the same vein that Hardin (1968) would approach the pastoral commons 14 years later, Gordon showed that unrestricted open access either would lead to overexploitation, or that rents would be dissipated if restrictions were placed on total extraction. In the context of externality problems and zero transaction costs, Coase showed that a clear assignment of rights would lead to Pareto-optimal outcomes, regardless of to whom the rights were assigned. An immediate result of these writings was that private property rights became universally extolled as the only efficient property regime. One reason for this was the confusion of common property and open access (Bromley, 1989b, 1991, 1992; Ciriacy-Wantrup and Bishop, 1975). The other reason was the perception that creation and maintenance of private property somehow is costless — a misconception that persists even today.

As early as 1950, Alchian had suggested that institutions were subject to competitive pressures, and that inefficient institutions would perish in the face of such competition. Developing these themes, and introducing the more realistic condition of significant costs of transacting, Demsetz produced a defining and much-quoted thesis of the property rights school:

> Changes in knowledge result in changes in production functions, market values, and aspirations. New techniques, new ways of doing the same things — all invoke harmful and beneficial effects to which society has not been accustomed. It is my thesis in this part of the paper that the emergence of new property rights takes place in response to the desires of the interacting persons for adjustment to new cost responsibilities. The thesis can be restated in a slightly different fashion: property rights develop to internalize externalities when the gains of internalization become larger than the costs of internalization. Increased internalization, in the main, results from changes in economic values, changes which stem from the development of new technology and the opening of new markets, changes to which old property rights are poorly attuned (Demsetz, 1967, p. 350).

Thus, shifts in relative prices may reverse a situation where transaction costs previously made it undesirable to bring marginal social and private costs into line. On the one hand the property rights school seeks to explain institutional evolution through changes in economic parameters, primarily relative prices. Where rights are unspecified, rent capture will come about through opportunistic behavior on the part of individual agents, leading to rent dissipation. Changes in relative prices can make it profitable to engage in bargaining and more detailed contractual specification, where such specification earlier was too costly. State intervention maybe warranted because the benefits of legislation have grown to a point where they exceed the costs. In other words, the costs of opportunistic behavior now exceed the costs of specification and enforcement of rights.[1] When land is abundant it has no price; since there is no shared cost associated with its use, there are no externalities. As capture attempts multiply in response to increasing scarcity, land becomes costlier relative to other factors, rent is dissipated through costly litigation, and it becomes profitable to remove land from the public domain into the hands of groups or individuals with clearly defined rights. The corollary of Demsetz's thesis to land is thus a transition from open access to a situation where all rights to land are specified and enforced. On the other hand, the theory often purports to show the superiority of private (or individual) — as opposed to common — property regimes because the former is said to permit less costly contracting and avoids free-rider and hold-out problems.

A number of publications have expounded on property rights theory, its application to land in general, and to developing countries in particular. Barzel (1989) has pointed out that certain attributes will always remain in the public domain — either because the gains from rights specification are too small, or the costs are too large. Thus, the absolute rights often attributed to freehold are an exaggeration, something that even a cursory perusal of Western land law will readily reveal. Platteau (1996) has summarized property rights theory and its more recent developments as they apply to land rights in sub-Saharan Africa, and dubbed it "The Evolutionary Theory of Land Rights." Extending Demsetz's thesis on the evolution of institutions, government provision of land titles is here treated as a market response to increasing rural demand. This feature is thoroughly critiqued in the paper by Platteau on both practical and theoretical grounds. North (1990) presents a subtler view of how institutions evolve; acknowledging the role of culture and norms, and emphasizing costs of information and rights enforcement, North abandons the concept of an efficient institutional evolution. His focus is not microeconomic, but some of the points regarding the scale of institutions are crucial — in particular how the demands of an increasingly complex economy require more universal institutions in the face of rising information costs. Other convincing misgivings about the theory and its relevance, also considered by Platteau (1996), include a general lack of available intensification technologies (implicit in the theory of induced technical change), the absence of accessible capital to invest in such technologies when they do exist, the persistence of cultural norms that run counter to privatization or its predicted effects, the inseparability of efficiency and equity, and second-best problems whereby the emergence of a single market, e.g., land, in a general market vacuum may increase inefficiencies. The most thoroughly tested hypothesis of the theory is the positive effect that government provision of titles will have on investment demand, credit supply, and productivity. Both supportive (Feder, 1987; Feder and Onchan, 1987) and critical (Migot-Adholla *et al.*, 1991; Pinckney and Kimuyu, 1994) studies exist. As far as costly rent capture is concerned, the usual example is costly litigation in connection with land disputes, although titling also has been found to increase litigation costs (Coldham, 1978).

The propositions of the theory, as regards problems related to tenure security and investment decisions in indigenous tenure regimes, can be summarized as follows. First, the lack of legal title of land reduces its value as collateral, thus increasing the price of capital and reducing the value of investments. Second, high transaction costs in establishing ownership will reduce the value of investments, or, conversely, any residual uncertainty about ownership will have the same effect since future returns may be lost. Third, the absence of a land market means that farmers cannot convert fixed land assets into other asset forms, thus reducing the value of investments to the farmer and preventing efficiency gains of trade. For the same reason, land becomes less attractive as collateral to the lender, again increasing the price of capital.

This paper specifically critiques the second of these assertions. This critique is based partly on the nature of indigenous rights — that is, whether such rights in fact are communal and ambiguous, and partly on the implied one-way link between security of tenure and investment demand. This, in turn, leads to a critique of the common assertions about opportunism, rent capture, and rent dissipation.

3. INDIGENOUS LAND RIGHTS, SECURITY, AND INVESTMENT: AN ALTERNATIVE VIEW

(a) *Land use and land appropriation under abundance*

The types of land use that develop under conditions of land abundance are naturally extensive, given the ready availability of land and the associated incentives to substitute it for other factors, notably labor. This substitution is, however, at some point curbed, not only by the increasing physical effort required in utilizing more land at greater distances, but also by the complementary nature of land and labor endemic to many traditional forms of cultivation. This issue has been explored in Bromley (1989b).

A key feature of traditional systems of shifting cultivation is mobility. When, after a period of cultivation, resources are considered insufficient for further exploitation, the community (family, kinship group, or village) will move to an unsettled area of bush and start over. Associated with mobility is often a paucity and impermanence of material possessions. The essential possession of a household required to move at frequent intervals from one location to another is its own labor power. Another characteristic is the lack of trade. The interlinked features of dispersed population, lack of material possessions, an emphasis on self-reliance and consequent equation of labor power and wealth, often impeded fruitful exchange of commodities, and the situation may be compounded by a general and far-reaching uniformity of the natural environment. This ecological uniformity narrows the range of products hence reducing the incentives for trade (except over very long distances). The absence of markets in turn influences the egalitarian nature and functions of traditional communities. Villages consisting of relatively small kinship groups and affines need to spread risk through the sharing of resources available within the community, and acute local food shortage is solved through migration to kin settled in a region where food is relatively plentiful.

The impermanence of residence and lack of material possessions, and the associated assignment of values, may in numerous ways inform the manner in which land is viewed. The resource over which a household has absolute and initial right is its labor. Thus, the key to possession of a resource or a good is the labor expended in its acquisition. In a sense, this can be seen as the "swapping" of labor for another benefit, the conversion of rights in labor to rights in the fruits of that labor. The important distinction, however, is not between goods acquired through labor and goods obtained through trade or barter; it is between the ultimate origins of a good. A good thus initially acquired through labor may then in turn be bartered or invested, and the new resource or good obtained will be subjected to equally strong rights of ownership.

This might ostensibly be interpreted as commensurate with a Lockean perspective on appropriation of land rights. Two points need clarification in this regard. First, appropriation of a good, and the subsequent assignment of a right, does not materialize in an institutional vacuum; a "social contract" — an agreement, tacit or explicit, on the legitimacy of ownership — must precede individual appropriation of resources

(Bromley 1991). Second, shifting cultivators do not perceive land in the established Western manner as geographical points on a grid. Land contains a certain collection of natural resources — resources that are not initially created or acquired through labor — and appropriation applies to these resources in a manner that is often independent of the coincidence of their location. Thus, one does not have rights over land as such; a right to one of the resources on the land is established through the visible expenditure of labor or of other goods thus acquired. The rights to the use of a tree may be established by planting it, felling it, or perhaps by simply marking it. But no one has the rights to a tree if its circumstance cannot somehow be ascribed to human effort.

If land is abundant and freely available — that is, initial rights over it do not exist — land, and the resources upon and within it, have no price.[2] But neither the condition of abundance nor the failure to recognize rights in undeveloped land implies that land is worthless. What is implied is that the potential value of land is realized only by mixing it with labor. Rights to land can be claimed only through the use of land, and only for the duration of that use. A crop field that is left fallow will, when evidence of human activity has faded, revert to the public domain. Land itself, since it is not originally obtained through human activity, cannot be permanently claimed or alienated. Any fruits of human activity, on the other hand, may be sold or exchanged; thus one may observe the frequent sale of crops on a piece of land, or the sale of huts and houses, but not the land itself. This distinction between land itself and the fruits of labor on any given section of land is important analytically, and especially with respect to investment.[3]

(b) *Rights in transition, security, and investment*

We have observed that rights in land are traditionally established through initial use and maintained through continued use. When land has been abandoned for a sufficiently long time, i.e. when evidence of use has vanished, anyone may claim the land. When land is abundant, however, this poses no problem, at least to the extent that one disregards land variability in quality and distance from dwelling. Since land may equally well be acquired elsewhere, no farmer will have any incentive to claim any particular field, and by the same token, no farmer will fret over its loss. In the language of property rights theory, the negligible external costs do not justify internalization.

How does land use change, from an initial condition of abundance, as land becomes more scarce? One obvious implication[4] is that the land to labor ratio decreases, and that more land will be under cultivation at any given time. Specific expressions of this in the context of shifting cultivation are a decline in fallow periods and the gradual conversion of swidden land to permanently cultivated land. Theoretically, more permanent land claims appear when fallow periods fall below a critical number — the period between the end of the crop rotation and the point at which a field reverts to the public domain — although the number may itself decrease as land becomes scarce. The logical result of a process where population pressure causes increasing land scarcity, however, is one where more and more farm land is cultivated in such a way — i.e. continuously or semi-continuously — that land does not revert to the public domain.

The fact that indigenous rights to land are contingent upon continued use is often perceived as a major problem by some commentators on African tenure. The persistence of the risk of losing land when fallowed hypothetically leads to myopic behavior and disincentives in terms of investments in long-term productivity and sustainability. The fact that proprietary rights may have beneficial incentive effects is often neglected, perhaps because these benefits only appear where markets in land, labor, or capital are imperfect. The possibility of eviction seems sensible, however, if land is scarce and the risk of absentee ownership is high. The requirement that land more or less continuously be used prevents such "waste" of idle land and would seem efficiency-enhancing in the short term at the very least,[5] with the important caveat that may apply if the institution itself is the cause of market imperfection.

The arrangement thus, in its basic form, may entail a benefit in the form of exploitation, or "coverage," and a cost in the form of long-term insecurity of tenure. If the right to use land is absolutely secure as long as use continues, then the infringement on absolute ownership that this arrangement entails is the inability to simultaneously maintain the right to retain ownership and the right not to cultivate the land.[6] A right to permanent use of land is contingent upon not exercising the right to fallow it, at least not for extended periods of time.

How relevant is this problem of insecurity of tenure in sub-Saharan Africa? First, the problem of not being able to abandon land might be trivial in the context of a community where land is truly scarce. To the extent that land is the major source of income and subsistence, there would be little incentive not to use the land every year anyway, so security would, in effect, be ensured. Moreover, a household which for some reason wished to abandon the land for a period of time but later reclaim it may have other strategies at its disposal, notably leaving the land in trust of relatives. Finally, long-term investments are not likely to be undertaken by people with a propensity for abandoning their land. A proprietary system of land rights may thus in fact help to weed out farmers with an indifferent attitude to farming.

Permanent use is one way to establish claims

to land. A method that is perhaps even more powerful is to invest in land. To the extent that the investment represents a visible commitment to the long-term productivity of the land, continued use of the land is implied, and the common assertion that tenure security is necessary to promote investment may — in many cases — be reversed. That is, investment is necessary to obtain security. Investments in trees, irrigation furrows, buildings, or other fixed structures may provide a litigant in a land dispute with an unassailable case. Thus, although insecurity of tenure is a disincentive to invest, it is — paradoxically —often also an incentive because investment will itself increase security.

This leads to a related issue. A common definition of security — or rather insecurity — of tenure is the perceived probability of losing ownership of the land. In communities where land is seen as a bundle of resources rather than a geometric area, and where multiple tenure determines the access to these resources, the above definition is inadequate. Barrows and Roth (1990, p. 292) state that tenure security "can also be defined more broadly as the perception of the likelihood of losing a specific right to cultivate, graze, fallow, transfer, or mortgage." One such right is the right to recover the returns on any investment made on a given parcel of land. Any two rights may or may not be interlinked. For example, the right to harvest the fruit from a tree may be linked to the right to cut down the tree; or the right to bequeath land may be linked to the right to sell it. One action may be sufficient to claim several rights that need not otherwise be related; or one behavioral code or norm may inform the rules regarding several different rights. The right to recover an investment need not, however, be related to the right to retain land. This is hardly a radical notion; in most Western countries, the loss of property in an ownership dispute is typically tempered by compensation for any fixed investments in the property that the loser of such a dispute has undertaken, at least as long as that property was not initially acquired illegally.

Similarly, when an African farmer loses an ownership dispute, that farmer may be compensated for any trees planted, buildings erected, or furrows dug. The rule is, of course, far from absolute. The law itself is often not written down; local African courts do not always follow the prescribed codes of procedure; decisions are often affected by the stature and authority of the litigants. Nevertheless, in cases where the loser in an ownership dispute has not clearly obtained the land through swindle, investments may be compensated. Even in cases of blatant fraud, compensation has been known to be given.

If one accepts that certain types of investment in land are a legitimate way of claiming more secure rights to land, and that investments may be recovered even when land is lost, the assertion that insecurity of land rights in indigenous tenure systems is a serious impediment to investment seems less convincing. The question of whether investment is more attractive under freehold or under the conditions outlined above is equivalent to the following question: will the increased expectation of retaining the natural land rent offset the risk of losing the investment, when the latter is a function of both the increased security in land and the expected recovery of investment even when land is lost?

(c) *The model*[7]

Consider a simple model of a farmer with the "absolute" rights afforded by freehold tenure. Net productivity prior to investment, termed rent, is a_0. The gains from an investment that gives a perpetual, annual increase in agricultural productivity from a_0 to a_1 at an interest rate of r will have a present value of

$$S_F = \frac{a_1 - a_0}{r} \tag{1}$$

Investment costs are here ignored since, from a present value perspective, they have no bearing on the relative advantage of the two tenure regimes. For simplicity, if the investment is in a fixed asset, it is assumed that a_1 includes a premium deducted from the productivity increase large enough to cover capital consumption. The corresponding gains for a farmer with user rights of the type described above, hereafter simply called "indigenous tenure," will consist of two distinct parts. First, there is the direct productivity gain from the investment itself, which, in addition to the above variables, will be a function of the probability of eviction after the investment and the likelihood of recovering all or part of the investment if evicted. This will be called the "recovery effect."

The second effect is the increased expectation of rent capture resulting from the lower probability of eviction generated by the investment. This is equal to expected rent after investment minus rent prior to investment, and will be called the "rent effect." Let d be the product of the probability and level of recovery of investment returns — that is, the discounted, perpetual increase in annual flows generated by the investment — even if evicted; p_1 is the probability of eviction after the investment, and p_0 is the probability of eviction before investment. Boundaries for p are given by $0 \leq p \leq 1$ and $p_1 \leq p_0$. The expected total returns for a farmer with indigenous tenure is given by the equation.[8]

$$S_I = \underset{(2a)}{\frac{a_1 - a_0}{r}} \times \underset{(2b)}{\frac{r(1-p_1) + p_1 d}{r + p_1}} + \underset{(2c)}{\frac{a_0}{r}} \times \underset{(2d)}{\frac{r(p_0 - p_1)(1+r)}{(r + p_1)(r + p_0)}} \tag{2}$$

The first product, (2a)×(2b), is the recovery effect; the second, (2c)×(2d), is the rent effect. If p_0 and p_1 are both 0 (no risk of eviction before or after investment) (1) and (2) become identical — both tenures provide equal investment incentives. Another expected corollary of the model is that if p_0 and p_1 are equal (no gain in tenure security from investment) and d is 0 (no possibility of recovery after eviction), then (2) reduces to $(a_1 - a_0)(1 - p_1)/(r + p_1)$, the standard formula for discounted perpetual annual flows under tenure insecurity, and the higher investment incentive of freehold is directly related to this insecurity.

Looking at the two effects in isolation reveals something of their relative power. If $d = 1$ (full investment recovery is guaranteed), and the worst-case scenario in terms of tenure security is assumed ($p_0 = p_1 = 1$; absolute certainty of eviction before and after investment), then (2) becomes

$$\frac{a_1 - a_0}{r(1 + r)} \tag{3}$$

The inferior incentive of indigenous tenure compared to freehold, even with certain immediate eviction, is merely a one-year discount of the capitalized investment gains, since the compensation is given only after the period (year 1) when land is lost. In general, if full recovery is guaranteed and investment does not reduce the risk of eviction ($p_0 = p_1$), (2) reduces to

$$\frac{a_1 - a_0}{r} \times \left(1 - \frac{rp_1}{r + p_1}\right) \tag{4}$$

The minimum of (4) is given by (3), the maximum is given by (1), when, as noted above, there is no risk of eviction before or after investment (in this case, level of recovery is irrelevant). The recovery effect cannot by itself render indigenous tenure equal to freehold in terms of investment incentives.

When investment does not improve tenure security, a high level of recovery or a small level of tenure insecurity will entail very small differences between the two tenure regimes. Figure 1 describes the recovery expectancy required to make the two tenures equal in terms of investment incentive for various changes in eviction probability, given an initial eviction probability of 20%. The discount rate is set at 10%.

The effect of increased tenure security is more complex. To isolate it, assume that recovery after eviction is infeasible ($d = 0$). Since $p_1 \leq p_0$, two extremes are provided by the cases $p_1 = 0$ and $p_0 = 1$. In the former case, when there is no residual uncertainty after investment (level of recovery after eviction is irrelevant), there is no loss of direct investment returns compared to freehold, and the higher investment incentive provided by indigenous tenure is given by the expected increase in rent capture. This is equivalent to the final segment in the new expression for total gains from investment under indigenous tenure:

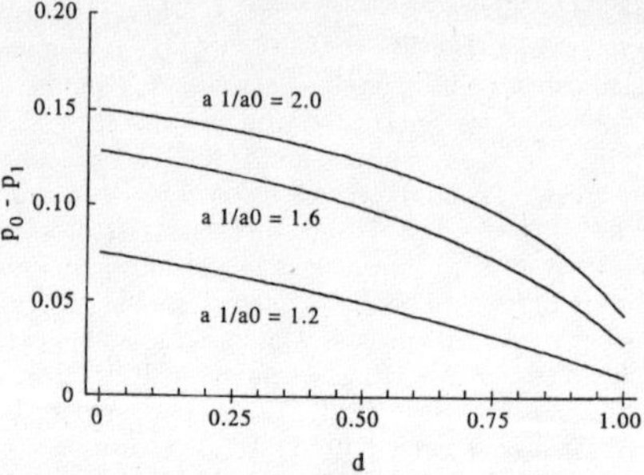

Figure 1. *The percentage decrease in probability of eviction, $p_0 - p_1$, required to provide indigenous tenure with investment incentive equal to that of freehold for different levels of expected investment recovery, d, when evicted. Initial probability of eviction, p_0, is 20%, and the discount rate, r, is 10%.*

$$S_I = \frac{a_1 - a_0}{r} + \frac{a_0}{r} \times \frac{1 + r}{1 + rp_0^{-1}} \tag{5}$$

This expected gain is again described in terms of rent multiplied by a ratio between 0 and 1, depending on the perceived likelihood of eviction prior to investment, p_0. The corresponding case when $p_0 = 1$ yields the following equation:

$$S_I = \frac{(a_1 - a_0)(1 - p_1)}{r + p_1} + \frac{a_0}{r} \times \frac{r(1 - p_1)}{r + p_1} = \frac{a_1(1 - p_1)}{r + p_1} \tag{6}$$

When both extremes occur, $p_1 = 0$ and $p_0 = 1$, (5) and (6) both reduce to

$$S_I = \frac{a_1 - a_0}{r} + \frac{a_0}{r} = \frac{a_1}{r} \tag{7}$$

and the higher investment incentive of indigenous tenure is (7)–(1) = a_0/r, the entire rent. A transition from absolute certainty of immediate eviction to absolute tenure security because of an investment is, perhaps, an unlikely scenario. In general, the difference in investment incentive between the two tenure regimes is given by (2)–(1), and the result is sensitive to small variations in the stated variables.

One striking feature revealed by the model is that if p_0 (initial probability of eviction) is small, even small changes in p will generate substantial increases in expected rent capture, whereas if p_0 is substantial, a small increase in p will entail a negligible rent effect. This can perhaps best be illustrated by an example. Assume recovery of investment returns after eviction is infeasible ($d = 0$). Consider three farmers who have identical land endowments in terms of both size and productivity, who have a discount rate of 20%, and who all face an identical investment decision that will increase agricultural production by 20%. One farmer has freehold tenure, and faces no insecurity before or after investment. A second farmer initially faces a 5% risk of eviction, which will be reduced by 1% after investment, so that p_1 is 0.04. The third farmer's tenure insecurity will be reduced by 20 percentage points — from an initial value of 50% to a residual value of 30%. Which of these farmers has the greater incentive to invest? From a present value criterion, they all have approximately the same incentive. Although the values of p here are sensitive to changes in interest rates and productivity increases, the general pattern holds: if initial insecurity is high, large changes in p are needed for indigenous tenure to provide equal investment incentives to freehold; if initial insecurity is low, very small changes are required. Which scenario is realistic? Although there are inherent problems in treating eviction risk as a fixed parameter, low rates are more relevant than large ones; a farmer who faces, say, a 30% annual risk of eviction is hardly likely to bother with land preparation at all. A farmer who faces an eviction rate of 30% has only a 17% chance of still owning his land after five years. Moreover, as mentioned, if initial eviction rates are low (smaller than 10%) and rent is at all substantial, the rent effect will be substantial for even small changes in p. This can be seen from Figure 2, where the percentage decrease in eviction probability required to render the two tenure regimes equal in terms of investment incentive is plotted against initial eviction probability. The stipulated productivity increase is 20%, and the recovery effect is assumed to be 0. The figure also reveals that the likelihood of indigenous tenure providing higher investment incentive generally will increase with the discount rate.

Another aspect is that, in general, in situations where the rent effect is negligible, the recovery effect will be important and vice versa. For example, the rent effect will decrease with an increase in p_1 (residual insecurity), whereas the recovery effect will increase with p_1. If the productivity increase from the investment is large compared to rent [if $(a_1 - a_0)/a_0$ is large], the rent effect will be small but the recovery effect will be large. Thus, if both effects are valid — and the thesis of this paper is that they often are — then investment incentives are unlikely to be significantly smaller under indigenous tenure than under freehold.

The size of the increase in productivity, relative to rent, is of general interest. The higher this ratio, $(a_1 - a_0)/a_0$, the lower the rent effect will be, and the more likely freehold is to provide higher investment incentives. As this ratio approaches 0, the rent effect becomes increasingly important, and it is thus possible that an "investment" will be undertaken even if it gives no productivity increase. Since in this case (2a)×(2b) = 0, such a scenario simply requires that the rent effect, (2c)×(2d), exceeds cost. This would, however, not be considered a conventional investment. We have here arrived at what is termed opportunistic behavior, where rent is dissipated in the capture of

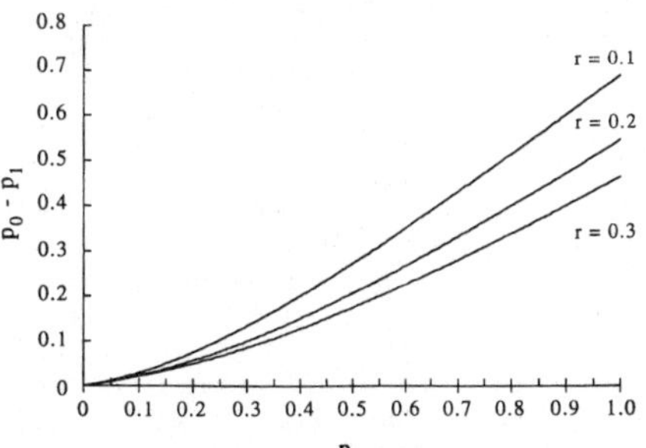

Figure 2. *Reduction in probability of eviction, $p_0 - p_1$, required to provide indigenous tenure with investment incentive equal to freehold for different values of initial eviction probability, p_0. Productivity increase is 20% and expected recovery if evicted is zero.*

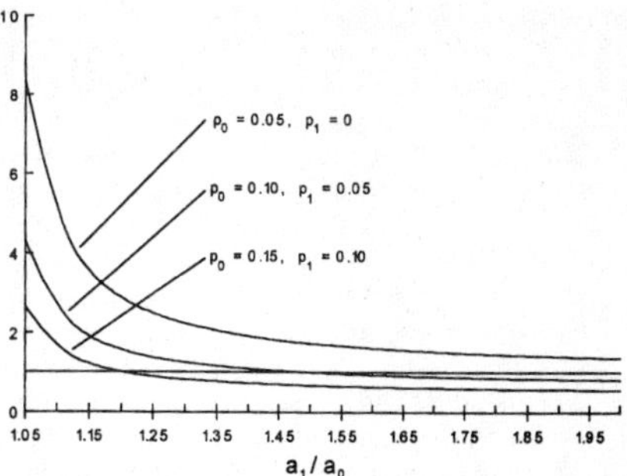

Figure 3. *The vertical axis is relative investment incentive of the two tenure regimes; a fraction where indigenous incentive, [2], is divided by freehold incentive, [1]. The horizontal line with a value of 1 represents equal investment — values higher than 1 denote situations where incentive is higher for indigenous tenure; values lower than 1 denote lower investment incentive for indigenous tenure. The horizontal axis describes changes in productivity resulting from the investment, given as a fraction with residual productivity divided by initial productivity, a_1/a_0. The discount rate, r, is 0.10 and expected investment recovery if evicted, d, is zero.*

resources in the public domain. The significant impact of the relative productivity increase is illustrated in Figure 3, where the relative investment incentive of the two tenure regimes, given as a fraction with indigenous incentive divided by freehold incentive, is plotted against residual productivity divided by initial productivity. Again, the recovery effect is assumed to be 0. The discount rate is set at 10% — the function is fairly robust against variations in the discount rate. Note that the points at which incentives are equal (the points where the curves cross the line where [2]/[1] = 1) will not be influenced by including positive costs; the slope of the curves will, however, increase with positive costs, thus accentuating the differences in incentive.

4. DISCUSSION

(a) *Types of investment and optimal investment*

At this point we need to relax some assumptions. The above model investigates incentives in the context of a single investment, given variations in certain key parameters. But an investment may possess a number of different attributes. A general model such as that in the previous section begs the question of what an investment actually is, and how investment attributes influence the variables of the model — in particular the probability of eviction. A farmer may face a number of investment opportunities; the tenure regime which he is under is likely to influence both the sequence in which he chooses them, and the amount of resources he commits to each one. Specifically, a farmer with indigenous tenure will choose an investment schedule that maximizes the combined effects of productivity increase and security increase; a farmer with freehold will be concerned only with productivity.

The significance of this can be seen by considering investment in movable and tradable assets. A farmer with freehold tenure will use the same productivity criterion when evaluating different types of investments. Since increased tenure security is inextricably linked to investments affixed to the land, however, a farmer with indigenous tenure will evaluate circumstances rather differently. The advantage of investing in movable and exchangeable assets, such as tractors or oxen, is that even if evicted, the farmer will retain his investment. This must be weighed against the advantage of increased tenure security that attends an investment in a fixed land asset such as irrigation structures or trees. If the recovery effect is substantial, it will nullify or reduce the advantage of investment in movable assets, and, *ceteris paribus*, create a bias toward investment in fixed land assets on the part of farmers and indigenous tenure.

An investment is often regarded as the acquisition or creation of productive physical assets, and this is the manner in which investments are understood in the model. More generally, however, investment can be understood as the swapping of current consumption opportunities for increased future consumption opportunities. Thus, two investments which have similar effects are longer fallows in order to enhance soil productivity, and planting leguminous trees for nitrogen-fixing purposes. It should be clear from earlier discussions, however, that the two will have opposite effects on tenure security. The former may be labeled an "inconspicuous" investment, as it does not involve the change or acquisition of an asset through labor or trade, but rather the "passive" enhancement of an asset through its return to a natural state. Such investments will reduce rather than increase security, and thus violate the model's assumption that investment enhances security. In a sense, tenure insecurity here causes land and farmer to part ways; what represents an investment in the land is not an investment to the farmer. This point is particularly important where sensitive ecosystems — and thus long-term sustainability considerations — are concerned. Such "inconspicuous" investments will, however, also go against the general grain of changes in land use implied by a process where land becomes scarce and rights are in transition. Unless one considers population pressure an endogenous variable, land-extensive cultivation methods at some point become untenable under either tenure regime. Indigenous tenure, by inducing conspicuous rather than inconspicuous investment, may in fact accelerate land use intensification.

Assuming that the effect on eviction probability is the same, the lower the productivity increase generated by the investment (relative to initial productivity; not to cost), the more likely indigenous tenure is to provide a higher investment incentive. Thus, it is possible to construct an example where, given otherwise identical conditions, a farmer with freehold will choose a productive investment such as terracing whereas a farmer with indigenous tenure will choose a nonproductive investment such as the construction of a house. If the degree of increased tenure security is linked to the extent to which the investment is seen as a commitment to the long-term productivity of the land, which it might well be, this will tend to negate the influence of productivity increase.

Economics is, however, not necessarily particularly concerned with how high investment demand is — at least not in the sense that higher is better. Excessive investment is as inefficient as underinvestment. Thus, if investment demand under freehold is efficient, and barring the unlikely event that a chance combination of circumstances should render indigenous and freehold tenure identical in all aspects of investment demand, indigenous tenure is inefficient regardless of the direction in which investment incentives diverge. The problem here, though, is the assumption that freehold incentives are socially optimal in rural African communities. What are the more realistic conditions, and in which ways are the lessons from the model likely to be relevant?

As the size of direct investment returns increases relative to rent, the rent effect decreases, and the likelihood that indigenous tenure will provide higher investment incentives decreases. Under which conditions is the productivity increase from an investment likely to be large relative to rent? One possibility is that rent is very low, and this may occur, e.g., when soils have been mined after repeated clearings. On severely degraded lands, indigenous tenure is therefore more likely to provide inferior investment incentives; farmers with any type of tenure may, however, be reluctant to engage in — or find it difficult to identify — viable investment opportunities on such land. If, on the other hand, rent is significant, investments that generate relatively large returns will probably also be capital-intensive; budget constraints may render investments of this type infeasible under all circumstances. Moreover, if inexpensive investments with high returns are available, these are likely to be undertaken by farmers regardless of tenure.

The key lessons of the model are as follows: (i) as the discount rate increases, the likelihood of indigenous tenure providing the higher investment incentive increases; (ii) as the productivity increase of an investment becomes smaller relative to rent, the likelihood of indigenous tenure providing the higher investment incentive increases; (iii) as the initial probability of eviction decreases, the likelihood of indigenous tenure providing the higher investment incentive increases, and; (iv) if the probability of recovering the investment even when evicted is high, a very small decrease in eviction probability is required to render investment incentive higher under indigenous tenure. The model is admittedly rudimentary, and conclusive statements about which regime provides the higher investment incentive cannot be given without measuring the variables for each specific case. When matched with a realistic view of conditions in sub-Saharan Africa, however, it seems to us that these effects increase the possibility that investments which would require low costs or low discount rates under freehold tenure may be undertaken with higher costs or discount rates under indigenous tenure. In particular, the possibility that the prospect of increased tenure security will lead a farmer with indigenous tenure to continue to commit resources to land improvement beyond the point where marginal costs and benefits normally would converge is important. In addition, to construe this as an incentive for overinvestment would fly in the face of the almost universal consensus that myopic behavior is one of the most critical obstacles to rural development in sub-Saharan Africa.

(b) *Rent capture and rent dissipation*

As we have seen, it is possible that an "investment" will be undertaken under indigenous tenure conditions even when no productivity increase results, because the rent effect may exceed cost. In some examples of open access, the entire rent is dissipated, as in Gordon's (1954) portrayal of the fishery, and in the example given by Mendelsohn (1990) for rent capture from land in frontier areas. The solution to this problem was initially seen to be the provision of private property rights — in the fishery, tradable quotas; for land, freehold tenure. Private property rights — we are told — would allow all costs to be internalized, and were conveniently assumed to be both "absolute" and costlessly supplied. The work of economists within the transaction cost genre has since dispelled these notions by recognizing that more detailed specification and more rigorous enforcement of rights is linked to increasing costs. The notion persists, however, that the problem reduced to a simple comparison of two types of costs: on the one hand, the cost of strictly rent-dissipating opportunistic behavior generated by the absence of certain rights, and on the other hand, the cost of rights specification and enforcement sufficiently elaborate to avoid such rent dissipation. In the context of increasing land scarcity, it is merely a matter of when it becomes economically efficient to specify rights of increasing detail in response to the change in relative prices.[9]

Mendelsohn's example of a recently opened frontier area is useful in examining some of these claims, although it should be noted that he does not claim universal validity for his models which are tailored to Latin American conditions:

> Suppose, however, that property rights over this new frontier have not yet been defined. Suppose that it is decided that each person's share of land at each distance will depend on the amount of some x_i that the person invests in defending or creating his property right. For example, each person can prematurely develop by building roads or clearing land before the land is profitable to use. Or possibly each person can pay guards to keep the other people away from the land. Or the person may destroy parts of the land (by cutting valuable forest cover) to secure ownership of the rest. [. . .] The Model reveals that individual maximizing behavior will lead competing colonists to spend as much money creating their property rights as the land is worth. Development will be physically sustainable but society will reap zero net benefits (Mendelsohn, 1990, p. 7).

Clearly, for the entire rent to be dissipated in the manner of this example, the following conditions must be fulfilled: (i) all feasible capture activities are strictly wasteful (have no beneficial effects); (ii) costlier capture activities are always superior to less costly ones and are available to the point where cost equals rent, and; (iii) no prior rights exist. It is possible that all of these conditions occasionally may hold for the fishery. Some of the conditions, in particular (ii) and (iii), may be closely matched in frontier areas in some parts of Latin America and Asia. Most important for our purposes, none of these conditions is likely to hold in rural Africa; even "frontier" areas where no prior land use exists will be subject to the established custom of the tribe. Rights are essentially instrumental in nature (Bromley, 1991). Agreement on rights which are detrimental to the community will not be reached. In the development of acceptable forms of claiming property, then, one would assume that wasteful strategies will not gain approval, at least not in the long run in communities with a relatively old and cohesive social structure. As for individual incentives, why would a farmer "invest" unproductively if a productive investment can achieve the same objective?

The point here is that rational, individual capture of resources in the public domain — opportunistic behavior — is not necessarily rent-dissipating. If continuous cultivation or investment in land assets enhance tenure security, then rent capture may generate tangible benefits. Moreover, even if these benefits are smaller than those that would be generated under freehold, the relevant comparison is between the difference in benefits and the costs of rights specification and enforcement, not between the simple costs and benefits of freehold as such. It is important to note here that even an "investment" which has no productive effect, as denoted in the model by $a_1 = a_0$, is not necessarily wasteful. The example where the erection of a building increases tenure security is pertinent; although the building has no effect on productivity, it still obviously provides benefits.

Just as capture attempts do not have to be rent-dissipating, some forms of capture may in fact dissipate more than rent provided the social costs of resource depletion exceed private costs. This can again be seen as an effect of the incongruity between the income potential from a particular piece of land and the income potential for a given household, given insecurity of tenure; an investment in the context of the household may be a divestment if considered per unit land. "Destructive" investments — investments that entail costs over and above complete dissipation of rent, and thus represent a net reduction in social wealth — may be rational if no other means of capture are available. Such "investments" not only dissipate rent in the manner modeled by Mendelsohn, but also permanently reduce or destroy the income potential from the land. Conversion of tropical rain forest to wasteland may indeed fit such a description.

Finally, a note on land disputes. Costly litigation is the predominant example of how rent is dissipated when rights are inadequately specified. But disputes do not always lend themselves to a simple tenurial analysis. First, although tenure insecurity will increase the uncertainty of the outcome of any given dispute, a typical conflict still requires "irrational expectations" in that "Disputants go to court only if they are optimistic about the outcome (indeed, between them, they must err in the direction of excessive optimism)" as Barzel (1989, p. 70) has pointed out. Second, insofar as a dispute is between heirs to an estate, tenure regime is relevant only to the extent that it incorporates laws of succession.

(c) *Concluding remarks*

The land market, or the lack of such, is not treated in detail here. Corollaries do exist. Under most traditional African tenures, land cannot be sold but improvements can. As for investments, these are tradable for both tenure regimes, although "rent" may be tradable only under freehold. If rent goes down, land value will increasingly be congruent with investments (improvements), and indigenous tenure may approach freehold in this respect. Strategies that subvert the traditional norm that prohibits land sales exist, e.g., rules specifying that the surrounding land accompanies any house that is sold. As land becomes scarce, its value will — to an increasing degree — be incorporated into such transactions. Since land cannot be moved, however, an activated land market implies an increasing intermix of different people and peoples, with consequences for the tight and largely self-governing communities that are found throughout much of rural Africa. As North (1990) has noted, increasingly, impersonal transactions will lead to higher information costs and a greater need for government action. Although state intervention is not required to establish markets, efficient markets — those with low transaction costs — require various forms of collective action (Bromley, 1993). Moreover, the very transactions facilitated by markets may themselves generate a need for state action. This is perhaps especially true of land markets. On the other hand, markets for agricultural land are in general slow, even in most Western countries, due to the complexity and variability of land, associated high information costs, and a lack of "interim markets" (Basu, 1986).

Another issue not considered here is the possibility that the tenure regime itself is the cause of market imperfections (Platteau, 1992, 1996). In general, however, we believe causality runs the other way; tenures arise to cope with the prevailing economic conditions, and will not profoundly influence markets. An important reservation in this regard is, perhaps, the credit market. It could be — indeed it has been — hypothesized that the issuing of land titles will generate the emergence of a financial market and thus more capital-intensive investment. The argument is that a title deed will provide the necessary security that lending institutions require. Norms dictating that land is essentially a common heritage may resist such moves. That is, codes preventing farmers from seeking permanent claims to land also prevent them from presenting that land to the bank as collateral. Many other reservations apply, including rationing rather than supply effects of land registration, with associated inequities (Carter, 1988), and the general second-best problems that attend an emerging market is a wider market vacuum (see, e.g., Jaynes, 1984).

This paper is, however, primarily concerned with the effects of tenure on investment demand rather than on redistribution or credit supply. We argue that: (i) most African farmers do not face a high risk of eviction; (ii) continuous use and "conspicuous" investments in land-based resources will further reduce this risk; (iii) even if land is lost in, for instance, a dispute, the investment may be partially or completely recovered, and; (iv) the more feasible investment alternatives among farmers in sub-Saharan Africa are inexpensive ones with modest absolute returns on — at worst — moderately degraded land.

Under these conditions, indigenous tenure is likely to provide significantly higher investment incentives than freehold, and very unlikely to provide significantly lower investment incentives. We also highlight the paradox that whereas tenure security — as such, or in its conventional tenurial guise of freehold — is routinely seen as a prerequisite for investment and prudent land use, the reverse link may be just as important; investment or prudent use may be a prerequisite for tenure security. The fact that land-based investment is low in rural African communities is not, therefore, due to the incentive structure of the indigenous tenure regime but to the general lack of investment opportunities as determined by the cost and availability of agricultural technology.

Moreover, the conventional propositions that indigenous tenure provides insufficient investment incentives, and at the same time leads to rent dissipation, are contradictory. Each may have some merit on its own, but both cannot hold at the same time. The very act of rent-dissipating capture is largely analogous to overinvestment — in the extreme case, an investment which yields no direct returns but only more secure rights to land. For sub-Saharan Africa, we argue that most cases are not extreme; the key to understanding this is to see that many of the activities related to farming have a dual function — one that is productive and one that is tenurial. If the general investment climate of a rural community is overly cautious — because of market failure, risk aversion, or for other reasons — it is possible that indigenous tenures may provide investment incentives that are superior to freehold, as well as a path toward tenure security more efficient than state intervention in the form of imposed titling programs.

In a dynamic context, the comparison of tenure regimes may seem contrived; at each stage of a transition process a farmer faces a set of opportunities unique to the rights defined by that stage. The analytical merit of counterfactuals — questions such as "what would productivity have been under a different tenure regime?" — shrinks as theory is superimposed on reality. The point here has been to illustrate that in that set are opportunities which, if taken, will push the process itself into a subsequent stage, and that these opportunities may be profitable in both a static and a dynamic context. Indigenous tenures may contain intrinsic mechanisms and incentives that, if allowed to unfold, trigger and sustain a transition to tenures that resemble the familiar Western institution of freehold. Thus, indigenous tenures may initially provide investment incentives that on the one hand may be equal to freehold, and on the other hand — and by these very incentives — propel them towards freehold.[10] To put it in plain language, tenure security is a result, as well as a cause of land use decisions.

NOTES

1. It is, of course, possible that a change in relative prices may cause the costs of rights specification and enforcement to decrease, thus providing lower costs of internalization — rather than increasing gains — as the motive behind institutional revision. But since, as Bardhan (1989) has pointed out, economics does not provide a theory of how (rather than why) institutions change, this notion is not thoroughly treated in the literature.

2. It is common, in relation to traditional tenure, to attribute ownership of land to chiefs. But chiefs primarily had rights over their subjects rather than the land on which they farmed, although certain important exceptions exist. The role of the chief was largely political, a role that the modern African state to some extent has filled in the post-independence era.

3. This distinction, though often ignored, is evident also in the way Western law denies exclusive rights to certain land resources, e.g., mineral rights in the United States and rights to minor forest products and recreation in much of Northern Europe.

4. Insofar as population pressure is behind increasing land scarcity.

5. Such exploitation may of course be undesirable in the long term if land use is generally unsustainable.

6. Rights of transfer (as opposed to price) are not necessarily linked to permanence of ownership.

7. There is, at times, the impression among economists that a "model" entails optimizing procedures, behavioral equations, and constraints. This view however, conflates the idea of optimization with the idea of "economic" and is therefore too restrictive; "economic" is not necessarily "economizing." Recall that an economic model is an abstract representation of reality incorporating variables and the relationships among those variables. The model permits a

depiction of outcomes of this relationship, and therefore facilitates explanation and prediction. Notice that "analysis" is a weaker idea — and a more meager activity — than is explanation and prediction. Notice, also, that there is more to economic models than mere prediction.

8. See the Appendix for elaboration of this formula.

9. It is a paradox that the ideological origin of the private property lobby is liberal (in the European sense) and anti-state, when the corollary of the theory itself in most cases is state intervention in property matters. This paradox rests perhaps on the aforementioned confusion of common property and open access, but mostly on the belief that free markets and the property assignments on which they depend are costless. As North (1990, p. 66) has put it, "... when economists talk about efficient markets, they have simply taken for granted an elaborate framework of constraints." We should point out that here that North is wrong to regard the institutional setup as consisting of only "constraints." Institutional arrangements, being "the working rules of going concerns" comprise both liberation and constraint to economic agents (Bromley, 1989a).

10. This has earlier been discussed in terms of the nature of property rights in land influencing economic use versus economic use influencing the nature of property rights in land (Bromley, 1989a).

REFERENCES

Alchian, A. A., "Uncertainty, evolution and economic theory," *Journal of Political Economy*, Vol. 58 (1950), pp. 211–221.

Ault, D. E. and G. L. Rutman, "The development of individual rights to property in tribal Africa," *Journal of Law and Economics*, Vol. 22, (1979), pp. 63–182.

Bardhan, P., "Alternative approaches to the theory of institutions in economic development," in P. Bardhan (Ed.), *The Economic Theory of Agrarian Institutions* (Oxford: Oxford University Press, 1989), pp. 3–17.

Barrows, R. and M. Roth, "Land tenure and investment in African agriculture: Theory and evidence," *The Journal of Modern African Studies*, Vol. 28 (1990), pp. 265–297.

Barzel, Y., *Economic Analysis of Property Rights* (Cambridge: Cambridge University Press, 1989).

Bassett, T. J., "Introduction: The land question and agricultural transformation in sub-Saharan Africa," in T. J. Bassett and D. E. Crummey (Eds.), *Land in African Agrarian Systems* (Madison: University of Wisconsin Press, 1993), pp. 3–31.

Basu, K., "The market for land: An analysis of interim transactions," *Journal of Development Economics*, Vol. 20 (1986), pp. 163–177.

Bates, R. H., "Some conventional orthodoxies in the study of agrarian change," *World Politics*, Vol. 26 (1984), pp. 234–254.

Besley, T., "Property rights and investment incentives: Theory and evidence from Ghana," *Journal of Political Economy*, Vol. 103, No. 5 (1995), pp. 903–937.

Bromley, D. W., *Economic Interests and Institutions: The Conceptual Foundations of Public Policy* (Oxford: Blackwell, 1989a).

Bromley, D. W., "Property relations and economic development: The other land reform," *World Development*, Vol. 17, No. 6 (1989b), pp. 867–877.

Bromley, D. W., *Environment and Economy* (Oxford: Blackwell, 1991).

Bromley, D. W., "The commons, common property, and environmental policy," *Environmental and Resource Economics*, Vol. 2 (1992), pp. 1–17.

Bromley, D. W., "Reconstituting economic systems: Institutions in national economic development," *Development Policy Review*, Vol. 11, No. 2 (June 1993), pp. 131–151.

Bruce, J. W., "Land tenure issues in project design and strategies for agricultural development in sub-Saharan Africa," LTC Paper No. 128 (Madison: University of Wisconsin-Madison, 1986).

Bruce, J. W., "Do indigenous tenure systems constrain agricultural development?" in T. J. Basset and D. E. Crummey (Eds.), *Land in African Agrarian Systems* (Madison: University of Wisconsin Press, 1993), pp. 35–56.

Carter, M. R., "Equilibrium credit rationing of small farm agriculture," *Journal of Development Economics*, Vol. 28 (1988), pp. 83–103.

Ciriacy-Wantrup, S. V. and R. C. Bishop, "Common property as a concept in natural resource policy," *Natural Resources Journal*, Vol. 15 (1975), pp. 713–727.

Coase, R. H., "The problem of social cost," *Journal of Law and Economics*, Vol. 3 (1960), pp. 1–44.

Coldham, S., "The effect of registration of title upon customary land rights in Kenya," *Journal of African Law*, Vol. 22 (1978), pp. 91–111.

Demsetz, H., "Toward a theory of property rights," *American Economic Review*, Vol. 57 (1967), pp. 347–359.

Dorner, P., *Land Reform and Economic Development* (Harmondsworth: Penguin, 1972).

Feder, G., "Land ownership security and farm productivity: Evidence from Thailand," *Journal of Development Studies*, Vol. 24 (1987), pp. 16–30.

Feder, G. and T. Onchan, "Land ownership security and farm investment in Thailand," *American Journal of Agricultural Economics*, Vol. 69 (1987), pp. 311–320.

Gordon, H. S., "The economics of a common property resource: The fishery," *Journal of Political Economy*, Vol. 62 (1954), pp. 124–142.

Hardin, G., "The tragedy of the commons," *Science*, Vol. 162 (1968), pp. 1243–1248.

Jaynes, G. D., "Economic theory and land tenure," in H. Binswanger and M. R. Rosenzweig (Eds.), *Contractual Arrangements, Employment, and Wages in Rural Labour Markets in Asia* (New Haven: Yale University Press, 1984), pp. 43–62.

Johnson, O. E. G., "Economic analysis, the legal framework and land tenure systems," *Journal of Law and Economics*, Vol. 15 (1972), pp. 259–276.

LTC, "Security of tenure in Africa" Mimeo (Madison: University of Wisconsin, Land Tenure Center, 1990).

Mendelsohn, R., "Property rights and tropical deforestation," Paper presented at the American Economic Association meeting (Washington, DC: 1990).

Migot-Adholla, S., P. Hazell, B. Blarel and F. Place, "Indigenous land rights systems in sub-Saharan Africa: A constraint on productivity?" *World Bank Economic Review*, Vol. 5 (1991), pp. 155–175.

North, D. C., *Institutions, Institutional Change and Economic Performance* (Cambridge: Cambridge University Press, 1990).

Pinckney, T. C. and P. K. Kimuyu, "Land tenure reform in East Africa: Good, bad or unimportant?" *Journal of African Economies*, Vol. 3 (1994), pp. 1–28.

Platteau, J. P., "Land reform and structural adjustment in sub-Saharan Africa — Controversies and guidelines," FAO Economic and Social Development Paper No. 107 (Rome: FAO, 1992).

Platteau, J. P., "The evolutionary theory of land rights as applied to sub-Saharan Africa: A critical assessment," *Development and Change*, Vol. 27, No. 1 (1996), pp. 29–85.

World Bank, "Land reform," Mimeo (Washington, DC: World Bank Development Series, 1974).

APPENDIX: ELABORATION OF INVESTMENT DEMAND MODEL FOR INDIGENOUS TENURE

An investment increases annual productivity from a_0 to a_1 (a_1 includes a capital consumption premium) and reduces annual risk of eviction from p_0 to p_1. Even if evicted, the farmer has a chance to recover all or part of the capitalized value of investment returns. The capitalized value of the perpetual increase in annual flows is:

$$\frac{a_1 - a_0}{r}$$

where r is the discount rate. The product of the probability and level of recovery, even if evicted, is termed d.

(a) *Returns from productivity increase*

The first part of the formula concerns the gains from the productivity increase, $a_1 - a_0$, that the investment generates. After the investment has taken place, the probability of eviction is p_1. The expected benefit in terms of direct investment returns in year 1 is:

$$(a_1 - a_0)(1 - p_1)$$

In the year 2, the corresponding expression is:

$$(a_1 - a_0)(1 - p_1)^2$$

And in year n:

$$(a_1 - a_0)(1 - p_1)^n$$

But even if evicted, the farmer may recover a part of the capitalized value of investment returns. Since the likelihood of being evicted after one year is p_1, and the expected level of recovery is d, then the expected benefit in year 1 is:

$$\frac{(a_1 - a_0)dp_1}{r}$$

In year 2 account must be taken of the probability, $1 - p_1$, that eviction already occurred in year 1. The expression for year 2 is thus:

$$\frac{(a_1 - a_0)(1 - p_1)dp_1}{r}$$

And in year n:

$$\frac{(a_1 - a_0)(1 - p_1)^{n-1}dp_1}{r}$$

The present value of expected returns from the productivity increase generated by the investment for any given year is the sum of the two expressions, discounted to the present by multiplying with $(1 + r)^{-n}$. In year one, this is:

$$[(a_1 - a_0)(1 - p_1) + \frac{(a_1 - a_0)dp_1}{r}] \times (1 + r)^{-1}$$

And in year n:

$$[(a_1 - a_0)(1 - p_1)^n + \frac{(a_1 - a_0)(1 - p_1)^{n-1}dp_1}{r}] \times (1 + r)^{-n}$$

Now, define:

$$X = (a_1 - a_0) + \frac{(a_1 - a_0)dp_1}{r(1 - p_1)}$$

Then the present value of the string of expected returns from year 1 to year n, termed S_A, can be written as:

$$S_A = \frac{X(1 - p_1)}{1 + r} + \frac{X(1 - p_1)^2}{(1 + r)^2} + \ldots + \frac{X(1 - p_1)^{n-1}}{(1 + r)^{n-1}} + \frac{X(1 - p_1)^n}{(1 + r)^n} \quad (1)$$

Multiply both sides of the equation by $(1 + r)/(1 - p_1)$:

$$S_A = \frac{1 + r}{1 - p_1} + \frac{X(1 - p_1)}{1 + r} + \ldots + \frac{X(1 - p_1)^{n-2}}{(1 + r)^{n-2}} + \frac{X(1 - p_1)^{n-1}}{(1 + r)^{n-1}} \quad (2)$$

Now subtract equation (1) from equation (2):

$$S_A = (\frac{1 + r}{1 - p_1} - 1) = X - \frac{X(1 - p_1)^n}{(1 + r)^n} \Rightarrow$$

$$S_A = \frac{X(1-p_1)}{r+p_1} \times \left(1 - \frac{X(1-p_1)^n}{(1+r)^n}\right)$$

The productivity increase is perpetual; when n approaches infinity, the expression becomes:

$$S_A \lim_{n \to \infty} = \frac{X(1-p_1)}{r+p_1} \times (1-0) = \frac{X(1-p_1)}{r+p_1}$$

Substitute for X:

$$\vec{S}_A = \left[(a_1 - a_0) + \frac{(a_1 - a_0)dp_1}{r(1-p_1)}\right] \times \frac{1-p_1}{r+p_1} \Rightarrow$$

$$S_A = \frac{a_1 - a_0}{r} \times \frac{r(1-p_1) + dp_1}{r+p_1} \qquad (3)$$

(b) *Returns from increased tenure security*

The second effect arises because the investment will reduce the probability of eviction from p_0 to p_1 and thus increase the expectation of retaining the rent from the land, a_0.

The present value of expected rent from the land from years 1 through n before investment is:

$$\frac{a_0(1-p_0)}{1+r} + \frac{a_0(1-p_0)^2}{(1+r)^2} + \ldots + \frac{a_0(1-p_0)^{n-1}}{(1+r)^{n-1}} + \frac{a_0(1-p_0)^n}{(1+r)^n}$$

The math here is analogous to that in the previous section — the above formula is identical to that in equation (1) except that a_0 has been substituted for X and p_0 has been substituted for p_1. Thus, when n approaches infinity, the present value of expected rent before investment is:

$$\frac{a_0(1-p_0)}{r+p_0}$$

The same math applies exactly to the present value of expected rent from the land after the investment, except that the new probability of eviction, p_1, is substituted for the earlier probability, p_0. Thus, this can be expressed as:

$$\frac{a_0(1-p_1)}{r+p_1}$$

The returns from increased tenure security, termed S_B, is the difference between the two:

$$S_B = \frac{a_0(1-p_1)}{r+p_1} - \frac{a_0(1-p_0)}{r+p_0} \Rightarrow$$

$$S_B = \frac{a_0}{r} \times \frac{r(p_0 - p_1)(1+r)}{(r+p_1)(r+p_0)} \qquad (4)$$

(c) *Total investment incentive*

The total gain from the investment, S_1, is simply the sum of the two effects, $S_A + S_B$:

$$S_1 = \underset{(a)}{\frac{a_1 - a_0}{r}} \times \underset{(b)}{\frac{r(1-p_1) + dp_1}{r+p_1}} + \underset{(c)}{\frac{a_0}{r}} \times \underset{(d)}{\frac{r(p_0 - p_1)(1+r)}{(r+p_1)(r+p_0)}}$$

(a) and (c) are expressions for discounted perpetual annual flows — (a) for productivity increase and (c) for rent. (b) and (d) are ratios with boundaries of 0 and 1.

[8]

Property rights, externalities and resource degradation: locating the tragedy

Bruce A. Larson and Daniel W. Bromley

1 Introduction

Two axioms dominate discussions of resource degradation and property rights. The first, here called the *composition axiom*, states that complete control of a resource must be vested in a well-defined group for socially efficient use. The second, called the *authority axiom*, states that the well-defined group must also act with a unified purpose. These two axioms come together in the received wisdom of resource use in that individual private property is offered as the solution to resource degradation. The logic of this conclusion is that there is but one person in the 'group', and the locus of authority resides in that one individual. Those inclined to support this position will suggest that once individual private property is established, the unity of both *composition* and *authority* is achieved and resource use will be efficient, and – by implication – socially optimal (Cheung, 1970; Demsetz, 1967; Posner, 1977).

The superiority of individual private property in natural resources, and the correlated indictment of group management regimes, is based on two premises. First, groups are said to be incapable of acting in a socially preferred manner toward the resources that they use. And second, individuals with unique and absolute authority over resource use rates are assumed to behave in a socially preferred manner with respect to the time stream of resource use. The power of the composition and authority axioms, when combined with these two premises, is legendary and well accepted; individual owners of natural resources will *not* use those resources in an inefficient – or antisocial – manner, while groups will *always* use resources inefficiently and at a rate that exceeds their natural regenerative capacity. Having accepted these two 'truths', it is easy to celebrate private property, and also to accept the validity of Hardin's (1968) so-called 'tragedy of the commons'.[1]

That resource degradation is a severe problem in the Third World is well known (Ruddle and Manshard, 1981; US Congress, OTA, 1983; World Bank, 1985). Resource degradation is largely driven by the demands of rural populations, living at or below a subsistence level, for fuelwood and land for agricultural production (Allen and Barnes, 1985; Bromley, 1986; Lundgren, 1983; Perrings, 1989; World Bank, 1985). And since resources in the Third World are often controlled through various systems of group management, the tragedy of the commons has been used to explain deforestation, declining soil quality, and excessive cattle grazing (Picardi and Seifert, 1976; Glantz, 1977). For example, Allen (1985: 61) suggests that 'common property woodland will be overharvested and will retreat'. As a result, private property to achieve unity of composition and authority and, therefore, halt the tragedy is suggested as a necessary condition to invest in resources and reduce degradation. This conclusion has been a major catalyst for the push towards individual tenure and land registration in Africa from the colonial period to the present (Noronha, 1985).

In this paper we address directly the authority and composition axioms that give rise to the presumed optimality of private (individual) property in natural resources, and the correlated indictment of group management regimes. To accomplish this task, we proceed in two stages. In section 2, we review and interpret the literature on the incentives for resource use over time under private and common property. Based on a clear understanding of the nature of property and the axiomatic foundations of private and common property analyses, we show that the two premises upon which received doctrine now rests are inconsistent with both theoretical results and empirical observations. The literature review also shows that resource degradation can be an optimal response to economic and environmental circumstances under a much wider range of property regimes than conventionally accepted. The sufficiency of the composition and authority axioms to protect resources, and by implication the uniform superiority of any property regime for halting resource degradation, is rejected.

Since the superiority of any particular property rights regime is rejected, our analysis of resource degradation turns in section 3 to the incentives for resource use under alternative property regimes. And since the farm household is the primary form of agricultural and pastoral production in the Third World (Singh *et al.*, 1986), we analyse the incentives for resource use over time with the aid of a simple dynamic farm-household model. With appropriate modifications, the model is used to compare the incentives for resource use under individual and a general form of common property. Based on a clear understanding of common property arrangements, we show that the household's time-rate-of-use problem does not imply that a resource will be depleted more severely under common than private property. The links between production technology, the ecosystem, and endowments in creating the incentives for resource degradation in the absence of property rights problems are explored.

Perhaps we should make a distinction between *depletion* and *degradation*; resource degradation has the negative connotation that an observed rate of resource use is somehow not the 'correct' path. If depletion is considered to be degradation, the cause of the incorrect path must be located before a solution can be offered. If externalities due to an incomplete specification of property rights are the problem, in which case the composition axiom is violated, then the lack of property rights provides a clear reason why resource depletion is considered to be degradation. But when property rights problems are not the cause of degradation, locating the tragedy behind resource degradation must also turn to the other elements of the economic problem – objectives, constraints, and endowments.

2 Review

2.1 *Property rights*

An individual property right *in* a resource is a claim of value that the owner of the right can expect to be enforced by some power. The word 'in' is highlighted here because it focuses on the fact that when one party holds a property right in a resource, the party does not necessarily hold all the rights. The existence of a property right that does not contain some restrictions, which implies that some other entity also holds rights in the resource, seems rare. While restrictions are often placed on certain behaviour by the state, restrictions also arise from other quarters (family, kinship group, religion).

Pure individual property, where one individual holds *all* the rights in the resource, is a rare extreme of the property continuum discussed in the literature that promotes private property as the solution to resource degradation. For example, authors have pure individual property in mind when it is argued that 'privately owned resources will always tend to be allocated to the highest value uses' (Furubotn and Pejovich, 1972: 1141), or 'if a single person owns land, he will attempt to maximize its present value...' (Demsetz, 1967: 355). But even the concept of 'ownership' in Western societies, where the full rights in a resource belong to an individual after certain governmental reservations are taken into account (Furubotn and Pejovich, 1972), recognizes that at least two parties have rights in the resource.[2]

To satisfy the composition axiom, the well-defined group that owns a resource is determined by a complete specification of individual property rights. There is little question that a complete specification of rights diminishes uncertainty and promotes efficient resource use (Furubotn and Pejovich, 1972). But in many parts of the world incomplete or unclear property rights – and the breakdown of authority to ensure compliance with those very rights – may be the basic cause of resource degradation. But the question still remains, what property rights regimes are able to reduce degradation and promote socially desirable use? Specifically, the first issue is to identify what property regimes are able to satisfy the composition and authority axioms.

2.2 *The presumed inability of group coordination*

Common property exists when more than one individual holds property rights in the resource, and when there exist restrictions on group size. Ciriacy-Wantrup and Bishop (1975) discuss both historical and current examples of resources under common property regimes. Baker and Butlin (1973) offer an exhaustive account of such systems in Britain.[3] A more current description of common property regimes throughout the Third World is found in the proceedings from the Conference on Common Property Resource Management (National Research Council, 1986), Bromley (1992) and McCay and Acheson (1987). It is important to emphasize that all parties do not necessarily hold the same property rights in the resource. Common property *does not* imply communal ownerships, which has been described as 'a right which can be exercised by all members of the community' (Demsetz, 1967: 353), *nor* does it imply 'free access by all to the resource' (North and Thomas, 1977: 234).

The inability of groups to act in a socially responsible manner – the first premise – is usually blamed on the impossibility of groups to coordinate and cooperate on a pattern of resource use (Demsetz, 1967; Gordon, 1954; Hardin, 1968; Scott, 1955). Thus, even though common property satisfies the composition axiom, the authority axiom is violated because members of the group are always presumed to have the incentive to cheat on any cooperative agreement (Livingstone, 1986). However, this argument often confuses common property with open access, which in turn violates the composition axiom; there is no 'group' since access is unlimited. For example, Cornes and Sandler (1983: 787) suggest that 'common property analyses demonstrate the overexploitation of a scarce fixed resource ... when access is free ...'. Free access, also known as open access, implies the absence of property because no individual (or entity) has a secure claim over the benefit stream arising from a resource. Thus the 'disaster' of open access has been attributed to common property without recognizing the important distinctions between the two regimes.

A situation of open access is often modelled as a prisoner's dilemma or isolation paradox. Assuming Nash behaviour, a non-cooperative equilibrium level of resource use is driven by the strict dominance of individual strategies (Runge, 1981; Sen, 1967). Since there are no incentives to conserve on the use of the resource (because others will surely use it), users exploit the resource at a rate that, although individually rational, eventually leads to its degradation. Even though it would be better for all to cooperate and limit the use of the resource, open access does not provide any mechanism to enforce the agreement. Since Pareto-superior strategies exist where less of the resource is used, the existence of externalities provides a clear reason why the depletion of a resource under open access implies degradation.

The strict dominance of individual strategies has been questioned when individual welfare depends on the actions of others in the group (Cornes and Sandler, 1983; Dasgupta and Heal, 1979; Runge, 1981; Sugden, 1984). Even though the returns to each member of the group may depend on the actions of others, the strict dominance of individual strategies still holds if: (1) the objective functions of the members of the group are separable with respect to the strategies of other members (Runge, 1981); and (2) each member can ignore the external costs of its actions on others in the group. But this structure of the group's choice problem must, by definition, violate the authority axiom, and is essentially identical to a situation of open access. Technology creates separable choice functions, property rights allow users to ignore the effects of their choices on others in the group, and individuals attempt to make themselves as well off as possible with no regard for the welfare of others in the group. Based on this simple analysis, which rules out cooperative behaviour and places the blame for degradation on group management, private property is advanced as the only possible solution to the overexploitation of a resource.

But private property as a 'solution' to resource degradation ignores three issues. First, dominant individual strategies are a direct artefact of the technical production conditions that create separable objective functions. If joint costs exist under common property arrangements, for example in agricultural or range land, dividing the land into parcels controlled by private property regimes *will not necessarily reduce or eliminate the technical interdependence that exists between (among) the users* (Wynne, 1986).

Second, the structure of property rights and other institutions allows the externality to exist. While production technologies may imply separable objective functions, individually optimal strategies only deviate from the social optimum when property rights allow the members of the group to ignore the cost of their choices on other members of the group.

And third, individuals and the state, which surely retains certain rights or places restrictions on individual rights, are assumed to play a cooperative game in which the state is able to enforce the new set of property rights. But this assumption does not necessarily hold in many parts of the world. The imposition of state control, either directly through state ownership or indirectly through individual private property, without the ability to enforce the arrangements, has been an important factor in resource degradation (Bromley and Chapagain, 1984; Commander, 1986; Thomson, 1977).[4] Also, due to incomplete knowledge of the process whereby rights in a resource are transferred to an individual, attempts to redefine property rights have often failed (Wynne, 1986). Such a failure essentially creates a situation of open access.

Rather than defining away the possibility of coordinated behaviour, the group incentives to use a resource controlled by a common property regime can be analysed as an assurance problem, which involves coordinating the expectations of strategies among the players of the game. The assurance problem is a non-cooperative game where the players do not have a dominant strategy to defect from all agreements (Lewis, 1986; Schotter, 1981; Sen, 1967; Ullman-Margalit, 1978). Specifically, dominant individual strategies do not exist when the choice functions of the members of the group are not separable with respect to the strategies of other members. When secure expectations of others' strategies are provided by property rights and other social institutions, the assurance problem recognizes that it may be possible for the group to coordinate use and satisfy the authority axiom.

A resource controlled by common property arrangements is similar to a *club good*, which is a good whose benefits are received by members of the club provided some mechanism exists to exclude non-members (Buchanan, 1965; Cornes and Sandler, 1986; Sandler and Tschirhart, 1980; Tiebout, 1956). Members of a club do not have the choice to either coordinate use or 'go it alone', but instead they have the choice either to become a member and accept the rules of the group or not to be a member and, therefore, not use the resource. While group membership may involve paying an initiation fee or toll, one of the more common exclusion mechanisms in developing countries has traditionally been family and village lineage (McCay and Acheson, 1987; National Research Council, 1986). Such exclusion mechanisms are one way to provide more secure expectations of the strategies of others.

We have shown in this section that common property regimes are theoretically consistent with both the composition and authority axioms. We have also shown that the first premise – that groups are incapable of acting in a socially preferred manner – is a direct artefact of the axiomatic foundations of the game-theoretic models that offer individual private property as the solution to resource degradation. Common property is either confused with open access, which violates the composition axiom, or the individual decision problem is structured so that the group cannot coordinate use, which violates the authority axiom.

2.3 *The presumed optimality of individual private property*

We now turn to the second premise, that individuals with unique and absolute authority over resource use rates will behave in a socially preferred manner with respect to the resources they use. The second premise also becomes relevant for common property regimes when the assurance problem is solved, and the composition and authority axioms are satisfied. Indirectly, we show that the composition and authority axioms are not sufficient to ensure that resources will not be degraded. Notice that the incentives for resource use under individual private property are not usually considered since, according to the first premise, groups are presumed to be incapable of using resources in a socially responsible manner.

As highlighted in the literature on soil erosion, renewable resource extinction, and land degradation due to agriculture, individual private property regimes can also violate the composition and authority axioms. And when these axioms are satisfied, private property may not ensure that an individual owner has the incentive to protect and invest in a renewable resource. For example, McConnell (1983) analyses the incentives for soil erosion when a farmer's objective is to maximize the present discounted value of profits. Assuming that there are no off-site costs of erosion, and that a well-functioning land market exists where land values depend on soil depth (a proxy for soil quality), the optimal strategy could well be to deplete the soil. There are no externalities in this case since all financial and environmental costs (decreases in future productivity due to soil erosion) are internalized into the owner's resource allocation problem. The farmer's optimal strategy would coincide with a social optimum only if the farmer's discount rate equals the social discount rate. However, worrying about a private discount rate's relation to a social discount rate is probably irrelevant since, for example, the land market in the US may *not* reflect prior investments in soil conservation (Barrows and Gardner, 1987), and agricultural externalities in the form of soil erosion and chemical runoff are a main source of nonpoint water pollution (Nonpoint Source Task Force, 1985).

That extinction of a renewable natural resource is potentially optimal for individual present-value maximization has been widely documented (Clark, 1973, 1976; Cropper *et al.*, 1979; Cropper, 1988; Lewis and Schmalensee, 1977; Smith, 1975). In a simple version of the time problem, the 'Iron Law of the Discount Rate' leads to extinction if the growth potential of the resource is less than the discount rate, and if it is profitable to harvest the last unit (Page, 1977).[5] Even if the growth potential is greater than the discount rate, Cropper *et al.* (1979) and Cropper (1988) show that in a more general model the 'Iron Law' still leads to extinction when the initial stock of resources is sufficiently small.[6] While extinction may not result from present-value maximization if harvest costs increase as the stock decreases (so that it is never profitable to harvest the last unit), the resulting stock could still be 'low'. That is, it has reached economic – if not physical – extinction. Since there are no externalities in these models, in other words the composition and authority axioms are satisfied, it is uncertain if and when resource degradation begins.

It is certain that resource degradation, whether in the form of soil erosion, deforestation, or water pollution are especially acute problems in the poor, agriculturally based developing countries (Anderson, 1987; Allen and Barnes 1985; Lundgren, 1983; Southgate *et al.*, 1984). In these countries poverty can be defined as a situation where dissavings exist in the form of resource degradation to maintain a subsistence level of consumption (Perrings, 1989). The link between poverty and degradation is not surprising since land and its associated resources are the main capital inputs in agriculture, which in turn is the main source of rural incomes.

Perrings (1989) develops a model of the open-agrarian economy that is operating at a minimum level of subsistence where resource degradation, due to intensified agricultural production, is an optimal response to adverse changes in the world economy.[7] As in the literature on renewable resource extinction, Perrings' model emphasizes how the ecological setting, the production technology, and the budget set can create the right incentives for resource degradation in the absence of property rights problems (that is, even with the composition and authority axioms satisfied). If prices are exogenous to the local market then the link between the budget set and the environment is broken since local prices will not reflect local scarcities. With a shift in the terms of trade, there may be no alternative but to increase agricultural production to maintain a subsistence income. Resource degradation occurs if the environment is sensitive to increases in production. Other shocks to this system – including drought, political turmoil, taxes, or alternative production possibilities – could lead to a similar chain of events.

The 'tragedy' in Perrings' (1989) model is the combination of poverty, ecology, and technology that produces resource degradation as a byproduct of a strategy to survive. Perrings (1989) concludes that:

> When the need to stave off starvation governs all current production decisions it may be expected that people will ignore the future consequences of these decisions. If the price of output falls, or the price of inputs rises, and if this drives agrarian income below the poverty line (minimum subjective subsistence level) agricultural activity will rise to compensate – even if the future costs approach infinity. Poverty may be expected to drive up their rate of time preference to the point where all that matters is consumption today.[8]

Risk aversion, which is equivalent to a large discount rate in Perrings' model, is likely to be great when subsistence is threatened (Hammer, 1986a, b). If poverty drives the marginal rate of time preference to infinity, then the future environmental effects of the current strategy are *optimally ignored*. While these effects are internalized into the decision-making process, their costs from the perspective of the resource users are zero due to the infinite discount rate. Therefore, while the resource users impose intertemporal effects on themselves, these effects are *Pareto irrelevant*. Recall that Pareto-irrelevant externalities are those effects that are optimally ignored in the decision-making process when the cost of internalization is greater than the benefits (Bromley, 1986; Buchanan and Stubblebine, 1962). While two parties are often viewed as trying to negotiate to internalize the effects, here we have in mind one party 'negotiating' with itself over the effects that it must bear in different time periods. Although the marginal rate of time preference provides structure to the bargaining process, it is not a variable to be bargained over. Given an infinite rate of time preference, it is optimal for the resource user to ignore future effects; the bargain has been struck. Although it may be reassuring to some that these future effects are Pareto irrelevant, those individuals who find it necessary to impose such effects on themselves may not be too intrigued with the concept of Pareto irrelevancy.

We have shown, through reference to the existing literature, that a range of property regimes can satisfy the composition and authority axioms. Nonetheless, these two axioms are insufficient to ensure that resource degradation is not an optimal response from the point of view of the individual and, by implication, a group that coordinates its use of a resource. Having rejected the superiority of any particular property rights regime, common or individual, our analysis of resource degradation now turns to the incentives for resource use under alternative property regimes.

3 A dynamic farm-household model for private and common property

3.1 The model

As stressed in Perrings (1989) and World Bank (1985), resource degradation in agrarian economies is directly related to agriculture. Land degradation in the form of soil erosion and deforestation is often a joint product of land clearing for crops and the demand for firewood, building materials, and fodder (Allen and Barnes, 1985; Anderson, 1987; Bromley, 1986; Lundgren, 1983). The farm household is also the primary form of agricultural and pastoral production in these economies (Singh *et al.*, 1986).[9] Therefore, a dynamic farm-household model is a natural framework for analysing the links between agricultural production and resource degradation under various property regimes.[10]

In this section we develop such a model and, following Perrings (1989) and McConnell (1983), assume that all future costs of household choices on the environment are internalized into the decision-making process.[11] But in contrast to the emphasis on the individual rate of time preference for degradation, which is found in the interpretation that poverty and risk aversion may imply a large discount rate (Hammer, 1986a; Perrings, 1989), we explicitly analyse the production and investment/degradation incentives of the household. Surely the rate of time preference is important, but here we focus on how resource endowments, production technology, ecosystem dynamics, prices, and preferences create the household's endogenous value of the environment or 'marginal cost of resource degradation'. We show that even though future environmental effects of resource-use decisions may be significant, the present value to the household of these effects can be 'small' even when the rate of time preference is 'low'. In other words, cheap resources which can occur without property rights problems provide the incentives for resource degradation.

We proceed by considering a hypothetical group of households – a village – that 'own' a well-defined area of land under a stylized form of private and common property. We then compare how the incentives for land use differ under the two property regimes. Since a given area of land does not necessarily have any technical characteristics that preclude either group management or partitioning into privately owned plots, this direct comparison illustrates that the incentives for resource degradation can exist under either property regime when property rights (or the technical characteristics of the resource) are not the fundamental problem, and that neither regime is uniformly superior in terms of protecting resources.

Under private property each household has complete control of and obtains all the proceeds from a portion of the village land. The household can sell its land at any time, although for simplicity it is assumed that households do not rent land. Under common property, each family holds exclusive use rights in and also obtains all the proceeds from a specific share of the village land. However, use rights cannot be sold or transferred to others, and rights are returned to the village if the household moves to another area (such as a city). The basic structure of private property is essentially fee simple ownership, while the structure of common property describes village-level land control throughout Africa (Fortmann and Roe, 1986; Noronha, 1985; Peters, 1986), and also characterizes the use of grazing commons and common field systems (Baker and Butlin, 1973; Netting, 1976; Rhoades and Thompson, 1975).[12]

The household is assumed to produce under a fallow-rotation system, where land is rotated between tillage and fallow periods for managing soil productivity. The ecosystem and the state of agricultural technology produce the need for a fallow-rotation system because continual cropping quickly reduces soil productivity. Fallow-rotation agriculture is commonly found in the Third World and exists along a continuum from temporary slash and burn practices to more permanent short-fallow systems (Raintree, 1985). In general, the household must make two land allocation decisions within a fallow-rotation system: (1) at any point in time the household's total land stock must be allocated between tillage and fallow; and (2) the length of the tillage and fallow periods on each piece of the household's land must be chosen.[13] To reduce the number of household choice variables in the model, some simplifying assumptions on the land allocation process allow these two, generally independent, decisions to be determined by the choice of one land-allocation parameter. At the beginning of the planning horizon $t_0 = 0$, the household allocates its fixed quantity of land A between tillage ΘA and fallow $(1 - \Theta)A$, where $0 \leq \Theta \leq 1$. While the land-allocation parameter Θ remains constant throughout the planning horizon, it is assumed that at each point in time a small (fixed) amount of land $(1/n)A$ is switched into tillage and out of fallow to keep the overall land allocation constant, where $0 \leq 1/n \leq 1$. Given any A and n, the length of the tillage and fallow periods are altered simply by a change in Θ; each piece of land $(1/n)A$ is in tillage for Θnt before returning to fallow for $(1 - \Theta)nt$.[14]

The household produces a staple crop $C(t)$ on its tilled land using labour $L_c(t)$ as a variable input according to

$$C(t) = C(L_c(t), Q(t), \Theta A), \tag{1}$$

where $Q(t)$ is an index of soil quality or productivity over *all* of the household's land, and the production function C is non-decreasing in L_c, Q, and Θ. The index $Q(t)$ is thought of as a weighted average of soil productivity over both the tillage and fallow land.[15]

The household also produces firewood $h(t)$ on the fallow land using labour $L_h(t)$ according to

$$h(t) = h(L_h(t), F(t), (1 - \Theta)A), \tag{2}$$

where $F(t)$ is total tree biomass which only grows on the fallow land, and the function h is non-decreasing in L_h and F, and non-increasing in Θ. In fallow rotation agriculture, trees and crops are usually produced on separate plots of land, although the model could be easily modified to include the case where trees and annuals are intercropped.

The dynamics in the ecosystem, represented by the soil productivity state variable $Q(t)$ and the tree biomass state variable $F(t)$, produce the need for fallow-rotation agriculture. In fragile ecosystems, where soil quality is quickly depleted during tillage, the fallow period and any tree growth play a dual role for the household. Fallow is a soil-building period during which trees help to increase nutrients and retain moisture in the soil and reduce erosion, as well as provide a source of products $h(t)$.

The net change in soil productivity at each t is

$$\dot{Q}(t) = q(L_c(t), Q(t), F(t), \Theta), \quad Q(0) = Q_0, \tag{3}$$

where Q_0 is the household's endowment of soil productivity at the beginning of the planning horizon; the growth function q is non-increasing in L_c and Θ and non-decreasing in F; and q is positive and increasing in Q beyond some critical point Q_c up to some level Q_m, beyond which q is decreasing in Q (see Smith, 1968: 411).

The net change in tree biomass at each t is

$$\dot{F}(t) = f(F(t), (1-\Theta)A) - h(L_h(t), F(t), (1-\Theta)A), \quad F(0) = F_0, \tag{4}$$

where F_0 is the household's endowment of tree biomass at the beginning of the planning horizon; and the function f, which describes the natural growth of tree biomass, is non-increasing in Θ; and f is positive and increasing in F beyond some critical point F_c up to some level F_m, beyond which f is decreasing in F.

Our objective is to analyse the incentives for resource degradation under alternative property regimes when property rights problems do not exist – that is, when the authority and composition axioms are satisfied. Therefore, we have assumed in equations (1)–(4) that there are no off-site externalities under both property regimes. In other words, the crop production and tree harvesting decisions of one household do not enter into the decision problem of other households. Externalities can be easily incorporated into the model by allowing the state equations (3) and (4) for a household j to depend on the level of its state variables, $Q^j(t)$ and $F^j(t)$, along with the state variables of some other household k, $Q^k(t)$ and $F^k(t)$. In this case, externalities that exist between the two households are driven by the technical relationships in the ecosystem, whether they 'own' the land under common or private property. The authority axiom would be violated unless the owners could agree to coordinate their use of the resource. If externalities exist between households, their coordination problem could be modelled as a non-cooperative differential game (see Intriligator, 1971).

For a given Θ and T, the present discounted value of household utility is[16]

$$J(Q_0, F_0, T{:}\ \Theta) = \max_{X_l, L_h, L_c} \int_0^T U(Y, X_l)\, e^{-\delta t} dt + e^{-\delta T} J^*(F(T), Q(T), T, \beta^*) \tag{5}$$

subject to the state equations (3) and (4), and

$$Y = w(L_e - X_l) + p_c C(L_c, Q, \Theta A) + p_h h(L_h, F, (1-\Theta)A) - w(L_c + L_h) + Y_e, \tag{6}$$

$$L_c, L_h, X_l, Q, \geq 0, \quad \text{and} \quad 0 \leq h \leq F, \tag{7}$$

where $U(X_l(t), Y(t))$ is the household's instantaneous utility function that depends on leisure $X_l(t)$ and an aggregate consumption commodity or income $Y(t)$; δ is the household's marginal rate of time preference; L_e is the household's total time endowment in each period; p_c is the price of the staple crop, p_h is the price of firewood, and w is the price of labour/opportunity cost of leisure, and it is assumed that the household can buy or sell all it desires at fixed prices; Y_e is an exogenous flow of income, such as remittances from family members in a city; and J^* is a terminal value function that depends on terminal time T, the terminal values for soil productivity $Q(T)$ and tree biomass $F(T)$, and a vector of parameters β^*.

In the household's budget constraint, (6), $L_e - X_l$ is total household labour supply, and $L_c + L_h$ is total household labour demand. When household labour supply is greater than labour demand, the household supplies excess labour to the market and earns the wage w; when labour demand is greater than labour supply, the household hires labour on the market at the wage w. Thus, the household simultaneously chooses X_l, L_c, and L_h to maximize the household's present discounted value of utility, while buying and selling labour at the wage w is needed to satisfy its labour market equilibrium.[17]

The function J is the household's indirect utility function, and, based on Bellman's fundamental recurrence relation (Intriligator, 1971), J^* is interpreted as the discounted-to-time-T value of household utility beginning at time T and continuing to some future period (possibly infinity). Given the specific definitions of private and common property used here, the fundamental difference between the two property regimes for the household model defined by equations (3)–(7) lies in the terminal value function $J^*(F(T), Q(T), T, \beta^*)$, which is assumed to internalize correctly all of the effects beyond T of household choices into the decision process. As a result, differences in the rate of resource use under the two regimes are driven by differences in the terminal value function.

Using the household model developed here, we proceed in two stages to investigate the implications of the dynamic household model for resource use. First, based on a given terminal value function J^*, we derive and interpret the necessary conditions for efficient resource use. And second, we discuss some possible differences between the terminal value function under private property, $J^p(F(T), Q(T), \beta^p)$, and common property, $J^c(F(T), Q(T), \beta^c)$, and then show what these differences imply for the rate of resource use under the two regimes. We show that resource degradation can be efficient under both property regimes, and that there is no reason to suggest, a priori, that either type of property regime better protects the resource base.

3.2 *Efficient resource use given any terminal value function J^**

The household's problem of maximizing the present value of utility, subject to its production functions (1) and (2), environmental state equations (3) and (4), and income constraint (6), yields common-sense allocative rules that provide insight into the incentives to deplete or invest in natural resources. Using the Maximum Principle, the necessary conditions for an optimum to the household's problem are provided in Appendix A. The costate equations of motion for the household's problem (see Appendix A, equations (A.5) and (A.6)) show that the soil and forest resources decrease in value to the household at the same rate at which they give rise to valuable outputs (Dorfman, 1969). Integrating the costate equations from t' to T and using the transversality conditions yields:

$$\lambda_1(t') = \int_{t'}^{T} \left[e^{-\delta t} \frac{\partial U}{\partial Y} p_c \frac{\partial C}{\partial Q} + \lambda_1 \frac{\partial q}{\partial Q} \right] dt + e^{-\delta T} \frac{\partial J^*}{\partial QT}, \tag{8}$$

$$\lambda_2(t') = \int_{t'}^{T} \left[e^{-\delta t} \frac{\partial U}{\partial Y} p_h \frac{\partial h}{\partial F} + \lambda_1 \frac{\partial q}{\partial F} + \lambda_2 \left(\frac{\partial f}{\partial F} - \frac{\partial h}{\partial F} \right) \right] dt + e^{-\delta T} \frac{\partial J^*}{\partial F(T)}, \tag{9}$$

where all the notation, variables, functions, and parameters are defined in equations

(1)–(7), except that $\lambda_1(t')$ and $\lambda_2(t')$ are the costate variables associated with the state equations (3) and (4).

From Bellman's optimality principle, the costate variables equal the change in the maximum value of the objective function starting at an arbitrary t' that results from a marginal change in the assets at t', $0 \leq t' \leq T$ (Intriligator, 1971). Thus, the opportunity costs of resource depletion at t', $\lambda_1(t')$ and $\lambda_2(t')$ are the marginal utility of an extra unit (shadow values) of the resources at t'. The marginal value of the resources includes current and future values that depend on three main factors: (1) the marginal effect of the stock at t' on future utility due to output changes; (2) capital gains/losses from t' to T due to a change in the stock at t'; and (3) the marginal effect of the stock at T on the salvage value function.

The incentives for the utility maximizing choices of labour provide the direct link between the household's existing income situation, crop production, tree harvesting, and resource depletion. The first-order condition for the efficient use of labour in crop production (Appendix A, equation (A.3)) can be rearranged to yield[18]

$$p_c \frac{\partial C}{\partial L_c} = w - \frac{\partial q}{\partial L_c} e^{\delta t} \lambda_1 [\partial U/\partial Y]^{-1}, \quad 0 \leq t \leq T. \tag{10}$$

From equation (10), the household chooses L_c so that its marginal value product equals its total marginal cost, where the total marginal cost at any t involves two distinct terms: (1) the exogenous market wage w; and (2) the endogenous marginal environmental cost. This environmental cost is determined by the fragility of the environment to crop production (represented by $\partial q/\partial L_c \leq 0$), which yields an equal change in $Q(t)$ through the state equation (3), the household's shadow value for soil productivity at $t(e^{\delta t}\lambda_1)$, and the inverse of the marginal utility of income at t. The marginal utility of income acts as the 'exchange rate' that translates the shadow value of soil productivity (in utility) into the household's shadow price (in income) for an extra unit of Q at t. Since the value of the soil resource lies predominately in its future income-generating effects (see equation (8)), the shadow price of $Q(t)$ can also be interpreted as the marginal rate of substitution between current and future income.

The first-order condition for the efficient use of labour in tree harvesting (Appendix A, equation (A.4)) can be rearranged to yield

$$\{p_h - e^{\delta t} \lambda_2 [\partial U/\partial Y]^{-1}\} \frac{\partial h}{\partial L_h} = w, \quad 0 \leq t \leq T. \tag{11}$$

The household also chooses L_h so that its marginal value product equals its marginal cost, where the net price of a unit of tree biomass involves: (1) the exogenous market price p_h; minus (2) the endogenous marginal environmental cost, where $e^{\delta t}\lambda_2[\partial U/\partial Y]^{-1}$ is the shadow price (in income) of a unit of biomass.

Equations (8)–(11) show how the elements of the household's decision problem (technology, prices, the ecosystem, income, preferences, endowments, along with the discount rate) create the incentives for efficient resource use that, nevertheless, can lead to resource degradation. The household recognizes that the choices of labour change the level of the resource stocks and, as shown in equations (10) and (11), internalizes correctly such effects into its optimal choices of labour. But the household determines an endogenous shadow price for this change – the marginal cost of degradation. Anything which decreases the shadow prices of the resources decreases the marginal cost of labour in crop production and increases the net price of tree biomass; both effects tend to increase the demand for labour and, therefore, increase soil degradation and deforestation.

For any terminal value function J^*, a combination of a fragile ecosystem, poverty (low income and high marginal utility of income), and low environmental endowments creates a situation where resources are efficiently degraded. While a fragile ecosystem would tend to decrease the demand for labour by either increasing the wage rate for L_c or decreasing the net price of harvested trees, the values of these effects to the household in income terms may be small due to a low income level (high marginal utility of income). As a result, anything that reduces household welfare and income will tend to reduce the shadow price of a resource and increase its use. As shown in Appendix A, the household is always made worse off with: (1) an increase in the price of a market purchased good X_m, which is equivalent to a decline in the household's terms of trade *vis-à-vis* the market; and (2) a decrease in exogenous income Y_e. Structural adjustment loans, which are often conditional on decreasing subsidies for urban consumption goods and increasing agricultural output prices, essentially increase the price of p_m and may also decrease Y_e by decreasing the amount of income that urban household members are able to send back to the farm household.

As in static household models and as shown in Appendix A, the effect on household income and welfare due to a permanent increase in w, p_c, or p_h is indeterminant and depends on whether the household is a net seller or net purchaser of labour, crops, and firewood over the planning horizon. Resource endowments are likely to be important here because the household is more likely to be a net purchaser of the staple and, therefore, be made worse off with a crop price increase when endowments are poor. With poor endowments, the marginal productivity of labour in crop production is likely to be small, and the household would have the incentive to rely on wage income and tree harvesting revenues to purchase stable consumption needs. Also, the marginal effects of soil productivity on crop production and the state equations may be small given sufficiently poor endowments Q_0 and F_0; intuitively, land that is relatively unproductive may remain unproductive over a range of improvements. In the extreme, when $\partial C(L_c, Q, \Theta A)/\partial Q = 0$ for attainable levels of Q given Q_0, the value of soil productivity to the household is derived exclusively from the terminal value function J^* (see equation (8)). And from equation (9), the value of trees to the household also tends to be smaller when soil productivity has less value. In turn, the lower tree value tends to increase tree harvesting from equation (11), lower the tree stock from equation (4), and decrease soil productivity from equation (3).

3.3 Comparing resource allocation under private and common property

In the previous section we discussed how the incentives for resource use can lead to resource degradation, and focused primarily on how low income levels and poor endowments set the stage for degradation. Property rights need not be the basic problem, and efficient use can be theoretically consistent with degradation for any property rights regime. In this section we use the household model to compare directly the incentives for resource use under common and private property by considering how the terminal value function J^*, which is endogenous to the household, differs under the two regimes.

The terminal value function under private property $J^p(Q(T), F(T), T, \beta^p)$ includes the discounted utility of consumption beyond time T that is purchased with: (1) the income from the sale of the land; and (2) the income from the household's alternative employment source if it continues beyond T. For the case of common property, which precludes land sales, the terminal value function $J^c(Q(T), F(T), T, \beta^c)$ includes the discounted value of consumption purchased with the income from the household's alternative employment source if it continues to exist beyond T. The parameters β^p and β^c represent other factors beyond T that influence the decisions problem, and in general could also be a function of T.

Bequest motives are another element of the terminal value functions J^p and J^c, which could be represented in the vectors β^p and β^c. Bequest motives toward future members of a family or village that influence household preferences for the terminal value of assets have been identified and studied in both market and non-market economies. Becker (1981) discusses the issue of pure altruism, while non-altruistic components are found in Kotlikoff and Spivak (1981), Bernheim *et al.* (1985) and Pollack (1988). The literature on economic development also discusses the motives of the parents to provide working capital (such as human capital), or in this case environmental capital, to children who will later provide old-age support (Hammer, 1986a). While bequest motives that are independent of land sale price may exist under private property, in which case the terminal level of the environmental assets affects more than just land sale values, there is every expectation that bequest motives for resources controlled under a common property regime are significant, especially since group membership is due to family lineage. Village conventions and institutions may also influence household preferences for the terminal levels of the resources.

An implication of the first premise concerning group resource management (groups cannot act in a socially responsible manner towards the resources they use) is that members of the group will tend to undervalue their resources because there are no market incentives to take into account the effects of current actions beyond the household's planning horizon. According to Demsetz (1967), common property implies that future generations have no say in the current use of the resource and that the current members of the group do not care about its future members, while private property allows all generations to have the correct influence on the current pattern of resource use through the perfect land market. With a perfect land market, the profit-maximizing land owner essentially acts with an infinite planning horizon (Samuelson, 1976). If common property implied that the terminal value function J^c was zero or did not depend on the states of the assets, which is implicit in Demsetz (1967), an inter-temporal externality would exist since the environmental costs of the group's choices that fall beyond the planning horizon are not internalized into the decision-making process. Besides ignoring the existence of bequest motives and assuming that profit rather than utility is the relevant objective function, Demsetz's (1967) assumption of a perfect land market is difficult to accept.[19]

While no externalities exist in our model, resource values differ due to differences in the terminal value functions under the common and private property regimes. But it *cannot be concluded that the household values its resources more highly under one property regime than the other*. Equations (8) and (9) show that a larger terminal value of a resource to the household, which is determined by the marginal effect of the terminal stock on the terminal value function, increases the shadow value of the resource in all periods. The property regime that is associated with larger shadow values for the resources will be associated with larger resource stock since the marginal cost of L_c will be larger and the net price of fuelwood will be lower (see equations (10) and (11)). Given the two resources of interest here, there are nine different relationships between the resource values under the two regimes that can exist depending upon the relative magnitudes of $\partial J^*/\partial Q(T)$ and $\partial J^*/\partial F(T)$ under private and common property; some are associated with lower resource values under common property, and some are associated with lower resource values under private property. Representing the terminal value function for private property as $J^c(Q(T), F(T), T, \beta^p)$ and that for common property as $J^c(Q(T), F(T), T, \beta^c)$ the nine different cases are all possible pairs (a_i, b_j), $i,j = 1, 2, 3$, made of individual draws from sets A and B, where:

$$A = (\partial J^p/\partial Q = \partial J^c/\partial Q, \partial J^p/\partial Q > \partial J^c/\partial Q, \partial J^p/\partial Q < \partial J^c/\partial Q), \quad \text{and}$$

$$B = (\partial J^p/\partial F = \partial J^c/\partial F, \partial J^p/\partial F > \partial J^c/\partial F, \partial J^p/\partial F < \partial J^c/\partial F).$$

There is no scientific knowledge that can rank the relative magnitudes of the terminal value under private property J^p and common property J^c, even assuming a perfect land market, or the relative magnitudes of the derivatives of these functions with respect to terminal stocks. For the case $(a_3, b_3) = (\partial J^p/\partial Q < \partial J^c/\partial Q, \partial J^p/\partial F < \partial J^c/\partial F)$, the household under common property places higher values on both soil productivity and trees for all time periods. Those who find comfort in the private property solution rule out eight cases and consider only the possibility of

$$(a_2, b_2) = (\partial J^p/\partial Q > \partial J^c/\partial Q, \partial J^p/\partial F > \partial J^c/\partial F). \tag{12}$$

As a final point, the household may also choose the optimal time T to sell its land under private property, or relinquish use rights under common property, and then move on to alternative economic opportunities. By the envelope theorem, the necessary condition for an optimal choice of T is

$$\partial J/\partial T = H(T) + [\partial J^*/\partial T - \delta J^*]e^{-\delta T} = 0, \tag{13}$$

where $H(T)$ is the present-value Hamiltonian (see Appendix A) evaluated along the optimum at T. Using the transversality conditions (A.7) and (A.8), equation (13) can be rearranged to yield

$$U(T) + \frac{\partial J^*(T)}{\partial Q(T)} q(T) + \frac{\partial J^*(T)}{\partial F(T)} [f(T) - h(T)] = \delta J^*(T) - \frac{\partial J^*(T)}{\partial T}, \tag{14}$$

where U, J, q, f, and h are evaluated at the optimum in equation (5) at T.

Equation (14) is an optimal stopping rule that is identical to an asset replacement criterion (Perrin, 1972; Samuelson, 1976). The household remains on the land until the marginal utility of continuing production through immediate benefits and capital gains equals the opportunity cost of not stopping. The term $\delta J^*(T)$ translates $J^*(T)$ into a constant flow of utility, while the term $\partial J^*(T)/\partial T$, which is expected to be negative, shows how the passage of time affects utility beyond T. The property regime that is associated with a higher opportunity cost of remaining on the land and lower terminal values of the resources will be associated with a shorter terminal time and higher rates of resource use. But we showed in the previous section that the relative magnitudes of $\partial J^*/\partial Q(T)$ and $\partial J^*/\partial F(T)$ as well as J^* under the two regimes cannot be ranked, and assert here that the relative magnitudes of $\partial J^*(T)/\partial T$ under both regimes is equally unknown. Therefore, no general conclusion, or presumption, about the optimal stopping time or terminal values under the alternative property regimes is warranted.

Although the model developed in this section allows for many possibilities, which may be troubling to those looking for the 'solution', we have proven our main thesis that degradation can exist in the absence of property rights problems. We have also shown that economic theory does not suggest which property regime is associated with higher resource values and, therefore, higher resource stocks. As a result, no specific property regime can be expected a priori to provide the solution to the tragedy of resource degradation.

4 Conclusion

In this paper, we address directly the authority and composition axioms that give rise to the presumed optimality of individual property in natural resources, and the correlated indictment of group management regimes. The logic of these conclusions is based on two premises which we have shown, through reviewing the literature on private and group resource management, to be inconsistent with theoretical possibilities and empirical observations. The review also showed that resource degradation can be an optimal response to economic and environmental circumstances under a much wider range of property regimes than conventionally accepted. Therefore, the sufficiency of the composition and authority axioms to protect renewable natural resources was rejected.

Using a simple dynamic model of the farm household, we showed that the household's decision problem under common property does not automatically suggest that resources are more likely to be degraded under common than private property. As such, the model is offered primarily to identify how poor resource endowments, low income (higher marginal utility of time), as well as high discount rates tend to decrease the household's endogenous value of the environment. In other words, the household may not ignore the consequences of its current decision on the future quality of the environment, but the value of these effects – the marginal cost of degradation – to the household can be small. Thus, as highlighted in this paper, the tragedy is located in the incentives for efficient resource use that, nonetheless, lead to resource degradation due to poverty, poor resource endowments, and a fragile ecosystem.

Appendix A

Substituting (6) directly into the utility function, the present-value Hamiltonian is

$$H = U(Y, X_l)\,e^{-\delta t} + \lambda_1 q + \lambda_2 (f - h) \tag{A.1}$$

where λ_1 and λ_2 are the costate variables for the equations of motion.

From the Maximum Principle, the optimal paths for the control, state, and costate variables for a given Θ and T satisfy (assuming an interior solution):

$$\frac{\partial H}{\partial X_l} = \mathrm{e}^{-\delta t}\left[-w\frac{\partial u}{\partial Y} + \frac{\partial U}{\partial X_l}\right] = 0, \tag{A.2}$$

$$\frac{\partial H}{\partial L_c} = \mathrm{e}^{-\delta t}\left[\frac{\partial U}{\partial Y}\left(p_c\frac{\partial C}{\partial L_c} - w\right)\right] + \lambda_1\frac{\partial q}{\partial L_c} = 0. \tag{A.3}$$

$$\frac{\partial H}{\partial L_h} = \mathrm{e}^{-\delta t}\left[\frac{\partial U}{\partial Y}\left(p_h\frac{\partial h}{\partial L_h} - w\right)\right] - \lambda_2\frac{\partial h}{\partial L_h} = 0, \tag{A.4}$$

$$\lambda_1 = -\left[\mathrm{e}^{-rt}\frac{\partial U}{\partial Y}p_c\frac{\partial C}{\partial Q} + \lambda_1\frac{\partial q}{\partial Q}\right], \tag{A.5}$$

$$\lambda_2 = -\left[\mathrm{e}^{-rt}\frac{\partial U}{\partial Y}p_h\frac{\partial h}{\partial F} + \lambda_2\left(\frac{\partial f}{\partial F} - \frac{\partial h}{\partial F}\right)\right], \tag{A.6}$$

$$\lambda_1(T) = \mathrm{e}^{-\delta T}\frac{\partial J^*}{\partial Q(T)}, \tag{A.7}$$

$$\lambda_2(T) = \mathrm{e}^{-\delta T}\frac{\partial J^*}{\partial F(T)}. \tag{A.8}$$

Using the envelope theorem, the optimal choice of Θ is determined by

$$\frac{\partial J}{\partial \Theta} = \int_0^T\left[\mathrm{e}^{-\delta t}\frac{\partial U}{\partial Y}\left(p_c\frac{\partial C}{\partial \Theta} + p_h\frac{\partial h}{\partial \Theta}\right) + \lambda_1\frac{\partial q}{\partial \Theta} + \lambda_2\left(\frac{\partial f}{\partial \Theta} - \frac{\partial h}{\partial \Theta}\right)\right]\mathrm{d}t = 0 \tag{A.9}$$

Assuming that a set of second-order conditions is also satisfied (see Kamien and Schwartz, 1981), equations (A.2)–(A.9), along with state equations (3) and (4) are necessary and sufficient for the solution to the household's resource allocation problem.

For reference, the household's optimal land allocation condition (A.9) can be rearranged to yield

$$\int_0^T\left[\mathrm{e}^{-\delta t}\frac{\partial U}{\partial Y}p_c\frac{\partial C}{\partial \Theta} + \lambda_1\frac{\partial q}{\partial \Theta}\right]\mathrm{d}t = -\int_0^T\left[\mathrm{e}^{-\delta t}\frac{\partial U}{\partial Y}p_h\frac{\partial h}{\partial \Theta} + \lambda_2\left[\frac{\partial f}{\partial \Theta} - \frac{\partial h}{\partial \Theta}\right]\right]\mathrm{d}t. \tag{A.9'}$$

The left-hand side of (A.9′) is the marginal utility of land in tillage, while the right-hand side is the marginal utility from land in fallow. Anything that increases the marginal utility of land in tillage or decreases the marginal utility of land in fallow will tend to increase the quantity of land in tillage and, therefore, decrease soil productivity. In the extreme, the household would set $\Theta = 1$ if it was always better off allocating land to tillage.

Since the budget constraint (6) is linear in prices and exogenous income, the indirect object function (5) is linear homogeneous in p_c, p_h, w, and Y_e. When aggregate household consumption Y is disaggregated into consumption of the staple (X_c), tree biomass

(X_h), and a market purchased good (X_m), in which case $Y = X_c p_c + X_h p_h + X_m p_m$ the household's real income budget constraint (in terms of the market purchased good) can be written as

$$X_m = (1/p_m)[w(L_e - X_l) + p_c C + p_h h - w(L_c + L_h) + Y_e - p_c X_c - p_h X_h]. \quad \text{(A.10)}$$

Writing the utility function as $U(X_c, X_h, X_m, X_l)$, substituting the real income constraint (A.10) into the utility function, and using the envelope theorem, the effects of permanent price increases on household welfare are:

$$\frac{\partial J}{\partial p_c} = \int_0^T e^{-\delta t} \frac{\partial U}{\partial X_m} \frac{1}{p_m} (C - X_c)\, dt, \quad \text{(A.11)}$$

$$\frac{\partial J}{\partial p_h} = \int_0^T e^{-\delta t} \frac{\partial U}{\partial X_m} \frac{1}{p_m} (h - X_h)\, dt, \quad \text{(A.12)}$$

$$\frac{\partial J}{\partial p_m} = -\int_0^T e^{-\delta t} \frac{\partial U}{\partial X_m} \frac{X_m}{(p_m)^2}\, dt \leqq 0, \quad \text{(A.13)}$$

$$\frac{\partial J}{\partial Y_e} = \int_0^T e^{-\delta t} \frac{\partial U}{\partial X_m} \frac{1}{p_m}\, dt \geqq 0, \quad \text{(A.14)}$$

$$\frac{\partial J}{\partial w} = \int_0^T e^{-\delta t} \frac{\partial U}{\partial X_m} \frac{1}{p_m} (L_e - X_l - L_c - L_h)\, dt. \quad \text{(A.15)}$$

As in static household models, the general effects of price changes on the optimal choices of labour, leisure, and consumption are indeterminate and depend on substitution and income effects and on the household's net production situation. Even in a simple two-period model of household production, unambiguous results are difficult to obtain (Max and Lehman, 1988).

Notes

1. One sees similar approaches to the problems of fishery management – the 'sole ownership' hypothesis of Gordon (1954) and Scott (1955). While recognizing that the composition of the group cannot be changed, unitization establishes one controlling management entity (the sole owner) that supersedes the wishes and discretion of all individual parties interested in resource extraction. For example, the 1976 Fishery Conservation and Management Act, which extended the US economic zone to 200 miles, addressed the authority issue by establishing Regional Fishery Management Councils to manage the fish resource (Anderson, 1977).
2. While the efficiency of a competitive world with a complete specification of individual property is well known (assuming one is willing to ignore distributional issues), using this ideal (and unattainable) world as the basis for comparing existing common property regimes lacks relevance. Also, the conclusion that 'private property' subject to the limitations imposed by the state provides for the correct incentives for resource use, found for example in Furubotn and Pejovich (1972), is based on an implicit theory of the state that assumes the individual takes the rights held by the state to be exogenously given (the state is able to enforce the limitations).
3. Also see Dahlman (1980) for an excellent account of the efficiency of common field agriculture in England.
4. Since many land titling and registration projects in the developing countries were predicated on the assumption of state enforcement, it is not surprising that the projects often failed to realize their goals (Green, 1987; Noronha, 1985).

5. If a resource growth function is $dx/dt = f(x)$, then $f'(0)$ is the growth potential.
6. When the discount rate is zero, Cropper (1988) shows that extinction can be optimal if the minimum viable resource stock is positive and the initial stock is sufficiently small.
7. Also see Perrings (1987).
8. Schultz (1980) also stresses the need for economics to provide a better understanding of the links between poverty and agricultural production.
9. Dynamic farm-household models have been used to analyse the effect of risk on production (Roe and Graham-Tomasi, 1986), credit constraints (McLaren, 1979), the effects of taxes on financially constrained farm households (Chambers and Lopez, 1984), and timber supply from non-industrial private forests (Max and Lehman, 1988).
10. Agricultural production by the household may include annual and perennial crops, forestry, animal husbandry, and may also include fallow periods on land where fragile soils are otherwise degraded by continual cultivation (Fortmann and Rocheleau, 1985).
11. Following Roe and Graham-Tomasi (1986), we also assume the household acts as a homogeneous decision unit, although we recognize that the homogeneity of the household has been seriously questioned, particularly in reference to gender-based differences in resource control at the household level (Folbre, 1986). Within-household distributional issues, as with group resource management in general, focus on the authority axiom, which we assume here is satisfied.
12. The empirical foundations for the institutional assumptions in the common property case are found in the many chapters of National Research Council (1986), and also see Netting (1976), Wade (1987) and Bromley (1992).
13. For example, with bush-fallow agriculture in Sudan, the household managed its land according to a 10–25 year rotation cycle with 25 to 50 per cent in crops during any given year. A household's total land was divided into plots, and on each plot crops were grown for 6–10 years before returning to fallow for 4–15 years (UNSO, 1983).
14. For example, if $A = 1$, $\Theta = 1/6$, and $1/n = 1/24$ is reallocated every period t, then each 1/24 piece of land is in tillage for $4t$ and fallow for $20t$. It is assumed that $(1/n)A$ is small so that the cost of reallocating the land can be ignored.
15. It may be more general to distinguish soil productivity on tillage as compared to fallow land, and specify separate state variables and state equation dynamics. The single index $Q(t)$ limits the number of state variables in our analysis.
16. J is also a function of other parameters, such as prices and discount rates. While uncertainty with respect to prices, weather, technical change, and ecosystem dynamics surely complicates the resource allocation process, these types of uncertainty are largely independent of the property rights situation and are specific to a particular situation. Therefore, to remain simple, we assume that prices remain constant, technology does not change, and there is no uncertainty. These assumptions are equivalent to the hypothesis of static household expectations with respect to prices, technology, and the dynamics in the ecosystem. The model is readily adapted for more specific analyses depending on a set of assumptions about uncertainty and the household's ability to acquire information.
17. The form of the utility function implies that the household is indifferent between on-farm and off-farm labour. To limit the number of assets, it is also assumed that there is no savings market and that the household spends all of its income on consumption in each period. A savings market can be easily incorporated into the model, but the results are essentially equivalent; the marginal utility of income influences optimal input choices whether or not a savings market exists.

    The consumption side of the model could be disaggregated to include the consumption of the staple (X_c), consumption of firewood (X_h), and consumption of a market purchased good (X_m) with price p_m, in which case aggregate consumption is

$$Y = p_c X_c + p_h X_h + p_m X_m. \qquad (7')$$

18. From equation (A.2), leisure and income are consumed up to the point where the marginal rate of substitution between Y and X_l is equal to their price ratio (price of Y is 1).
19. The ability of the household to internalize all the relevant effects into the decision process is heavily dependent on its ability to observe correctly the relationships between production choices and the environment (the state equations (3) and (4)), and the ability of the scrap value function J^* to internalize all the effects of current choices on the environment. The reasonableness of these assumptions may be seriously questioned when analysing specific situations, but the plausibility of these assumptions are not necessarily conditioned by the structure of property.

References

Allen, J.C. (1985), 'Wood energy and preservation of woodlands in semi-arid developing countries: the case of Dodoma Region, Tanzania', *Journal of Development Economics*, **19**, 59–84.

Allen, J.C. and D.F. Barnes (1985), 'The causes of deforestation in developing countries', *Annals of the Association of American Geographers*, **75**, 163–84.
Anderson, D. (1987), *The Economics of Afforestation: A Case Study in Africa*, Baltimore, MD: Johns Hopkins University Press.
Anderson, L.G. (ed.) (1977), *Economic Impacts of Extended Fisheries Jurisdiction*, Ann Arbor, MI: Ann Arbor Science Publishers.
Baker, A.R.H. and R.A. Butlin (eds) (1973), *Studies of Field Systems in the British Isles*, Cambridge: Cambridge University Press.
Barrows, R. and K. Gardner (1987), 'Do land markets account for soil conservation?', *Journal of Soil and Water Conservation*, **42**, 232–6.
Becker, G.S. (1981), *A Treatise on the Family*, Cambridge, MA: Harvard University Press.
Bernheim, B.D., A. Shleifer and L.H. Summers (1985), 'The strategic bequest motive', *Journal of Political Economy*, **93**, 1045–76.
Bromley, D.W. (1986), 'Natural resources and agricultural development in the tropics: is conflict inevitable?', in A. Maunder and U. Renborg (eds), *Agriculture in a Turbulent World Economy*, Oxford: Gower, 319–27.
Bromley, D.W. (1992), *Making the Commons Work: Theory, Practice, and Policy*, San Francisco: ICS Press.
Bromley, D.W. and D.P. Chapagain (1984), 'The village against the center: resource depletion in South Asia', *American Journal of Agricultural Economics*, **66**, 868–73.
Buchanan, J.M. (1965), 'An economic theory of clubs', *Economica*, **32**, 1–14.
Buchanan, J.M. and W.C. Stubblebine (1962), 'Externality', *Economica*, **29**, 371–84.
Chambers, R.G. and R.E. Lopez (1984), 'A general, dynamic, supply-response model', *The Northeastern Journal of Agricultural and Resource Economics*, **13**, 142–54.
Cheung, S.N.S. (1970), 'The structure of a contract and the theory of a non-exclusive resource', *Journal of Law and Economics*, **13**, 49–70.
Ciriacy-Wantrup, S.V. and R.C. Bishop (1975), 'Common property as a concept in natural resource policy', *Natural Resources Journal*, **15**, 713–27.
Clark, C.W. (1973), 'Profit maximization and the extinction of animal species', *Journal of Political Economy*, **81**, 950–61.
Clark, C.W. (1976), *Mathematical Bioeconomics: The Optimal Management of Renewable Resources*, New York: Wiley.
Commander, S. (1986), 'Managing Indian forests: a case for the reform of property rights', *Development Policy Review*, **4**, 325–44.
Cornes, R. and T. Sandler (1983), 'On commons and tragedies', *American Economic Review*, **73**, 806–14.
Cornes, R. and T. Sandler (1986), *The Theory of Externalities, Public Goods, and Club Goods*, Cambridge: Cambridge University Press.
Cropper, M.L. (1988), 'A note on the extinction of renewable resources', *Journal of Environmental Economics and Management*, **15**, 64–70.
Cropper, M.L., D.R. Lee and S.S. Pannu (1979), 'The optimal extinction of a renewable natural resource', *Journal of Environmental Economics and Management*, **6**, 341–9.
Dahlman, C.J. (1980), *The Open Field System and Beyond*, Cambridge: Cambridge University Press.
Dasgupta, P.S. and G.M. Heal (1979), *Economic Theory and Exhaustible Resources*, Cambridge: Cambridge University Press.
Demsetz, H. (1967), 'Toward a theory of property rights', *American Economic Review*, **57**, 347–59.
Dorfman, R. (1969), 'An economic interpretation of optimal control theory', *American Economic Review*, **59**, 817–31.
Folbre, N. (1986), 'Cleaning house: new perspectives on households and economic development', *Journal of Development Economics*, **22**, 5–40.
Fortmann, L.R. and D. Rocheleau (1985), 'Women and agroforestry: four myths and three case studies', *Agroforestry Systems*, **2**, 5–40.
Fortmann, L.R. and E.M. Roe (1986), 'Common property management of water in Botswana', in *Proceedings from the Conference on Common Property Resource Management, National Research Council*, Washington, DC: National Academy Press, 161–80.
Furubotn, E. and S. Pejovich (1972), 'Property rights and economic theory: a survey of recent literature', *Journal of Economic Literature*, **10**, 1137–62.
Glantz, M.H. (ed.) (1977), *Desertification: Environmental Degradation in and Around Arid Lands*, Boulder, Co: Westview Press.
Gordon, H.S. (1954), 'The economic theory of a common property resource: the fishery', *Journal of Political Economy*, **62**, 124–42.
Green, J.K. (1987), 'Evaluating the impact of consolidation of holdings, individualization of tenure, and

registration of title: lessons from Kenya', LTC paper 19 (Land Tenure Center, University of Wisconsin, Madison, WI).

Hammer, J.S. (1986a), 'Children and savings in less developed countries', *Journal of Development Economics*, **23**, 107–18.

Hammer, J.S. (1986b), 'Subsistence first, farm allocation decisions in Senegal', *Journal of Development Economics*, **23**, 355–69.

Hardin, G. (1968), 'The tragedy of the commons', *Science*, **162**, 1243–8.

Intriligator, M.D. (1971), *Mathematical Optimization and Economic Theory*, Englewood Cliffs, NJ: Prentice Hall.

Kamien, M.I. and N.L. Schwartz (1981), *Dynamic Optimization: The Calculus of Variations and Optimal Control in Economics and Management*, Amsterdam: North-Holland.

Kotlikoff, L.J. and A. Spivak (1981), 'The family as an incomplete annuities market', *Journal of Political Economy*, **89**, 372–91.

Lewis, D. (1986), *Convention: A Philosophical Study*, Oxford: Basil Blackwell.

Lewis, T.R. and R. Schmalensee (1977), 'Nonconvexity and optimal exhaustion of renewable resources', *International Economic Review*, **18**, 535–52.

Livingstone, I. (1986), 'The common property problem and pastoralist economic behaviour', *Journal of Development Studies*, **23**, 5–19.

Lundgren, B. (1983), 'Global deforestation, its causes and suggested remedies', *Agroforestry Systems*, **3**, 91–5.

Max, W. and D.E. Lehman (1988), 'A behavioral model of timber supply', *Journal of Environmental Economics and Management*, **15**, 71–86.

McCay, B. and J. Acheson (1987), *The Question of the Commons*, Tucson, AZ: University of Arizona Press.

McConnell, K. (1983), 'An economic model of soil conservation', *American Journal of Agricultural Economics*, **65**, 83–9.

McLaren, K.R. (1979), 'A dynamic model of a joint firm-household', *Australian Economic Papers*, **18**, 294–307.

National Research Council (1986), *Proceedings from the Conference on Common Property Resource Management*, Washington, DC: National Academy Press.

Netting, R. (1976), 'What alpine peasants have in common: observations on communal tenure in a Swiss village', *Human Ecology*, **4**, 135–46.

Nonpoint Source Task Force (1985), Final report of the Federal/State/Local Nonpoint Source Task Force and recommended national nonpoint source policy, Washington, DC: Office of Water, US Environmental Protection Agency.

Noronha, R. (1985), 'A review of the literature on land tenure systems in sub-Saharan Africa', Report ARU 43, Washington, DC: World Bank.

North, D. and R.P. Thomas (1977), 'The first economic revolution', *Economic History Review*, **30**, 229–41.

Page, T. (1977), *Conservation and Economic Efficiency: An Approach to Materials Policy*, Baltimore, MD: Johns Hopkins University Press.

Perrin, R.K. (1972), 'Asset replacement principles', *American Journal of Agricultural Economics*, **54**, 60–67.

Perrings, C.P. (1987), *Economy and Environment: A Theoretical Essay on the Interaction of Economic and Environmental Systems*, New York: Cambridge University Press.

Perrings, C.P. (1989), 'Optimal path to extinction? Poverty and resource degradation in the open agrarian economy', *Journal of Development Economics*, **30** (1), 1–24.

Peters, P.E. (1986), 'Concluding statement', in *Proceedings from the Conference on Common Property Resource Management, National Research Council*, Washington, DC: National Academy Press, 615–20.

Picardi, A.C. and W.W. Seifert (1976), 'A tragedy of the commons in the Sahel', *Technology Review*, **78**, 42–51.

Pollack, R.A. (1988), 'Tied transfers and paternalistic preferences', *American Economic Review*, **78**, 240–44.

Posner, R.A. (1977), *Economic Analysis of Law*, Boston, MA: Little Brown.

Raintree, J.B. (1985), 'Agroforestry, tropical land use and tenure', International Council for Research in Agroforestry, Workshop on Tenure Issues in Agroforestry, Nairobi, Kenya.

Rhoades, R.E. and S.J. Thompson (1975), 'Adaptive strategies in alpine environments: beyond ecological particularism', *American Ethnologist*, **2**, 535–51.

Roe, T. and T. Graham-Tomasi (1986), 'Yield risk in a dynamic model of the agricultural household', in I.J. Singh, L. Squire and J. Strauss (eds), *Agricultural Household Models*, Baltimore, MD: Johns Hopkins University Press, 255–76.

Ruddle, K. and W. Manshard (1981), *Renewable Natural Resources and the Environment – Pressing Problems in the Developing World*, New York: United Nations University.

Runge, C.F. (1981), 'Common property externalities: isolation, assurance, and resource depletion in a traditional grazing context', *American Journal of Agricultural Economics*, **63**, 595–606.

Samuelson, P. (1976), 'Economics of forestry in an evolving society', *Economic Inquiry*, **14**, 466–92.

Sandler, T. and J. Tschirhart (1980), 'The economic theory of clubs: an evaluative survey', *Journal of Economic Literature*, **18**, 1481–521.

Schotter, A. (1981), *The Economic Theory of Social Institutions*, Cambridge: Cambridge University Press.

Schultz, T.W. (1980), 'Nobel lecture, the economics of being poor', *Journal of Political Economy*, **88**, 639–51.

Scott, A. (1955), 'The fishery: the objectives of sole ownership', *Journal of Political Economy*, **63**, 116–24.

Sen, A.K. (1967), 'Isolation, assurance, and the social rate of discount', *Quarterly Journal of Economics*, **81**, 112–24.

Singh, I.J., L. Squire and J. Strauss (eds) (1986), *Agricultural Household Models*, Baltimore, MD: Johns Hopkins University Press.

Smith, V.L. (1968), 'Economics of production from natural resources', *American Economic Review*, **58**, 409–31.

Smith, V.L. (1975), 'The primitive hunter culture, pleistocene extinction, and the rise of agriculture', *Journal of Political Economy*, **83**, 727–56.

Southgate, D., F. Hitzhusen and R. MacGregor (1984), 'Remedying Third World soil erosion problems', *American Journal of Agricultural Economics*, **66**, 879–84.

Sugden, R. (1984), 'Reciprocity: the supply of public goods through voluntary contributions', *Economic Journal*, **94**, 772–87.

Tiebout, C.M. (1956), 'A pure theory of local expenditures', *Journal of Political Economy*, **64**, 416–24.

Thomson, J.T. (1977), 'Ecological deterioration: local-level rule making and enforcement problems in Niger', in M. Glantz (ed.), *Desertification: Environmental Degradation in and Around Arid Lands*, Boulder, CO: Westview Press.

Ullman-Margalit, E. (1978), *The Emergence of Norms*, New York: Oxford University Press.

United Nations Sudano-Sahelian Office (UNSO) (1983), *The Gum Market and the Development of Production*, Geneva, New York: UNSO.

US Congress, Office of Technology Assessment (1983), 'Sustaining tropical forest resources', background paper no. 1, *Reforestation of Degraded Lands*, Washington, DC: US Government Printing Office.

Wade, R. (1987), 'The management of common property resources: finding a cooperative solution', *World Bank Research Observer*, **2**, 219–34.

World Bank (1985), *Desertification in the Sahelian and Sudanian Zones of West Africa*, Washington, DC: World Bank.

Wynne, S.G. (1986), 'Information problems involved in partitioning the commons for cultivation in Botswana', in *Proceedings from the Conference on Common Property Resource Management, National Research Council*, Washington, DC: National Academy Press, 359–89.

Oxford Agrarian Studies, Vol. 22, No. 1, 1994

Co-management or No Management: The Prospects for Internal Governance of Common Property Regimes through Dynamic Contracts

BRENT M. SWALLOW & DANIEL W. BROMLEY

ABSTRACT *It has been suggested that African rangelands would be utilized and managed on a more sustainable and profitable basis if they were governed by co-management arrangements, with state governments defining group rights and governing inter-group interactions and local organizations governing interactions among members within particular groups. In this paper we develop a discrete-time dynamic model of a rangeland to investigate the possibilities for internal management of resource use interactions within a common property regime. We find that there can be effective internal management without any formal institutional structure within the regime if: (1) group members are confident that the boundaries of the regime will be effectively protected; (2) the group of resource users is kept relatively small; (3) future pasture potential is not overly sensitive to changes in the current stocking rate; and (4) individuals do not discount future payoffs too heavily.*

1. Introduction

Sustainable exploitation of Africa's natural resources requires innovation in the techniques used to harness resource benefit streams and of the institutions that govern the use and consumption of those benefits. The needs are pressing. Across the continent, 0.2% of the total land area, 30 000 km^2, is deforested each year. In the ten countries with the greatest areas of dense tropical forests, the annual rate of deforestation is 0.6%, or 11 000 km^2 (World Resources Institute, 1990). This deforestation is reducing Africa's biological diversity, depleting its energy reserves and damaging its soil fertility. In the densely populated Ethiopian highlands, an average of between 90 and 130 tonnes of soil are eroded from each hectare of cropland every year (Constable, 1984, p. 24).

Population growth and poverty will continue to be the main forces driving the processes of environmental degradation in the coming decades. In the 1980s, high population growth (3.2% per year), together with a paltry 1% annual growth of gross domestic product and a decline in agricultural production, produced a large net decrease in living standards (World Bank, 1990; USDA, 1990). Now 30% of the people of sub-Saharan Africa are classified as being extremely poor (less than $275

Brent M. Swallow, Agricultural Economist, International Livestock Centre for Africa, P.O. Box 46847, Nairobi, Kenya. Daniel W. Bromley, Anderson-Bascom Professor of Agricultural Economics, University of Wisconsin-Madison, Madison, 53706, U.S.A.

4 *B. M. Swallow & D. W. Bromley*

annual consumption in 1985 US dollars), and the vast majority of them live in rural areas (World Bank, 1990).

Institutional innovation is needed to enhance individuals' incentives to internalize the environmental costs of their production practices, to invest in more productive and sustainable production techniques, and to mitigate resource-use conflicts. One imperative is for innovation of more effective institutions for governing the use of public domain resources—resources for which individualized property rights are not recognized. This includes the large percentages of Africa's rangeland, wildlife, forest and water resources that are governed by state property regimes, common property regimes, or are truly open access. Individualized property is an unlikely alternative for many of those resources given their non-divisibility, their relatively low potential to generate economic rents, the high private costs associated with the protection of boundaries (e.g. the construction and maintenance of fences), and the high costs and inefficiencies of public land registration and litigation systems (Runge, 1986; Noronha, 1985; Bromley, 1991, Chapter 7).

The state agencies that have been given responsibilities to directly manage public domain resources have generally proved to be ineffective in sub-Saharan Africa. Several factors have contributed to these failures: (1) state agencies tend to be rigid in their application of rules (e.g. the forest codes in Francophone West Africa as discussed by Lawry, 1989); (2) state agencies usually ignore, or even attempt to undermine, indigenous political structures and institutions (Bromley, 1991, Chapter 6; Moorehead, 1989); (3) state agencies often lack the power, authority and/or will to implement rules proscribed at regional or national levels (Lawry, 1990); and (4) state employees who are responsible for the enforcement of resource-use rules are often remunerated, legally or illegally, through the collection of fines (Lawry, 1989).

Lesotho's Range Management and Grazing Control Regulations of 1980 and 1986 illustrate many of these problems. The regulations direct principal chiefs to operate under the direction of Ministry of Agriculture officers to enforce a strict set of controls to limit livestock numbers, control the locations of cattleposts, enforce opening and closing dates for highland grazing areas, and prohibit grass burning. The regulations have had very little impact on those who are responsible for their enforcement, and even less impact on those who are meant to comply with the rules (Shoup, 1987; Swallow, 1991, pp. 251–252).

Frustrations with the performance of state organizations have amplified the calls for greater local participation in the definition and enforcement of institutions for the management of public domain resources (e.g. Shanmugaratnam *et al.*, 1991). Proponents of community management are able to refer to a variety of ethnographic and historical studies showing that local-level institutions have been effective for many of Africa's public domain resources. Examples of effective local management of rangeland resources have been described for the Basotho in Lesotho (Shoup, 1987), the Boran in Ethiopia (Helland, 1982), the Barabaig in Tanzania (Lane, 1991), the Berber in Morocco (Giles *et al.*, 1992), and the Turkana (McCabe, 1990), Gabbra (Stiles, 1992) and Maasai (Kituyi, 1990) in Kenya. Runge (1986) argues that three characteristics of village life have fostered the development of those local-level common property institutions: (1) because of their poverty, people are unable to afford the transaction costs associated with private property; (2) because of people's dependence on natural resources that vary greatly in quality and productivity, exclusive use rights would result in a highly inequitable distribution of productive potential; and (3) their poverty and dependence on a variable natural resource base gives people incentives to develop a variety of cooperative and reciprocal relationships.

Unfortunately, however, many of the analysts who have described successful common property regimes also recognize that a number of political and economic processes have been continually undermining the authority of customary authorities and the socio-economic bases for local collective action. Customary authorities have been weakened by the intentional and unintentional actions of both colonial and post-colonial governments (Bromley, 1991, chapter 6; Lawry, 1990) and by reductions in the bases of their economic power. Artz *et al.* (1986), Starr (1987) and Swallow (1991, Chapter 6) describe these processes for cases in Morocco, Niger and Lesotho. The economic and political bases for local collective action have also been reduced. Collectives that share resources are becoming more heterogeneous in terms of their access to new techniques (Behnke, 1988), degree of commercialization (Swift, 1977), and access to political power (Moorehead, 1989). In many cases, the village economy is becoming more integrated into increasingly open regional or national economies. As a result, local area residents are taking greater advantage of external economic and political opportunities (Sperling, 1987; Lawry, 1988) and more non-residents are exploiting village resources (Little, 1985).

The overall result, according to Lawry (1990, pp. 419–20) is "a hiatus, in which economic and political changes have combined to forestall effective local action, and state regulation is ineffectual." One way out of this hiatus, Lawry (1990, p. 420) suggests, is co-management—cooperative management arrangements between state and local organizations in which states assign group rights to specific resources, establish overall guidelines for inter-group interactions, and help to create more positive environments for the operation of local organizations. The latter then mobilize local participation in resource management and advise the state on the desirability of proposed management practices. Co-management is becoming the norm for many public domain resources in North America (e.g. Acheson, 1989).

In the remainder of this paper we examine the possibilities for effective resource management in a relatively low-cost, flexible type of co-management regime. A state government assigns and protects group rights, enforces restrictions on group membership, and protects boundaries from incursions by outsiders. That is, the state governs relationships between common property regimes, provides external legitimacy for the group of resource users within regimes, but does not support any particular form of governance within regimes. At the community level, the users having exclusive rights to the resource may develop any type of resource management institution that they identify as being appropriate. In the next section we argue that community management institutions often take the form of tacit agreements about "appropriate" or "cooperative" resource-use patterns. We then develop a difference game model of an African rangeland to study factors affecting the support for such informal agreements, or dynamic (implicit) contracts. Several research and policy implications follow regarding the institutional and organizational innovations that would be consistent with effective co-management of Africa's public domain resources.

2. External and Internal Order in Common Property Regimes for African Resources

There are several contemporary cases in which African governments have been effective in protecting boundaries and providing external legitimacy for common property regimes. For example, residents of eleven villages in the Sehlabathebe area of Lesotho have been granted exclusive grazing rights to an area of 31 000 hectares including village grazing areas, mountain grazing areas and arable land surrounding the villages.

The Lesotho government supports these rights by restricting grazing permits to residents, sanctioning the right of the grazing association to impound outsiders' livestock, and providing advice on grazing management within the grazing area (Lawry, 1988). Since 1984, the Senegalese government has also recognized the rights of pastoral groups to register group title to local grazing areas. Pastoral units created under the Eastern Senegal Livestock Development Project have begun to administer grazing rotations, coordinate members' grazing and watering activities, and coordinate agricultural and livestock activities in the area (Bromley & Cernea, 1989; Associates in Rural Development, 1989). In Zimbabwe, the government has supported the development of grazing schemes in which fences delineate the boundaries between common property regimes (Cousins, 1992).

The institutions providing the internal order of common property regimes are seldom as formal or rigid as those providing the external order. For example, Niamir (1989) reviews many cases from West Africa in which institutions that have been successful in governing the behaviour of members of common property regimes have been enforced by the actions of the members themselves. A review of the ethnographic literature reveals five types of internal punishments that have been, and in many cases continue to be, used by African pastoral groups to enforce community norms of behaviour and resource management. In order of increasing severity they are: fines, temporary exclusion, physical punishment, permanent banishment, and curse. Fines are often payable in kind: among the Barabaig of Tanzania fines are payable in terms of honey beer for minor offences and cattle for more serious offences (Lane, 1991, p. 251). Temporary exclusion, or exclusion from a particular resource, is also practised by the Barabaig. An individual who abuses a particular water source may be punished by being excluded from future use of that source (Lane, 1991, p. 250). Physical punishment is frequently employed among the Karimojong of Uganda. Karimojong elders have the prerogative to "... call for the chastisement of anyone who is disrespectful or disobedient. Men of the junior sets or generation are generally quick to respond to this command by restraining and abusing, and frequently beating, their errant fellow" (Quam, 1976, pp. 102–103).

Banishment and curse are more severe punishments that are usually reserved for serious crimes or for people who fail to respect punishments for less serious offences. Banishment is an extreme form of exclusion in which a culprit is excluded from using common resources, all social networks, and all types of personal contact. Among the Barabaig "this usually results in his departure from Barabaig society and a life of anonymity elsewhere" (Lane, 1991, p. 251). When all of the normal punishments fail, more severe punishments can be imposed by recourse to supernatural powers. For example, pastoralists of the Rhiraya tribe in the High Atlas mountains of Morocco believe that the spirit of their patron saint, Sidi Fars, watches over their pasture and can be called upon to punish illegal use of the common pasture. Individuals who are so cursed are expected to become the victims of natural disasters and disease (Giles *et al.*, 1992).

3. A Rangeland Difference Game

To investigate the prospects for internal governance of common property regimes, it is necessary to examine the incentives, expectations and conjectures of current and potential resource users. To that end a difference game model of a livestock-rangeland system is developed in this section.

Suppose that n independent economic agents, who may be individuals, families, or herding groups, have exclusive rights to keep livestock on a well-defined area of rangeland for T-1 discrete time periods. The average physical product generated by each animal kept on the rangeland during any period (APP_t) is a function of the aggregate stocking rate (X_t) and the state of the rangeland (A_t) (equation (1)). The state of the rangeland is defined by its "pasture potential"—the output that would be generated by a single animal kept alone on the rangeland for that period. Pasture potential is constant within growing periods but changes between periods as the matrix of forage species is affected by climatic conditions, livestock grazing pressures, and the "herd effect" caused by livestock trampling and agitating the grassland. A non-linear equation of motion for pasture potential is given in equation (2).

$$APP_t \quad = f1(A_t, X_t) \text{ where } \frac{\partial f1}{\partial A_t} > 0; \frac{\partial f1}{\partial X_t} < 0 \tag{1}$$

$$A_{t+1} - A_t = f2(A_t, X_t) \text{ where } \frac{\partial f2}{\partial A_t} < = > 0; \frac{\partial f2}{\partial X_t} < 0; \frac{\partial^2 f2}{\partial^2 X_t} < 0. \tag{2}$$

The problem faced by one of these agents, agent i, is to choose the amount of livestock capital for each period of the planning horizon (Xi_t) that maximizes the expected sum of discounted future profits derived from the sale of livestock products plus the expected terminal value of the individual's ownership share in the terminal period T (equation (3)).[1] Since herding is the major variable factor used in the production of livestock in Africa, costs are specified only as a function of the number of livestock (i.e. cost of input function). The terminal value of the rangeland is a positive function of pasture potential:

$$\underset{\{\underline{Xi_t}\}}{\text{Max}} \sum_{t=0}^{T-1} \{\beta^t P\, APP_t(A_t, X_t)Xi_t - C(A_t, Xi_t)\} + \beta^T F(A_T) \tag{3}$$

where $X_t = \sum_{i=1}^{n} Xi_t$

$$\frac{\partial C}{\partial Xi_t} \geq 0 \text{ and } \frac{\partial^2 C}{\partial^2 Xi_t} \leq 0; \frac{\partial C}{\partial A_t} \leq 0 \text{ and } \frac{\partial^2 C}{\partial^2 A_t} \leq 0; \frac{\partial F}{\partial A_T} \geq 0;$$

$\beta \equiv$ discount factor = 1 / (1 + discount rate);
$P \equiv$ fixed price per unit of livestock output;
$C \equiv$ cost of herding input;
$T =$ terminal date;
$F \equiv$ terminal value of the individual's ownership share.

The first-order necessary conditions (assuming an interior solution) are given by equations (4) to (7). Second-order sufficient conditions are satisfied.

$$\frac{\partial L}{\partial Xi_t} = P \frac{\partial f1}{\partial X_t} \frac{\partial X_t}{\partial Xi_t} + P\, APP_t - \frac{\partial Ci}{\partial Xi_t} \tag{4}$$

$$- \mu_t \frac{\partial f1}{\partial X_t} \frac{\partial X_t}{\partial Xi_t} = 0 \qquad t = 1, \ldots, T-1$$

$$\frac{\partial L}{\partial A_t} = P \frac{\partial f1}{\partial At} - \frac{\partial Ci}{\partial A_t} + \mu_t\left(1 + \frac{\partial f2}{\partial A_t}\right) - \frac{\mu_{t-1}}{\beta} = 0. \qquad t = 1, \ldots, T-1 \tag{5}$$

$$\frac{\partial L}{\partial A_T} = \frac{\partial F}{\partial A_T} - \mu_T = 0 \tag{6}$$

$$\frac{\partial L}{\partial \mu_t} = A_{t+1} - A_t - f2(A_t, X_t) = 0 \qquad t = 1, \ldots, T-1 \tag{7}$$

Beginning from the initial period ($t = 0$) and initial state (A_0), the agent makes a series of marketing and purchasing choices on the basis of calculations regarding the present value of expected future profits. With no restrictions on purchases or sales, the agent will keep the amount of livestock capital such that the marginal benefits and marginal costs are equal for the last unit marketed or purchased. The optimality condition given in equation (4) indicates that the amount of livestock capital is optimal when the value of marginal product for livestock capital is equal to the sum of marginal herding cost and marginal rangeland user cost in terms of its impact on future pasture potential. We assume that the market price of the output is insensitive to the level of output from a particular area of rangeland.[2]

The specification of the optimality condition clearly indicates that agents do not have dominant strategies: the prisoners' dilemma model is not an appropriate game-theoretic formulation of the problem since non-separable externalities affect the value of the marginal product (an intra-temporal externality) and marginal rangeland user costs (an inter-temporal externality) (Runge, 1981). Expectations are thus crucial. Agents forms expectations about entry and exit (their own and others'), the behaviour of other incumbents and potential entrants, and how others' behaviour will be affected by changes in their own behaviour (i.e. conjectural variations). Those expectations depend upon the institutional arrangements governing resource use: entry and exit expectations depend upon the rights, duties and rules governing resource access; conjectural variations depend upon the rules, conventions and contracts governing resource use within the regime.

The model is appropriate for analysing agents' incentives and expectations under a variety of internal institutional arrangements. Following the discussion above, the remainder of the paper focuses on the possibilities for internal governance when there are external restrictions on entry and exit that limit resource access to a fixed group of users, but no external or group mechanisms that enforce internal institutions. In game-theoretic terms, we assume that the agents cannot make binding commitments and that the strategy choice of each agent is made at the beginning of each period with perfect recall of all past actions but no information about others' current strategy choices. While we agree with Reinganum & Stokey (1985) that these assumptions are not generally appropriate for modelling the interdependent actions of agents in common property regimes, they allow us to identify minimal conditions for effective internal management within common property regimes whose boundaries are protected by external agencies.

4. Dynamic Contracts

In an earlier section we discussed five types of internal punishments—fines, temporary exclusion, physical punishment, permanent banishment, and curse—that have been used by African pastoralist groups to maintain social order. Hirshleifer & Rasmusen (1989) have shown that one of the less severe of these punishments, exclusion, can support dynamic contracts in non-cooperative games with finite and certain end-points such as the one considered here. In this section we investigate the incentives and expectations of agents involved in such dynamic interactions within a common property regime. We show that there are plausible circumstances in which exclusion punishments can be maintained by the actions of the agents themselves. In the next section we employ a simulation analysis to examine factors affecting the strength of those contracts.

Each agent has the following expectations: the n current users will have access to the benefit streams in all periods of the planning horizon; no other agent will enter the group during the planning horizon; current-period actions are unknown when the other $n-1$ agents choose their actions; agents' actions become public information at the end of each period.

Agents following exclusion strategies condition their current-period actions on others' actions in the preceding period. An exclusion strategy proscribes different actions depending upon those actions and the period of the game.

(a) The cooperative phase—if $t < T-1$ and all agents acted cooperatively in period $t-1$, keep Xc_t amount of livestock capital in period t, where $(Xc_t n)$ is the stocking rate that maximizes joint profits.
(b) The punishment phase—if $t < T-1$ and any of the other agents deviated in period $t-1$, report the deviant(s) and keep the amount of livestock capital that is consistent with the Nash equilibrium for the remaining players (XN).
(c) The terminal phase—if $t = T-1$, keep the amount of livestock capital that is consistent with the Nash equilibrium.

It is assumed that any group member can be temporarily excluded if the other group members take appropriate actions. It is also assumed that temporary exclusion is costless both to the individual who makes the accusation and to those who enforce the punishment (although it can be shown that dynamic contracts can also be viable if exclusion is costly). And it is further assumed that all accusations can be costlessly verified at the end of the period and that false accusations will be punished in the same manner as deviant stocking rate actions.

Proposition. There are ranges of feasible values for the parameters of the dynamic livestock/rangeland model such that a subgame perfect Nash equilibrium exists with agents playing the compliance phase of exclusion strategies in periods 1 to $T-2$ and the terminal phase in period $T-1$.[3]

Proof. To prove this proposition it must be shown that all single-period games have Nash equilibria and that there are combinations of feasible parameter values such that no player who follows an exclusion strategy has an incentive to deviate from that strategy.[4]

There are three ways that an agent can deviate from an implicit contract: (1) by stocking at a level greater than Xc_t when no one is accused of deviating in the previous period; (2) by falsely accusing another agent of deviating in the previous period; or (3) by failing to report the deviation by another agent in the previous period.

Consider a time period t $(0 < t < T-2)$ following a period in which all agents complied with the terms of the contract. An individual has an incentive to deviate only if the expected present value of deviation during period t is greater than the expected present value of compliance during periods t and $t+1$ as shown in equation (8)). Expectations regarding periods following $t+1$ do not enter into the calculations. Under the rules of the game the agent expects to re-enter with a clean slate after a single period of punishment:

$$\pi c_t + \beta \pi c_{t+1} > \pi d_t \tag{8}$$

where $\pi c_t \equiv$ single-period payoff to compliance;

$\pi d_t \equiv$ single-period payoff to deviation.

There are two types of deviation that the agent could consider in this situation: (1) stocking at a level greater than Xc_t, or (2) falsely accusing another agent of deviating in period t. Assuming that the potential deviant expects no other agent to deviate in either the current period or the following period, the expected two-period payoff from deviation of type (1) is given in equation (9) as $Vd_t(1)$, the expected two-period payoff from deviation of type (2) is given in equation (10) as $Vd_t(2)$, and the expected two-period payoff from compliance is given in equation (11) as $Vc_t(1,2)$:

$$Vd_t(1) = \pi d_t$$
$$= P\ APP_t\ (A_t,\ Xd_t + Xc_t(n-1))\ Xd_t - C\ (A_t,\ Xd_t) \quad (9)$$

$$Vd_t(2) = \pi d_t$$
$$= P\ APP_t\ (A_t,\ XN_t(n-1))\ XN_t - C(A_t,\ XN_t) \quad (10)$$

$$Vc_t(1,2) = \pi c_t + \beta \pi c_{t+1}$$
$$= P\ APP_t\ (A_t,\ Xc_t n)\ Xc_t - C\ (A_t,\ Xc_t)$$
$$+ \beta[P\ APP_{t+1}\ (A_{t+1},\ Xc_{t+1} n)\ Xc_{t+1} - C\ (A_{t+1},\ Xc_{t+1})] \quad (11)$$

where Vd_t ≡ expected two-period payoff from deviation;
Vc_t ≡ expected two-period payoff from compliance;
Xc_t ≡ stocking rate consistent with maximization of group profits;
Xd_t ≡ stocking rate consistent with maximization of short-term individual profits.

Now consider another time period t $(0 < t < T-2)$, following a period in which one of the agents deviated from the contract either by stocking at the level of Xd_t or by falsely accusing another agent of deviation. An individual who is aware of the deviation has an incentive to deviate from the dynamic implicit contract—that is, to ignore the other agent's deviation in the previous period and deviate herself in the current period—if the single-period payoff to deviation, $Vd_t(3)$, is greater than the two-period payoff to compliance, $Vc_t(3)$. The specification of $Vd_t(3)$ in equation (12) assumes that the agent who deviated in period $t-1$, without being punished, will again deviate in period t:

$$Vd_t(3) = P\ APP_t\ (A_t,\ 2Xd_t + XN_t(n-2))\ Xd_t - C(A_t, Xd_t) \quad (12)$$

$$Vc_t(3) = P\ APP_t\ (A_t,\ XN_t(\mathrm{n}-1))\ XN_t - C(A_t, XN_t)$$
$$+ \beta[P\ APP_{t+1}\ (A_{t+1}, Xc_{t+1} n) Xc_{t+1} - C(A_{t+1}, Xc_{t+1})]. \quad (13)$$

Similar computations are germane for an agent considering deviation in period $T-2$ (the second to last period of play). The only difference is that the second period payoff from compliance will always be defined by the Nash equilibrium stocking rate. Equation (14) defines the expected payoff from compliance in period $T-2$ following universal compliance in period $T-3$, while equation (15) defines the expected payoff from compliance in period $T-2$ following a deviation in period $T-3$:

$$Vc_{T-2}(1,2) = P\ APP_{T-2}\ (A_{T-2},\ Xc_{T-2} n)\ Xc_{t-2} - C\ (A_{T-2},\ Xc_{T-2})$$
$$+ \beta[P\ APP_{T-1}\ (A_{T-1},\ XN_{T-1} n)\ Xc_{T-1} - C\ (A_T,\ XN_{T-1})] \quad (14)$$

$$Vc_{T-2}(3) = P\ APP_{T-2}\ (A_{T-2},\ XN_{T-2}(n-1))\ XN_{T-2} - C\ (A_{T-2}, XN_{T-2})$$
$$+ \beta[P\ APP_{T-1}\ (A_{T-1},\ XN_{T-1} n)\ Xc_{T-1} - C\ (A_{T-1},\ XN_{T-1})] \quad (15)$$

Now we can investigate whether or not there are empirical specifications of the livestock owner's problem as defined in equations (1), (2) and (3) such that equation (8) holds for the three types of deviation described above. Simulations showed that there is, in fact, a range of plausible empirical specifications for which those conditions do hold.[5] The simulations also raise several hypotheses about factors affecting the strength of dynamic implicit contracts in common property regimes. The results of that analysis and the hypotheses it supports are detailed in the next section.

5. The Strength of Dynamic Implicit Contracts

The simulation analysis needs specific versions of the average physical product function, the equation of motion, the cost of input function, and the terminal value function. To begin, specific versions of the average physical product equation (1) and the equation of motion (2) were specified from available secondary data. The stocking rate experiments described by Jones & Sandland (1974) and Sandland & Jones (1975) support the assumption of a linear relationship between average physical product, the number of animals and the rangeland's pasture potential as given in equation (16). Experimental results suggest that rangelands are least sensitive to changes in stocking rate at relatively high and relatively low levels of pasture potential (Holechek, *et al.*, 1989). To capture this effect, a variable called 'pasture sensitivity' (S_t) is defined over the feasible range (0,1) in equation (17). Equation (18) indicates that changes in pasture potential are a non-linear function of pasture sensitivity, livestock capital, and parameters whose values depend on rangeland area and ecological conditions:

$$APP_t = A_t - BX_t \tag{16}$$

$$S_t = A_t\,(1 - A_t) \tag{17}$$

$$A_{t+1} - A_t = S_t\,(A_t - dX_t - hX^2_t)\,g \tag{18}$$

Next, specific versions of the cost function and the terminal value function were formulated. To keep the analysis as simple as possible, it was assumed that the marginal cost of input is constant for all stocking rate levels. This implies that the only intra-temporal externality is that which works through the average physical product function. Also, it was assumed that the terminal value function is invariant to the level of pasture potential. A planning horizon of 200 periods is assumed.

The model was solved for the optimal stocking rate levels, Xc_t and Xd_t, and the short-term payoffs, Vc_t and Vd_t, for various combinations of the biological parameters (*B, d, h* and *g*) and economic parameters (*P, mc*, β). The results indeed indicate that the returns from compliance are less than, or greater than, the returns from deviation, depending upon the levels of the various biological and economic parameters. Most noteworthy are the relationships between strength of contract and rangeland sensitivity, the discount factor, and group size.

To summarize the results it is useful to define the concept of *strength of contract* as the difference between the payoff to compliance and the payoff to deviation. The stronger the contract, that is, the greater the difference between the payoff to compliance and the payoff to deviation, the more likely it is to remain effective despite changes in biological and economic parameters. For example, Figure 1 plots strength of contract against group size. *Ceteris paribus*, the contract will be effective for groups with between 0 and n_c members. The contract will not be effective for groups with more than n_c members.

The sensitivity of future pasture potential to changes in current stocking rate is represented by the parameters *d, h* and *g* in the specific version of the model. A series of simulations illustrated that strength of contract is very sensitive to changes in those parameters. *Ceteris paribus*, the less sensitive is pasture potential (i.e. the lower the levels of *d, g* and *h*), the stronger the contract. The causality is as follows: the less influence that current actions have on future payoffs, the lower the 'user cost' of current actions, the more similar are optimal resource use patterns from the short-term and long-term perspectives, and the less the short-term gains from deviation from the long-term social optimum.

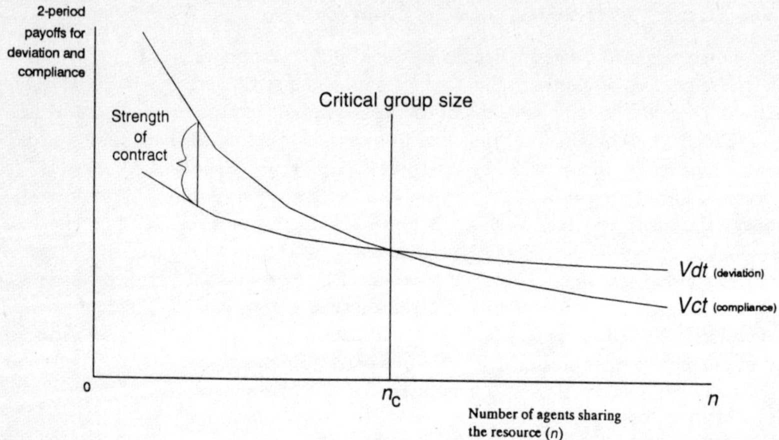

Figure 1. Strength of contract and critical group size in internal contracts for common property regimes.

A special case of the above model is the case in which pasture potential does not change from period to period—this is equivalent to assuming no intra-temporal externality (assuming that g is equal to zero is sufficient to produce such a case). Simulations of this case show that strength of the contract is positively related to the discount factor and the marginal cost of production, and negatively related to size of the group and the price of the output. The results are relatively insensitive to changes in either the level of pasture potential or the level of forage competition, but very sensitive to changes in group size (see Figure 2).

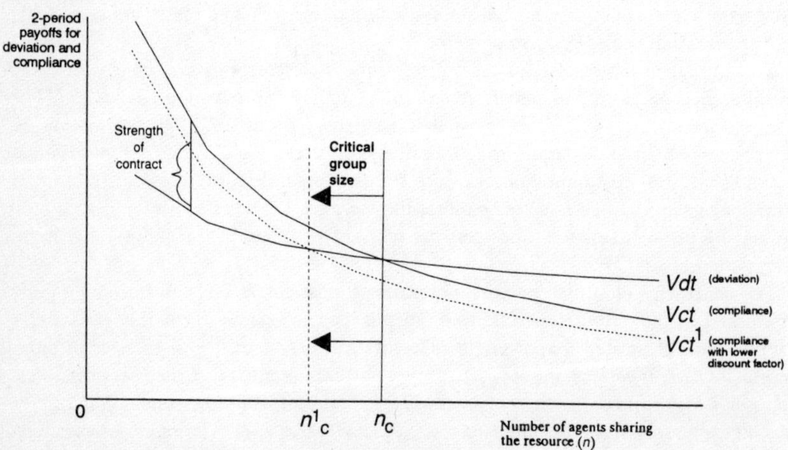

Figure 2. Effect of a reduction in the discount factor on strength of contract and critical group size.

The analysis shows that dynamic implicit contracts, of the type considered above, are likely to be effective only when the group size is fairly small—that is, less than 10 members. Additional analyses show that these contracts can be effective in larger groups (that is, up to 50–60 members) if:

(1) members can credibly impose longer periods of exclusion against deviants—banishment is practised by many groups of African pastoralists;
(2) members agree (explicitly or tacitly) to keep a total number of livestock that is greater than the joint profit-maximizing level but less than the Nash equilibrium level—Swallow & Brokken (1990) found that the joint stocking rate in Lesotho was very similar to their estimate of the rate that maximizes production; or
(3) there are financial, market, or cultural restrictions that limit the ability of potential deviants to take advantage of profit opportunities—McCabe (1990) argues that financial and market restrictions are very important in limiting herd build-ups among the Turkana.

6. Possible Extensions

There are possibilities for extending this analysis to increase the variety of cases to which the results are applicable. For example, the random variables affecting single-period revenues can be incorporated explicitly. Rotemberg & Saloner's (1986) analysis of dynamic contracts in oligopolistic markets with fluctuating demand supports the hypothesis that dynamic contracts will be less effective when stochastic variables result in single-period revenues that exceed the mean, and more effective when stochastic variables result in single-period revenues less than the mean. Stochastic climatic variables are particularly important for Africa's arid and semi-arid rangelands because of the inverse relationship between mean rainfall and variability of rainfall. New conceptual frameworks are being developed for understanding rangeland ecology in those 'non-equilibrial' systems (Behnke *et al.*, 1993).

The model can also be extended to consider the situation of groups sharing multiple resources. Bernheim & Whinston (1990) consider dynamic contracts in situations in which firms have multiple-market contact. Their results suggest that the users of multiple resources can use excess enforcement power from one resource-use situation to strengthen contracts in other situations. This result provides support for Runge's (1986) assertion that the degree of interdependence among community members is important to the strength of community institutions.

The model can also be extended to consider internal contracts that are enforced through active 'hedging' arrangements involving hostages, collateral, hand-tying actions, gain sharing, or partial surrender of autonomy (Kronman, 1985).

7. Discussion and Conclusions

The analysis presented above illustrates conditions in which common property institutions may develop 'spontaneously' through the actions of individual resource users. According to Young (1989), imposition, negotiation and spontaneity are the three primary processes by which institutions originate. We show that institutions that develop spontaneously may operate without any formal internal structure if: (1) the boundaries of the regime are protected by some external government agency; (2) the groups are relatively small; (3) future pasture potential is not overly sensitive to changes in current stocking rate, and (4) individuals did not discount future payoffs too heavily.

Unfortunately, various factors are undermining the bases of support for dynamic contracts and other, more formal, local institutions. One, the increased scarcity of land resources in rural Africa is resulting in the conversion of land use from grazing to cropping and mixed crop/livestock systems, and the spontaneous assertion of individual rights (Lane, 1991, p. 208; Behnke, 1988). Two, increased access to alternative social networks and sources of livelihood means that community-based sanctions—multiple-market dynamic contract, exclusion, curse—are becoming less effective in controlling individual behaviour (Lane, 1991; Lawry, 1990; Bromley, 1991; Runge, 1986). Three, external political developments are increasing the desire of many pastoralists to secure individual claims to their grazing resources (Solomon Bekure *et al.*, 1991).

Nonetheless, groups of local resource users remain in unique positions to assess resource productivity, monitor other agents' compliance or deviation with resource use institutions, draw upon traditional social sanctions, and adjudicate resource use disputes among members. Given the limitations on the effectiveness of state governments in local-level resource management that were described above, it is evident that government organizations must work in partnership with local community organizations to support the development of effective co-management regimes for rangeland resources. At the minimum, government organizations can be effective in maintaining the boundaries of common property regimes. Within regimes, governments have opportunities to support internal order by recognizing and enforcing the legal right of local agencies to define resource use rules and enforce sanctions on deviants.

Notes

1. The results generated from this model are invariant to the choice of function among the class of expected utility functions. For the sake of simplicity, the expected profit function is used. Assuming that stocking rate is the only control variable simplifies the problem and makes the exposition more transparent. It is important to note, however, that there are many other range management options available to the co-owners of collectively used rangelands: burning, livestock breed improvement, herd movement regulations, and closing and opening dates for key resources.
2. This is one of the factors that makes the analysis presented in this paper distinct from previous analyses of the dynamics of common property regimes such as those of van der Ploeg (1986), Karp (1992) and Reinganum & Stokey (1985).
3. Subgame perfection is the standard test of equilibrium in non-cooperative dynamic games. An equilibrium is subgame perfect "if the relevant portions of an equilibrium strategy are Nash equilibria for every subgame of the original game, whether or not that subgame is reached in equilibrium" (Hirshleifer & Rasmusen 1989, p. 93).
4. By the Kakutani fixed-point theorem, a game has at least one Nash equilibrium if: (1) agents have complete information; (2) strategy sets are compact and convex; (3) payoff functions are defined, continuous, bounded for all strategies and players, and concave with respect to other players' strategies; and (4) strategy choices are made without prior knowledge of others' choices (Friedman, 1986, pp. 25–39). Conditions (1), (3) and (4) hold by construction. Condition (2) can be satisfied by restricting stocking rate choices to be not less than zero and not more than the amount at which average physical product is zero.
5. It is important to understand that the equilibrium to this non-cooperative repeated game does not 'unravel' from the last period, despite the fact that the agents have complete certainty that the game will terminate in period T. While all agents deviate in the last period of play because they know that they cannot be punished, they have incentive to comply in the second last period because they know that they can be excluded from the last period (Hirshleifer & Rasmusen, 1989, p. 93). It is worth noting that compliance is least likely in the second to last period, however, because the foregone payoffs in the last period are defined by the Nash equilibrium rather than the cooperative equilibrium.

References

Acheson, J.M. (1989) Where have all the exploiters gone? Co-management of the Maine lobster industry, in F. Berkes (ed.) *Common Property Resources: Ecology and Community-based Sustainable Development*, pp. 199–217 (London, Belhaven Press).

Artz, N.E., Norton, B.E. & O'Rourke, J.T. (1986) Management of common grazing lands: Tamahdite, Morocco, in *Proceedings of the Conference on Common Property Management*, pp. 259–280 (Washington, D.C., National Academy Press).

Associates in Rural Development (1989) Options for promoting user-based governance of Sahelian renewable natural resources. Paper prepared for presentation at the CILSS-sponsored conference, *Regional Encounter for a Better Socio-Ecological Balance in the Rural Sahel*, Bamako, Mali.

Behnke, R. (1988) Range enclosure in central Somalia, *Pastoral Development Network Paper* No. 25b (London, Overseas Development Institute).

Behnke, R., Scoones, I. & Kerven, C. (1993) *Range Ecology at Disequilibrium: New Models of Natural Variability and Pastoral Adaptation in African Savannas* (London, Overseas Development Institute).

Bernheim, B.D. & Whinston, M.D. (1990) Multimarket contact and collusive behaviour, *Rand Journal of Economics*, 21(1), pp. 1–26.

Bromley, D.W. (1991) *Environment and Economy: Property Rights and Public Policy* (Oxford, Basil Blackwell).

Bromley, D.W. & Cernea, M.M. (1989) *The Management of Common Property Natural Resources: some Conceptual and Operational Fallacies*, World Bank Discussion Paper 57 (Washington, DC, The World Bank).

Constable, M. (1984) *Ethiopian Highlands Reclamation Study: The Degradation of Resources and an Evaluation of Actions to Combat It* (Addis Ababa, Ethiopia, Land Use Planning and Regulatory Department, Ministry of Agriculture and Food and Agriculture Organization of the United Nations).

Cousins, B. (1992) *Managing Communal Rangeland in Zimbabwe: Experiences and Lessons* (London, Commonwealth Secretariat).

Friedman, J.W. (1986) *Game Theory with Applications to Economics* (Oxford, Oxford University Press).

Giles, J.L., Norton, B.E. & O'Rourke, J.T. (1992). Oukaimadene, Morocco: a high mountain agdal. In D. W. Bromley (ed.) *Making the Commons Work: Theory, Practice and Policy*, pp. 281–304 (Washington, National Academy Press).

Helland, J. (1982) Social organization and water control among the Borana, *Development and Change*, 13, pp. 239–258.

Hirshleifer, D. & Rasmusen, E. (1989) Cooperation in a repeated prisoners' dilemma with ostracism, *Journal of Economic Behaviour and Organization*, 12, pp. 87–106.

Holechek, J.L., Pieper, R.D. & Herbel, C.H. (1989) *Range Management* (Englewood Cliffs, Prentice-Hall).

Jones, R.J. & Sandland, R.L. (1974) The relation between animal gain and stocking rate, *Journal of Agricultural Science, Cambridge*, 83, pp. 335–342.

Karp, L. (1992) Social welfare in a common property externality, *International Economic Review*, 33(2), pp. 353–372.

Kituyi, M. (1990) *Becoming Kenyans: Socio-economic Transformation of the Pastoral Maasai* (Nairobi, Kenya, ACTS Press).

Kronman, A.T. (1985) Contract law and the state of nature, *Journal of Law, Economics and Organization*, 1(1), pp. 5–32.

Lane, C.R. (1991) *Alienation of Barabaig Pasture Land: Policy Implications for Pastoral Development in Tanzania* (Ph. D. dissertation, University of Sussex).

Lawry, S.W. (1988) *Private Herds and Common Land: Issues in the Management of Communal Grazing Land in Lesotho, Southern Africa* (Ph. D. dissertation, University of Wisconsin).

Lawry, S.W. (1989) *Tenure Policy and Natural Resource Management in Sahelian West Africa* (LTC Paper 130, Land Tenure Center, University of Wisconsin).

Lawry, S.W. (1990) Tenure policy towards common property natural resources in Sub-Saharan Africa *Natural Resources Journal*, 30, pp. 403–422.

Little, P.D. (1985) Absentee herd owners and part-time pastoralists: the political economy of resource use in northern Kenya, *Human Ecology*, 13(2), pp. 131–151.

McCabe, J.T. (1990) Turkana pastoralism: a case against the tragedy of the commons, *Human Ecology*, 18, pp. 81–103.

16 *B. M. Swallow & D. W. Bromley*

Moorehead, R. (1989) Changes taking place in common-property management in the inland Niger delta of Mali, in F. Berkes (ed.) *Common Property Resources: Ecology and Community-based Sustainable Development*, pp. 256–272 (London, Belhaven Press).

Niamir, M. (1989) *Herders' Decision-Making in Natural Resources Management in Arid and Semi-Arid Africa* (Community Forestry Note No. 4, Rome, Food and Agriculture Organization of the United Nations).

Noronha, R. (1985) *A Review of the Literature on Land Tenure Systems in Sub-Saharan Africa* (World Bank Discussion Paper No. ARU 43, Washington, DC, World Bank).

Quam, M.D. (1976) *Pastoral Economy and Cattle Marketing in Karamoja, Uganda* (Ph. D. dissertation, Indiana University).

Reinganum, J.F. & Stokey, N.L. (1985) Oligopoly extraction of a common property natural resource: the importance of the period of commitment in dynamic games, *International Economic Review*, 26(1), pp. 161–173.

Rotemberg, J.J. & Saloner, G. (1986) A supergame-theoretic model of price wars during booms, *American Economic Review*, 76, pp. 390–407.

Runge, C.F. (1981) Common-property externalities: isolation, assurance, and resource depletion in a traditional grazing context, *American Journal of Agricultural Economics*, 63, pp. 595–607.

Runge, C.F. (1986) Common property and collective action in economic development, *World Development*, 14(5), pp. 623–635.

Sandland, R.L. & Jones, R.J. (1975) The relation between animal gain and stocking rate in grazing trials: an examination of published theoretical models, *Journal of Agricultural Science, Cambridge*, 85, pp. 123–128.

Shanmugaratnam, N., Vedeld, T., Mossige, A. & Bovin, M. (1991). *Resource Management and Pastoral Institution Building in Dryland Africa*. Report to the World Bank. Norwegian Centre for International Agricultural Development, Agricultural University of Norway.

Shoup, J. (1987) *Transhumant Pastoralism in Lesotho: Case Study of the Mapoteng Ward* (Maseru, Lesotho, Land Conservation and Range Development Project).

Solomon Bekure, de Leeuw, P.N., Grandin, B.E. & Neat, P.J.H. (eds.) (1991) *Maasai Herding: An Analysis of the Livestock Production System of Maasai Pastoralists in Eastern Kajiado District*, Kenya (ILCA Systems Study 4, Addis Ababa, Ethiopia, International Livestock Centre for Africa).

Sperling, L. (1987) Wage employment among Samburu pastoralists of north-central Kenya, in B. Isaac (ed.) *Research in Economic Anthropology*, 9, pp. 167–190 (Greenwich, C. JAI Press).

Starr, M.A. (1987) Risk, environmental variability and drought-induced impoverishment: the pastoral economy of central Niger, *Africa*, 57(1), pp. 29–50.

Stiles, D. (1992) The Gabbra: traditional social factors in aspects of land-use management, *Nomadic Peoples*, 30, pp. 41–52.

Swallow, B.M. (1991) *Common Property Regimes for African Rangeland Resources* (Ph.D. dissertation, University of Wisconsin-Madison).

Swallow, B.M. & R.F. Brokken (1990) Information and the 'optimal control' of an African rangeland resource. Paper presented at the American Agricultural Economics Association Annual Meeting, Vancouver, Canada.

Swift, J.J. (1977) Pastoral development in Somalia: herding cooperatives as a strategy against desertification and famine, in M. H. Glantz (ed.) *Desertification: Environmental Degradation in and around Arid Lands*, pp. 275–305 (Boulder, Westview Press).

USDA (United States Department of Agriculture) (1990) *World Agriculture: Trends and Indicators, 1970–89* (Statistical Bulletin 815, Washington, DC, USDA).

van der Ploeg, F. (1986) Inefficiency of oligopolistic resource markets with iso-elastic demand, zero extraction costs and stochastic renewal, *Journal of Economic Dynamics and Control*, 10, pp. 309–314.

World Bank (1990) *World Development Report 1990: Poverty* (Oxford, Oxford University Press).

World Resources Institute (1990) *World Resources 1988–89* (New York, Basic Books).

Young, O.R. (1989) *International Cooperation: Building Regimes for Natural Resources and the Environment* (Ithaca, Cornell University Press).

[10]

Institutions, Governance and Incentives in Common Property Regimes for African Rangelands

BRENT M. SWALLOW[1] and DANIEL W. BROMLEY[2]
[1] *International Livestock Centre for Africa, P.O. Box 46847, Nairobi, Kenya*; [2] *University of Wisconsin-Madison, 427 Lorch Street, Madison, Wisconsin, U.S.A.*

Abstract. The general distinctions between open access, state property, common property and private property are now well established in the academic literature. When applied to African rangelands, however, common property admits a wide variety of resource management regimes. To formulate effective policies it is necessary to understand the structure and operations of particular regimes. In this paper we discuss three examples of common property regimes, two from the southern African nation of Lesotho and one from the west African nation of Senegal, to illustrate some of the key characteristics of common property regimes. In particular, it is important to understand the structure of governance, the types of institutions that govern behavior, and the compatibility between governance, institutions and individual incentives. A common property regime can only be effective if its institutions are compatible with the structure of governance. The extent of its effectiveness also depends upon the incentives and expectations of individuals expected to enforce the rules of the institutions or comply with their terms. At present, most African governments lack the organizational capacity and political will necessary to implement state property regimes, official regulations on resource use, or individual property rights for rangelands resources. In many cases it is more appropriate for governments to define and enforce group rights to particular resources, then help to establish conditions in which internal group dynamics yield efficient resource management outcomes.

Key words: Common property, property rights, rangelands, Africa, Lesotho, Senegal

1. Introduction

Africans keep about 14 percent of the world's cattle and 21 percent of the world's sheep and goats on a land base that comprises 25 percent of the world's total area of rangelands. The number of people engaged in extensive livestock production is higher in Africa than in any other region of the world. Of the 30 to 40 million pastoralists in the world – people who rely on extensive livestock production for at least half of their income and subsistence needs – over half reside in Africa (Galaty and Johnson, 1990; Sandford, 1983). Livestock contribute about 35 percent of Africa's agricultural domestic product and 17 percent of the dietary protein in human diets (Winrock International, 1992: pp. 12–16).

The forage and water resources emanating from most African rangelands are shared by several individuals, households or village groups. This shared use of natural resources received its early indictment in the fisheries literature when writers began, unfortunately, to refer to the open access fishery as

Environmental and Resource Economics **6**: 99–118, 1995.

a 'common property resource' (Gordon, 1954; Scott, 1955). Garrett Hardin, seeking to make a point about uncontrolled population growth, coined the allegorical phrase, 'the tragedy of the commons' (Hardin, 1968). To make his point, he invoked the proverbial grazing pasture in which each separate owner of livestock has little incentive to control livestock numbers. For some reason, few questioned the Hardin link between parents deciding to have more children, and a community of grazers deciding how many animals to place on the range. Indeed, it is precisely this difference which is central to natural resource policy – and which Hardin should have used in his appeal for population control. By mixing metaphors, Hardin missed a wonderful opportunity, and he managed to induce an entire generation of economists and development assistance experts to believe that livestock management was no different from couples having babies. While it may be difficult to control the breeding behavior of humans, social groups certainly have many ways to control greedy and obstreperous livestock keepers. Those intent on individualizing (i.e., 'privatizing') African land tenure so as to make it conform with ideological precepts found much comfort in the Hardin allegory. A paper about population policy became, instead, the 'theoretical' foundation for grazing policy across an entire continent.

Repeated challenges to the applicability of the 'tragedy of the commons' model has prompted a surge of interest in common property (Berkes, 1989; Bromley and Cernea, 1989; Ciriacy-Wantrup and Bishop, 1975; McCay and Acheson, 1987; National Academy of Sciences, 1986). Analysts familiar with particular situations often point out that collectively-used natural resources are governed by resource management regimes that approach the conceptual essence of common property (*res communes*). For example, analysts have described common property regimes governing rangeland use in Lesotho (Shoup, 1987), Ethiopia (Helland, 1982), Tanzania (Lane, 1991), Morocco (Gilles *et al.*, 1992) and Kenya (McCabe, 1990; Stiles, 1992; Kituyi, 1990). Here we consider a *common property regime* to be a set of institutional arrangements that define the conditions of access to, and control over, a range of benefits arising from collectively-used natural resources (Bromley, 1989, 1991; Bromley and Cernea, 1989; Ostrom, 1986; Young, 1989).

In this paper we argue that there are resource management regimes with a wide range of institutional arrangements and governance structures that are consistent with this definition of common property. Different types of economic and environmental problems may arise depending upon the structure of governance and the types of institutions. Different policies and interventions may thus be appropriate for solving those problems. Herein we offer a political-economy framework for analysis of resource management regimes that fall within the broad class of common property. The framework recognizes the importance of the socio-political structures that set the institutional context for individual behavior and collective action. We apply the framework to common property regimes for African rangelands. We begin with brief reviews of rangeland regimes from Lesotho and Senegal to motivate the framework.

2. Examples of Common Property Regimes for African Rangelands

In this section we review three regimes, two from Lesotho and one from Senegal, that represent some of the variety of rangeland regimes that prevail across Africa. In these descriptions we draw heavily upon our previous analyses of those regimes (see Swallow *et al.*, 1987; Swallow and Brokken, 1990; Swallow, 1990, 1991; Bromley and Cernea, 1989). While all of the regimes meet the definition of common property regime as presented above, all have different political and institutional structures. At the outset it is important to note that all three regimes operate in geographical areas that receive high average annual rainfall compared to rangelands in many other areas of Africa.

2.1. LESOTHO'S MABOELLA REGIME

Lesotho's extensive grasslands are utilized under two resource management regimes: the *maboella* regime governs the use of village common lands in the lowlands and foothills and the cattlepost regime governs the use of mountain grazing areas. The lowlands and foothills comprise a narrow belt of land around the western borders of the country with about 25 percent of the country's land base. Elevation ranges from 1,520–1,830 metres above sea level and average annual rainfall is 750 mm. Over half of the country is classified as mountainous. Elevation in the mountains varies from 1,830 to over 2,700 metres above sea level and the average annual rainfall is 1,000 mm. The foothills are a transition zone between the lowlands and mountains.

Maboella was established in the mid-1800s by Lesotho's first Paramount Chief, Moshoeshoe, at the height of his political and economic power. *Maboella* was instituted in order to protect areas of common lands for special uses during particular times of the year. Some forms of *maboella* governed the utilization of natural stands of edible plants, medicinal herbs, woodlots, grasses, and reeds, while other forms reserved pasture areas for utilization during certain seasons or prohibited grazing on certain areas to allow their regeneration (Eldredge, 1986; Sheddick, 1954).

The rules for *maboella* were promulgated at the national level by the Paramount Chief and enacted at the village level by the Paramount Chief's designates. At the local level, the *molisa oa lethobo*, or warden of enclosures, was appointed by the village chief to be responsible for the enforcement of *maboella* rules. Wardens were allowed disproportionate allocations of thatching grass as compensation for enforcing *maboella* rules. Village chiefs had incentives to impose fines on those who violated the rules since they received income from fines levied in their courts.

In most villages there is now relatively little enforcement of *maboella* rules on village residents. The external and internal bases for *maboella* have gradually weakened during the last hundred years. Externally, the advent of the colonial and post-colonial governments and courts reduced the political and legal support for village chiefs and wardens to enforce *maboella* rules. A number of alternative policy organizations – political parties, village development committees, donor agencies and government agencies – have come to compete with chiefs for external authority and legitimacy. Many of these organizations have attempted to 'modernize' or otherwise 'reform' the customary institutions.

Internally, chiefs and wardens no longer receive financial rewards for *maboella* enforcing rules. Legislation passed in 1946 resulted in a 90 percent reduction in the number of recognized indigenous courts and a prohibition on chiefs receiving income from fines levied in their courts (Machobane, 1990: pp. 226–277). The primary motivations for chiefs to enforce *maboella* regulations have become personal and political. Chiefs who support the government of the day, or own large numbers of livestock, have greater interests in collective grazing lands. Contemporaneous changes in the distribution of wealth and economic opportunities in South Africa have made rural residents less dependent upon the economic power of chiefs. Households with migrant workers have become more dependent upon remittances and less dependent upon natural resources for their subsistence or economic livelihoods (Lawry, 1988).

Shoup (1987) documents the case of one lowland village, Ha Nchele, that has initiated a successful village grazing regime with very little external assistance. In about 1976 the village leaders initiated a rotational grazing scheme on village-grazing lands as an alternative to taking their animals to cattleposts in the mountains. The regime has been successful in enforcing rules on its members regarding access and allocation of the village-grazing areas. Shoup (1987) suggests several reasons for this success: (1) The village chief had a personal interest in the success of the regime because he held the greatest number of livestock, but did not abuse his power as chief. (2) The chief and the Village Development Committee shared leadership in defining the operations and evolution of the regime. (3) The regime built upon the customary institution of *maboella*.

2.2. LESOTHO'S CATTLEPOST REGIME

Increased exploitation of the country's expansive mountainous regime enabled Lesotho's human and livestock populations to expand at the end of the nineteenth century and beginning of the twentieth century (Swallow *et al.*, 1987). By the beginning of the twentieth century, a system of seasonal transhumance between the lowlands and mountains was established. Animals were kept on village grazing areas and harvested fields during the winter months (governed by *maboella*) and moved to mountain rangelands areas – cattlepost areas – for the summer months.

The cattlepost regime was established in the 1920s to coordinate the activities of the increasing number of people grazing their animals on mountain pastures and to protect the mountain rangelands from over-exploitation. The regime was enforced by the Paramount Chief and the Principal Chiefs. Any livestock owner who sought to use a specific cattlepost area had to request permission from the relevant chief. Chiefs were not allowed to withhold permission to any Masotho on the basis of the person's residential location or social status. With permission, the person could build a cattlepost hut and paddock and graze their animals in specific areas during designated times of the year. Exclusive rights were not granted to individuals; individuals were prohibited from blocking access to others who had also been granted permission (Sheddick, 1954).

It appears that the cattlepost system performed the coordination function more effectively than the regulation function. Lesotho's populations of cattle, sheep and goats grew rapidly during the first three decades of the twentieth century so that cattle and smallstock populations reached their historic peaks in 1921 and 1931 respectively (Swallow and Brokken, 1987). Concern about the ecological impacts of these large numbers of livestock (e.g., Pim, 1935) prompted the colonial government to commission an extensive survey of the mountainous region. Staples and Hudson (1938) estimated that the overstocking of Lesotho's mountain pastures had resulted in the encroachment of inedible bushes, noxious weeds and less palatable grasses into areas formerly dominated by palatable perennial grasses. The 'carrying capacity' of the pastures was dramatically reduced as a result.

In the early 1970s a grazing-permit system was introduced to help monitor seasonal movements of livestock and to restrict the numbers of livestock kept on particular areas of rangeland. Permits issued by, or on behalf of, the principal chiefs specify the location where an individual is permitted to graze his animals and also the number of animals allowed. Under the Range Management and Grazing Control Regulations of 1980 and 1986, Principal Chiefs operated under the direction of officers of the Ministry of Agriculture to enforce a strict set of controls including: grazing permits, limitation of livestock numbers to the 'carrying capacity' of the local area, specifications on the location of cattlepost kraals, dates at which cattlepost areas were opened and closed for grazing, and prohibitions on grass burning.

The stated objectives of these interventions were to arrest the deterioration of both lowland and mountain rangelands, to bring livestock numbers in line with the 'carrying capacity' of rangelands, and to increase the value of livestock products produced in Lesotho. The evidence – continued rangelands deterioration (Swallow, 1991: pp. 238–241), a decline in the quantity and quality of livestock products (Hunter, 1987), ignorance of the rules (Shoup,

1987) – indicated that these interventions had, in general, not achieved the (perhaps unrealistic) objectives set for them.

An institutional innovation that has achieved some success in governing resource management in the mountain grazing areas is the grazing association. The grazing association that is now being used as a model for Lesotho and other areas in southern Africa is the Sehlabathebe Grazing Association.

The Sehlabathebe Grazing Association was established in 1982 with support from the U.S.A.I.D.-funded (United States Agency for International Development)-Land Conservation and Range Development Project as a mechanism for the residents of mountain areas to take greater control over the grazing resources in their areas. The area allocated to the grazing association, 30,720 hectares, included village grazing areas, cattle post grazing areas, and 11 villages. Residents of the 11 villages were granted exclusive grazing rights to the area, a concept project which personnel labelled 'controlled' communal grazing (Weaver, 1986). The enforcement of exclusive use by local residents resulted in an immediate reduction in the number of livestock grazed in the area. The consequent decrease in competition for forage has resulted in a recuperation of the rangelands and improvement in the condition and productivity of local animals.

The chief, the project manager, and the grazing association have been quite successful in enforcing the regime's boundary. They have been far less effective, however, in enforcing rules within the regime. Frustration over the project with the grazing association resulted in the project playing an increasing role in the active management of the association. As of August 1986, it was the project manager, not the executive committee, who directed the range riders, set the dates for grazing rotation, and administered the finances of the association (Lawry, 1988).

2.3. EASTERN SENEGAL'S PASTORAL UNITS

Eastern Senegal is the site of one of the World Bank's most successful experiences with collective management of African rangelands. The project covers an area of approximately 14,000 square kilometres that is populated by about 70,000 people of the Peul, Wolof and Mandingo ethnic groups. Average annual rainfall is 700 mm in the north of the area and 1,400 mm in the south. Most of the permanent residents are agro-pastoralists who live in permanent villages. Approximately four percent of the area is planted to crops (Shanmugaratnam *et al.*, 1992: pp. 34–35).

The traditional authority system that governed access and use of the pasture lands was based on lineage and caste. A project pre-appraisal undertaken by the World Bank during the mid-1970s noted that the traditional authority system was no longer effective. The nationalization of land ownership in 1964 undermined the basis of the customary system. Drought conditions in the Fero area of northern Senegal and Mauritania resulted in an influx of transhumant pastoralists. Problems of local over-grazing and land-use conflicts between livestock and cultivation were on the rise. The former common property regime had essentially become and open access situation (Bromley and Cernea, 1989: p. 34).

During the first phase of the project (1976–1983), 53 pastoral units were established in the area. Each pastoral unit was comprised of eight to ten small villages and 1–2,000 agro-pastoralists. The pastoral units collaborated with the project in the delivery of supplemental feed and veterinary supplies and served as collective credit guarantors. Loan repayment rates were excellent.

During the project's second phase (1984–88), the pastoral units began to take on common-property rangeland management as a secondary activity. In 1984, a Protocol Agreement was passed that permitted the pastoral units to register legally-defensible communal rights to grazing lands and watering points (Vedeld, 1992). The pastoral units began to administer grazing rotations to coordinate the grazing and watering activities of their members as well as agricultural and livestock activities in the area (Associates in Rural Development, 1989; Bromley and Cernea, 1989).

2.4. SUMMARY AND COMPARISON OF THE CASE STUDIES

The common property regimes from Lesotho and Senegal have general similarities and specific differences. First, in each case the effectiveness of the customary regime depended upon the strength of the *authority structure* on which it was based. The *maboella* and cattle post regimes of Lesotho were based on the authority of the chieftaincy, while the customary regime of eastern Senegal was based on lineage and the caste system of nobles and slaves. In both countries the customary authority structures weakened with the advent of colonialism and the increased commercialization of the rural economies. Weaker authority structures resulted in less effective implementation of the *institutions* that governed the behavior of individuals and groups.

Second, each of the current cases of effective common property management was based on a combination of customary authority, new organizations and the de-centralized actions of individual livestock owners. The success of the Ha Nchele regime in the lowlands of Lesotho depended upon the actions of the chief as customary leader and wealthy livestock owner, the leadership of the Village Development Committee, and the willingness of all livestock owners to comply with the grazing regulations and enforce compliance by their neighbours (Shoup, 1987). The Sehlabathebe regime in the mountains of Lesotho depended upon the leadership and strength of the Principal Chief, cooperation between several village chiefs, technical advice and assistance provided by representatives of the Ministry of Agriculture, and the actions of the elected Range Management Association (Lawry, 1988).

The pastoral units of eastern Senegal are new organizations (Groupements d'Interêt Economique) that are based on the customary caste system (i.e., all board members of the new organizations are former nobles) and are empowered by new national laws that provide them with recourse to the national legal system. About half of the potential members of a GIE in a given locality are actual members (Shanmugaratnam *et al.*, 1992).

Third, each regime consists of a constellation of institutional arrangements. In the Ha Nchele area every permanent resident of the village has the *right* to graze animals on village pastures – but they must follow certain regulations restricting where they can graze their animals at different times. Those regulations are a combination of *rules* enforced by village authorities and *contracts* enforced by all livestock owners. In the Sehlabathebe area, every permanent resident of the eleven villages in the area has the right to graze animals in the village areas and mountain pastures covered by the Range Management Association (RMA). Residents of other areas are not permitted to bring animals into the RMA. Rules covering the use of the areas by members of the RMA are specified but are seldom enforced. In Senegal the members of the pastoral units have recognized rights to use land and water resources in their local areas. The pastoral units also provide mechanisms to resolve conflicts between crop and livestock uses of land. It is not clear, however, whether the pastoral units have any right to exclude outsiders.

3. Alternative Institutional Forms

The case studies illustrate that African rangeland regimes consist of diverse constellations of institutional arrangements that are supported by various external and internal enforcement mechanisms. The sub-section 2.4 that summarizes and compares the case studies introduces several concepts that are useful for analyzing the operation of common property regimes. Rights, rules and contracts were mentioned as types of institutions. In this section we define those and other types of institutions and discuss examples. Wherever appropriate, we draw upon the case studies presented above.

A *rule* is a 'standard setting forth actions that agents are expected to perform (or refrain from performing) under appropriate circumstances' (Young, 1989: p. 16). African governments are often tempted to pass legislation to enact strict rules designed to govern livestock owners' behavior. For example, Lesotho's Range Management and Grazing Control Regulations of 1980 and 1986 decreed that principal chiefs should operate under the direction of officers of the Ministry of Agriculture to enforce a strict set of controls including: grazing permits, limitation of livestock numbers to the 'carrying capacity' of the local area, specifications on the location of cattleposts, dates at which cattlepost areas are opened and closed for grazing, and prohibitions on grass burning (Government of Lesotho, 1980). In practice these rules have had little impact on rangeland utilization in the country. For example,

Shoup (1987) found that the ward chief in the area he studied made no attempt to limit either the number of animals grazed by any individual livestock keeper or the total number of livestock in any cattlepost area. In fact, he considered it his duty to facilitate his subject's access to mountain pastures.

To understand African rangeland regimes sufficiently to design appropriate institutional innovations, it is essential that we move beyond the formalism of official rules and into another domain.

3.1. RIGHTS

Much of the current literature on common property speaks in terms of the concept of 'property rights.' To clarify, we consider a *right* to be a guarantee given by a collective authority system to those who comprise – are part of – the entity. An individual or group has a right to opportunities or benefits from a policy that advances the enjoyment of that opportunity is preferred over one that does not, regardless of the implications for the collective goals of the society (Dworkin, 1977). *Property rights* – rights to potential future benefits – are rarely unconditional guarantees. Usually they are qualified by: (1) the types of agents holding rights and bearing duties; (2) the conditions necessary for their realization; and, (3) their level of abstractness. Rights and duties vis-à-vis rangeland resources are held by states, directly by individuals, or indirectly by individuals through their membership in groups. Property rights can be held by all individuals in a society or only by the occupants of certain social roles. Rights can be superior to collective goals, conditional on the advancement of those goals, or derived from those goals (Becker, 1977; Dworkin, 1977).

There have been many situations, particularly in French West Africa, in which colonial governments, and later post-colonial governments, have declared customary right structures to be void and declared state 'ownership' of collectively-used rangelands. The results vary, but few post-colonial governments have been effective in governing local-level resource use and management. In eastern Senegal, state declaration of ownership may have had some positive consequences by reducing the power of the established elites and providing legal machinery for a more equitable distribution of rangeland rights (Bromley and Cernea, 1989). More common, however, have been the instances in which only negative social impacts were apparent. In the Niger River delta of Mali the *dina* common property regime has been undermined by French colonial rule and by the 1960 declaration of state ownership of all natural resources. In some areas of the delta, powerful groups and individuals – founding lineages, merchants, retired soldiers – have been able to establish exclusive access to the most productive resources. Other areas of the delta now have characteristics of open access. These areas have come under increased stress from herders, fishers and rice producers. The level of conflict among users has been high and the quality of the resource base has deteriorated (Lawry, 1989; Moorehead, 1989).

Rights can also be general, specific, or particular. While a general property right may entitle an individual to some unspecified ownership right to rangeland benefits; a specific property right would identify the specific benefit – forage and water generated by the rangelands – to which the individual is entitled. A particular property right would further indicate the particular area of rangelands over which the right extended.

From the case studies presented above, it appears that customary rangeland rights are often expressed in specific but not particular terms. Under Lesotho's cattlepost regime, Basotho livestock keepers have specific rights to products emanating from Lesotho's mountain rangelands. To be effective, however, those rights had to be enforced by someone from a national-level institution such as the Paramount Chief. With the deterioration in the authority of the chieftaincy, however, it has become important that rangeland regimes can be enforced at the local level. For locally-enforced institutions to be effective, rangeland rights must be specified in particular terms. The grazing rights of individual livestock keepers must be associated with particular areas of the rangeland. This has been a primary outcome of the Sehlabathebe grazing association.

3.2. CONVENTIONS

Runge (1981, 1986) hypothesizes that the internal order of common property regimes can often be self-enforced by the actions and expectations of the individual resource users themselves. In general, a self-enforcing social institution that provides agents with assurance regarding others' behavior is called a *convention*. Runge used the customary rangelands tenure regime in Botswana to support this hypothesis:

> . . . the traditional institutional structure provided a relatively stable and cooperative basis for resource use and the exchange and trade of basic commodities. These 'rules of the game' were sufficient to assure each individual that his rights, duties, liberties and exposures would be respected by others (1981: p. 301).

3.3. CONTRACTS

An institutional arrangement that has received little explicit attention by analysts of common property regimes is the *contract*. A contract is an agreement among agents that is supported by the actions of a third party, in the case of externally-enforced contracts, or by the actions of the agents themselves, in the case of internally-enforced contracts. The need for a contract can arise in any situation in which there is 'transactional insecurity,' that is, any situation in which agents' actions of compliance or deviation from the terms of an agreement do not occur simultaneously (Kronman, 1985).

Alternatively, agents' actions may occur simultaneously but information about those actions may be expensive to collect. This inter-temporal dimension makes contracts inherently a dynamic phenomena.

Because common property has generally been neglected in the current literature, we focus primarily on internally-enforced contracts in this paper. Internally-enforced contracts can either be explicit or implicit: the difference is the type of enforcement mechanism supporting the contract. Explicit contracts are enforced by the deliberate actions of the contracting agents, while implicit contracts are enforced by implicit threats of future retaliation for current deviations. Deliberate actions taken to secure explicit contracts might include hostage taking, collateral requirements, hand-tying, gain sharing, or partial surrender of autonomy.

Dynamic contracts are enforced by strategies containing credible threats of future punishments for current deviations from the terms of the (explicit or implicit) agreement. Punishment strategies considered in the theoretical literature include trigger strategies, stick-and-carrot strategies, exclusion, and tit-for-tat. Briefly, an agent following a trigger strategy will comply as long as everyone else complies, but will revert to Nash equilibrium behavior if anyone ever deviates (Friedman, 1986). An agent following a stick-and-carrot penal code will respond to others' deviations by imposing a harsh but short-lived punishment, followed by compliance (Abreu, 1986). An agent following an exclusion penal code will take steps to exclude deviants from future access to the resource (Hirshleifer and Rasmusen, 1989). And an agent following a tit-for-tat penal code will mimic others' actions: cooperation will be rewarded with cooperation, deviation will be punished by deviation (Axelrod, 1984).

The customary rangeland tenure system of the pastoral Fulani of Senegal and elsewhere in West Africa has been described by a number of analysts in terms that are very similar to the conceptual notion of the dynamic contract. From a review of empirical studies of African pastoralists, Niamir (1989) distinguishes between what she calls active coordination and passive coordination among herding units. Active coordination refers to situations where herding units follow formal and informal rules that are created and recognized by a group of herding units. Passive coordination refers to situations where 'no formal agreements are made between tribes but where coordinated movements result from the wish to avoid other tribes' (p. 40). Passive coordination is maintained through 'informal rules,' or, in the terminology suggested here, dynamic contracts (Swallow and Bromley, 1994).

4. Governance and Institutions

Fundamental to the operations of common property regimes are the authority systems that sanction rights, enforce rules, and define the contexts in which conventions and contracts are negotiated. Authority systems are concerned with *governance*, and governance is the process of deciding what a collective will do and how it will do it. *Governments* exist for the process of governance; that is, governments are created to carry out governance. *Institutions* are defined by the process of governance to provide order to the relations among the members of a collective and to constrain what governments may do to the members in the name of governance (Bromley, 1989). To understand institutions, therefore, it is necessary to consider the nature of the authority system, process of governance, and the implications of those processes for the implementation of institutions.

4.1. GOVERNMENTAL DIVERSITY

Besides institutional diversity, rangelands regimes also exhibit considerable governmental diversity. Mair (1977) identified three types of customary government that prevail (or have prevailed) among the livestock-keeping peoples of Africa: (1) centralized governments; (2) diffused governments; and (3) minimal (or non-existent) governments. Societies with centralized governments have hierarchical political structures in which '. . . a single supreme authority is recognized, and public affairs are regulated, decisions taken, and obedience claimed by persons acting in his name' (Mair, 1977: p. 138). Many agro-pastoral groups in Eastern and Southern Africa have or had centralized governments in which chiefs perform executive, legislative and judicial functions. During the days of Moshoeshoe I (circa 1796–1886) the people of Lesotho had one of the most hierarchical governments of all the livestock-keeping peoples of Africa. The Paramount Chief had authority to perform a variety of functions:

> He everywhere represents his people in their dealings with outsiders, and organizes such communal activities as war, collective labour, and certain types of ritual. . . . He is both legislator and judge, with power to inflict capital punishment; he claims many forms of tribute, in both labour and kind; he controls the distribution and use of land, coordinates agricultural activities, provides for the poor and needy, and rewards those who serve him well (Shapera, 1956: pp. 40–41).

In contrast to this centralized structure, most pastoralist groups in Eastern and Western Africa have customary governments that are characterized as being 'diffused' or 'minimal.' Those with diffused customary governments include the Maasai, Kipsigi, Pokot, Nandi and Samburu of Kenya, and the Karimojong of Uganda (Mair, 1977; Quam, 1976). In those societies legislative and judicial authority is held by relatively egalitarian elders' councils. The enforcement of elders' decisions depends upon the type of case: the coercion of younger age-sets is used to enforce judgements in criminal cases, while social sanctions and coercion of individual litigants combine to enforce judgements in most civil cases (Mair, 1977). For example, among the Maasai:

> . . . the primary institution for the resolution of conflict and social accountability is a council of elders. . . . The range of affairs dealt with include conflicts between local residents, access

to communal resources, and interpretation of proper conduct as deemed consistent with being Maasai. The council derives its powers from and is a practical expression of the age-based principle of organization. The council's authority is underpinned by its collective curse on any member who persistently fails to heed decisions and the cohesion of age-set leaders who enforce subordination to the collective wisdom manifest in council decisions (Kituyi, 1990: p. 114).

Societies identified as having minimal governments include the Turkana of Kenya, the Fulani of West Africa, and the Western Dinka, Nuer, and Mandari of Sudan. These groups have neither chiefs nor elders' councils with the authority or power to enforce rules. Designated individuals or councils may arbitrate disputes but have no power to enact punishments. Individuals and coalitions have responsibilities to assess the fairness of the judgements reached by their chiefs or elders' councils and undertake actions necessary to impose sanctions on deviants. Each individual or coalition will therefore consider their own welfare (short-term or long-term) when they make such decisions.

The nomadic Fulani, as well as most of the semi-nomadic ones, seem to be anarchic in their political organization. Their chiefs act as guides, arbitrators, and spokesmen for extended family groups that tend to move about more or less together. These chiefs have no real power of coercion over their followers, nor can they make binding agreements on their behalf (Riesman, 1978: p. 27).

4.2. IMPLEMENTATION OF INSTITUTIONS

The structure of government under which a common property regime operates – whether it be centralized, diffused, or minimal – determines the type of institutions that can be implemented to govern relations among members and between members and non-members. The most demanding type to govern is that concerning rights. To be implemented rights must be: (1) formulated and promulgated, (2) communicated to those to whom they apply (members and non-members alike), (3) interpreted, (4) enforced, (5) legitimized with the persons or groups to which they apply, and (6) adapted to changing needs and circumstances (Bull, 1977: pp. 56–57).

To implement the rights of groups – that is, those at the boundaries of regimes – a body performing these functions must also be able to interpret the aims of the larger society in which the groups are established, to judge between the rights and duties of competing groups, and enforce sanctions on individuals, groups and collectives of groups. Such a body must be capable of enforcing sanctions on the individuals and groups who hold rights and duties and on collectives of groups. To implement the rights of individuals as members of groups – that is, rights within regimes – the body must interpret the aims of the group, judge between competing rights, and enforce sanctions on individuals and collectives of individuals.

Evidence from Lesotho, Senegal and Zimbabwe (Cousins, 1992) suggests that national governments are better suited to the enforcement of group rights than individual rights. In those countries, the national governments have achieved some successes in defining boundaries between group resources and in supporting groups to identify and punish those who violate those boundaries. Governments have been less successful in enforcing order on the internal operations of rangeland regimes. The Sehlabathebe Grazing Association has been keen to use external authority to exclude outsiders but reluctant to apply that same authority to enforce internal grazing rules.

Conventions and contracts, because they are not 'rights,' can be implemented without central government units. They can be effective, therefore, in social groups with central, diffused, minimal or non-existent governments. Conventions and internally-enforced contracts can also govern relations between groups of resource users (at the boundaries of regimes) and within groups (within regimes). It is unlikely, however, that internally-enforced contracts will be simultaneously effective on both levels in the absence of some other institutional arrangements. That is, for a group of resource users to be successful in maintaining an implicit internal agreement they must have confidence that future entry into the group will be restricted, or at least limited to a known number of potential entrants. A minimum condition for the effective operation of dynamic implicit contracts may therefore be that there is some social authority that enforces rights or rules regulating the entry of new individuals or groups, the mobility of individuals between groups, and the mobility of groups between sovereign polities.

An example that supports this hypothesis is provided by Ha Nchele in Lesotho. Because the boundaries between most Lesotho villages are relatively clear and well-known, the residents of Ha Nchele have encountered few difficulties in excluding outsiders from their village common areas. Membership of the grazing association was naturally restricted to the resident households who kept cattle. At Ha Nchele this was a relatively small number, 29 out of a total of 128 households. Even with that small number of households, grazing rules were not self-enforcing. People violated rules and were punished. Anyone who violated the clearly-articulated rules had their animals impounded and was charged a fine. Group members enforced rules themselves by identifying deviants and helping to collect fines. No external enforcement was necessary.

5. Expectations, Incentives and Institutions

The structure of governance determines the necessary, but not sufficient, conditions for the successful implementation of institutions regarding common property regimes. Implementation of these institutions requires action on the part of particular individuals. Individuals respond to their own incentives and expectations.

Consider first the incentives and expectations of the individuals who are responsible for defining and enforcing the rights and rules that comprise common property regimes. Local leaders – customary, appointed or elected

– often perform important roles in common property regimes. Their incentives depend upon their relationships with the external political and legal system and their relationships with the group of resource users and other local constituents. The incentives they have to enforce restrictions on resource use also depend directly on their use of the resource and the benefits and costs they derive from enforcing the rules.

Government employees are often responsible for advising local groups in group organization and technical aspects of resource management. They may also be responsible for mediating relationships between groups of resource users. The incentives and expectations of government employees depend upon the government system of incentives, the tolerance of nepotism and corruption, the resources that are available to them to fulfil their assigned roles, their personal affiliations with one group or another, and possibly their own goals regarding resource use.

Now consider the incentives and expectations of resource users themselves: Swallow (1991: pp. 156–156) shows that the user of a collectively-used rangeland has an incentive to demand a resource use rule; at the same time he or she also has an incentive to deviate from such a rule. The incentive to deviate depends upon the external gains from deviation, the probability that other resource users will comply or deviate, the probability of being caught and punished, and the likely severity of the punishment.

Runge (1986) hypothesizes that the incentive of an individual to deviate from a stocking-rate rule generally decreases with the number of other agents with which he expects to comply. Results from a multiple-period simulation model, presented in Swallow and Bromley (1994), challenge the validity of that hypothesis. Those results indicate that, *ceteris paribus*, the incentive for an individual to deviate from a stocking-rate rule actually increases with the number of agents with which he expects to comply. Further, individuals have incentives to deviate from stocking-rate rules in almost all cases, and time periods. Generally, therefore, internal stocking-rate rules will not be self-enforcing.

The literature on internally-enforced contracts suggests other mechanisms by which internal agreements (explicit or tacit) on resource allocation can be maintained without external enforcement. Internally-enforced contracts can operate within a set of articulated rights, rules, and codified contracts (Bowles and Gintis, 1988; Williamson, 1985) or within a 'state of nature' in which 'individuals and groups must arrange their transactions without the aid of an independent enforcement mechanism whose powers are significantly greater than their own' (Kronman, 1985: p. 9).[1]

Swallow and Bromley (1994) show that the strength of a dynamic contract – the difference between the payoff to compliance and the payoff to deviation – is positively related to: (1) the marginal cost of production and (2) the duration and severity of the punishment, and negatively related to: (1) the discount rate, (2) the size of the group, (3) the price of the output, and

(4) the number of other agents expected to comply. The strength of contract is very sensitive to changes in group size. Dynamic contracts are unlikely to be effective in groups with more than 30–40 members.

6. Policy Implications

To address the problems of African livestock-rangelands development, feasible policy objectives must be established and feasible policy instruments designed to advance those objectives. A nation-wide system of individual property rights and duties is only a feasible objective if legitimate central authorities have the power, will (incentive) and managerial capacity – external legitimacy – necessary to protect individuals against collectives and adapt institutions to changing circumstances. To be enforceable under current conditions, property rights must be defined in specific terms. For example, the common property innovations that have been successful in Lesotho and Senegal have defined specific rangelands and water resources to which people have rights. The more variable the environment, the more difficult the tradeoff between the need for specificity and the need to allow flexibility in grazing patterns (van den Brink *et al.*, 1995).

Group property rights are feasible under a broader range of circumstances. Implementation of group property rights requires a central authority that can arbitrate between the interests of broad groups of the population and enforce boundaries and agreements between groups. Unambiguous membership criteria are a pre-requisite for effective group rights.

Effective group rights will only lead to efficient resource allocation if there are effective mechanisms for internal governance. The effectiveness of a formal structure of internal governance will depend upon the incentives of the individuals whose roles are to enforce rules and other individuals who are expected to comply with the rules. Internally-enforced contracts are mechanisms for internal governance that can be effective with little or no internal authority system. Internal contracts can be enforced through such explicit mechanisms as collateral, hostages, or gains sharing arrangements, or through implicit threats of future retaliation for current deviations (dynamic contracts). External agencies can facilitate internal contracts by: (1) providing assurance that agents will have long-term interactions with the same group of resource users; (2) increasing information about agents' preferences and their compliance or deviation from contracts; (3) increasing the points of contact between resource users; or (4) absorbing some of the transaction costs associated with the maintenance of contracts.

Political structures and the institutions they support are continually changing: what might have been feasible with customary government structures may not be feasible with current structures. Common property regimes, polities, and ecologies are systems that are evolving, co-evolving through their repeated interactions, and responding to exogenous political, economic and ecological shocks. At the present time, the factors that are having the greatest impact on the common property regimes for African rangelands include: (1) greater competition for livestock, land and water between pastoralists, cultivators, and conservationists; (2) reductions in the economic and political power of customary authorities; (3) inter-ethnic and international conflicts between pastoralist groups; (4) declarations of 'ownership' of rangelands by African governments (Lawry, 1989); (5) adoption of new water provision techniques and tsetse-control techniques (Behnke, 1988); (6) increasing importance of non-livestock and non-agricultural opportunities for employment and income generation; and (7) increased concentration concerning the ownership of livestock among pastoralists and increased ownership of livestock by external investors (Little, 1987).

These processes are serving to undermine the efficacy of status quo institutional arrangements. In this context policy makers need to search for ways to facilitate institutional change that will make regimes more resilient and better able to allocate resources to the mutual benefit of those who share their access. Priority should be given to group rights and the internal institution-building capacity of local groups and communities.

Acknowledgements

Earlier revisions of this paper were presented at the 'International Conference on African Economic Issues', Abidjan, Côte d'Ivoire, in August 1992 and the 'Workshop on New Directions in African Range Management Policy', Matopos, Zimbabwe in January 1992. Useful comments have been provided by David Pratt, Peter de Leeuw, Roy Behnke, Maryam Niamer-Fuller and Ian Scoones. We also appreciate the constructive comments provided by the anonymous reviewers.

Note

[1] Kronman (1985) points out that his state of nature is somewhat different from the Hobbesian state of nature as a 'war of every man against every man.' A Hobbesian state of nature involves 'transactional insecurity' – in a non-simultaneous exchange, at least one party is exposed to the danger that another party will not complete the exchange – and 'vulnerability of possession' – the objects possessed by an individual are subject to attack at any time. Kronman's state of nature, on the other hand, involves transactional insecurity and possessive security.

References

Abreu, D. (1986), 'Extremal Equilibria of Oligopolistic Supergames', *Journal of Economic Theory* **39**, 191–225.

Associates in Rural Development (1989), 'Options for Promoting User-Based Governance of Sahelian Renewable Natural Resources', paper prepared for presentation at the CILSS-sponsored conference, 'Regional Encounter for a Better Socio-Ecological Balance in the Rural Sahel', Bamako.

Axelrod, R. (1984), *The Evolution of Cooperation*, Basic Books, New York.

Becker, L. C. (1977), *Property Rights: Philosophical Foundations*, Routledge & Kegan Paul, Boston.

Behnke, R. H. (1988), 'Range Enclosure in Central Somalia', Pastoral Development Network Paper No. 25b, Overseas Development Institute, London.

Berkes, F. (ed.) (1989), *Common Property Resources: Ecology and Community-based Sustainable Development*, Belhaven, London.

Bowles, S. and H. Gintis (1988), 'Contested Exchange: The Political Structure of Competitive Markets', Department of Economics, University of Massachusetts, mimeo, Amherst, MA.

Bromley, D. W. (1991), *Environment and Economy: Property Rights and Public Policy*, Basil Blackwell, Oxford.

Bromley, D. W. (1989), *Economic Interests and Institutions: The Conceptual Foundations of Public Policy*, Basil Blackwell, Oxford.

Bromley, D. W. and M. M. Cernea (1989), *The Management of Common Property Natural Resources: Some Conceptual and Operational Fallacies*, World Bank Discussion Paper 57, The World Bank, Washington, D.C.

Bull, H. (1977), *The Anarchical Society: A Study of Order in World Politics*, Columbia University Press, New York.

Ciriacy-Wantrup, S. V. and R. C. Bishop (1975), ' "Common Property" as a Concept in Natural Resources Policy', *Natural Resources Journal* **15**, 713–727.

Cousins, B. (1992), *Managing Communal Rangelands in Zimbabwe: Experiences and Lessons*, Commonwealth Secretariat, London.

Dworkin, R. M. (1977), *Taking Rights Seriously*, Harvard University Press, Cambridge.

Eldredge, E. A. (1986), *An Economic History of Lesotho in the Nineteenth Century*, Ph.D. dissertation, University of Wisconsin-Madison.

Friedman, J. W. (1986), *Game Theory with Applications to Economics*, Oxford University Press, Oxford.

Galaty, J. G. and D. L. Johnson (1990), 'Introduction: Pastoral Systems in Global Perspective', in J. G. Galaty and D. L. Johnson, eds., *The World of Pastoralism: Herding Systems in Comparative Perspective*, New York: The Guilford Press, pp. 1–15.

Gilles, J. L., B. E. Norton and J. T. O'Rourke (1992), 'Oukaimadene, Morocco: A High Mountain Agdal', in D. W. Bromley, ed., *Making the Commons Work: Theory, Practice and Policy*, San Francisco: ICS Press, pp. 229–258.

Gordon, H. S. (1954), 'The Economic Theory of a Common Property Resource: The Fishery', *Journal of Political Economy* **62**, 124–142.

Government of Lesotho (1980), *Range Management and Grazing Control Regulations 1980*, Legal Notice No. 39, Government Printer, Maseru.

Hardin, G. (1968), 'The Tragedy of the Commons', *Science* **162**, 1234–1248.

Helland, J. (1982), 'Social Organization and Water Control Among the Borana', *Development and Change* **13**, 239–258.

Hirshleifer, D. and E. Rasmusen (1989), 'Cooperation in a Repeated Prisoners' Dilemma with Ostracism', *Journal of Economic Behavior and Organization* **12**, 87–106.

Hunter, J. P. (1987), *The Economics of Wool and Mohair Production and Utilization in Lesotho*, Institute of Southern African Studies Research Report No. 16, National University of Lesotho and Research Division Report RD-R-80, Ministry of Agriculture and Marketing, Roma and Maseru.

Kituyi, M. (1990), *Becoming Kenyans: Socio-economic Transformation of the Pastoral Maasai*, ACTS Press, Nairobi, Kenya.

Kronman, A. T. (1985), 'Contract Law and the State of Nature', *Journal of Law, Economics and Organization* **1**, 5–32.

Lane, C. R. (1991), *Alienation of Barabaig Pasture Land: Policy Implications for Pastoral Development in Tanzania*, Ph.D. dissertation, University of Sussex.

Lawry, S. W. (1989), *Tenure Policy and Natural Resource Management in Sahelian West Africa*, LTC Paper 130, University of Wisconsin, Land Tenure Center, Madison.

Lawry, S. W. (1988), *Private Herds and Common Land: Issues in the Management of Communal Grazing Land in Lesotho, Southern Africa*, Ph.D. dissertation, University of Wisconsin-Madison.

Little, P. D. (1987), 'Land Use Conflicts in the Agricultural/Pastoral Borderlands: The Case of Kenya', in P. D. Little and M. M. Horowitz, eds., *Lands at Risk in the Third World*, Colorado: Westview Press, Boulder.

Machobane, L. B. B. J. (1990), *Government and Change in Lesotho, 1800–1966*, St. Martin's Press, New York.

Mair, L. (1977), *Primitive Government*, Indiana University Press, Bloomington.

McCabe, J. T. (1990), 'Turkana Pastoralism: A Case Against the Tragedy of the Commons', *Human Ecology* **18**, 81–103.

McCay, B. and J. M. Acheson (1987), *The Question of the Commons: The Culture and Ecology of Communal Resources*, University of Arizona Press, Tuscon.

Moorehead, R. (1989), 'Changes Taking Place in Common Property Resource Management in the Inland Niger Delta of Mali', in F. Berkes, ed., *Common Property Resources: Ecology and Community-Based Sustainable Development*, London: Belhaven Press.

National Academy of Sciences (1986), *Common Property Resource Management*, National Academy Press, Washington, D.C.

Niamir, M. (1989), *Herders' Decision-making in Natural Resources Management in Arid and Semi-Arid Africa*, Community Forestry Note 4, Food and Agriculture Organization of the United Nations, Rome.

Ostrom, E. (1986), 'Issues of Definition and Theory: Some Conclusions and Hypotheses', in National Academy of Sciences, *Proceedings of the Conference on Common Property Resource Management*, Washington, D.C.: National Academy Press, pp. 597–614.

Pim, A. W. (1935), *Financial and Economic Position of Basutoland*, His Majesty's Stationary Office, London.

Quam, M. D. (1976), *Pastoral Economy and Cattle Marketing in Karimoja, Uganda*, Ph.D. dissertation, Indiana University.

Riddell, J. C. (1982), *Land Tenure Issues in West African Livestock and Range Development Projects*, LTC Research Paper No. 77, University of Wisconsin-Madison, Land Tenure Center, Madison.

Riesman, P. (1978), 'The Fulani in a Development Context: The Relevance of Cultural Traditions for Coping with Change and Crisis', Report written under USAID contract, no. REDSO/WA-78-138, U.S. Agency for International Development, Washington, D.C.

Runge, C. F. (1981), 'Common-Property Externalities: Isolation, Assurance and Resource Depletion in a Traditional Grazing Context', *American Journal of Agricultural Economics* **63**, 595–607.

Runge, C. F. (1986), 'Common Property and Collective Action in Economic Development', *World Development* **14**, 623–635.

Sandford, S. (1983), *Management of Pastoral Development in the Third World*, John Wiley and Sons in association with the Overseas Development Institute, Chichester.

Scott, A. (1955), 'The Fishery: The Objectives of Sole Ownership', *Journal of Political Economy* **63**, 116–124.

Shoup, J. (1987), *Transhumant Pastoralism in Lesotho: Case Study of the Mapoteng Ward*, Land Conservation and Range Development Project, Maseru.

Shanmugaratnam, N., T. Vedeld, A. Mossige and M. Bovin (1992), *Resource Management and Pastoral Institution Building in the West African Sahel*, World Bank Discussion Paper 175, The World Bank, Washington, D.C.

Shapera, I. (1956), *Government and Politics in Tribal Societies*, Schocken Books, New York.

Sheddick, V. (1954), *Land Tenure in Basutoland*, Her Majesty's Stationary Office, London.

Staples, R. R. and W. K. Hudson (1938), *An Ecological Survey of the Mountain Area of Basutoland*, His Majesty's Stationary Office, London.

Stiles, D. (1992), 'The Gabbra: Traditional Social Factors in Aspects of Land-use Management', *Nomadic Peoples* **30**, 41–52.

Swallow, B. M. (1991), *Common Property Regimes for African Rangelands Resources*, Ph.D. dissertation, University of Wisconsin-Madison.

Swallow, B. M. (1990), *Strategies and Tenure in African Livestock Development*, LTC Paper 140, University of Wisconsin Land Tenure Centre, Madison, Wisconsin.

Swallow, B. M. and R. F. Brokken (1987), 'Cattle Marketing Policy in Lesotho', *African Livestock Policy Analysis Network*, Network Paper No. 14. Addis Ababa, International Livestock Centre for Africa, Ethiopia.

Swallow, B. M. and R. F. Brokken (1990), 'Information and the "Optimal Control" of an African Rangelands Resource', paper presented at the American Agricultural Economics Association Annual Meeting, Vancouver, Canada.

Swallow, B. M., R. F. Brokken, M. Motsamai, L. Sopeng and G. G. Storey (1987), *Livestock Development and Range Utilization in Lesotho*, Institute of Southern African Studies Research Report No. 18, National University of Lesotho and Research Division Report RD-R-82, Ministry of Agriculture and Marketing, Roma and Maseru.

Swallow, B. M. and D. W. Bromley (1994), 'Co-Management or No Management: The Prospects for Internal Governance of Common Property Regimes through Dynamic Contracts', *Oxford Agrarian Studies* **22**(2), 3–16.

van den Brink, R., D. W. Bromley and J.-P. Chavas (1995), 'The Economics of Cain and Abel: Agro-Pastoral Property Rights in the Sahel', *Journal of Development Studies* **31**(3), 373–399.

Vedeld, T. (1992), 'Local Institution-Building and Resource Management in the West African Sahel', *Forum for Development Studies* **1**, 23–50.

Weaver, L. C. (1986), 'Planning for Grazing Associations in Lesotho', in *Proceedings from the Workshop on Grazing Associations in Lesotho*, Maseru, Ministry of Agriculture and USAID Land Conservation and Range Development Project.

Winrock International (1992), *Assessment of Animal Agriculture in Sub-Saharan Africa*, Winrock International, Morrilton, Arkansas, U.S.A.

Williamson, O. (1985), *The Economic Institutions of Capitalism*, Free Press, New York.

Young, O. R. (1989), *International Cooperation: Building Regimes for Natural Resources and the Environment*, Cornell University Press, Ithaca, New York.

[11]

Economic dimensions of community-based conservation[1]

Community-based conservation (CBC) of biological resources recently has come to be regarded as a feasible concept with which to augment or supplant traditional approaches. These older models, based on the idea that only national governments could bring sufficient knowledge and authority to the task, are now largely discredited. The traditional approaches did not work for two fundamental reasons.

First, biological resources cannot be managed by proclamation alone, and many national governments – having declared certain areas part of a system of national reserves or parks – were powerless to implement what they had declared. Governments do not 'own' what they cannot control. Lacking effective means of matching proclamations with actions, many national reserves became inviting targets for people on the very margin of survival.

The second reason for failure, which is related to the first, is that creation of such islands of biological abundance in areas often suffering from severe resource degradation offers enticements that no amount of enforcement and wardens could overcome. In a word, the incentives were clearly awry. The problem is now of far greater importance than previously. With the declaration of the 1992 Convention on Biological Diversity, the international community appears prepared to expand the nature and extent of biological reserves on a scale deemed impossible only a decade ago. The failures of the traditional model would simply be compounded many times over if it were the only institutional form on which governments could draw in implementing this expansion. Fortunately, there are alternatives, and CBC appears to be the method of choice at the moment.

Community-based conservation seems compelling because it starts from the most fundamental principle: individuals will take care of those things in which they have a long-run, sustained interest. National preserves – the traditional model – violate this principle by driving a legal and bureaucratic wedge between local people and the resource base in need of protection. Community-based conservation seeks to locate arenas of mutuality between those who want biological resources to be managed on a sustained basis and those who must rely on these same biological resources for the bulk of their livelihood.

The major problem to be addressed in community-based conservation is how to structure the working rules of such resource-management regimes so that local people have a robust and durable interest in the conservation of biological resources of interest to the larger international community. The answer, in brief, is to be found in the structure of entitlements (often called property rights) and in the constellation of incentives and sanctions that emanate from them. If we think of these new entitlement structures as resource-management regimes, then the incentives and sanctions constitute the working rules of those regimes. These working rules define domains of choice for local people as participants in the sustainable management of biological resources. The economic problem is to craft working rules that are incentive-compatible for CBC.

Incentive compatibility

The economic dimension of CBC centres around the search for new institutional arrangements that will align the interests of local people with the interests of non-local – and often distant – individuals and groups seeking sustainable management of particular ecosystems. In essence, we seek new resource-management regimes in which the interests of those living in such regimes coincide, to the greatest extent possible, with the interests of those living at some remove.

Economics usually is thought to concern markets, prices, or the buying and selling of particular objects. While these are indeed part of the economist's domain, at the most fundamental level, economics is about particular behaviours in response to specific choice domains. Economists are interested in the choices that people make, given the context in which individuals find themselves at a particular moment. The economic dimension of CBC is precisely concerned with the context of choice throughout a hierarchy of biodiversity conservation interests. The connection between behaviour and reward is found in incentives – grounded in entitlements – that define choice domains for individuals.

If the relatively rich in the industrialized North are able to enjoy the benefits of biodiversity conservation at scant individual cost – while restricting the choice domain of poor individuals in the tropics, where a particular ecosystem such as Rondônia in Brazil has attracted international attention – then incentive problems abound. This situation is unworkable because the interests of local people – on whom the fate of ecosystems depends – are discounted relative to the interests of those who care for the ecosystem but not for its human inhabitants.

Incentive compatibility is established when local inhabitants acquire an economic interest in the long-run viability of an ecosystem that is important to people situated elsewhere. The interests of locals need not be identical to those of the international conservation community; sustained conservation of local resources requires only that the local stake in conservation becomes somewhat greater than in the previous resource-use patterns deemed inimical to conservation. Such ecosystems represent benefit streams for both parties: those in the industrialized North who seek to preserve biodiversity and those who must make a living amid this genetic resource.

The world's genetic resources are under constant threat from a range of land-use changes and economic pressures. This threat is the more serious because of the failure of existing institutional arrangements to guide and control individual and group behaviours with respect to these genetic resources. Recent international efforts, including the 1992 Earth Summit held in Rio de Janeiro, suggest that many of the world's leaders are prepared to make a commitment to the preservation of biodiversity. New policy initiatives with respect to biodiversity conservation are being pursued on several fronts. These initiatives must be understood as only part of a larger institutional transformation necessary to affect the way in which local people use and manage genetic resources.

Public policy with respect to community-based conservation of biodiversity consists of three components: the goals or intentions of CBC; a structure of new institutional arrangements predicated on these intentions; and a constellation of enforcement mechanisms that will induce compliance with the intentions. That is, policy is more than just the expression of abstract goals by national leaders. Policy must be seen as a coherent process whereby goals are transformed into meaningful operational strategies and programmes that will render them attainable. The starting point of any (new) policy is the intention(s) that it aims to achieve.

Figure 1 depicts what can be called the policy hierarchy. At the policy level, goals and intentions are discussed and articulated. From these flow a set of institutional arrangements with the purpose of creating organizational structures – or modifying existing organizations – so that various aspects of biodiversity conservation can be improved. The Convention on Biological Diversity can be regarded as the policy declaration, which is then followed by specific rules to be followed by the contracting parties. These rules – the new institutional arrangements – will call for the designation of protected areas, guidelines for management of those areas, the restoration of degraded ecosystems, and systems to regulate the use and management of such areas in the future.

These institutional arrangements hold organizational implications, as the figure suggests. Some governmental agencies will be created, while existing agencies will be given new writs with the intent of carrying out the policy intentions of the convention. In Figure 1, this is the organizational level. Here, a lower level of institutional arrangements will be formulated. Examples include particular criteria for designating certain areas worthy of protection, management guidelines for allowable uses and activities in those areas, and so on. These second-level institutional arrangements then bear on behaviours at the operational level. At this level, individuals interact with each other – and with environmental resources – in a way that is either conducive to sustainable management of such resources or leads to their destruction.

Finally, Figure 1 illustrates the feedback that is part of any policy process. The patterns of interaction among local people – their economic activities, land-use practices, and individual and collective use of the local ecosystem – result in particular outcomes that may or may not be conducive to sustainability of the ecosystem. Mechanisms and procedures for assessing outcomes against the declared purposes of conservation policy, and allowing correction and modification when discrepancies arise, must be in place. That feedback can pertain to either the policy or the organizational level. At the policy level, perhaps the goals and intentions were unrealistically optimistic or too vague. At the organizational level, perhaps bureaucratic turf battles have precluded the development of a coherent policy-implementation framework.

Regardless of where in the hierarchy the fault lies, the fundamental problem is that the institutional arrangements defining choice domains at the operational level are inappropriate. That is, the resulting patterns of interaction fail to bring about individual and group behaviours that will result in conservation of biological resources.

These points suggest that local individuals can become part of a system of community-based conservation if they are given an interest in the benefit stream flowing from the newly managed biological domain. However, it is important to pay particular attention to the relationship between systems of property rights and economic incentives.

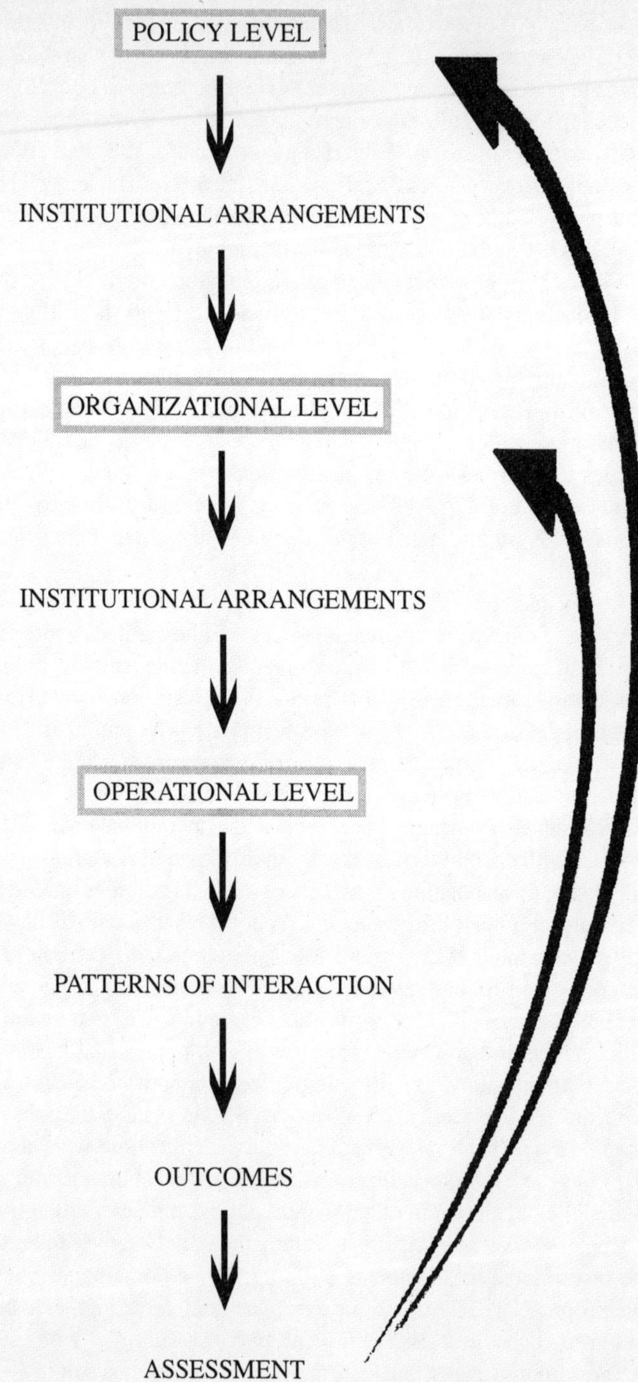

Figure 1 The policy hierarchy

Entitlements

A fundamental issue is how institutional arrangements in general, and systems of property rights in particular, constitute an essential structure of economic incentives that operate on individual economic agents. Customarily, the outcomes of market processes – prices, quantities, and costs – are regarded as 'economic incentives' while the legal arrangements – property rights – are regarded as 'constraints' on economic behaviour. This view has the twin disadvantages of being both incomplete and comprising a fallacy of composition. Prices and costs are simply artefacts of the prevailing institutional structure that indicates which factors of production must be paid for and which can be obtained free of charge. Hence, 'cost' is a function of underlying legal arrangements.

The economic incentives at the operational level in Figure 1 are embedded in a particular legal structure. If property rights are unclear or perverse, then human action that degrades the environment will proceed without any mechanism for making the responsible party bear the costs of such behaviour. The destruction of local habitat in the trekking regions of Nepal illustrates this problem. Similarly, poaching of wildlife in southern Africa reflects incentives at the operational level, which programmes such as 'Campfire' seek to rectify. The prevailing property structure therefore forms the very core of economics – and therefore of the incentives that individuals face (Bromley, 1989, 1991).

In the language of property relations, we say that current resource users stand in a position of privilege with respect to the interests of those who care about biological resources. This means that resource users are free to disregard the costs their actions impose on others. Under the prevailing legal set-up, those who care about biological resources have no rights.

In Madagascar, the logging of timber threatened the habitats of the golden bamboo lemur and the greater bamboo lemur (Wright, 1993). Under the prevailing legal set-up, loggers were free to disregard the costs imposed on those who hoped to protect the lemur's habitat. In other words, both the government and the loggers dismissed as unimportant the interests of those who care about the lemur. The loggers and those who care about habitat preservation were defined by the legal correlates of privilege and no rights respectively. Loggers were free to harvest timber at the lowest possible cost of those things for which they must pay: labour, fuel, machinery, permits, operating capital, and the like. For the loggers, the associated habitat was not a resource, but merely an impediment to the expeditious removal of timber.

The legal structure, in this way, defines what constitutes a resource. The legal system (and the embedded property regime) creates incentives for behaviour through its recognition – or non-recognition – of what is a 'cost'. The destruction of genetic resources in the vicinity of logging was not a 'cost' to loggers because the prevailing legal relations failed to force the government to regard them as such. Therefore, changes in property regimes can offer fundamental changes in the economic incentives for loggers and others whose behaviours hold important implications for the world's biological resources.

The essence of the Ranomafana National Park Project was redefinition of the legal relations between those who saw only the forest's trees and those who saw the forest as habitat for a complex of biological resources. Under the new legal regime –

Ranomafana National Park – loggers face vastly different incentives. These different incentives flow inexorably from a different legal structure. The loggers now have a duty to protect genetic resources on pain of financial sacrifice, and those who care about biodiversity conservation have a right to expect careful treatment of the area's biodiversity. Ranomafana National Park is simply a new legal regime for resource management.

Community-based conservation is an effort to assign rights and duties to local communities so that they behave in certain ways with respect to particular biological resources. The rights come in terms of the secure expectation that local management in the interest of biological conservation will be rewarded in some way. The duties come in terms of the obligations that local groups agree to undertake in order to reap the benefits of biological conservation.

These rights and duties concern who is excluded from use of the biological resource, how that exclusion will be defined, monitored, and enforced, how the group will create new rules when circumstances dictate, and how the group will interact with external bodies – both national and international – in redefining rule structures. These rules, and the rights and duties of which they are a part, constitute the necessary conditions for the existence of the new resource-management regime. The management of that regime is then defined by a secondary set of rules that indicate acceptable behaviour on the part of all who use the biological resources, procedures for assuring compliance with the management rules, criteria for deciding when the existing rule structure no longer serves its purpose, and procedures for changing the constellation of management rules.

In the international sphere, when we say that a particular nation has rights over its biological resources, it means that others – whether individuals or nation-states – have duties with respect to those biological resources. The Ranomafana National Park is a perfect example of international collaboration in the redefinition of legal regimes over biological resources.

The international Convention on Biological Diversity aims to bind nation-states together in a structure of quasi-right–quasi-duty relations that will carry the force of moral – if not legal – authority. The governments of various nations will have a moral commitment to protect biological diversity within their sovereign territories. The critical missing element, of course, is an ultimate authority that will prevent nation-states, having accepted the conditions of the convention, from defecting. Long-run compliance, however, might be secured through a number of means including changes in foreign economic assistance, trade sanctions, or withholding of other 'benefits' of the international community (Young, 1989).

These and other issues will require careful analysis if the international community is to succeed in crafting durable and incentive-compatible means for managing the world's biodiversity on a sustainable basis.

Economic incentives

In biological conservation, a fundamental problem is understanding the critical interrelation between the interests of individuals, groups, and national governments as manifested in behaviours with implications for the world's genetic resources. Behaviours, informed and driven by interests, are mediated through various property regimes that entail prospects of perceived gains and losses for various agents in the system. In brief, individuals and governments face incentives for certain behaviours. Some of these are often thought to be economic in nature, but rarely are incentives regarded as legally based. As the foregoing makes clear, however, economic incentives cannot exist without predication upon some legal relation.

If the destruction of biological resources – by virtue of the legal arrangements – is of no consequence to the responsible party, then there is no incentive with which to encourage greater care in preventing such damage. On the other hand, if the legal regime shifts, so that parties responsible for resource destruction are also responsible for compensating those harmed, the economic incentives shift dramatically as the potentially responsible party now contemplates the financial implications of the required compensation payments.

Economic instruments for biological conservation cannot be regarded in isolation from the legal regime that makes those economic instruments both relevant and binding to economic agents. A situation in which those who cause destruction of genetic resources stand absolved of compensation requirements is the very essence of a perverse economic incentive. The perversity can be corrected not by finding some more clever economic instrument, but by changing the legal regime within which the particular economic instruments are embedded. A shift from a legal situation of privilege to one of duty for polluters is precisely the necessary first step in rectifying perverse economic incentives.

The challenge of community-based conservation is to create mechanisms for articulating values in biodiversity conservation and then permit those values to be manifested in incentive-compatible policy instruments. Finally, compliance procedures must be implemented to ensure that conservation actually results. CBC programmes with any hope of success will contain all three elements.

Facilitative policies build on the existing conservation tendencies of individuals living among valuable biological resources. Such policies are pertinent when the interests of the local community coincide with the interests of those who seek to conserve biological resources. Here, CBC could succeed if the policy process simply reinforced certain pre-existing tendencies among the local population. 'Campfire' discusses an effort to align the interests of local individuals in Zimbabwe with enhanced prospects for biological conservation. Programmes such as 'Campfire' seek to give local inhabitants a stake in the sustainable management of a range of ecological resources. Kakadu National Park in Australia, created from a combination of commonwealth and Aboriginal land, also seems to have borne this element in mind.

When the interests of local communities are not consistent with enhanced conservation of biological resources, then it will be necessary to move beyond facilitative policies to actions that appear more regulatory in nature. Where it is possible to rely on inducement of certain conserving activities, then the domain of volition is largely preserved. Where compulsion is necessary to realize conserving activities, then the domain of choice for individuals is constrained.

Inducing policies attempt to realign incentives so that individuals and groups will be more inclined to engage in CBC activities. 'Annapurna' presents one example of this phenomenon. In this case, the drastic increase in trekkers to the Annapurna region of Nepal threatens a range of biological resources. The local inhabitants had become unwitting participants in the degradation of the ecosystem as commercialization of the area proceeded unchecked. While local residents certainly benefited from the increased commercial activity, the new development path was not sustainable. The Annapurna Conservation Area Project seeks to reintegrate local individuals into decision making so that they can retain some control over their immediate surroundings. The communities undertake both small-scale conservation measures and efforts to provide alternative energy sources to preserve the area's dwindling forest resources. The intent is to reintegrate local individuals into decisions about local biological resources so that they manage those resources in a sustainable fashion. This is an example of policies that induce change in local behaviours.

Policies that compel certain behaviours attempt to force individuals to avoid actions that threaten biological conservation. The traditional approach to biological conservation – national parks, preserves, and other protected areas – is an example of compulsion in practice. The essence of community-based conservation is to replace compulsion with a mixture of facilitative and inducing approaches.

Property regimes in resource management

Two general types of property regimes are pertinent to community-based conservation programmes. The first (and traditional) way in which biological resources are protected is by creating national parks or national reserves. This is known as a state-property regime. In these regimes, ownership and control of environmental resources rests with the state, while management is carried out through its agents (government). Individuals and groups may be able to make use of the environmental resources, but only with the forbearance of the administrative agency charged with carrying out the wishes of the larger political community. The state may either manage and control the use of state-owned environmental resources directly, through government agencies, or it may lease the resources to groups or individuals, who are then given usufruct (use) rights for a specified period of time. In the extreme, state-property regimes result in the complete eviction of those with customary-use rights.

State-property regimes remove most managerial discretion from the user and generally convey no long-run expectations in terms of tenure security. To be successful, such regimes require governmental structures and functions that can match policy pronouncements with meaningful administrative reach.

The conservation community seems divided about the record of such regimes. A state-property regime is an example of compulsion. Those who live in or near such areas are generally prevented from using most parts of the local ecosystem. One graphic illustration of this is found in Amboseli, where such exclusion certainly does not appear to be conducive to aligning the interests of the Maasai with long-run conservation in Kenya.

Recently, buffer zones have been established around some biological reserves. These buffer zones still operate as examples of state-property regimes, with the provision that certain uses are allowed. These are still basically compulsory regimes, with strict rules originating outside the group of locals prescribing acceptable resource-use patterns and rates.

While buffer zones were thought to solve the enforcement problems associated with the artificiality of preserves, the solution is only partial. The next logical step is to recognize that conservation may be best enhanced if local people can be incorporated directly into the ecosystem as part of the management regime. Indeed, at the extreme, conservation is often enhanced to the extent that local people can be vested with a long-run interest in resource management.

Two approaches can be pursued. The first, as illustrated by Kakadu, is to create a state-property regime on lands that are acknowledged to belong to local people. Kakadu National Park in the extreme north of Australia encompasses both Aboriginal land (under lease) and commonwealth land. Along with this joint ownership of land, a system of joint decision making governs many aspects of park use and management. Under this co-management arrangement, local people become an integral part of the structure of resource use.

Where this option is not available, it is possible to develop an alternative ownership regime that gives locals a stake in the future benefit streams arising from the ecosystem. This ownership structure would resemble what we call a common-property regime. Of course many common-property regimes around the world have been destroyed as a result of the relentless march of 'modernization' and individualization. However, as suggested earlier, the essence of a common-property regime is that it strives to get the incentives right in a most fundamental way. Granting ownership rights to a group of local inhabitants and allowing them to craft a set of management rules for controlling use of their biological resources potentially resolves much of the conflict of interest that attends the preservation of local biological resources.

The literature concerning the feasibility of common-property regimes is broad (Bromley, 1991,1992; McCay and Acheson, 1987; Ostrom, 1990; Stevenson, 1991). Much of this literature addresses the robustness of common-property regimes against competing claims from those outside the group of co-owners. As with private property, a common-property regime requires the willing legitimacy of the political hierarchy in which it is located. Private property would be nothing if the owner(s) did not have the capacity to call upon some authority system to enforce the sanctity of the regime. The same condition of authority also must exist for common-property regimes if they are to survive.

Is the legitimacy of that ownership drawn from the community or the nation-state? The answer hinges on the question of who the local community turns to when the legitimacy of its claim is challenged by outsiders. Arguing that legitimacy rests with the locals when the very security of the local natural resource is under threat from others who covet its bounty is not enough. Community claims address only the origins of the ownership interest of local people, not how that property right is to be upheld against potential incursions by others.

Whether we like it or not, the only authority available for that task is the nation-state and its government. Indeed, as suggested elsewhere, the breakdown of many common-property regimes is traceable to the fact that the nation-state regarded local communities as politically marginal and therefore not worthy of the effective protection that only the state can provide. There are no rights in a state of nature; rights only exist in the presence of an authority system that agrees to protect, with violence if necessary, the interests it finds legitimate. Individuals effectively have only those rights that the nation-state agrees to protect with its monopoly on coercion. The protection brought to those interests by the state consists of duties for non-owners. Only with effective duties assigned to others can rights exist (Bromley, 1992, 1993).

The community reserves of the Peruvian Amazon appear to meet this condition of external legitimacy for the common-property regime and the internal legitimacy for the rule-making authority of the group. The government acts as an authorizing agent for these management regimes but seems to rely on the local inhabitants to operate the regime. When resource degradation becomes too severe, non-residents are precluded from extracting resources. This decision apparently is the foundation of a renewed commitment on the part of locals to manage the resource base in a sustainable fashion.

The impetus for the community management scheme came from locals reacting to the extraction of resources they regarded as their own. With external legitimacy recognized by the nation-state, the way was clear for the locals to undertake the hard work of crafting improved management rules conducive to enhanced resource management over the long run.

As with a number of similar situations, in formulating policies for CBC, careful analysis of the feasibility of rehabilitating these common-property regimes is essential. However, it is necessary to recall that policy requires more than good intentions. Coherent policy also requires rules of implementation and rules of enforcement. The history of destruction of common-property regimes is dominated by failures of rules and by failures of enforcement mechanisms.

A true common-property (*res communes*) regime requires, at a minimum, the same thing as private property: exclusion of non-owners. While property-owning groups vary in nature, size, and internal structure across a broad spectrum, they are all social units with definite membership and boundaries, certain common interests, some interaction among members, some common cultural norms, and their own endogenous authority systems. Tribal groups and subgroups, subvillages, neighbourhoods, small transhumant groups, kinship systems, or extended families are all possible examples of meaningful authority systems within common-property regimes. These groupings hold customary ownership of certain natural resources such as farmland, grazing land, and water sources. In the absence of authority, there can be no property. When the authority system breaks down, the coherent management of environmental resource use can no longer exist. Under these circumstances, any property regime – private, common, state – degenerates into open access (*res nullius*).

The various property regimes elaborated upon here reflect economic conditions of land and related environmental resources, as well as the social overlay that reflects how those resources are to be used for the benefit of individual users – and those individuals from outside the immediate area who seek to influence how local biological resources are used and managed.

An essential element of biological conservation is to determine which areas should remain in the freehold domain, which areas should remain state property, and which areas should be restored to common-property regimes. In some places, national governments will need to declare their commitment to owning and managing certain critical areas. Existing national parks and preserves fit this notion. But state-property regimes may be created, as well, where several competing user groups are unable to reach sustainable agreements among themselves.

In other areas, governments only need to ensure the external legitimacy of boundaries, thus allowing the evolution of common-property regimes over large expanses of important biological resources. Note that national governments may be required to protect new common-property regimes from intrusion by others, but they can then delegate management to the users themselves. Under this assured boundary protection, co-owners are presumed to be able to innovate institutional arrangements for managing natural resources on a sustainable basis. This management, in addition to concern for the nature and extent of natural resources use, also would be concerned with mobilizing and implementing investments in these resources. Such investments, in all probability, would constitute joint property among the co-owners of the regime.

Governance issues in community-based conservation

Community-based conservation strategies will be successful only with recognition that the local management entities ('communities') are themselves embedded in a political regime that may be indifferent to conservation and the role of local communities in that process. At this stage, national governments must be presumed to have agreed to a programme of enhanced biological conservation and that the problem is how to devolve that new (or enhanced) interest down to the local community, whose actions will be central to successful conservation outcomes. In other words, national governments will face the problem of determining the best locus for engaging in a particular policy discussion about biological conservation, formulating particular policies that will bring about enhanced biological conservation, and implementing the working rules and enforcement mechanisms associated with a particular policy.

First, there is a need to develop criteria whereby the policy dialogue on biological conservation can be properly located in a vertical dimension. The failure in most environmental policy discussions is that they do not start with a logic for identifying which level in the political hierarchy is the necessary and sufficient one for choice about particular environmental matters. 'Political hierarchy' here means the national level, the regional level, and the local level. Most environmental policy fails to articulate a coherent reason why practically all policy dialogue is presumed to be at the national level, while the regional and local levels are ignored or assumed to be so subservient to the national level that no conversations need be held there. This failure led to the traditional approach, in which national governments presumed that they were the only entities competent to protect and manage biological resources.

The task of developing criteria that will help national governments understand that some environmental issues are best addressed at the local level, some at the regional level, and still others at the national level is still before us. Given the extreme sensitivity to local and regional concerns in many nations, these issues will continue to plague the development of conservation policy.

The second imperative is to understand the proper role for executive, legislative, and judicial decisions. Of course, nations differ in how these three functions work and interact, and it is not possible to develop, in great specificity, a template that works in all places. In spite of this, some general conceptual work to help explain the logic of certain actions being determined in an arena of bargaining (the legislature), certain actions being determined in the arena of administrative rules (the executive), and other actions being determined in the arena of conflict resolution (the judiciary) clearly is needed.

The interplay between the legislative domain and the executive domain is often the most troubling. Legislatures are given to grand proclamations that are passed to executive branch departments for implementation. Before these sweeping goals can be implemented, however, they must first be rendered coherent and meaningful. What, for instance, does a legislature mean by 'protecting' biodiversity? What does a legislature mean when it declares that it wants the nation's waters to be 'clean'? And how does it perceive 'sustainable development'? Executive branch agencies are left with the difficult task of giving content to such broad declarations.

Similar problems will arise under various programmes to promote community-based conservation. Which aspects of local ecosystems will become the focus of conservation? Which levels of use will be regarded as consistent with conservation? Who will arbitrate disputes over decisions that have been taken? Policy development for community-based conservation must include careful attention to these matters.

As a third point, most environmental discussions and environmental programme proposals are silent on the critical link between individual economic agents and the new policy environment intended to change individual behaviours. Predictions about the good things about to happen as a result of a particular programme leave out the role of the individuals whose large and small behaviours – which must be modified as a necessary condition for change – led to the current undesirable situation.

The relationship between the individual economic agent and the state usually is treated as a box into which new programmes are dumped. By assumption, behaviours will be instantly modified, so that a better environment automatically results. Unfortunately, there are at least two forms of slippage in this policy. First, its makers often fail to understand the primary causes of environmentally destructive behaviours, and so the presumptive corrective policy instruments are ineffectual or miss the mark. Second, policy-makers too commonly assume that compliance with the new policy will be immediate and total.

Policy-makers need some guidelines that help them see the critical role of incentives in inducing compliance at minimal cost. Merely passing laws or developing administrative rules can be trivial and often counterproductive if compliance does not follow. Indeed, most environmental problems arise not from the absence of laws, rules, guidelines, and mandates but, rather, from the fact that individual economic agents can ignore those strictures with impunity. Often, a nation does not need more laws or rules, only smarter laws and rules that are cunning in their effect. Cunning rules induce different behaviour in ways that minimize the individual's interest in cheating. In economic terms, cunning rules are incentive-compatible rules.

Finally, we come to the problem of deciding a logical sequence of steps. A meaningful programme of biological conservation requires criteria for identifying problems that require immediate attention, those that can be addressed next, and, finally, those that do not currently represent a serious threat to the society under consideration. The great need here is development of environmental assessment criteria that are not dependent upon the disciplinary composition of a particular team of experts charged with conducting an assessment of the biological resources in particular places. This requires a wide range of environmental knowledge as an underpinning, but the pay-off from more comprehensive assessment seems obvious. This work must also develop criteria for deciding which problems require immediate attention, and in what form.

By way of general guidelines, care should be taken to investigate current patterns of environmental resource use in particular locales, with special attention given to management of these resources in the commercial and subsistence sectors. Development of indices of local resource degradation and an understanding of the current situation in terms of long-run sustainability will be important. Throughout, it will be essential to pay particular attention to local power structures; existing laws, rules, and customs influencing natural resources use; and household responses to these institutional conditions in terms of their survival strategies.

Helpful steps can be taken to engage local communities in a participatory process to determine desired future development scenarios. These scenarios must recognize environmental sustainability, the economic and social empowerment of local people, and the reorientation of natural resources-use regimes toward community needs and aspirations. The work should call attention to impediments to reallocating various natural resources, and it should suggest local, regional, and national mechanisms and instrumentalities with which to effect reallocation.

Individual and group access to particular natural resources must be documented and the major factors – or lack thereof – that influence that access determined. Special attention should be paid to current use patterns, the causes of resource degradation, sources of current conflicts over environmental resource use, and the institutional arrangements – rules, laws, customs – that have given rise to this situation.

For each local area, it will be essential to develop several feasible scenarios of natural resources use. These development scenarios should emphasize environmental sustainability, the economic and social empowerment of local people, and the gradual reorientation of resource use towards community needs and aspirations. Probable impediments to reallocations of various natural resources should be made and local, regional, and national mechanisms and instruments to effect that reallocation suggested.

Resource values and resource valuation

The economic approach to biological conservation is often thought to require that markets be established so that 'economic values' might be revealed. This confusion of price with value not only gives rise to disparaging jokes about the density (or arrogance) of economists, it confuses sources of value. Values, as artefacts of prevailing social norms, reside in the minds of individuals (Vatn and Bromley, 1994). Not until diamonds became associated – through clever and relentless advertising – with durable love did they acquire such 'value', thereby allowing a 'market' in which high prices seemed eminently 'reasonable' to work.

Markets do not exist to reveal true values; markets simply allow willing buyers and sellers to come together for mutual gain. The prices emanating from the market carry no normative significance in the absence of a long list of assumptions that allow us to infer, if the assumptions hold, that exchange prices reveal true social values. But if genetic resources are not to be bought and sold like loaves of bread, we need not despair that we cannot discover their true value. The social problem is not to discover 'true values' for genetic resources (for such a quest is bound to fail) but to ensure that genetic resources are managed under legal regimes that prevent their destruction at zero cost to the responsible parties. After all, if legal regimes are non-perverse, and if the potentially responsible parties are thereby precluded from making decisions about genetic resources with little financial sacrifice, then we would find rather more 'conservation' of genetic resources taking place. Is it 'enough' conservation? Who knows? But it is an improvement over the status quo in which certain economic interests are at liberty to squander valuable biological resources at no personal cost.

Values, after all, can be articulated through several mechanisms. Yosemite National Park did not need to spend its early years embroiled in some market process that enabled individuals and groups to ascertain its very considerable 'value'. Its social value was determined by intuition and reason, not by empirical observation. Economists tend to be wary of such 'political' (or extramarket) revelations of value, warning that free-riders will thereby be able to 'overstate' the value of such places in order to preserve them without actually having to pay for them. Of course, we often forget that such objections not only beg the ultimate question of what represents 'true value' but also seem to imply that markets will reveal such truth. Markets *may* reveal truth – but they may not. When irreversibilities are present, it may be prudent to take steps to avoid the small probability that our actions may set in train events leading to the disappearance of certain presumptively valuable biological resources. We call this the safe-minimum-standard of conservation (Bishop, 1978, 1980; Pearce and Warford, 1993).

Many questions on how to value resources, define policy, design property regimes, institute legal structures, decide equity, and arbitrate differences and disputes must be present at the heart of any coherent policy dialogue over biological conservation. It seems reasonable to consider a dual approach to the problem of biodiversity conservation. The first step is to move quickly to ensure that existing biodiversity is preserved; this is the short-run imperative. Next, it will be necessary to set in place legal and economic regimes that enhance long-run sustainable management of diverse biological systems. That is, the future must first be secured from destruction. Only then can we implement coherent management regimes of long-run benefit to all participants in this complex human and biological system.

To date, the Convention on Biological Diversity provides only the first component – a set of intentions or goals – of public policy. The hard part, now, is to create new institutional arrangements that will transform good intentions into modified behaviours on the part of both individuals and national governments. Articulating good intentions is the easy part and, although necessary, is very far from sufficient to ensure biodiversity conservation over the long run. Biological conservation is enhanced to the extent that we are clear about the sources of 'value' in biological resources and create institutional arrangements to recognize and distribute part of that value to those who undertake the hard work of resource management in the interest of conservation.

Two essential aspects of the value of biological conservation are implicit in the foregoing discussion. The first, called the intrinsic approach, sees value in biological resources independently of any direct use by humans. This view regards the conservation of biological resources as important in its own right without any further justification. The intrinsic approach starts from the ethical position that humans lack the moral sanction to destroy natural habitat. The second, the utilitarian approach, regards biological conservation as important because of the need to preserve the option that we may some day discover valuable products from such resources. This position is one of consequentialism and proceeds from the notion that nature is our storehouse. Biotechnology based on the extraction of genetic materials is part of the utilitarian view of biological conservation.

These two world views are not necessarily at odds in a practical sense. Indeed, both views together support the widest possible preservation or conservation of biological resources. Under the right terms, the moral position of the intrinsic value approach might well accede to the extraction of certain genetic material for utilitarian pursuits. But the essential trait of both these views is that biological resources must be conserved at almost any cost.

The problem, of course, is that the 'cost' of this preservation is likely to fall on those least able to pay. Suppose the maintenance of large reserves of genetic materials – undertaken to please a number of signatories to the Convention on Biological Diversity – requires a sacrifice in the living standards (or cultural practices) of local people. How can this new structure of imposed rights and duties be made to seem fair to the locals who must bear much of the cost of biodiversity conservation? A more subtle 'cost' arises when local people, who may have nurtured a particular genetic complex, fail to enjoy the enormous economic wealth that arises from commercial application of genetic resources. How can the extraction of genetic material be conducted so that those who 'created' this particular genetic complex will share in the future income stream from its widespread use?

We have here an economic problem with two distinct components. The first concerns the potential benefits from ecosystems that are maintained in their 'natural' state against the onslaught of 'development'. In other words, indigenous peoples must be compensated for the reduced level of economic and social well-being that maintaining particular ecosystems in their 'natural state' may necessitate. The second concerns how local people might share in the benefits. This involves developing contracts with the protectors and managers of indigenous ecosystems with the prospect of future pay-offs from commercial development of local materials. Clearly, the two aspects of the problem are not unrelated. Part of the potential compensation from the simple act of sustained management may well be the probability of a significant windfall from the commercialization of genetic materials it has preserved. I call these the economics of forbearance and the economics of serendipity.

The economics of forbearance

The economics of forbearance refers to resource-management regimes crafted to manage local ecosystems on a sustainable basis. The word *forbearance* is appropriate for the simple reason that the choices indigenous communities make in favour of conservation may relegate them to a lower level of economic 'development' than otherwise might be possible. Sustainable management of important ecosystems does not automatically sentence communities to relative penury, but the presumption is necessary in order to anticipate possible threats against the resource base.

In such instances, we must imagine two possible developmental trajectories for local communities and reckon the difference in economic well-being arising from the one that is imposed from the outside in the interest of biological conservation. As previously mentioned, when relatively wealthy inhabitants of the industrialized world impose developmental trajectories on poor peoples in the agrarian tropics, incentive compatibility suffers severe distortion. The incidence of benefits and costs from this situation is not only inimical to durable conservation behaviour in the local area but manifestly inequitable. Cost-sharing schemes to remunerate local 'managers' of externally valued ecosystems are essential on pragmatic grounds, as well as on grounds of simple equity.

The economics of serendipity

Particular ecosystems, managed on a sustained basis by indigenous peoples, occasionally produce natural resources or genetic materials that give rise to prodigious wealth for the party able to control the associated income streams. The economics of serendipity refers to the need for careful institutional crafting to ensure that local groups enjoy the fruits of commercial developments arising from locally produced genetic materials.

As a model, we might consider fashioning such income-sharing schemes along the lines presently used in the extraction of hydrocarbons, plus a bonus for the embedded effort that has gone into the development of that genetic resource. Note that fossil fuels are entirely passive with respect to the local community, while genetic materials must be understood as the wilful product of human action and choice. The Lockean idea of acquiring some presumptive claim to an income stream from the expenditure of labour is pertinent here. Royalty schemes prevalent in the fossil-fuel business therefore represent a minimal approach to compensation of local resource managers.

Conclusions

The economic dimension of community-based conservation seeks to emphasize the critical role of incentives operating on those who will have the responsibility of resource management and on those who insist – from their distant material comfort – upon conservation of biological resources. The incentives must be right at the community level before indigenous peoples will knowingly enter into such agreements. Getting the incentives right at the international level, so that those who declaim the wonders of biological conservation are not absolved of the financial responsibility conservation implies, is equally important. After all, celebrating the wonders of biodiversity preservation is cheap and facile if no costs are thereby incurred. It is doubly disingenuous if the declaimers stand to reap untold wealth through the careful marketing of derivative products made possible by the sweat and forbearance of the unseen poor.

Within the nation-state, community-based conservation must be seen as an essential reform in nations' environmental policies. At the most fundamental level, programmes to enhance CBC necessarily locate different rule-making powers at different levels (at the centre, at the regional level, at the local level) in a national system. Emphasis must be given to the implied organizational structure and institutional dimensions of environmental policy in general and land-use policy in particular.

The international community can facilitate community-based conservation to the extent that the citizens of the industrialized North are prepared to underwrite a good share of the perceived opportunity costs of widespread conservation of areas that might otherwise fall under the curse of modernism. This will require collaborative programmes with the sovereign governments in places where biological conservation is desired. Incentive problems are therefore pertinent down through the nested structure of interests. CBC will be successful only if the rules – and the incentives – are right all the way through that hierarchical system.

Note

1. The author wishes to thank the editors, Shirley Strum, David Western, and Michael Wright, and the copyeditor, Lisa Lawley, for their help in making this chapter more readable.

References

Bishop, R.C. (1978), 'Endangered species and uncertainty: the economics of a safe minimum standard', *American Journal of Agricultural Economics*, **60**, 10–13.

Bishop, R.C. (1980), 'Option value: an extension and exposition', *Land Economics*, **58** (1), 1–15.

Bromley, D.W. (1989), *Economic Interests and Institutions: The Conceptual Foundations of Public Policy*, Oxford, England: Basil Blackwell.

Bromley, D.W. (1991), *Environment and Economy: Property Rights and Public Policy*, Oxford, England: Basil Blackwell.

Bromley, D.W. (ed.) (1992), *Making the Commons Work*, San Francisco: ICS Press.

Bromley, D.W. (1993), 'Regulatory takings: coherent concept or logical contradiction?', *Vermont Law Review*, **17** (3), 647–82.

McCay, B.J. and J.M. Acheson (eds) (1987), *The Question of the Commons*, Tucson, Arizona: University of Arizona Press.

Ostrom, E. (1990), *Governing the Commons*, Cambridge, England: Cambridge University Press.

Pearce, D.W. and J. Warford (1993), *World Without End*, Oxford, England: Oxford University Press.

Stevenson, G.G. (1991), *Common Property Economics*, Cambridge, England: Cambridge University Press.

Vatn, A. and D.W. Bromley (1994), 'Choices without prices without apologies', *Journal of Environmental Economics and Management*, **26** (2), 129–48.

Wright, P. (1993), 'Ranomafana National Park, Madagascar: rainforest conservation and economic development', case study prepared for the Liz Claiborne Art Ortenberg Foundation Community Based Conservation Workshop, 18–22 October, Airlie, Virginia.

Young, O.R. (1989), *International Cooperation: Building Regimes for Natural Resources and the Environment*, Ithaca, New York: Cornell University Press.

jei JOURNAL OF ECONOMIC ISSUES
Vol. XXVIII No. 2 June 1994

The Enclosure Movement Revisited: The South African Commons

Daniel W. Bromley

The Legacy of Apartheid

As I have said elsewhere in relation to the European conquest of North America, "Private property is not necessarily theft, as Proudhon put it, but a good deal of theft has ended up as private property" [Bromley 1991, 25]. Nowhere is this more true than in South Africa.

The term "enclosure" in my title is also appropriate to the South African setting. The two great English enclosures–the first beginning in the mid-fifteenth century and continuing into the seventeenth century, and the second covering approximately 80 years near the end of the eighteenth century–entailed the eviction of tillers from the land and their replacement first by sheep and then by emerging agricultural technology. The object of attention in both these institutional transformations was the changing economic value of people on the land in comparison with other forms of agricultural technology or with new agricultural enterprises. Recall that the people being evicted were not displaced for reasons pertaining to them as individuals, but were removed by the more powerful landowning class for reasons owing to the perceived imperatives of economic change sweeping rural England. While those displaced may have taken small comfort in

---

The author is Anderson-Bascom Professor of applied economics, University of Wisconsin-Madison. *This paper was presented at the annual meeting of the Association for Evolutionary Economics, Boston, Massachusetts, January 3-5, 1994.*

this subtle distinction, it offers a profound contrast to the enclosure movement in South Africa.

There we find a history of displacement that has little to do with sheep versus men or with promising new technology. That is, those being evicted were not the incidental by-product of some economic imperatives to keep agriculture "competitive." Moreover, the evictees were not simply sent off to an urban sector that was undergoing its own economic transformation. In South Africa, the term "enclosure" must be regarded not as something that was done to land, but as something that was done to people. Indeed, those Africans evicted from areas coveted by the white population were first simply displaced. It was not until the full flowering of apartheid following World War II that they were "enclosed" in large areas euphemistically referred to as "homelands." This is an enclosure movement with a particularly venal connotation.

Finally, I have chosen to emphasize the South African "commons" because the institutional restructuring now underway will, in large measure, restore the traditional South African commons to its rightful owners. The current story concerns how that might occur.

First a little background. In 1652, Jan van Riebeeck, under contract with the Dutch East India Company to provision the growing ship traffic around the Cape of Good Hope, arrived near Cape Town. The subsequent colonial history–at least until the rise of Hitler in the early 1930s–was neither better nor worse than colonial history throughout the world. Local inhabitants were moved out of the way, killed, subjected to rather standard humiliation and deprivation, and generally abused in the fashion of the day. The aggressively Calvinist Dutch Reformed Church provided a special brand of heavenly inspiration for such treatment. But aside from this divine guidance provided by the "civil religion" of South Africa, Afrikaner colonialism and subjugation was rather like that found throughout the smaller latitudes.

But Hitler's rise to power, and the Afrikaner identification with Aryan superiority, provided serious impetus to what was to become the most complete and brutal isolation of a people in world history. Fifty years after the first seeds of apartheid were sown, and as apartheid was beginning to crumble, that troubled nation "had the widest gap between rich and poor of any country in the world for which data are available. Eighty-seven percent of its land, and 95 percent of its industrial undertakings, are in white hands" [Sparks 1991, 388]. Nor was the economic concentration only in terms of race. At that same time, more than 82 percent of the market capitalization of the Johannesburg Stock Exchange was controlled by just six conglomerates–four of whom controlled almost 78 percent of total capitalization. To say that the South African economy was created for a very few white people would not be an exaggeration.

My primary concern here is with land control in South Africa, for it is here that the clash between modernism and traditional African customs will be played out. The institutional transition in South Africa focuses on land precisely because land was the fundamental instrument of apartheid. Of course, our own country has a sad history of racial barriers. But to imagine South Africa in American terms is to miss the essence of apartheid.

Blacks were not allowed to live in the cities in which they worked. Those who worked there had to leave each evening for the squatter settlements on the urban fringe. All were required to show "passes" in order to move about. More than 18 million arrests were made for violations of the "pass laws." The residents of traditional black settlements, if found to be in areas desired by whites, were hauled off in the middle of the night. More than three million blacks were forcibly evicted from their residences–their homes were then burned and the rubble plowed under. Better known are the "homelands," where most of the nation's black population were "enclosed." More than 75 percent of the total population was forced to live on less than 13 percent of the land area. And it is the worst land to be sure. These areas, seriously overpopulated for decades and now even more seriously degraded, account for less than 3 percent of the nation's GNP.

The evolving political and economic transformation in South Africa provides economists with a rare opportunity to watch a revolution play out in slow motion. It is clear that control of the machinery of state will change in a drastic way. Blacks, who comprise approximately three-fourths of South Africa's population, have never been allowed to vote. The white governments of apartheid have ruled by acquiring slim majorities from less than 15 percent of the population. As this institutional transition proceeds, there are two important land-related issues that commend themselves. The first concerns the actual process of land redistribution to the victims of apartheid. The second concerns the content of current "ownership" by whites. We will focus, in other words, on both the winners and the losers of the current political transformation.

Redistributing the Landed Estate

There are two dimensions of land redistribution in South Africa. The first of these concerns the restoration of land to those who were displaced by apartheid. This is *land restoration*, and it will need to be addressed immediately by the new democratic government. Note that restoration addresses the past by corrective actions taken in the present. Land restoration will require the extinguishment of current title and the transfer of the ownership interest to successful claimants. I will discuss the case for compensation of current owners below.

The other dimension of land redistribution is less concerned with the past than it is with the future. Apart from the restoration process, there will be an important interest in the acquisition of housing parcels, agricultural estates, commercial and industrial locations, and other uses from which Africans have been precluded via the strictures of apartheid. This is the *land acquisition* dimension. Note that *acquisition* may take two forms.

First, it could occur immediately as Africans, now free to enter the land market, seek to acquire parcels for a variety of uses. Some of these acquisitions will come from white owners, and the market will be the means of effecting the transfer. This process, if carried out immediately, is fraught with risks since the legitimacy of the current title–pending completion of land restoration–is subject to dispute. The second component of acquisition will concern lands that will have been recently awarded to Africans under the process of land restoration. That is, once the awards are complete, others may seek to acquire those lands.

Returning to the restoration dimension, millions of black South Africans will come forward with land claims seeking the restoration of traditional areas. These claims will move through a judicial system, the outcome of which will be a decision about the restoration of specific parcels of land. The successful claims will likely fall into two classes: (1) those awards that are physically and economically impossible to honor; and (2) those awards that are possible to honor, although existing uses must be terminated.

In the former category, we have lands that are now occupied by major urban places, by reservoirs, or by major conservation areas such as Kruger National Park. Here, precise restoration of specific lands will be impossible, and so the claimants must necessarily be satisfied with compensation. This compensation could be in the form of alternative land parcels or other instruments of value—cash, annuities, or vouchers.

For those lands that can be feasibly restored, most are currently in use by others. These lands will bear two burdens—*specific awards* in which direct restoration of specific parcels to previous occupants is possible, and *replacement awards* in which alternative sites are offered as part of a compensation program. Replacement awards may also be necessary if two or more competing claimants seek the same parcel of land. Notice that *land acquisition* cannot safely proceed before the *land restoration* process because a particular parcel may become the focus of a subsequent restoration award. Land acquisition can only occur for those parcels whose provenance has been shown to be known and secure from subsequent claims.

Following restoration, land and associated improvements may move to others. The new owners of these lands could be Africans, or they could be any other individual in South Africa. Indeed it is not impossible to imagine that a white owner, displaced in the restoration process, might well purchase his original holding from the recipient of a restoration award. There also may be lands now in white commercial farms that will not be awarded as part of restoration processes but rather will move directly from white owners to black owners who wish to undertake agricultural production. These buyers will bring as-yet unspecified instruments to the rural land economy–their own cash and financing capacity, cash grants, vouchers, annuities, etc.

On the Ownership of the Landed Estate

The interesting economic questions pertain not to the judicial process of land restoration, but rather to the matter of compensation of current owners of parcels awarded to the victims of apartheid. This brings us, immediately, to the fundamental question of the empirical content of "ownership" of existing white commercial farms. There may indeed be good reasons to allow white farmers to walk away from the commercial sector with some liquidity. Some will argue that the treatment of these individuals will play a profound role in assuring potential investors in the newly democratic South Africa.

Leaving aside these larger macroeconomic considerations, what about the case for compensation to current landowners on their own terms? After all, they have served the former South African state well. They have worked hard, they have suffered the vagaries common to farmers the world over, and they have brought forth bounteous harvests. On the assumption that the new government of South Africa wishes to be more compassionate than have its predecessors, some form of *severance* recommends itself. Simple decency augurs against expropriation of the white estate without some form of compensation.

However, one could make a strong case that compensation of current owners, even if called for, is less straightforward than it may seem at first glance. First, we must note that the larger part of the current "value" of white commercial farms is merely an artifact of all of the prior taxpayer largess. Commercial agriculture in South Africa was a central part of the political and economic structure of apartheid. On this ground alone, one might surmise that the economic and political legitimacy of ownership claims within that structure are seriously undermined. To a very large extent, South African commercial farms existed for the same reason that Soviet collective farms existed–to control the political tenor of the rural hinterland and to permit the state to command the delivery of necessary food and fiber products.

Unlike its Soviet counterpart, nominal ownership of the land and machinery in South Africa was given to the farm operator. And of course, the "owner" was free to manage the estate as he wished. Yet, at the boundary of the enterprise, where the "owner" interacted with the "market," the situation became one of extreme state control. Prices were set, there were few buyers (often only one) for the output, and conditions of exchange were severely circumscribed. In return for the political protection–and the pronounced economic generosity–of the South African regime, farmers were expected to produce certain products for domestic consumption or for international markets. Inputs were heavily subsidized.

This is a useful reminder that gross institutional forms–private versus state–are often fundamentally misleading. If one ignores the nominal ownership of land and other capital, the differences between Soviet agriculture and South African agriculture are less than they may seem at first glance. Both systems owe their origins to the imperative to control the politics of the hinterland, and so both owe their operational structure to the political imperative of their creation.

The obvious question becomes: is compensation of white commercial farmers justified on economic grounds? Put somewhat differently, what is this compensation to cover? Is it to compensate them for agricultural machinery purchased with subsidized loans and totally expensed off of income in the year in which the machinery was purchased? Is it to compensate for land incorrectly brought into arable production by the availability of subsidies for irrigation and other inputs? Is it to compensate for inflated yields made possible by immoderate input subsidies? Is it to compensate for land whose value is artificially enhanced by subsidized irrigation schemes? Is it to compensate for the loss of use of groundwater–the extraction of which was made cheaper by subsidized pumps and electricity? In this case, if compensation is to be forthcoming, what adjustment is to be made if that water extraction imposed non-trivial costs on those in the black community who formerly depended upon that groundwater? Or finally, is compensation to be given white farmers for all of their hard work since undertaking to populate rural South Africa for political reasons?

On balance, there is probably a modest case in favor of some compensation for those whose agricultural estates are implicated in land restoration under a new South African government. The exact magnitude of that compensation will, however, need to be negotiated. Whatever the magnitude of compensation, there is an important issue of how it is regarded by the new government as well as by the possible recipients.

Indeed, there is a compelling case for assuring that such transfers be regarded as *severance payments* rather than as *compensation*. Compensation payments would bestow *ex post* political and economic legitimacy on the prior circumstances. That history, in which white farmers participated in the displacement and elimination of millions of Africans, is not something for which compensation can be considered morally compelling.

On the other hand, severance payments offer a clean break with the past. Such transfers to displaced whites would defuse a serious political problem for the new government. However, such payments to displaced white commercial farmers must not be allowed to get mixed up with the purchase price for the new agricultural assets under land acquisition schemes. To do so would be to strap black purchasers with debt–or needless stigma in the case of grants–to acquire back what many will regard as having been theirs in the first instance. The African community has already paid a very steep price indeed for the establishment and maintenance of the existing white commercial sector. Now to ask black farmers to pay some arbitrary "market" price–in other words, to buy the agricultural assets–so that "compensation" can be given to the instruments of their erstwhile white oppressors has little basis in economics, and even less in morality.

Conclusions

The transition to democracy in South Africa will include the restoration of the commons in that many activities will reinstate the collective use and management of the landed estate. Existing white occupants will be displaced through land restoration and land acquisition. A modest case for "compensation" of such displaced occupants exists, provided payments are seen as severance packages, not as compensation for assets taken over by the new government.

Notes

1. The term "enclosure" in England's rural history comes from the extensive individualization and subsequent hedging of the large common fields. These "great fields" had been communally plowed and pastured, but with the spread of sheep production it became advantageous to demarcate individual pastures. Hedges provided the means, and in doing so, "enclosed" the sheep in pastures. Those who imagine that England's quaint fields and hedges date back to Roman times will be disappointed to learn that most of the English countryside has looked as it now does for only several hundred years. If one wants to get a glimpse of rural England in medieval times, the large grain fields of East Anglia will offer a reasonable approximation. There the hedges have been ripped out with a vengeance.

2. It is estimated that approximately 40 percent of commercial agricultural enterprises are in financial default to the credit sector. The necessity of compensation in such cases is obviously more difficult to sustain.

References

Bromley, Daniel W. *Environment and Economy: Property Rights and Public Policy.* Oxford: Blackwell Publishing, 1991.

Sparks, Allister. *The Mind of South Africa.* London: Mandarin Paperbacks, 1991.

Oxford Development Studies, Vol. 24, No. 3, 1996

Necessity and Purpose in Chinese Agriculture: 1949–95

ZHIQUN XUE-LASCOUX & DANIEL W. BROMLEY

ABSTRACT *The evolution of institutional arrangements in Chinese agriculture is looked at through the twin concepts of necessity and purpose. Nested agency relations are examined from the state planning apparatus down through levels of village officials and individual households. The emerging diversity of institutional arrangements must be understood as logical outcomes of the pragmatic evaluation of material and institutional conditions in the Chinese countryside. This diversity shows up in the domain of property regimes in land, and in the organization of production on the land.*

1. Introduction

Since the late 1970s, a series of reforms have been carried out in the rural sectors of China, among which the development of institutional arrangements guiding agricultural production have been the most profound. The decade beginning in 1978 witnessed first, an orchestrated convergence of the various forms of the production responsibility system (PRS) into the household responsibility system (HRS), and then a second phase of autonomous dispersion of institutional arrangements within the HRS. By the late 1980s, China faced once again the problem of establishing innovative institutional arrangements to guide agricultural production.

In this paper we address the nature and extent of that institutional dispersion since the late 1980s. At one level, the changes would seem to suggest fundamental reform in the domain of "landed property rights" in China. At another level, however, they relate only to the regime of incentives operating at an interpersonal level among the millions of Chinese engaged in agriculture. While land is certainly central to agriculture, it has to be remembered that all land in China is still owned by the state. Hence to talk of changes in property rights is both to overstate the nature of reforms, and to miss the more important institutional transformations occurring in agriculture, quite apart from any affecting property rights.

A multi-level principal agent model is used to show that the institutional changes arose from the recognition of different purposes in different locations within China. While the material conditions at the village level differ significantly across the country, the interests at that level have never differed markedly from the interests at the centre, namely to secure ample production of food and fibre from an arable land base that is

Zhiqun Xue-Lascoux and Daniel W. Bromley, Department of Agricultural and Applied Economics, University of Wisconsin-Madison, 427 Lorch Street, Madison, WI 53706, USA.

among the most meagre, per capita, in the world.[1] When the term "interests" is used it is meant in the sense of purpose. In essence, the evolving institutional diversity is the logical outgrowth of variations in local material conditions operating against a rather uniform purpose up through the principal-agent hierarchy.

A household labour-allocation model is constructed to demonstrate how different combinations of purpose and material conditions (though they are also influenced by local custom) affect the selection of local-level institutional arrangements governing production regimes. Particular attention is given to the important roles played by: (1) production and marketing quotas; (2) the opportunity to produce high-valued crops; and (3) the availability of off-farm employment.

2. The Setting

A variety of rural reforms have been carried out continuously in China since 1979. The first reform package, introduced in 1979, has been regarded as the cause of the rapid growth achieved between 1979 and 1984 in all major sectors of agriculture. Between 1978 and 1983 the gross value of agricultural output grew by about 7% per year compared to an annual growth rate of 3% over the two decades prior to the reforms. Rural incomes per capita more than doubled over this same period. In 1978, per capita savings in rural areas averaged Y18, while by 1983 rural savings per capita had increased to Y60 (Bruce & Harrell, 1989). Since these results occurred immediately following the move to the HRS, so-called "decollectivization" is often said to be their cause; but the early steps in rural reform are properly regarded as a move to the PRS.

The PRS was a set of rules differing substantially from those operating under the collective era (1958–78). Institutional arrangements under the PRS initially took several forms: (1) a reduction of the size of the basic working group; (2) a decentralization of decision making in the production process; and (3) a change of distribution scheme aimed at promoting work incentives (Kueh, 1984). However, within 4 years (1979–83), the various forms prevailing at the beginning converged to one basic institutional structure that is now referred to as the HRS.

The essence of the HRS was the replacement of the production unit by the individual household as the basic unit of operation, income distribution, and accounting in agriculture. Under the HRS, cultivated land in a village was assigned to each household through contracts, typically specifying the amount of land to be cultivated, the nature and amount of inputs to be supplied by the collective, the expected level of production, an agreed quota of staple crop production to be sold to the state, the amount to be handed over to the collective and, in some cases, the number of days of labour to be contributed to maintenance of public works (Bruce & Harrell, 1989). The burden of agricultural taxation was also shifted to households. Draft animals and divisible farm equipment, previously under the possession of the production team, were also allocated to households for their use. Initially, the duration of contracts was 3–6 years.

Within this institutional structure, the distribution of arable land to households was guided by an egalitarian principle, with three popular rules of assignment. The first was distribution on a per capita base. Land of different quality or character (fertile and exhausted land, grain fields and cotton fields, seedling fields and main fields, cultivated fields close to the homestead and far away from it, etc.) in a village was divided into equal parcels, and each household was assigned a share in all types of land according to the number of people in the household. A household's contracted land thus often consisted of small parcels of different qualities and was geographically scattered.

The second method of land distribution differed from the first only in that the assignment was done on a per work force basis. The amount of land a household could contract depended on the number of household members in the work force.

The third method was based on a combination of the previous two schemes. Land in a village was divided in two parts, the subsistence field and the responsibility field. The subsistence field was assigned on a per capita basis, while the responsibility field was assigned on a per worker basis.[2] The former occupant of the land under the HRS would remain with the production team which would now be known as a village co-operative. However, households were granted conditional use rights on a certain amount of collective land and became residual claimants over their contracted land.

Until 1984 the prevalence of the HRS had caused little controversy. The system was typically perceived as being more productive than the previous institutional arrangements because it offered work incentives through the provision of a closer link between reward and effort as measured by output (Nolan & Paine, 1986; Lardy, 1986; Lin, 1987, 1988, 1992; Huang, 1993; He, 1993). After 1984, however, the alleged benefits of the HRS began to be questioned.

It was noticed that there was a serious absence of incentives for peasants to invest in, and to maintain, agricultural land. That is, use rights alone did not seem sufficient to ensure productivity over the longer term. The efficacy of the land-assignment scheme under the HRS was also questioned. The argument was advanced that the scheme encouraged small-scale farming, excessive scattering of plots and inappropriate land/labour ratios (Kueh, 1985; Wen, 1989; Bruce & Harrell, 1989). Crop output, especially in grains, stagnated after 1985.

The late 1980s, therefore, witnessed yet another wave of discussions concerning proper institutional arrangements in agriculture. After the "illusion" of having successfully concluded the previous experiments on land policies, including the 1950 land reform, the 1958 collectivization, and the 1978–83 devolution to the HRS, the search for "optimal institutions" was once again on the agenda.

Unlike in the previous nation-wide programmes, first when small-farmer agriculture was emphasized (1950), and then when collectivization was imposed (1958), this new search did not result in yet another universal solution. Research staff, and those responsible for policy, engaged in continuing disagreements and no single group was able to impose its own favoured solution on others. Dating from 1984, when the central government was unable to resolve the disagreements, and during which time it was unwilling to incur the political risk of initiating yet another standard system, *dirigisme* dissolved into pragmatism.

Local authorities were granted great latitude in the design of agricultural institutions, and local experiments were explicitly encouraged. Unlike in the initial period of the HRS, households were permitted to employ, or sell, labour for farm work. Sub-leasing was sanctioned so that the undesirable land/labour ratios resulting from the land-assignment scheme could be adjusted. The land contract period was extended for up to 15 years to promote long-term commitments to land improvement.

As a result, a wide variety of institutional arrangements for production and land use emerged in different regions of the country (Yao & Carter, 1994). Some of the systems kept the basic features of the early HRS, while others did not. The problem is, therefore, to interpret and explain this diversity in institutional arrangements.

Are some institutional arrangements better than others? Is there one optimum towards which all institutional arrangements will eventually converge once again? Will this convergence, should it occur, provide the central government with a new rationale for universal imposition?

Both the HRS, and the variety of institutional arrangements that later emerged, constitute a set of norms or rules that concern two primary issues: (1) the property relations over arable land; and (2) the organization of production activities. The two issues are clearly interrelated because the choice set of organizational forms for production is defined, to a large extent, by the rules that specify the right/duty relationships among people with respect to the use and control of land. Of particular concern here is who has access to particular plots of land, what are the conditions of access to it, and who has a presumptive right to the products from the land?

The differences in institutional arrangements embedded in property relations, and reflected in the organization of production, encompass three aspects: (1) the nature and size of the working group; (2) the organization of the production process itself; and (3) the distribution of income arising from production activities.

2.1 *The Working Group*

Production groups differ in size from a single household, to groups formed by several households, to large farms based on the whole team. The nature of the working group ranges from general household farms, to specialized farms, and ultimately to an agricultural–industrial–commercial (AIC) complex.

A general household farm refers to a single household-based production group that produces, apart from the necessary quota products, any crops suitable to the household's purpose. A household farm (or a farm comprised of several households) is regarded as a specialized farm if: (1) a majority of the labour force is engaged over 60% of the time in certain specialized work; (2) the return from the work has a share of more than 60% in the total return to the enterprise; (3) the marketed share of output from specialized production accounts for at least 80% (60% in the case of grain producers); and (4) sales revenue are at least double those of a "normal" farm in a county (Kojima, 1988).

The scale of an AIC complex in the crop sector is usually larger than a household or several households farming as a unit. In the typical case an AIC evolves out of a former state farm. These enterprises usually carry out both production activities directly, as well as related activities such as the supply of agricultural inputs and the processing and sale of farm outputs.

2.2 *Organization of Production*

Institutional arrangements vary mainly in terms of the degree of collective involvement in the production process. Some village cooperatives have assumed an active role in the provision of technical assistance, infrastructure and part of the inputs. There are two general types of active collective involvement. One takes the form of direct engagement in farming activities, and the other is through indirect subsidies. Direct engagements are usually done through unified management of some of the productive activities, and require in turn a certain level of planning at the village level. The role of the collective in decision making is usually strengthened by this type of involvement.

The exact extent of collective management in production at the national level is hard to measure. However, according to a survey carried out by the Ministry of Agriculture's Policy Research Centre, in 1200 villages that have contracted out over 95% of their arable land to households, 40% of the land was under unified plowing, 45% of irrigated land was under unified irrigation and approximately one-third of all inputs were obtained through collective supply. Moreover, 63% of the surveyed villages had their crop layout and rotations decided at the village level and 58% of the surveyed villages set plans for basic farmland construction. The interesting fact is that this kind of direct management took place, primarily, in eastern regions of the country (Sicular, 1993). The role of the collective in farm management decisions is somewhat weaker in the central and western regions, with the latter being the least influenced.

The indirect role of the collective in production is exercised mainly through targeted subsidies to households financed by earnings from village-run, and often township-run, enterprises. Both types of collective involvement in agricultural production under the HRS are supposed to have resulted from the policy of using industry to subsidize agriculture.

In areas where collectives have assumed this indirect role, villages typically provide various subsidies to households involved in agricultural production either directly on labour time, on an output basis, or indirectly through free services or subsidized input supply. The necessity of such services is of course related to the operating scale of the households. When a certain concentration of land has occurred and some households, through lease-ins or auction, have acquired large areas of contracted land, the availability of these services becomes important. A contract signed with an active village co-operative by a specialized household would, for instance, include a general commitment by the village to: (1) provide scientific and technical advice and services (with costs specified for mechanized operations); (2) supply water and electricity for particular farm operations; (3) construct warehouses to be rented to the households; and (4) provide an initial "working fund" on a "per mu" basis (Bruce & Harrell, 1989).[3]

In areas where the role of the collective in production is relatively insignificant, very few services are provided to households. Transfers from industry to agriculture are usually not carried out, and households involved in agricultural production tend to diversify their activities into high-value cash crops and food processing (Wang, 1993).

2.3 Income Distribution

Institutional arrangements for income distribution also differ across villages. In those where a standard HRS model has been in place, the distribution scheme involves the retention by the household of the output from the contracted land that is in excess of the marketed quota. The household in this arrangement is the basic unit of distribution and is the residual claimant. In villages where production is organized more centrally by the collective, individuals from the village may take up membership in the farm and receive fixed and often-subsidized wage payments. Some villages have a combined system in which households engaged in crop production are both residual claimants on their contracted land, and recipients of fixed payments from the village collective based upon their labour time in agriculture.

3. Analysing Chinese Institutional Arrangements

When addressing the question of why institutional arrangements for agricultural production differ across villages it is important to remember that institutions are the rules and norms that define individual behaviour, formulate interpersonal relationships, and govern transactions in human society.[4] Institutions determine the choices available to individual decision-making units, and therefore the outcomes of millions of autonomous economic transactions. In particular, institutional arrangements determine the distribution of costs and benefits among various economic entities (Bromley, 1989).

To understand institutional variation in China requires that we view policy as a process involving three essential levels—a policy level, an organizational level and an operational level. The policy level can be perceived as the top of a hierarchical decision making process which usually deals with questions relating to social goals (Bromley, 1989). In the Chinese context a policy-level decision is represented, for example, by the view that the means of production shall be owned not by individuals but by the collective and state.

The general goals and purposes formulated at the policy level are then translated, through a set of institutional arrangements, into organizational structures whose task it is to carry out the implications of the stated purpose and goals from the policy level. In China these are the agencies whose task it is to formulate production and procurement plans in the agricultural sector. Notice that the institutional arrangements promulgated at the organizational level then define the operating domain—or the choice sets—of individual agricultural decision-making units at the village level. That is, institutional arrangements from the organizational level determine the domains of choice of households and firms at the operational level.

Institutional arrangements which are formulated at—and operate on—the different levels of the policy process serve different functions. Between the policy and the organizational level they form the larger legal and economic environment of a society and provide a general boundary for the actions of all decision making units. These institutional arrangements serve to co-ordinate the activities of different organizations, and to allocate each organizational unit to a role-specific position in the social framework. Between the organizational and the operational level, institutional arrangements provide an incentive structure for individual decision-making units. The institutional arrangements spell out for each unit a set of horizontal and vertical relationships with others, in the form of a set of rights and duties. Norms and rules at this level also help each individual unit to formulate reasonable expectations regarding the behaviour of others, and provide for the required stability for long-term planning. In a market economy, for example, elaborate contract and bankruptcy laws both liberate and constrain the behaviour of participating parties so that each decision unit can be reasonably certain about the range of actions that others may take and formulate its strategies on basis of those expectations (Bromley, 1993).

In order to understand the emergence of institutional variation within the same sector—in this case Chinese agriculture—we argue that three factors must be considered: (1) purpose; (2) material conditions; and (3) existing institutional conditions or local customs.

3.1 Purpose

Economic agents operating under different institutional settings are led to behave differently and they will, therefore, generate varying economic outcomes, both in terms of resource allocation and income distribution. These potential outcomes play an important role in the choice of one particular institution as opposed to another. The clever policy maker will base the choice of institutional arrangements on a comparison between the expected outcomes of different institutional arrangement and those thought to be desirable. In other words, the policy maker is concerned with ends and means, or with both purpose and instruments.

The purpose of particular institutional arrangements is quite simply to serve the purpose of those in a position to define desired end states. The evolution of these working rules is a process characterized by conflicts and struggles among various interest groups, each of which bring their own idea of purpose to bear on the policy process. At a given time, the purpose of a community may include several distinct objectives, each serving the interests of one or some of the groups within it. The distribution of political power among different groups will, of course, have a strong influence on the notion of the community's purposes. Since a community, in this case an entire nation-state, is seldom an entity with homogeneous interests, the identification of purposes involves conflicts and power struggles that underlie compromise and reconciliation.

3.2 Material Conditions

The material conditions central to institutional variation can be thought of as the physical and technological features of an economy. They include the nature and availability of certain technologies, and the ecological conditions in which a technology is used to produce food and fibre. While both technology and ecological circumstances are, to some extent, the result of prior institutional arrangements, we can think of the material conditions as somewhat exogenous at any particular moment in the policy process. In a sense, this relationship between natural and man-made capital determines the feasibility of certain institutional arrangements. Irrigated rice production, to take one example, and the institutional arrangements that render it a "mode of production", is the outcome of a complex of ecological and technological artifacts. The material conditions determine the range of feasible means for achieving the objectives—or the purposes—of the policy makers.

3.3 Fixed Institutional Conditions

The design of new institutional arrangements governing agricultural production is itself influenced by a prior structure of relations that, in their totality, are somewhat fixed, and thus define Chinese society. One of these prior institutional arrangements is that land remains under the ultimate control of the nation state. Another would be the structure of rules and norms that reflect and reinforce the notion of community over individuality. Some may choose to call these aspects Chinese "culture". At this point it does not matter what nomenclature is used. It is only essential to admit that these prior institutional structures provide a matrix within which new and innovative institutions pertaining to agriculture must fit.

The interrelationships among institutions may be vertical as well as horizontal. A vertical interrelationship prevails, for example, when the rules and norms directing the behaviour of operational units are bounded and constrained by arrangements made at the policy level. Horizontal interrelationships, on the other hand, are revealed in cases where rules and norms in one community of decision-making units are dependent on those in another community. In fact, the impacts of the general institutional framework on the establishment of a particular institution have been emphasized in many analyses of different land tenure arrangements. Institutional features relating to markets in capital, labour and insurance, for instance, are frequently used to explain a particular tenancy arrangement (Bardhan, 1989).

4. Towards an Explanation of Institutional Diversity in China

Differences among villages in terms of material conditions are the most obvious preconditions for institutional variability in Chinese agriculture. China occupies an area of 9.6m km^2. Different regions in the country are exposed to very different climate and weather, and they are endowed with various combinations of water resources, topography and soil types. As a result crop production conditions vary widely.

Four major differences are relevant. First, the composition of cropping differs. Some villages are able to grow crops with high economic values, while others must be content with planting those of lower value. Second, different topographical and demographic features in the various regions pose constraints on the choice of production technique. Regions with relatively low population density and flat topography, for instance, typically have a higher level of farm mechanization (Putterman, 1993). Third, the structure of the rural economy differs as a result of interregional differences in terms of income, degree of industrialization, and the development of commercial activities. Rural agriculture-based industry is often better developed in regions with higher levels of income, hence there is greater demand for diversified food products. In some regions, township- and village-run enterprises are strong in the rural non-agricultural sector while in others private family-based enterprises have a predominant role. Fourth, rural employment structure differs. The share of rural labour engaged in non-agricultural activities differs and so do the job opportunities for rural labour outside villages.

The differences in the institutional conditions across villages lie mostly in the "horizontal" direction. In principle, all Chinese villages are subject to the same set of guidelines for institutional arrangements for land issued by the central government. However, in each village, institutions for land are also constrained by the different features in labour or capital arrangements. In some, collective agriculture has been carried out extensively in the past. Crop production and income distribution are mostly planned and organized by the collective. Consequently, farm machinery used in large-scale production has also been bought with the savings of a collective. The use of this machinery is usually guided by a scheme consistent with collective production. In other villages, where collective agriculture has been less successful, there is little collective saving, and as a result little collectively-owned or controlled machinery. Existing arrangements for the use of farm machinery would thus place different constraints on the choice of institutions for land.

In some regions, rural labour "traditionally" has a higher propensity to migrate and to take up seasonal jobs outside the village or the region. With the passage of time, farmers in such regions build up contacts with the surrounding cities and are more likely to obtain off-farm jobs within them. Different opportunities for rural labour to work outside villages would again pose different constraints on the choice of institutions for land.

Finally, we come to the least obvious inter-village differences, namely those of purpose. Since the purpose of a community is determined in a specific social and political context, which is essentially local in nature, an investigation of purpose must start in that context.

In an assessment of the unsuccessful economic performance of the socialist countries, Roemer used a three-level principal-agent model (Roemer, 1994), which is modified here to encompass a four-level structure (Table 1) to depict Chinese political reality. Notice the interdependence among various actors at different levels; the principal at each level can simultaneously be an agent at a higher level. Interdependence among economic actors results in the special interest and general well-being of each becoming mututally related. At any particular level, an economic actor, being simultaneously a principal and an agent, would identify concrete purposes according to this dual identity. The identification of purpose is then necessarily followed by the design of institutional arrangements that facilitate the activities, or transactions, necessary for

Table 1. The principal-agent structure of China

Level	Principal	Goal of the principal	Agent	Goal of the agent
1	Public (economic agents)	Increase the material well-being of each citizen and build an acceptable society	Political elites in the ruling regime	Keep position and avoid social unrest
2	Political elites	Design policy guidelines and control the general direction of the country's development	State planner	Keep positions
3	State planner	Design and carry out a concrete set of (central) plans that are consistent with the policy guidelines	Local planner	Keep positions
4	Local planner	Carry out the central plan and advance local interests	Economic agents in the local community (a part of the general public)	Maximum material well-being

the accomplishment of the purpose. These institutions assign different roles for agents, and structure the interrelationships among the differently "located" agents. In this institutional environment agents are expected—or induced—to behave in a specific way and to perform different tasks. An incentive-compatible mechanism would ensure that it is in the best interests of an economic actor to accomplish an expected (assigned) task when involved as an agent. In addition, the accomplishment of this task will become, in turn, a natural argument in the purpose of the actor in the role of a principal.

We see that purposes at different levels are interrelated through institutions. Within the hierarchy there is a certain group at each level (the leaders) possessing the capacity to design and enforce rules (institutions) to serve their own interests (their purpose).

In the post-1978 rural reforms in China, new institutional arrangements arose at three different levels—between the political élite and the state planners, between the state planners and the local planners, and between the local planners (village leaders) and the individual economic agents (households). Much of the interest here is in the position of households, though that depends on interactions within the system.

By the end of the 1970s the ruling élites came to realize the necessity of shifting the policy priority from "class struggle" to an improved standard of living. With respect to the crop sector, this general policy objective—or purpose—was interpreted in terms of higher incomes for crop producers, and greater production which would benefit all Chinese. These concerns derived from the necessity for political stability. The élites relied on both organizational changes and new institutional arrangements, primarily because at that time it was impossible to depend only on price inducements in agriculture. Rationed and low-priced staples had been provided to urban residents since the 1950s in order to sustain low urban wages and high profits for state industry. The structure of the economy resulting from this policy constituted a serious barrier to higher producer prices for staple crops.

Institutional arrangements at the first and second levels were thus characterized by a coexistence of central planning and control on crop production, though with a substantial role for decentralized decision-making in the production process. Since farmers were expected to seek higher income if provided with an opportunity to do so they were granted a certain amount of discretion. More importantly, they were granted residual claimancy over their responsibility land, and were thus encouraged to increase their own income through harder work and more care. However, since the conflict between higher farm income and low prices for staples remained unresolved, policy makers retained control of staple crop production, simply to prevent diversion of land away from lower priced items. Hence fixed production targets for key crops were maintained and became part of the contract conditions. State planners—being agents of the ruling élites—designed a set of rules for controlling and co-ordinating local production activities in order to meet targeted outputs, while new institutional arrangements were introduced to encourage producers to seek higher income through their own initiative. However, although planners at different locations in the hierarchy were interested in advancing the will of the ruling élites, the objectives followed were often quite different.

In other words, different purposes of planners at the organizational level caused endless inter-sector conflicts. State planners faced large regional differences in terms of resource endowments and general economic development. Since they had to be concerned with the total yield of each crop for the nation as a whole, it was logical for them to assign targets and tasks according to the perceived or expected capabilities of each region. Some local planners, particularly those in charge of the regions with good records in crop delivery, would thus receive higher mandatory targets than others.

The original purposes identified by the ruling élites were formalized into a set of specific tasks and targets and then delegated in different proportions to various planners at the village level. The principals at this level, being also the agents for their superiors in the hierarchy, were placed in very different positions. Some village leaders were assigned heavy quota loads. Others were less burdened with quota obligations and could consider income improvements for the village. Also, the objectives of their subordinates (mostly peasants in the village), and their abilities to advance these objectives under prevailing material and institutional conditions, were clearly different. For instance, in places where farmers could easily find higher paid jobs off the farm, village leaders had to seek means of compensation in order to ensure that enough villagers would be available to maintain quota production. In villages where off-farm opportunities were rare, village leaders did not worry so much about the income levels of their subordinates.

5. A Model of Institutional Variation and Individual Choice

In this section a simple household labour allocation model is used to demonstrate how different combinations of quota, crop types, and employment opportunities may result in different institutional arrangements for land. The mathematical version of the model is presented in the Appendix. The intuitive implications of the model are summarized in Figure 1.

Several assumptions are made. First, a household is treated as a single unit of decision-making and so intra-household differences in terms of preferences or individual objectives will be ignored. Second, it is assumed that the allocation of household

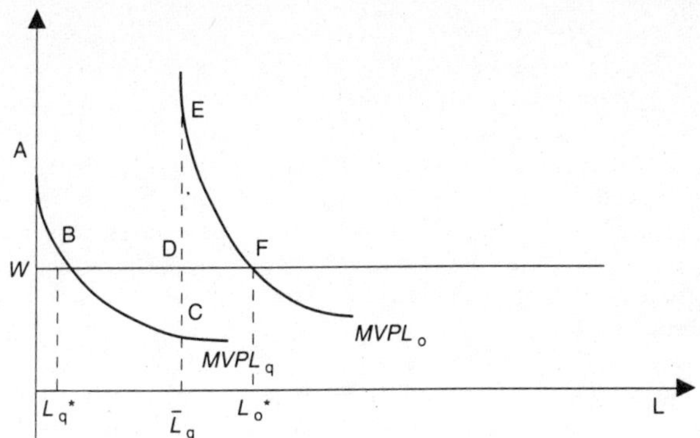

Figure 1. The basic model.

labour is motivated solely by concern for incomes. Village leaders, on the other hand, are assumed to be concerned only with the fulfilment of quota production. The combination of the two objectives gives us the village-level purpose. Third, the assumption is made that households in a village face the same material conditions (production technology and off-farm opportunities) and the same institutional preconditions (prices, duties, regulations and permissible activities). Inter-household differences in terms of preferences and labour productivity are disregarded. Fourth, we assume that the income of a typical household arises from three sources: (1) the production of a quota crop with a fixed procurement price; (2) the production of another crop with a higher price in the market; and (3) the sale of household labour to the wage sector. Fifth, we assume that crop production on the responsibility land takes only land and labour. The production function is increasing at a diminishing rate in both inputs. Finally, it is assumed that the contracted area to be devoted to crop production is just half of the total amount of the responsibility field assigned to each household.

A standard HRS in this model corresponds to the HRS before 1984, which was described earlier. We begin by ignoring inter-household differences in terms of preferences and labour productivity. The vertical axis measures the return to labour and the horizontal axis measures labour units. $MVPL_q$ depicts the marginal value product of labour devoted to quota crop production, while $MVPL_o$ to that of the "other" crop. In the latter case the origin for measurement of labour input on the horizontal axis begins from the level of labour input used in quota crop production. This point will appear later. The prevailing wage rate is w. Both $MVPL_q$ and $MVPL_o$ are downward sloping due to the decreasing marginal product of labour on a fixed amount of land. If drawn from the same origin $MVPL_o$ would lie above $MVPL_q$ for all levels of labour input.

Suppose that the amount of labour necessary for the required level of quota production is at $\bar{L}_q$. After the quota is met the household could use labour on the "other" crop and move on $MVPL_o$. In that case, bearing in mind that the origin for labour input starts at $\bar{L}_q$, the benefit to the household is measured in the conventional way by the area DFE. If the household was not constrained by a quota it would only allocate L_q^* to the production of quota crop (the income would be wBA). The requirement actually to use $\bar{L}_q$ results in the value of the marginal product (given the price received for quota crop) falling below w, tracing out the area BCD as a loss from income. In effect the the sum of the areas *w*BA, BCD and DFE represents the net benefits (costs) for the household to allocate labour on the responsibility field. The sum of these areas corresponds to the left side of equation (21) in the Appendix. It is obvious from the graph that the household would only wish to allocate labour to the responsibility field if the sum of the areas is larger than zero or in other words if *w*BA–DFE > BCD. Notice that if $\bar{L}_q$ lies on, or to the left of L_q^*, the net result of the participation in the HRS is unambiguously positive. This corresponds to the case in which the quota constraint is not binding so that the area BCD would not appear.

In that case the quota obligation imposed on the household would not prevent it from maximizing its income under a given set of crop prices and the prevailing wage rate. A standard HRS in this situation will be perfectly consistent with both the objective of income maximization set by the household and the objective of quota fulfilment set by the village leadership and various agents at higher levels in the policy hierarchy. The direct implication of this is that the quota obligation, in terms of the labour time of each household, is an important determinant for the "fitness" of a standard HRS. The principal-agent relations at various levels of the policy hierarchy lead to the incorporation of production quotas in the selection of purpose at the village level. The institutional arrangements for land will be designed in accordance with the quota requirement.

It is clear from the graph that, apart from the level of $\bar{L}_q$, the relative sizes of the areas *w*BA, BCD and DFE are also determined by the positions of w, $MVPL_q$ and $MVPL_o$. This suggests that the propriety of the standard HRS in a particular village depends directly on: (1) the prevailing wage rate in the economy of the larger area; (2) prices for the crops produced in the village; and (3) the level of labour productivity in the various crop sectors.

Here the level of w directly reflects the material conditions of the village, because the prevailing wage rate depends on: (1) the level of industrialization in the region; (2) the general level of regional income; and (3) the degree of diversification of the village economy. In some villages, the prevailing wage rate could simply be zero because there might be little possibility for rural households to be engaged in non-farm productive activities. Notice also that the wage is itself an artifact of the institutional conditions which, among others, permit rural residents to pursue non-farm activities when those are available.

Crop prices and labour productivity are jointly represented by the levels of $MVPL_o$ and $MVPL_q$. Here the existence of a quota and the fixed low prices for several quota crops clearly reveal the larger institutional setting in which economic activities take place. Labour productivity is a function of material conditions, depending as it does on the crops involved and the available production techniques. All can vary depending on the physical features and demographic characteristics of the various regions of the country.

In villages where the combinations of the above factors are such that the potential income from agriculture is low (recall the areas *w*BA, BCD and DFE in the figure), households could find it more profitable to quit farming activities and take up full-time wage jobs either in a township-village enterprise, or in nearby cities. The most direct consequence of this action would be a failure of the village to fulfil its quota, which would clearly not be a satisfactory outcome for village leaders. During the collective era, when village leaders possessed substantial administrative control on the movements of households, quota fulfilment was almost guaranteed. Now that reforms have seriously weakened such administrative controls, village leaders must resort to a suitable incentive structure in order to achieve a satisfactory outcome.

The above analysis reveals that the "fitness" of a standard HRS for a particular village is dependent on the combined effects of the material conditions, institutional conditions and local purposes. When changes occur in some, or all, of the influential factors the relative income consequences of different productive activities, and institutional arrangements for land will deviate from a standard HRS.

Depending on the specific material and institutional conditions of a village, and the level of the quota obligations, different rules and entitlement structures will be needed for the achievement of various purposes. The purpose of a village in the present case can be assumed to be the fulfilment of its quota, and the maximization of household income in the village. Production quotas assigned to each village specify the types of crops that must be produced and the amount of each obligatory crop to be delivered to the state at a fixed price. Since quota crops usually have low economic values, the village leaders must maintain substantial control over the use of land in order to ensure that households, given their income objectives, meet the quota. This explains the persistence of the right of the collective to manage the responsibility land under the standard HRS system. The households are allowed to make decisions in the production process but they are not entitled to choose crop types. In fact, no variant of the standard HRS could allow a complete delegation of decisions to the households given the institutional structure of the larger Chinese economy and its quota requirements.

Under the "correct" combination of quota levels, crop types, crop prices and wage rates, a delegation of the right to use the responsibility field to each household (and the right to the income) is sufficient for the achievement of the purpose. The combination of productivity levels and crop prices in this case would generate enough income incentive for households to take part in the standard HRS and deliver the quota. Although the income concern of a household may induce it to produce other crops than those specified by the quota, the limited rights it has with respect to its responsibility field poses an effective constraint on the range of its choices. The collective (led by the village leaders) has in its ownership bundle most of the ownership rights with respect to land. Only the right to use and the right to the income are delegated to the households. Households, on the other hand, have limited ownership rights with respect to use on the responsibility field. In particular, they may not transfer or receive income from the use right. Most of the decision making in the process of crop production is decentralized since households are residual claimants and are supposed to be responsible for the results of their production. Except for controlling the choice of crop types and the agreed delivery, village leaders have little influence on the productive activities of the households.

For a given quota, the higher the wage rate the less desirable it becomes to take part in the HRS. Similarly, for a given wage rate and *MVP* in the relevant crop sectors (and if the quota is binding), the higher the quota level, the smaller the rewards. This suggests that a standard HRS may be unsuitable for the given purpose in three situations: (1) when quota loads are excessively high; (2) when wage rates are very high; and (3) when MVP in the relevant crop sectors is very low.

The prevailing wage rate and the quota load are beyond the control of village leaders, and can be taken as given parameters. This means that if the standard HRS turns out to be unsuitable for a particular village, its leaders must raise the levels of the *MVP* through other entitlement structures or different organization of crop production. Since crop prices are not determined at the village level, the levels of the *MVP* can only be raised through production subsidies, through a rise of the marginal product of labour, or through a combination of the two. Depending on the village-specific material conditions, different property relations and production organizations can be used to administer the needed subsidies, or to achieve a higher level of labour productivity.

It is appropriate to introduce here the element of inter-household differences in labour endowments. Since households may differ in many respects, it is possible that some households may regard the standard HRS as a suitable scheme for their income maximization (the quota constraint is not binding for them), while others prefer wage jobs. However, since the village quota can only be fulfilled when each household accomplishes its share of the target, it is important for the village leaders to have all households participating in the standard HRS. If the pooling of the village land and labour could generate the required scale for using an alternative technology, and if its use could enable each household to receive a higher income than under the standard HRS (possible only when the productivity increase is very high), it will be both desirable and possible to adopt new methods. That, however, would obviously require a change in the property relations for land in the village.

The full bundle of ownership rights on land would need to be redefined by the collective (represented by the village leaders), or more rights (in particular the right to possess the use right) must be delegated to households, so that they can form a co-operative. Since most of the large-scale farm machinery associated with advanced technologies is usually indivisible, and is therefore owned collectively, the first alternative of redefining property relations seems to be more suitable. As a result of the change in property relations, crop production will also be organized differently. It should be noticed that the political power of the collective is also an important factor for the establishment of this type of property relations. Households are more likely to believe in a collective farming system in areas where collective agriculture in the past has been relatively successful. For this type of collectively organized production at the village level, it is important that the village leaders have the right to possess land, and the right to manage that land.

Even with a new technology, the total amount of labour in the village may still be excessive, relative to the total amount of land, for achieving a high marginal productivity of labour. Village leaders would need to restrict the number of people in crop production, and also create additional income-generating activities for the excess village labour force. In other words, village leaders must be able to control the villagers' access to land, and to decide which villagers are to work on the field and which are not. Village leaders must also have the right to the income from land so that they can use part of the income to support other activities if necessary. The organization of an AIC fits this type of situation quite well.

In cases where scale economies can be achieved without the pooling of resources in the whole village, leaders could seek means for achieving the required concentration of land in the hands of a few specialized households. Since, under a standard HRS, the distribution of collectively owned land is based on labour quantity, and not on labour quality or skills, households endowed with different kinds of labour may have very different perceptions about the profitability of crop production. Some households may find it more profitable to cultivate the responsibility field, and to fulfil the corresponding quota requirements, if land allocation is altered.

With an enlarged land area, for example, either the quota constraint will not be binding for such households, or the income from crop production will be larger than the income from wage jobs, even when the quota constraint is binding. For households endowed with a strong and skilful labour force, an increase in land area may raise the marginal product of labour significantly. For households less well endowed, an increase in land area may not change the comparison between income from farming activities and from wage jobs.

The task of village leaders in this situation is to create an institutional structure in which land-use rights could be transferred among village households as they wish. Households in which wage jobs are more profitable should be able to lease out their land-use right and avoid the quota associated with that land. The lease-in households, presumably those for whom the quota constraint will not be binding given a sufficiently large land area, would benefit more from cultivating the (enlarged) responsibility field and fulfilling the corresponding quota requirement (also enlarged) than from taking the available wage jobs. It is obvious that property relations would have to change in order to accommodate this kind of movement.

The right to possess on the collectively "owned" land should now be delegated to the households so that they may admit other workers to their responsibility field. As a result, property relations for the land must change accordingly. Possession of the land-use right must be included in the household's ownership bundle. So must the right to the income from the land. Households which offer to pay more for the lease-in of the use right on additional land must logically be the ones with higher levels of productivity and higher expectations on income. Compensated transfers of land use rights should, in general, enable the required concentration of use rights in the hands of the more skilful households. The collectives, however, could not interfere much in these transfers, or in the organization of production, given the relatively limited amount of ownership rights in their bundle.

6. Conclusions

Chinese agriculture is not made up of one system—it has many, in each of which institutional variability is pronounced. The reasons can be summarized in the following paragraphs.

Institutions are rules and norms that serve to co-ordinate individual actions for the accomplishment of specified purposes. Institutions establish an incentive and entitlement structure for economic activities through the definition of a cost-benefit framework for the economy, and a specification of the right-duty relationships among economic actors with respect to each other, and with respect to productive resources. Consequently, the institutional structure of an economy determines the set of attainable allocations or distributive outcomes. The rationale behind a particular set of institutional arrangements lies, most importantly, in the intended outcomes (purpose). Institutional arrangements must be understood in terms of their capacities for serving certain purposes. The allocative or distributive outcomes of a particular institutional framework constitute an important piece in the analysis of institutions, but the outcomes must be evaluated in relation to specific purposes in order to offer any hope for the understanding of institutional forms.

The diversity in institutional arrangements for Chinese agriculture is reflected both in the diversity of property relations for land, and in the different forms of production organization. Diversity must be understood in terms of the differing purposes, material conditions, and local customs and traditions in different places. While variation in material conditions may often be taken to result from natural factors (a point to be learned and accepted) differences in purposes and local customs are endogenous.

Given the current structure of the Chinese economy, with close inter-sectoral dependence and multi-level principal-agent relations, the formation of purposes at the village level is inevitably related to the purposes at the higher levels of the policy making hierarchy. The latter are motivated primarily by the interest of the political elites in maintaining the current regime. Institutional arrangements made at levels above the village define an incentive and entitlement structure in which the various villages can have different rights and duties, and in which the performance expected and required can vary. The role-specific tasks of a particular village in turn constitute a part of the village's "purpose".

Institutional arrangements for land as represented by a standard HRS are motivated, in part, by the need (as identified at the highest level of the policy—making hierarchy) to secure staple crop production and to improve the associated income levels. The income objective was achieved through incentive-boosting residual claimancy granted to crop producers, and delegation of a limited amount of decision power to the cultivators. The quota objective was achieved through the retention of most of the ownership rights in the hands of the collective—a property relation which makes it imperative for crop producers to comply with the quota plans. Institutional arrangements for land diverge from a standard HRS when the right and duty relationships specified within it fail to lead to a satisfactory accomplishment of the objectives.

The observed institutional diversity in Chinese agriculture is inevitable given the purposes and the different material and institutional pre-conditions under which the purposes must be accomplished. A proper understanding of this diversity cannot be obtained through the investigation of some universal "efficiency" property of various institutional arrangements. Rather, one must start by considering the context, since "efficiency" cannot be understood without a prior concept of purpose and necessity down through the policy hierarchy.

The nature of institutional change and dispersion, as described here, suggests that the production problems of the past had little to do with the intrinsic properties of any single system. Small-owner-agriculture could have been appropriate in some regions for certain purposes and under a certain set of customs and material conditions; so could collective farming under a different set of conditions, and for different purposes. The principal-agent structure among economic actors is an artifact of the prevailing institutional structure of the Chinese economy. Combinations of congruent and conflicting interests in different places is the result of their varied material and institutional conditions. It follows, therefore, that one would expect to find considerable diversity of institutional arrangements covering land and production relations.

The practical implication to be drawn from this analysis is that the Chinese government, as it searches for adaptive and incentive-compatible institutional arrangements in agriculture, will (and should) continue to encourage institutional diversity and resist the temptation to impose a centrally designed and standardized system for the whole country. It is more important to design a set of sound incentive mechanisms, to operate at each level of the principal-agent structure, so that the purposes at each level of the policy-making hierarchy will be reflected in each other. Moreover, institutional arrangements will, and must, continue to be structured in accordance with both necessity and purpose.

Notes

1. While the world's average of cropland (in hectares) per capita is 0.27, China has but 0.08 ha of cropland per capita. This puts it on a par with Bangladesh, ahead of Japan (0.04 ha per capita), but in the same grouping as The Congo, Djibouti, Bhutan, Israel, South Korea, Oman and Switzerland.

2. To maintain an egalitarian outcome, the contract period was often for 3–6 years, after which a reallocation of land would occur.
3. A mu is approximately one-fifteenth of a hectare.
4. A distinction can be made between institutions as norms or conventions and institutions as rules or entitlements. A few people writing on institutions have noted this difference explicitly. For a discussion of the different forms of institutions see Lewis (1969), Schotter (1981) and Bromley (1989).

References

Bardhan, P. (1989) Alternative approaches to the theory of institutions in economic development, in: P. Bardhan (Ed.) *The Economic Theory of Agrarian Institutions* (Oxford, Clarendon Press).

Bromley, D.W. (1989) *Economic Interests and Institutions: The Conceptual Foundations of Public Policy* (Oxford, Basil Blackwell).

Bromley, D.W. (1993) Reconstituting economic systems: institutions in national economic development, *Development Policy Review*, 11, pp. 131–151.

Bruce, J. & Harrell, P. (1989) *Land Reform in the People's Republic of China 1977–1988*, Research Paper No. 100, (Wisconsin-Madison, Land Tenure Center, University of Wisconsin-Madison).

He, D. (1993) Reform in land policy at the village level (in Chinese: "Cunji Nongdi Zhidu de Biange") in: *State Council's Development Centre, Land Reform in China: Proceedings of the International Conference on the Chinese Land Reform* (in Chinese: Zhongguo Nongcun Tudi Zhidu de Biange: Zhongguo Nongcun Tudi Zhidu Guoji Yantao Hui Lunwen Ji) (Beijing, Beijing University Press).

Huang, Q. (1993) A review of the Chinese land policy and the current problems (in Chinese: "Zhongguo Nongcun Tudi Zhengce de Huigu yu Mianling de Wenti") in: *State Council's Development Centre, Land Reform in China: Proceedings of the International Conference on the Chinese Land Reform* (In Chinese: Zhongguo Nongcun Tudi Zhidu de Biange: Zhongguo Nongcun Tudi Zhidu Guoji Yantao Hui Lunwen Ji) (Beijing, Beijing University Press).

Kojima, R. (1988) Agricultural organisation: new forms, new contradictions, *China Quarterly*, 116, pp. 706–35.

Kueh, Y.Y. (1984) China's new agricultural policy program: major economic consequences, 1978–1983, *Journal of Comparative Economics*, 8, pp. 353–375.

Kueh, Y.Y. (1985) The economics of the 'second land reform' in China, *China Quarterly*, 101, pp. 122–131.

Lardy, N.R. (1986) Agricultural reforms in China, *Journal of International Affairs*, 39, pp. 90–104.

Lewis, D.K. (1969) *Convention: a Philosophical Study* (Cambridge, MA, Harvard University Press).

Lin, J.Y. (1987) The household responsibility system reform in China: a peasant's institutional choice, *American Journal of Agricultural Economics*, 69, pp. 410–415.

Lin, J.Y. (1988) The household responsibility system in China's agricultural reform: a theoretical and empirical study, *Economic Development and Cultural Change*, 36, pp. 199–224.

Lin, J.Y. (1992) Rural reforms and agricultural growth in China, *American Economic Review*, 82, pp. 34–51.

Nolan, P. & Paine, S. (1986) Towards an appraisal of the impact of rural reform in China, 1978–95, *Cambridge Journal of Economics*, 10, pp. 83–99.

Putterman, L. (1993) *Continuity and Change in China's Rural Development* (Oxford, Oxford University Press).

Roemer, J.E. (1994) *A Future for Socialism* (Cambridge, MA, Harvard University Press).

Schotter, A. (1981) *The Economic Theory of Social Institutions* (Cambridge, Cambridge University Press).

Sicular, T. (1993) Ten years of reform: Progress and setbacks in agricultural planing and pricing, in: Y.Y. Kueh & R.F. Ash (Eds) *Economic Trends in Chinese Agriculture: the Impact of Post-Mao Reforms* (Oxford, Clarendon Press).

Wang, X. (1993) Case studies on land tenure systems in China (in Chinese: "Zhongguo Gengdi Zhidu de Gean YanJiu") in: *State Council's Development Centre, Land Reform in China: Proceedings of the International Conference on the Chinese Land Reform* (in Chinese: Zhongguo Nongcun

Tudi Zhidu de Biange: Zhongguo Nongcun Tudi Zhidu Guoji Yantao Hui Lunwen Ji) (Beijing, Beijing University Press).

Wen, G.J. (1989) The current land tenure and its impact on long term performance of the farming sector: The case of modern China, PhD Dissertation, University of Chicago.

Yao, Y. & Carter, M.R. (1994) *An Economic Analysis of the Property Rights Evolution in Post-Reform Rural China* (Department of Agricultural and Applied Economics, University of Wisconsin-Madison, mimeographed).

Appendix: The Household as Maximizing Agent

Given the six assumptions made in Section 5 of the paper, for any production cycle, a typical household will maximise its income:

$$M = P_q Q_q + P_o Q_o + wL_w \tag{A1}$$

where M stands for income, P_q is the state fixed procurement price for the quota crop, Q_q is output of quota crop, P_o the price for the other crop, Q_o the output of the other crop, w the wage rate and L_w the household labour time spent on the wage job.

The household faces a number of constraints. First, the technology constraint can be represented by the production functions:

$$Q_q = Q_q(L_q, T_q) \tag{A2}$$

$$Q_0 = Q_o(L_o, T_o) \tag{A3}$$

T_o stands for land devoted to other crop production and T_q for land devoted to quota-crop production. By the fifth assumption $\partial Q_q/\partial L_q \geq 0$, and $\partial^2 Q_q/\partial L_q^2 < 0$. By the sixth assumption, $T_o = T_q$ and we can treat T_o and T_q as fixed parameters for a particular household. The household also faces a time constraint:

$$L_t \geq L_q + L_o + L_w \text{ and } L_q \geq 0,\ L_o \geq 0,\ L_w \geq 0 \tag{A4}$$

where L_t stands for the total amount of household labour time. In a standard household responsibility system, the household must deliver, depending on the parameter T_q, a certain amount of quota crops to the state at fixed prices. This poses a third constraint on the labour allocation of the household. The output quota constraint can be written as:

$$Q_q \geq \bar{Q}_q \tag{A5}$$

where $\bar{Q}_q$ stands for the obligatory quota-crop output. Given the production function and the parameter T_q, this quota constraint can be transformed into a labour time constraint:

$$L_q \geq \bar{L}_q \tag{A6}$$

The household's income maximization problems becomes:

Maximize

$$M = P_q Q_q(L_q, T_q) + P_o Q_o(L_o, T_o) + wL_w \tag{A7}$$

subject to

$$\begin{aligned} &L_t \geq L_q + L_o + L_w \\ &L_o \geq 0 \\ &L_q \geq 0 \\ &L_w \geq 0 \\ &L_q \geq \bar{L}_o. \end{aligned}$$

Define the Lagrangian:

$$L = P_q Q_q(L_q, T_q) + P_o Q_o(L_o, T_o) + wL_w + \lambda_1(L_t - L_o - L_q - L_w) + \lambda_2(L_q - L_q).$$

The solutions to this maximization problem can be represented by the Kuhn–Tucker conditions:

$$\frac{\partial L}{\partial L_q} = P_q \frac{\partial Q_q}{\partial L_q} - \lambda_1 + \lambda_2 \geq 0, \text{ if } >, L_q = 0 \tag{A8}$$

$$\frac{\partial L}{\partial L_o} = P_o \frac{\partial Q_o}{\partial L_o} - \lambda_1 \geq 0, \text{ if } >, L_o = 0 \tag{A9}$$

$$\frac{\partial L}{\partial L_w} = w - \lambda_1 \geq 0, \text{ if } >, L_w = 0 \tag{A10}$$

$$\frac{\partial L}{\partial \lambda_1} = L_t - L_q - L_o - L_w \geq 0, \text{ if } >, \lambda_1 = 0 \tag{A11}$$

$$\frac{\partial L}{\partial \lambda_2} = L_q - \bar{L}_q \geq 0, \text{ if } >, \lambda_2 = 0. \tag{A12}$$

Let us first consider the case in which the obligatory quota constraint is not binding. That is to say, the optimized labour supply in quota-crop production (L_q^*) is larger than the required labour supply ($L_q^* > \bar{L}_q$). From equation (A12), we can see that $\lambda_2 = 0$. This is equivalent to the situation in which no quota constraint exists. We can examine the first order conditions associated with some possible solutions. At the optimum solution, if L_q^*, L_o^*, L_w^* all are positive, the first order conditions become:

$$P_q \frac{\partial Q_q}{\partial L_q} = P_o \frac{\partial Q_o}{\partial L_o} = w. \tag{A13}$$

This says that at the optimal solution, the marginal value product of labour in all three sectors is the same. It is also possible that at the optimum, L_q, L_o are positive, L_w equals zero; or L_q, L_w are positive and L_o zero (the design of the HRS excludes the possibility of having a positive L_o when L_q equals zero. In other words, one can not use the responsibility field to plant only the non-quota crop). The first order conditions for the first case will become:

$$P_q \frac{\partial Q_q}{\partial L_q} = P_o \frac{\partial Q_o}{\partial L_o} > w \tag{A14}$$

and the first order conditions for the second case are:

$$P_q \frac{\partial Q_q}{\partial L_q} = w > P_o \frac{\partial Q_o}{\partial L_o}. \tag{A15}$$

These first order conditions show that the optimal allocation of labour, the marginal value products of labour (*MVPL*) are the same in the two sectors in which the household is engaged and the *MVPL* in the third sector is lower than the *MVPLs* in the two sectors at the optimal level of labour supply.

Consider now the case in which the optimized labour supply to quota-crop production is smaller than required ($L_q^* < \bar{L}_q$). This implies that the quota constraint as represented by equation (A12) will be binding and $\lambda_2 > 0$ if the household takes part in the HRS. The household must supply $\bar{L}_q$ amount of labour to the quota-crop sector, even though it is not optimal for its income maximization. The maximization conditions for the boundary solutions in the case where L_q, L_o, L_w are all positive will be:

$$P_q \frac{\partial Q_q}{\partial L_q} + \lambda_2 = P_o \frac{\partial Q_o}{\partial L_o} = w. \tag{A16}$$

Again, it is possible that the optimal allocation of labour implies a zero labour supply to either the wage job or the other crop sector. In this case, the first order conditions associated with these solutions will become:

$$P_q \frac{\partial Q_q}{\partial L_q} + \lambda_2 = P_o \frac{\partial Q_o}{\partial L_o} > w \tag{A17}$$

and

$$P_q \frac{\partial Q_q}{\partial L_q} + \lambda_2 = w > P_o \frac{\partial Q_o}{\partial L_o}. \tag{A18}$$

The maximization conditions represented by equation (A16) show that with the boundary solutions, the *MVPL* in the quota crop sector is lower than in the other crop and the wage job sector. If household labour is only allocated in two of the three sectors, the first order conditions as represented by equations (A17) and (A18) only tell us that at the optimum, the *MVPL* in the quota-crop sector is lower than in the other sector in which the household is engaged. It is unclear whether the *MVPL* in the quota crop sector at the contracted level of labour supply is larger or smaller than the *MVPL* in the "uninvolved" sector.

When the optimized labour allocation in all sectors is positive, and the quota constraint is not binding, the standard HRS with an obligatory quota delivery is perfectly consistent with the household's objective of income maximization. Targeted output for the quota crop will be produced and household income will be maximized simultaneously. However, under a binding quota constraint, the supply of household labor to the quota-crop sector is larger than in the case of no constraint. This follows from the decreasing marginal product of labour. In other words, the obligatory quota delivery prevents the household from allocating its labour optimally for its income maximization. Targeted output for the quota crop will be produced (if the household does not exit the HRS) but household income will not be maximized. In this situation, the household has two options—either to stay in the HRS or to exit. If the first option is chosen, the household will allocate its labour according to the maximization conditions represented by equations (A16), or (A17) and (A18) and the obligatory amount of quota crop will be produced. If the second option is chosen, the household will use all its labour in the wage sector and no crops will be produced. An income maximizing household will choose to stay in the HRS and fulfil its quota duties only if

$$P_q\bar{Q}_q + P_o Q_o^* + wL_w^* > L_t w. \tag{A19}$$

This choice rule can be written alternatively as:

$$P_q\int_0^{L_o} \frac{\partial Q_q}{\partial L_q} + P_o\int_0^{L_o^*} \frac{\partial Q_o}{\partial L_o} + wL_w^* > wL_t \tag{A20}$$

or

$$P_q\int_0^{\bar{L}_q} \frac{\partial Q_q}{\partial L_q} - w\bar{L}_q + P_o\int_0^{L_o^*} \frac{\partial Q_o}{\partial L_o} - wL_o^* > 0 \tag{A21}$$

PART III

EMPIRICAL ISSUES

[14]

Reprinted from
AMERICAN JOURNAL OF AGRICULTURAL ECONOMICS
Vol. 66, No. 5, December 1984

Renewable Resource Management in Developing Country Agriculture (Pierre Crosson, Resources for the Future, presiding)

The Village Against the Center: Resource Depletion in South Asia

Daniel W. Bromley and Devendra P. Chapagain

We are interested in the institutional environment that defines the resource-use behavior of villagers in South Asia. It is that environment—consisting of the conventions, norms, and rules—that dictates daily behavior with respect to the natural resource base on which villagers are so dependent. Our title emphasizes tension between the village level and the "center." It is our hypothesis that this tension has been ignored in much of the literature on development in general and particularly in that literature concerned with the role of natural resources in economic development.

To ignore the tensions between the village and the center is to miss the essence of natural resource policy in many parts of the world, but especially is this the case in South Asia. By tensions we do not necessarily mean open hostilities, though that is possible. The sort of tensions we have in mind show up in terms of different priorities in resource use, different objectives regarding that use, and certainly different means for addressing conflicts among users at the local level—or between local and non-local users.

For the bulk of history the village was the consumption and production unit for most natural resources. A few items were traded, but for the most part local production was driven by local demand. As villages became unified under a variety of rulers, production decisions often were dictated by tribute necessities. When those rulers made economic exchanges with other rulers, the notion of foreign trade became an important aspect of natural resource use. Colonialism and imperialism were two logical extensions of early trade agreements, both driven by varying degrees of concern for secure expectations on the supply side. Britain's interests in India progressed from mere trade, through colonialism (targeted administration and control), and on to imperialism (rule).

With the flood of independence for Asian and African countries following World War II, erstwhile royal and colonial administrations gave way to fledgling states. Many were guided in their conception and formation by democratic principles borrowed from western nations with some experience in governance.

That the new governments of these countries—many of which attempted to aggregate extremely diverse ethnic, religious, and tribal entities—faced a formidable challenge cannot be denied. Missing in all of the concern for high-minded governance concepts was an equally pertinent recognition of the importance of administrative and enforcement mechanisms to replace those stripped away at independence.

It is the final era in the above sequence, namely state building, that is of greatest interest to those of us concerned with resource depletion in South Asia. And it is here also that we encounter an essential ingredient in contemporary village resource-use matters. The Indian village is characterized by the concept of *nistar*. This term describes the fact that members of the village have certain "rights" to utilize some specified areas for the gathering of fuelwood, fodder, dung, and other products such as vegetative residues for their own subsistence.

We point out that this access system bears absolutely no relation to the much-maligned—and mislabeled—notion of a "commons" as introduced into economics over twenty years ago (Gordon). In contrast to the true commons, where definite institutional arrangements exist to regulate group size as well as utilization per member, *nistar* rights in South

Session jointly held with the Association of Environmental and Resource Economists.

Daniel W. Bromley is a professor and chair, Department of Agricultural Economics, University of Wisconsin; Devendra P. Chapagain is in the Ministry of Agriculture, Kathmandu, Nepal.

The authors acknowledge the assistance of Michael Carter and Bruce Flory.

Asia more closely resemble those rights attaching to forests and wastelands of medieval times (Bloch, Duby).

The Asian village economy was one in which the very best agricultural and forest land was under the control of influential and wealthy landlords who were inclined to serve the interests of the rajas or their equivalent. But the village resource situation was one in which the masses who controlled no land still had access to the residual—to roadsides, to ditchbanks, and to other areas too poor or too isolated for effective control and cultivation. They scavanged, as it were. As colonial rule subsided and as the nascent state took shape, the issue of resource control became of central importance. Lands that had formerly been controlled by local political entities came under the administration of the national or regional government. The use of those lands by villagers suddenly became subject to an entirely different set of reciprocal rights and obligations. While *nistar* lands may not have been much affected by the rise of the central state, forest lands, whose control was transferred from a local ruler to the state, became something apart from the local economy. No longer was resource access something that might be negotiated for. Now legislative and administrative arrangements were determined at some remove from the village.

The 1951 revolution replaced a central authority with democratic ideals, promising much to a people that had long lived under an abundance of duties and obligations. A new constitution promised much and placed the state in the position of guarantor of individual liberties and planned economic development. As is often the case, Nepal embarked upon a "five-year plan" with grand themes and admirable objectives, the realization of which would require foreign assistance of both a technical and a monetary nature.

The rising expectations at the village level exceeded the ability of the state to deliver and, as so often happens, cynicism and distrust set in. Of course village governance was not attuned to the radical developmental themes emanating from the center; and so, in addition to their physical isolation from the center, there was a more serious isolation, one that roads alone could not overcome. While we can assume that those in the villages were as much interested in "development" as those at the center, the process was (and usually is) totally dominated by the latter. And that domination soon took the form of new institutional arrangements with a direct impact at the village level.

Our interest here is in one particular aspect of imposed institutional arrangement, namely the nationalization of all forest lands in Nepal. This action, taken in 1957, upset centuries of traditional patterns of resource control and of the village governance structure over resource use; the existing political structure, with its attendant rights and duties, was rendered quite irrelevant (Chapagain). Prior to the Private Forest Nationalization Act villagers made use of contiguous forest lands for a variety of products. Although there was no binding legal claim attached to the lands, they were usually considered to be "private" and so that word appears in the legislation.

The state was moved to nationalize forest lands for several reasons. First, medical technology had reduced infant mortality, and so Nepal's population was suddenly increasing quite rapidly, putting more pressure on local resources. Second, malaria control programs had made the terai lands (the lower hills and plains) habitable, and so relatively pristine areas were being cleared for agriculture. And, third, the new conviction arose at the center that ultimate resource control should rest with the state rather than with a larger number of isolated villagers.

As might be expected, nationalization in such a setting was destined to fail for two very obvious reasons: (*a*) villagers wre left with no alternative source of supply for the many products formerly collected on such lands, and (*b*) the center was unable to enforce the new institutional arrangement. The new structure was also hampered by the realization on the part of the villagers that it was intended as a revenue source for the state in the form of receipts from timber sales. There is some evidence that the Nationalization Act increased the rate of forest destruction as villagers hurried to convert affected lands into agricultural uses so as to exempt them from the transfer (Chapagain).

Nationalization shifted the locus of resource concern from the village to the center. When responsibility for control is taken away, there is little doubt that the village loses something in terms of its own sense of responsibility toward the resource. It is this perception on the part of villagers that has been of interest to us. To this end we recently conducted interviews among 140 households in a Nepal village. Our interest was to learn about intended resource use patterns and how the expectations of what other villagers would do might influence those use patterns.

The Model

The presumption among many economists is to suggest that resource depletion problems are best solved by the creation of private ownership arrangements over the threatened resources. The fact that serious resource depletion problems exist on private lands seems not to dampen the enthusiasm among those with a predisposition toward this particular institutional form. A second impediment is that privatization is also individualization and that the very existence of externalities rests in the individualization of decisions that carry collective implications (Bromley). To individualize decision making in a cultural setting with centuries of collectivist tradition is not only to confront essential social norms but it is to reintroduce the very spillover problems that joint action is so often called upon to mediate.

A south Asian village is a decision-making unit. In a sense we have the "private" control of resourse use—where private is taken to mean the village rather than a single individual. After all, much that we call private in the West is controlled by more than one individual. The matter of private control over resources refers to the ability to exclude others, not to how many individuals share in the decision making by those not excluded.

As discussed earlier, much of the decision-making power of the village has been preempted in South Asia by the center. The only way in which that resource control can be rekindled and reinvigorated is to recognize the interests of the village as a management entity and to search for ways to coordinate the independent actions of villagers.

We suggest that a necessary first step in that process is to understand the nature of group choice over collective assets. Every sophomore in economics is convinced that the "rational" individual will free ride rather than contribute to a public good. This faith carries over into more advanced discussions about the behavior of resource users around the world. Observations by anthropologists that Asian villagers do cooperate on resource-use decisions are considered quaint anecdotes of doubtful generality for resource policy in the developing world. Economic theory says that individuals will free ride, and therefore any data to the contrary are immediately suspect. Our interest, therefore, is to attempt to learn something of the free-riding tendencies of Asian villagers with respect to collectively used natural resources.

We take as our starting point the theoretical literature on institutions, of which the work of Frohlich and Oppenheimer, Runge (1981, 1984), Schotter, and Sen are of the greatest interest. The essential social role of institutions is to reduce uncertainty by defining and stabilizing expectations of a group of economic agents. Institutions "organize, process, and store the essential information required to coordinate human behavior" (Runge 1984, p. 162). A single individual (or household) in the village must determine how much to contribute to a collective good; such contribution may take the form of cash or labor commitments to the maintenance of a village forest, or it may be in the form of foregoing an opportunity to harvest the resource so that depletion is prevented.

The key to the contribution of individuals to a collective good is a mechanism whereby they might coordinate their expectations regarding the likely actions of others with respect to the same resource. To the extent that village-level institutional arrangements include such mechanisms, and to the extent that they are reinforced rather than undermined by the center, then depletion of collective natural resources is not automatic.

The Findings

Our experimental work follows in the tradition of Marwell and Ames. We asked the heads of 140 (400) households in Belkot Panchayat, Nepal, about their intentions with respect to a willingness to contribute toward the enhancement of a village asset (the forest). It should be clear that we were attempting to measure their behavioral intentions rather than their actual behavior. Each respondent was presented with a hypothetical situation in which they were told that they would receive an amount roughly equivalent to the current average annual tax burden. At the time of our survey (April 1983) this was Rs.100.

Each respondent was asked to allocate that windfall between a private use (one that would benefit only the household) and a public use (one that would benefit the collectively used village forest, or a community irrigation ditch). Both investment alternatives were said to return 10% per year. In addition, the public investment allocation from each household would be exactly matched by the national government. It was stressed that all villagers would continue to benefit from the collective resource whether or not they agreed to contribute anything.

The mean investment in the collective good from the Rs.100 windfall was Rs.49.29, with the remainder going to private investments (Rs.50.71). That is, the 140 households split the windfall almost evenly between the collective good and their own private investment. Fifty-one households (36%) donated the full amount of the windfall to the collective good, and an additional 30 households (21%) donated Rs.50. Combined, 81 households (57%) contributed at least one-half of the windfall to the collective good. Only 48 households (34%) refused to contribute anything to the collective good.

We found an interesting relationship between the size of the contribution to the collective good and the caste of the household. Specifically, low-caste households with less than one-half hectare contributed, on average, Rs.31.25 as opposed to Rs.68.75 for high-caste households owning more than 3 hectares.

We asked for all 140 respondents to indicate how much of the windfall would constitute a "fair" contribution to the collective good. While one-quarter of the respondents had no opinion on this, the mean of those who responded (105) was Rs.61.50. This estimate of a fair contribution exceeds by 25% the mean contribution of all 140 households (Rs.49.29). Approximately 70% of the responding households considered it "fair" to contribute at least Rs.50 to the collective good. Two-fifths of the respondents (44) considered it "fair" to donate the entire windfall of Rs.100 to the collective good. Only one respondent considered it "fair" to donate nothing to the collective good.

In a slight variation on the above experiment, we attempted to determine how the household heads would respond to a situation of unequal windfalls. Specifically, we told 36 respondents that they would be given Rs.200 (rather than the original Rs.100), and that the other 104 households would be given Rs.66. The mean contribution of both groups to the collective good remained almost the same—at slightly under 50% of their windfall; a finding consistent with that of Marwell and Ames. Interestingly, the proportion of free riders increased to 40% (from 34%) among households receiving the small windfall (Rs.66) when compared to a uniform windfall of Rs.100 for all households. For the larger windfall (Rs.200), free riding went from 34% of the households down to 25%.

Respondents were then asked to imagine that a nearby forested area had been opened up to the village for the collection of firewood, and that thirty bundles of firewood per year per household could be harvested by villagers on a sustained-yield basis; this quantity of firewood is slightly less than one-third of the annual firewood consumption by village households.

The mean quantity of firewood that respondents said they would harvest was twenty-four, with nearly 60% of the respondents (82) indicating that they would harvest less than the sustainable yield of thirty bundles per household. An additional 30% of the households (48) said that they would take exactly thirty bundles; only 10% of the respondents indicated that they would take more than thirty. Ninety percent of the households considered it "fair" to harvest at or below the sustainable yield. This intended cutting behavior was unaffected by another aspect of the interview that asked how their behavior would change if they knew that a privileged group in the village was taking more than the sustainable yield.

Our final experiment concerned the grazing of livestock on a newly acquired pasture area near the village. Respondents were told that the pasture could support 1,200 cattle per year, or an average of 3 cattle per household in the village. It should be noted that the average number of cattle in the village is currently about 3.8 per household. Here, as opposed to the firewood case, one-third of the households (45) indicated that they would exceed their "share" of the village use and that they would graze between 4 and 12 cattle. The remaining households (two-thirds) indicated that they would graze three or fewer cattle.

The mean number of cattle that all households considered "fair" to graze on the pasture was 3.6, exactly the mean number for how many cattle all respondents would like to put on the pasture. As with the firewood experiment, intended grazing behavior was not affected by the prospect that a privileged group of villagers might exceed their share of the use.

Implications for Natural Resource Policy

The idea that free-riding is the dominant strategy among economic agents is a venerable one in the literature. Do Nepal villagers free ride? Even recognizing the limitations of our survey we are not persuaded that they do. We asked the 140 respondents whether or not the likely behavior of others influenced what they would do with respect to their natural resource use, and in each of the experiments approximately 60% said that it would not. Thirty-five percent of the households said that they would be influenced by the amount of contribution made by other households in the case of the Rs.100 windfall, but when it came to cattle grazing only 10% of the respondents said that they cared what others would do. We stress that this independent behavior exists regardless of whether the respondent intend to free ride, or to be "a good citizen."

It seems safe to conclude that we find a substantial interest on the part of our respondents to contribute to a collective village asset and to refrain from exploitive behavior with respect to a village asset. At the same time, a majority indicated that their behavior was not much affected by the likely behavior of others. A clear majority do not free ride, nor would they if they thought others would. Village resource use behavior seems to be very much influenced by a sense for the collective well being. This does not mean that some would not overuse collective resources—especially in the case of grazing. But the magnitude of that overuse is not considered to be large.

The model that guided this investigation links one individual's contribution to a collective good to the anticipated actions of others in the same social unit. Across all of our experiments we found that approximately one-third of the respondents considered the likely actions of others to be decisive in their own resource-use decisions. This might be taken as rather weak support for the model. At the same time we found that a majority of the respondents said they would make contributions to the collective good. Hence, while the villagers seem to imply that they do not much care about what others intend to do, we believe it is reasonable to assume that the villagers know what is expected of them, and that others know likewise. Hence, while claiming that the actions of others are not generally of concern to them, they may be secure in the knowledge that the resource-use decisions of the others will not be greatly out of line with some accepted norm.

We hypothesize the presence of a "background ethic" or norm that influences collective resource use decisions. This norm has evolved over time as the members of a village struggle with the daily task of making a living. The majority care about the collective welfare, a minority will take more than is "safe or fair," and both will do so irrespective of what they think others will do. This is not striking unless one believes that all individuals are greedy free riders.

But working against this background ethic are two serious threats—one coming from the villagers themselves, and the other from the state. The first is population pressure. The second is the kind of resource policy formulation discussed at the outset; national governments passing laws and formulating administrative policies that threaten the existence of individual households. Such external influences are critical in the process of pitting villagers against themselves and of ultimately shifting resource stewardship away from the village. When resource responsibility is taken away from the village, so is the concern for the viability of the resource. It is the "patron syndrome" turned on its head; villagers do not care much for things that the state gives to them, and the same thing would seem to apply to the things that the state takes away. We should not be surprised.

We find a residue of concern for collective natural resources in a country that has been characterized as one of the most seriously exploited and where the state has usurped local resource management in name but not in deed. The lessons for the formulation of resource policy would seem to be several. First, the state must not decree what it cannot enforce; to nationalize the forest in name yet to leave it unmanaged and unadministered is probably worse than having done nothing. Second, supply-side policies that restrict local resource access must be matched by innovative policy on both the supply side—in the form of providing alternative supplies—and on the demand side in the form of helping to develop techniques and institutions that will dampen the need for the threatened resource.

In the absence of these aspects of a resource

policy, the center is simply exacerbating an already serious situation. More critically, it is undermining its possible future role for providing solutions to problems that will surely get worse before they get better.

References

Bloch, Marc. *Feudal Society*. Chicago: University of Chicago Press, 1961.

Bromley, Daniel W. "Land and Water Problems: An Institutional Perspective." *Amer. J. Agr. Econ.* 64 (1982):834–44.

Chapagain, Devendra P. "Managing Public Lands as a Common Property Resource: A Case Study in Nepal." Ph.D. thesis, University of Wisconsin, 1984.

Duby, Georges. *The Early Growth of the European Economy*. Ithaca NY: Cornell University Press, 1978.

Frohlich, N., and Joe Oppenheimer. "I Get By With a Little Help From My Friends." *World Politics* 23(1970):104–20.

Gordon, H. Scott. "The Economic Theory of a Common-Property Resource: The Fishery." *J. Polit. Econ.* 61(1954):124–42.

Marwell, Gerald, and R. Ames. "Economists Free Ride, Does Anyone Else?: Experiments in the Provision of Public Goods IV." *J. Public Econ.* 15(1981):295–310.

Runge, C. F. "Common Property Externalities: Isolation, Assurance and Resource Depletion in a Traditional Grazing Context." *Amer. J. Agr. Econ.* 63(1981): 595–606.

———. "Institutions and the Free Rider: The Assurance Problem in Collective Action." *J. Politics* 46(1984): 154–79.

Schotter, Andrew. *The Economic Theory of Social Institutions*. Cambridge: Cambridge University Press, 1981.

Sen, A. K. "Isolation, Assurance, and the Social Rate of Discount." *Quart. J. Econ.* 81(1967):112–24.

[15]

The Economics of Cain and Abel: Agro-Pastoral Property Rights in the Sahel

ROGIER VAN DEN BRINK,
DANIEL W. BROMLEY and
JEAN-PAUL CHAVAS

The complementarity of the economic systems of nomads and farmers is often overshadowed by the conflicts inherent in the competition over the control of land. The conflict is one of property rights. A dynamic programming model of the West African Sahel is presented that simulates the emergence of a dual economy based on the comparative advantage of the farmer and the pastoralist. The model illustrates that exclusive private property rights have no claim to optimality. The analysis of risk in an intertemporal framework suggests the optimality of another type of property right – the right to flexible adjustment typically claimed by the pastoralist. Multiple property regimes provide optimal settings for farmers and pastoralists.

I. INTRODUCTION

> Some say that the quarrel arose at Earth's division between the brothers, in which all land fell to Cain, but all birds, beasts and creeping things to Abel. They agreed that neither should have any claim on the other's possessions. As soon as this pact had been concluded Cain, who was tilling a field, told Abel to move his flocks way. When Abel replied that they would not harm the tillage, Cain caught up a weapon and ran in vengeful pursuit across mountain and valley, until he overtook and killed him
>
> [*Graves and Patai*, 1964: 91].

We draw on the story of Cain and Abel to focus attention on the differing property rights regimes inherent in sedentary agriculture and in

Rogier van den Brink, Agriculture and Environment Operations Division, Southern Africa Department, World Bank; Daniel W. Bromley and Jean-Paul Chavas, Department of Agricultural Economics, University of Wisconsin-Madison.

The Journal of Development Studies, Vol.31, No.3, February 1995, pp.373–399
PUBLISHED BY FRANK CASS, LONDON

pastoralism. This perspective is necessary in light of the recent rather widespread belief among development experts that private – individualised – and exclusive title to land in Africa is the *sine qua non* of improved economic performance [*Feder and Noronha, 1987; Feder and Feeny, 1991*]. This new perspective is also timely given the recent developments in property rights theory, particularly with respect to land uses at the extensive margin [*Bromley, 1992; 1991; 1989; Bromley and Cernea, 1989; National Academy of Sciences, 1986; Larson and Bromley, 1990; McCay and Acheson, 1987*]. Finally, this perspective strongly amplifies the recent developments in the field of rangeland management suggesting the need for more flexible strategies of natural resource use [*Cousins, 1992; Behnke and Scoones, 1991*].

The conflict between Cain – the farmer – and Abel – the herder – should be understood as one of property rights. In agriculture as well as livestock production, property rights emerge to secure income streams generated by production activities. The nature of the income stream, then, may affect the type of property right that is likely to be established. The crucial difference between sedentary farming and nomadic livestock production is that they differ in ability to react *ex post* to temporal uncertainty; in other words, they differ in flexibility.[1]

Unfortunately, property rights essential for livestock production in the Sahel have been eroded by a long history of conflicts. More recently, a number of state interventions that expropriated pastoralists of property rights crucial to their economic systems have clearly favoured farmers over pastoralists in the allocation of private property rights. These changes have created general uncertainty over property rights to natural resources, thereby inducing a *de facto* open access situation. The resulting tragedy of open access, induced by public policy, has substantially increased the costs of running the pastoralist economy (that is, its transaction costs) and adversely affected the pastoralists' ability to overcome periods of drought. Ever since the publication of Sen's [*1981*] seminal essay on the relation between famines and entitlements, the implications of the loss of property rights to the Sahelian nomads need no further elaboration.

In this article we develop the case for property regimes as *instrumental variables* in development policy, and we show that highly diverse and variable agricultural eco-systems demand property regimes that allow quick human response to new exigencies. We establish the microeconomic relationship between environmental variability, choice of technique, and property rights in a dynamic, partial equilibrium context. We demonstrate the importance of flexibility as an optimal strategic response of individuals faced with input uncertainty and develop a model simulating a dual economy that arises as the result of rational choice by individuals faced with temporal uncertainty. Such rational choice includes the choice of optimal property rights regimes which allow capture of the income streams of techniques appropriate for a particular agroecosystem.

The model, while in the vein of Demsetz [*1967*], does *not* lead us to conclude that exclusive private (individualised) property rights in land are necessarily optimal. Given spatio-temporal risk, other types of property regimes may be more appropriate. Over-exploitation of natural resources in the Sahel has often been associated with the introduction of techniques that allowed for a more intensive use of a given range without the formulation of the type of property rights regimes that could regulate and coordinate such use. As development policies reassess the role of livestock in Africa and elsewhere, it is essential that programmes be formulated with clarity and coherence so as to avoid the mistakes of the past when 'private' or 'group' ranches were regarded as the solution to pastoralist 'problems.'

In the second section of the article we develop a theoretical model of the dual economy of Cain – the farmer – and Abel – the nomad. The Biblical parallel is used to emphasise both the urgency and the universality of the problem. The model simulates a dual economy based on the comparative advantages of two different production techniques faced with environmental uncertainty. An economic theory of optimal production techniques and property rights is developed in a context of dynamic risk. In the third section we use the model to describe the agro-pastoral production system of the West African Sahel. In the fourth section we touch upon policy issues, both in a historical as well as in a current framework.

II. A DYNAMIC MODEL OF AGRO-PASTORAL PRODUCTION

Economists have generated an extensive literature on the effects of risk and uncertainty on economic decision making. However, risk is commonly modelled as if it were 'timeless'. The formulation of the problem in terms of timeless risk precludes the theory to investigate important economic behaviour such as learning and the use of adaptive strategies – dynamic decisions influenced by new information that becomes available over time. Once we introduce temporal risk, a wider variety of economic behaviour under risk can be modelled.[2]

If economic institutions are a response to risk of various types, it seems logical not to restrict analytical attention to only one type of risk. In other words, the recognition that risk is not timeless, but changes over time, is important for the analysis of economic behaviour and institutions in general, and property rights in particular. If a farmer puts up a fence around his fields and establishes an exclusive property right to the land, he reduces the risk that others may claim the field, and he assures himself of the full benefits of any investments he would care to undertake in his fields. He establishes *ex ante* certainty to the exclusive use of the land. The higher and the more certain the income stream he can derive from the exploitation of his field, the more he will be willing to pay for the 'fence', that is, the exclusive property right.

However, where there is *ex post* uncertainty there is a positive economic value attached to the capacity to adjust *ex post*. Thus, the *ex ante* certainty that a nomadic pastoralist would acquire by fencing his range in a situation of extremely variable rainfall, and with a limited potential to improve the productivity of the range, does not represent high economic value. The nomad, then, might not be interested in an exclusive property right to a particular field. He might be more interested in establishing a property right that would enable him to *ex post* adjust to temporal uncertainty. In particular, he would value property rights that assured him spatial mobility.

Such property rights assure the right holder of a secure income stream. From a pastoralist perspective, establishing tenure security means establishing the security of such property rights as are best suited to capture the income stream of a spatially mobile economic activity.

In the following, an economic model is presented that captures the dominant characteristics of the production systems of nomads and farmers in a stylised Sahelian environment. The model simulates a dual economy based on the comparative advantages of two different production techniques with respect to environmental uncertainty.[3] Choice of technique and choice of property regime become a function of particular eco-zones [*Bromley, 1989*].

In the model, the climate in the world inhabited by the farmer, Cain, and the nomad, Abel, is not a constant, but a variable. The north is arid and rainfall is extremely variable. Moving south, average rainfall increases while the variability is reduced. Each isohyet runs perfectly west–east over the region. Thus, movements along a particular isohyet do not cause changes in mean or variability of rainfall. This is a stylised approximation of the climatic conditions found in the Sahel. The simulated rainfall regime incorporates this basic pattern.[4] Every grid on the imaginary map of the world in which Cain and Abel live falls under some specific rainfall distribution. Laterally (that is, grids from west to east on an isohyet), each grid exhibits realisations from probability density functions with the same moments. North–south movements perpendicular to the isohyets exhibit realisations drawn from density functions that incorporate simultaneous changes in E(e) and Var(e). This climatic variable defines different eco-zones and is central to the following model.

Cain and Abel live in a simple two-period world in which it can rain in both periods. To optimise fodder availability for his herd, Abel attempts to stay perpetually mobile (for two periods in the model). Given actual rainfall in period 1 (represented by the realisation of the random variable e) he makes his location decision x_1. This may also be called his *ex ante* choice. After Abel has observed rainfall in period 2, he decides to move his herd to a new location x_2, exploiting the new grazing opportunities which present themselves. This is his *ex post* choice.

If we solve Abel's problem recursively, that is, through backward induction from period t = 2 to t = 1, we would take the following steps. The optimal choice of period 2 location (x_2) is given by the maximand of a function f representing '*ex post* utility'. The function f is assumed to be strictly concave in its arguments. We postulate that this choice of period 2 location will in general depend on his period 1 location, the period 2 rainfall, and the property rights regime in place. Nomadic *non-exclusive* property rights are defined as property rights that secure the profit stream of the livestock production activity *wherever* such production takes place. Note that non-exclusivity does *not* necessarily mean open access. Non-exclusivity implies that, *ex ante*, exclusive rights to a particular production location do not exist, but that rights of access exist which are restricted to a well-defined number of property right holders. We leave the exact definition of these rules of access unspecified at this point. Suffice it to say that such rules generally solve a coordination problem, which – in the empirical case of Sahelian pastoralists – are typically solved in a common property regime. Under open access, no coordination would exist, and the number of potential users could be unrestricted.

Consequently, Abel's problem in period 2 is the following:

$$\max_{x_2} f(x_1, x_2, e, Z) \tag{1}$$

x_1 = location at time t = 1

x_2 = location at time t = 2

e = rainfall distribution in period 2: not known at t=1, but known at t=2.

Z = variable representing property rights. If Z=0, property rights are non-exclusive. Such rights allow Abel to change location in period 2. If Z=1, exclusive property rights exist which prevent locational mobility.

The above optimisation problem yields the optimal period 2 location:

$$x^*_2 = x^*_2 (x_1 , e, Z) \tag{2}$$

Working backwards to the period 1 problem, we can formulate the choice of location as based on Abel's subjective expectations with respect to rainfall distributions and the profits incurred through relocation to x_2 after a particular rainfall. Optimal locations x_1 and x_2 are governed by the following dynamic programming problem:

$$\underset{x_1}{\text{Max}}\ E_1\{\underset{x_2}{\text{Max}}\ f(x_1, x_2, e, \delta, Z)\} \tag{3}$$

where E_1 is the expectations operator in period t = 1 over the random variable e, and δ represents a transaction cost parameter associated with movements.[5] We allow for transaction costs since the establishment of property rights, whether exclusive or non-exclusive, will normally involve costs associated with information gathering, contracting and enforcement.

Figure 1 compares the *ex post* utility obtained under three assumptions.[6] The first alternative assumes perfect mobility. The second alternative has transaction costs imposed on mobility. The third alternative, labelled 'immobility', assumes that Abel stays in the same location during both periods. Utility under perfect mobility is graphed as the solid line. In this case, that is, if movements are costless, Abel does not have an a priori preference for a given location. If transactions costs on movement are imposed, the expected utility is reduced and a southern location becomes more desirable. The expected value of utility if Abel remains at his period 1 location (under an immobile production scheme) is indicated by the lowest dotted line in Figure 1. Abel would want to move south given the higher expected value of rainfall and lesser variance there. At some point Abel might even prefer to settle in the south and establish himself as a rancher with a fixed location.

Property rights that allow Abel to secure the benefits derived from a strategy based on flexible response to environmental variability have positive economic value. In general, the value of flexibility F (measured in utils) is given by:

$$F = \underset{x_1}{\text{Max}}\ E_1\{\underset{x_2}{\text{Max}}\ f(x_1, x_2, e, \delta, Z)\} - \underset{x_1=x_2}{\text{Max}}\ E_1\{f(x_1, x_2, e, \delta, Z)\} \geq 0 \tag{4}$$

The value of the non-exclusive property regime (Z = 0) is derived from the value of *ex post* flexibility F. Abel assesses the value of non-exclusive nomadic property rights by comparing the result of the maximisation problem under full mobility with the result of a maximisation

FIGURE 1

EX POST UTILITY OF ABEL UNDER THREE MOBILITY ASSUMPTIONS

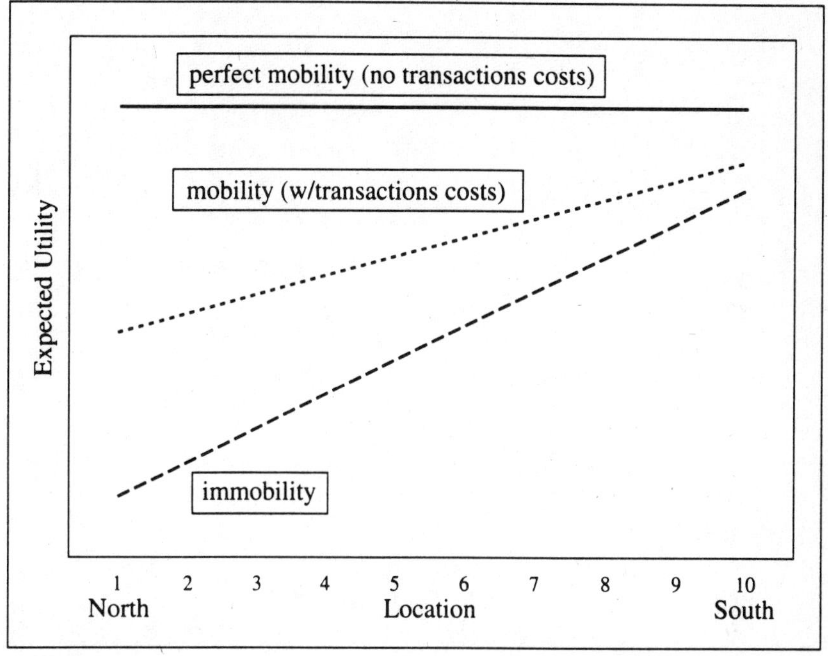

Source: see note 3.

problem under no mobility. The absence of such nomadic rights would constrain Abel's choice of x_1 to be equal to x_2. If $x_1 = x_2$, it can be shown that $F = 0$.

The expected value of flexibility with and without transactions costs is shown in Figure 2. The solid line represents the value of flexibility without transactions costs; the dotted line represents its value with transactions cost taken into account. As expected, the value of flexibility is highest in the North and lowest in the South, whereas the introduction of transactions costs lowers the value of flexibility for every point of the grid. Note that an increase in demographic pressure can be modelled as an increase in transaction costs.

What would be Abel's maximum willingness to pay for a nomadic property regime which, after all, is not costless to uphold? If we express the problem in monetary values, we can introduce initial wealth w. Abel's willingness to pay for non-exclusive property rights $Z = 0$ would be implicitly defined by the following equation:

FIGURE 2

THE VALUE OF FLEXIBILTY

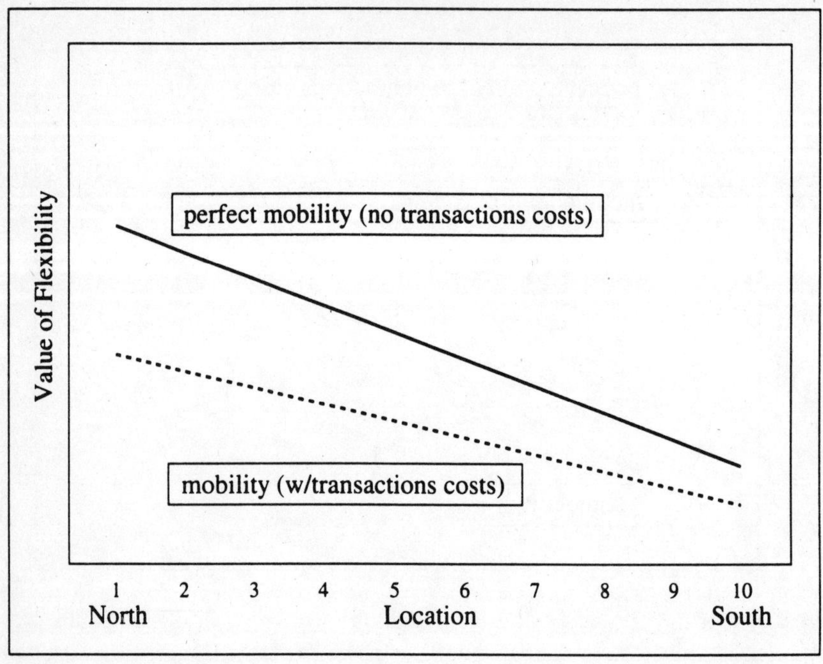

Source: see note 3.

$$\underset{x_1}{\text{Max}}\, E_1\{\underset{x_2}{\max}\, f(w - WTP, x_1, x_2, e, \delta, Z = 0)\} = \qquad (5)$$

$$\underset{x_1 = x_2}{\text{Max}}\, E_1\{\max f(w, x_1, x_2, e, \delta\ Z = 1)\}$$

w = initial wealth
WTP = Willingness to Pay

This equation gives an implicit definition of Abel's willingness to pay for property regime Z = 0. If his willingness to pay is positive, Abel will demand non-exclusive property rights, that is, Z = 0. The willingness to pay for such a property regime will in general increase with the value of flexibility. As shown in Figure 2, the value of flexibility is highest in the north. Extreme rainfall variability increases the value of an adaptive strategy *vis- à-vis* a non-adaptive strategy, and, thus, the likelihood that a non-exclusive property rights regime would be established.

Whereas the optimal domain of such a regime in our model is in the north, its territory (a particular set of *ex post* locations) is not a priori defined. Only *ex post* movement following a particular realisation of the random rainfall variable will define actual territorial occupation.

We have shown that Abel's production technique induces a demand for property rights that enable him to capture the benefits of flexibility. The base comparison of expected utility (with or without transactions costs) was always with a situation in which his pastoralist activity was restrained by immobility. For Cain, the farmer, the problem is different. Being a farmer, Cain makes the *ex ante* choice of location for the two periods. By definition, he does not move his farm between the two periods. Cain's technology of sedentary farming is an inferior choice in the arid north. Furthermore, as one moves south the comparative advantage gradually shifts from pastoralism to farming.

Cain's maximisation problem is defined as:

$$\underset{x_1=x_2}{\text{Max}}\ E_1\{g(x_1, x_2, e, \delta, Z)\}, \qquad (6)$$

where g(.) is Cain's utility function.

Cain's choice of property regime is also derived from a comparison between two maximisation problems. Cain compares expected utility of crop production under an exclusive property regime with the expected utility of sedentary livestock production. Thus, we assume that initially Cain is a sedentary pastoralist, who ponders whether he should switch production technology, given the ecosystem in which he finds himself. In making this choice, Cain realises that he will have to secure the benefits of crop production by establishing exclusive rights to the location. For instance, Cain will need to protect his crops against possible incursions of Abel's herds. Such exclusive cultivation rights are indicated by the variable $Z = 1$. Introducing initial wealth w, Cain's willingness to pay for an exclusive property rights regime will implicitly be given by the following equation:

$$\underset{x_1=x_2}{\text{Max}}\ E_1\{g(w - WTP, x_1, x_2, e, \delta, Z = 1)\} = \qquad (7)$$

$$\underset{x_1=x_2}{\text{Max}}\ E_1\{g(w, x_1, x_2, e, \delta, Z = 0)\}$$

If, for a given location, Cain's willingness to pay is greater than zero, he will demand an exclusive cultivation property right $Z = 1$.

Given the above model, it is now possible to endogenise the choice of technique and property rights regime given the rainfall probability distribution of a particular location. Ruling out the settlement of conflicting claims by violence, we could evaluate for each location x the maximum willingness to pay of each individual. The property rights regime governing the location will then depend on whether the WTP of Abel is greater than, equal to, or smaller than the WTP of Cain. We know from (4) that for Abel an adaptive strategy performs always at least as well as a non-adaptive strategy:

$$\max_{x_1} E_1\{\max_{x_2} f(x_1, x_2, c, \delta, Z=0)\} \geq \max_{x_1=x_2} E_1\{f(x_1, x_2, c, \delta, Z=0)\} \quad (8)$$

However, we do not know a priori for a given grid on the map whether Abel's WTP is larger or smaller than Cain's WTP. The relative magnitude of these WTP for a given location determines the optimal production technique and property rights regime (see Figure 3). By comparing these WTP, we can assess the optimal property regime and therefore endogenise the choice of particular economic institution. Figure 3 identifies an equilibrium point where the two WTP are equal.

The area to the north of the equilibrium point will be the optimal domain for livestock production and fall under Abel's non-exclusive nomadic property rights. The area to the south, *ceteris paribus*, will be the optimal domain for crop production governed by Cain's exclusive cultivation property rights. The domain of Abel's technology – with technology here defined as the combination of the optimal technique and the appropriate property right – does not imply exclusive territory. For Cain's technology, however, optimal domain does imply territorial exclusivity. The choice of technology in the model is made given period 1 location.

III. THE AGRO-PASTORAL PRODUCTION SYSTEM OF THE SAHEL

For the Sahel the stylised north–south sequence of agricultural resource exploitation largely conforms to the model presented in the previous section. Pure pastoral nomadism is practised in the arid Saharan north characterised by extremely variable rainfall of less than 200 millimeters per year. Pure nomadism can conceptually be defined as a perfectly mobile system of extensive livestock production with virtually no permanent place of abode, and no crop production. As one moves south, rainfall patterns become more stable, with average rainfall increasing to more than 800 millimeters for the Guinean savannah zone. The Sahel roughly occupies the transition zone between the Sahara and the Guinean savannah zone. In this transition from low and highly variable rainfall to high and more stable rainfall patterns, one finds the fully

FIGURE 3

CHOICE OF TECHNOLOGY AND PROPERTY RIGHTS REGIME

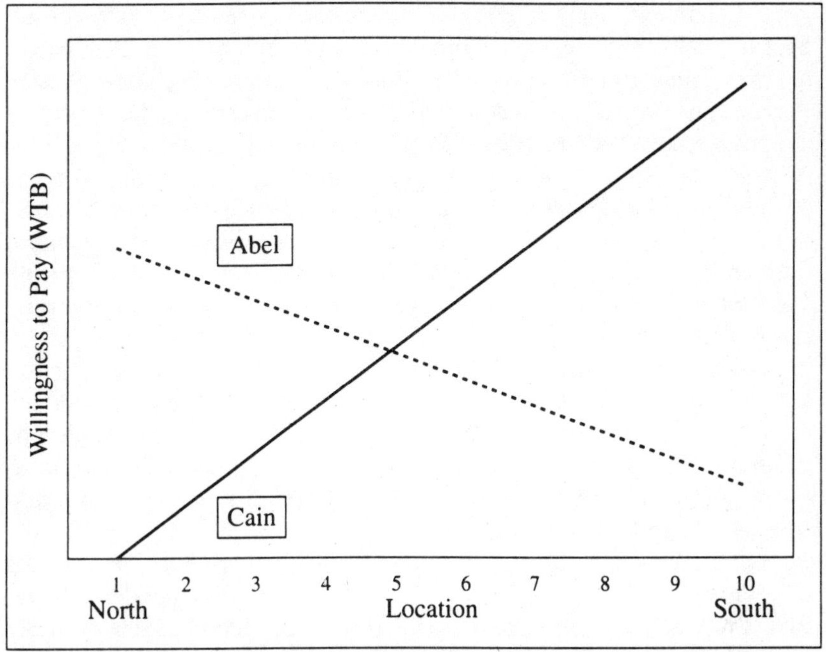

Source: see note 3.

mobile livestock production systems gradually associated with some form of crop production.[7] Such systems can be classified as semi-nomadism. Much of the southern Sahel is characterised by transhumance systems. Under the latter systems, trek routes are shorter, while part of the population is sedentary and engaged in crop cultivation.

Sahelian pastoralists typically employ several routes for the annual movement from dry-season pasture in the south to rainy season pasture in the north. The routes can range between 100 and 400 kilometres and are 'anchored' on one or more relatively sure waterpoints, such as a lake or a flooded valley. The more southern Sahelian transhumance systems employ shorter routes. However, multiyear periods of extreme and prolonged drought are a recurrent phenomenon across the Sahel, and they trigger pastoral movements over long distances. It is not unusual for such migrations to cause the crossing of several national borders, while the return to the original country may only occur several years later. The existence of such 'drought contingency routes' is a vital part of any pastoral strategy in the Sahel [*Starr, 1987*].

Two countervailing forces oppose southward movements of pastoralists. The first is the incidence of diseases detrimental to human and animal health, such as river blindness and trypanosomiasis. The second countervailing force is the increase of the farming population density. Population pressure reaches a relative maximum in the so-called 'sorghum belt', where large Sahelian population centers such as N'Djamena, Kano, Sokoto, Niamey, Ouagadougou, and Bamako are found. The area further south, however, is generally less densely populated. This is caused by increasing health hazards associated with a more humid climate and by a particularly unfavourable interaction between the shorter length of the dry season and increased leaching of the relatively shallow soils.

A closer look at property regimes associated with pastoral production systems reveals that the capacity for flexibility in movement is at the basis of their definition. Instead of making all production decisions *ex ante*, which would preclude the use of new information, the pastoralist adopts a strategy that allows for an *ex post* reaction to new information about rainfall and pasture conditions or, in other words, the temporal resolution of risk. Consequently, property rights of pastoralists emphasise the possibility for contingent, that is, state-dependent, movements – exactly as modelled in the previous section. Such property regimes do *not* attempt to establish exclusive rights to a particular piece of land *per se*. Thus: 'The pastoral Fulani displayed little concern with territorial identity or the defence of particular grazing areas; they were more interested in rights of access to pastures, water, and salt for their cattle than they were in the ownership of land' [*Frantz, 1986: 18–19*].

Typically, the tribal organisation of a nomadic property regime enables each economic unit to be continuously mobile since no single permanent trek route would be optimal under environmental uncertainty. The property regime, then, does *not* define a fixed territory for its members [*Baroin, 1985; Clanet, 1975*]. On the contrary, the relational aspects of property rights are stressed as pastoral peoples need to continually move around [*Neale, 1969*]. Movements need to be *coordinated* with other lineages and tribes, as well as with farming populations. The different itineraries of annual transhumance may be coordinated in advance by an assembly of lineages in order to minimise the risk of interference. Under such property regimes, lineage heads function as stewards of the system, while cattle are private property [*Lainé, 1982*]. The lineages thus form a management group that establishes rights and duties with respect to the use of pastoral resources (access to trek routes, pasture, water and so on). Nomadic property regimes, then, achieve a mix between individual incentives and group incentives mediated by – indeed, defined by – institutional rules.

Even the more 'sedentarised' pastoralists of the southern Sahel who practise restricted seasonal movements within zones of 30 to 50 kilometres, will typically not claim exclusive property rights to their potential grazing area. Lineages' management rights constitute property regimes that are not directly exclusive in terms of territory: they define priority access rights to water and pasture. The management right of lineage, however, needs to be asserted or 'activated' by the digging of wells, the erection of camps, and actual grazing. To the extent that nonmembers do not interfere with members' management and access rights, nonmembers also have access to the resources. However, the grazing areas are not open access regimes. Rules specifying priority access to water effectively regulate the usage of the territory by non-members whenever needed. Territorial exclusion, then, is indirectly achieved when needed by controlling the access to the crucially scarce factor but not by directly claiming exclusive territorial title to the land as such. Pastoralist property regimes of the Sahel are best described as common property regimes [*Wade, 1992*]. Unfortunately, the 'tragedy of the commons' as described by Hardin [*1968*] has tended to associate resource over-exploitation with common property regimes. However, empirical work on common property regimes has shown that over-exploitation is caused by the *absence* of common property rules, not by the *presence* of such arrangements. This suggests that the 'tragedy of the commons' should be relabeled the 'tragedy of open access' [*Bromley and Cernea, 1989*].

The claim for exclusive territorial title to the land is properly associated with sedentary farming systems. Whereas pastoralist mobility capitalises on the ability to adjust *ex post* to the variable environment, farming systems of the semi-arid tropics employ a number of cultivation techniques that stress *ex ante*, as well as *ex post*, adjustment to environmental risk. Here, risk reduction is obtained through portfolio diversification (an *ex ante* risk reducing technique) by choosing production activities and assets that exhibit low or negative covariances with respect to each other. Intercropping and plot scattering can be seen as good examples of such portfolio diversification. In this context, exclusive private property rights can emerge as the appropriate property regime.

For farmers, another set of production strategies, for example, variable planting dates and replanting is designed to adjust *ex post* to temporal risk in a manner comparable to the 'nomadic' adjustment to risk [*Chavas, Kristjanson and Matlon, 1991*]. Moreover, from a similar perspective, general techniques of shifting cultivation and crop rotations are themselves *ex post* adjustments, permitting the farmer to adjust to the variable productivity of the resource base [*Warren and Maizels, 1977*]. In Niger, one observer described a farming system as 'agricultural nomadism' in view of the continuous movement of farms in search for fertile soils [*Cissé, 1982*]. Even intensive and sustained manuring may not allow for permanent cultivation in some parts of the Sahel; the compound and the animal parkings are continuously moved in a rotational pattern so as to spread the benefits of manuring and to avoid over-exploitation of a particular plot [*Thomson, 1982*].

Typically, the individual farmer can obtain the use rights of a particular plot out of a common pool of plots managed by the lineage head. As long as the farmer uses the plot, he or she has exclusive property rights over the yield of the plot. However, given the limited scope for permanent cultivation of a particular plot, there emerges an option value for *ex post* adjustment, that is, the value of having access to a different plot at some point in the future. The membership of the community bestows a right to *farm*, but not necessarily to a *particular* farm. In this respect, the common property regimes of farming communities are basically similar to the pastoralist regimes. The similarity is caused by the need to solve a similar problem of coordination, since in both cases individuals are likely to make *ex post* adjustments that need to be coordinated within the group, or else risk causing negative externalities to others.

Common property regimes typically evolve to solve such coordination problems by specifying access rules to resources and enforcing them over a well-defined membership. In other words, the common property regime provides the market across which internalisation of the negative externalities can be negotiated. In cases where common property regimes are said to cause 'tenure insecurity' for the individual, the community may in fact be preventing individuals from (re)creating a negative externality by disassociating themselves from the common property rules. The benefits of exclusive, individualised property, then, need to be weighed against the social cost of the externality.

In summary, the agro-pastoral production systems of the arid and semiarid tropics typically incorporate a mix of mechanisms that allow for adaptive strategies to changing environmental conditions. In the case of Sahelian nomadism, the economic value of such flexible strategies has found its expression in continuous movements of the production unit over time, that is, 'spatio-temporal flexibility'. Empirically, one can observe a relation between the riskiness of the environment and the importance of flexibility-based adaptive strategies to the agricultural production system.

Property rights theory suggests that a pluralistic property rights regime under which both private and common property regimes could coexist and co-evolve would be efficient in capturing the economic value of different adaptive strategies. Nomadic property regimes allow pastoralists to implement adaptive strategies to environmental uncertainty. An adaptive strategy and its associated property regime generally require *ex post* coordination between economic actors. By contrast, a non-adaptive strategy typically requires only *ex ante* coordination. Thus, the informational requirements of adaptive strategies will induce the establishment of a common property regime if coordination between individuals is less costly under centralised management at the group level than under a system of private contracting between independent actors.

IV. POLICY ISSUES

Policy-makers and analysts often speak of a 'nomadic dilemma' when referring to the predicament of nomads in the Sahel and elsewhere in Africa. The 'nomadic dilemma' is seldom understood as a problem of property rights, but, rather, as one of nomads 'lacking modern education, ignoring frontiers and spreading cattle diseases' [*Adamu and Kirk-Greene, 1986: xiii*]. Additionally, 'Pastoral nomadism tends to be regarded as anachronistic, unconducive to good administration or education, and is expected to be superseded in time by "resettlement" programmes' [*Mortimore, 1989: 223*]. Thus, a commonly held assumption is that nomadism is ultimately doomed and that efforts should be geared towards making this outcome as painless as possible. See, for example, Lowe [*1986*]. This attitude is best illustrated by a proposal for a principal motion at the Fifteenth International African Seminar on Pastoralists of the West African Savannah that bluntly states that it is not in the interests of the pastoralists to continue to lead a nomadic way of life. Instead, they should settle down, while the governments of the region should take care 'to preserve whatever is worth preserving in their culture, including their languages' [*Adamu and Kirk-Greene, 1986: xvii*].

The empirical reality of the resilience and economic importance of pastoral production systems provides a stark contrast to the above presumptions. Perhaps 25 per cent of the total population of West Africa can be classified as pastoral [*Sihm, 1989*]. In Sahelian West Africa (Senegal, Mali, Burkina Faso, Niger, and Chad) livestock production typically accounts for 30 to 40 per cent of total agricultural value added. Shapiro [*1979*] estimated that cattle originating in Mauritania, Mali, Burkina Faso, Niger and Chad constitutes more than 50 per cent of all slaughter cattle in the wider West African region, whereas only one-tenth of West African cattle production can be attributed to sedentary livestock production systems. The so-called 'low-productivity' Sahelian livestock production systems operate at levels of animal protein production per hectare that significantly exceed the levels for comparable regions in the United States and Australia [*Breman and de Wit, 1983*]. Comparisons between transhumant and sedentary livestock production invariably show greater animal productivity under the former production modes [*Penning de Vries, 1983*].[8]

The supposedly 'subsistence oriented' and 'backward' nomadic economy supplies all major urban centers in West Africa with a steady flow of meat [*Swift, 1986*]. This flow is assured by an elaborate international trading network that links the Sahelian pastoralists with the major consumption centres on both sides of the Sahara desert. Paradoxically, the nomads' alleged poverty and backwardness do not seem to inhibit the governments of the region in levying a plethora of direct taxes on cattle trade. Similar direct taxation of farmers is virtually non-existent. Moreover, the balance of political and economic power between pastoralists and farmers in the West African savannah has steadily been shifting towards farmers. At worst, the process has led to the simple annulment of pastoral property rights. At best, transaction costs have increasingly been shifted on to the pastoralist production system. The undermining of pastoralist property rights is probably first and foremost related to a decline in political influence. Additionally, population pressure has increased the opportunity costs of arable land. The end result is that Abel's 'domain' has shrunk dramatically.

From the thirteenth century onwards, incited by the demand for slaves emanating from the trans-Saharan trade, the horse-riding peoples of Saharan origin had engaged in predatory activities on their Southern neighbours of Niger-Congo origins. This predatory pattern reached its climax during the eighteenth and nineteenth centuries, when pastoralist tribes effectively colonised large portions of the West African savannah through an imperialist expansion strategy based on professional warfare. This system rested on the mobilisation of large armies of slaves, on the mobility of cavalries – which explains why the invasions stopped short of the tsetse fly infected forest zones – and on the effective control over tribute-paying farming populations [*Bah, 1986; Franke and Chasin, 1980*].

The French colonisers attempted to pacify the region through the sedentarisation of the nomads and the abolition of slavery. Policies of *divide et impera* were employed to reduce the political power of the nomads, but at times the attacks on the nomadic hegemonies, such as the

1917 massacre of the nomadic aristocracy at Tanut in Niger, were direct and brutal [*Lainé, 1982*]. When the upkeep of the slave economies became infeasible and feudal taxation revenues dwindled, the nomadic empires quickly collapsed.

The voluntary or involuntary incorporation of sedentary farming populations in the nomadic political economy was a key strategy pursued by the nomads of the West African savannah [*Lovejoy and Baier, 1976; Konczacki, 1978*].[9] In some cases, transfers between the two systems were part of a formal political economy ruled by 'urbanised' pastoralists who monopolized the trans-Saharan trade routes, while assuring themselves of a steady food supply through the operation of slave plantations. In other cases, the transfers occurred as part of a pattern of opportunistic raids of nomads into the southern farming zones. Finally, and probably in the majority of cases, a symbiotic relationship existed between the rural pastoralists and their farming neighbours, based on the complementarity of the two production systems [*Baier, 1976; Mortimore, 1989; Forde, 1960*].

In the last decades, however, there has been a marked increase of conflicts between nomads and farmers, generally at the expense of the nomads. In particular, what has been called the 'colonisation' of the Sahel by the farming population greatly reduced the spatial flexibility on which the pastoralist technology was based. Nomads had to circumvent larger cultivated areas, lengthening their routes and increasing the costs of operating the pastoralist system considerably.[10] Additionally, new irrigation schemes typically occupy large areas of valley bottom lands, which constitute crucial pastoral resources during the dry season.

Unfortunately, both Sahelian and coastal governments of the region often identify with the farming population, viewing nomads as strangers, transients, and non-citizens with no legitimate claim to property rights to natural resources. The effect of this persistent 'farmer bias' is that changes in property rights regimes introduced by these states have usually completely annulled pastoral property rights. Nomads were simply expropriated by the declaration that all *terres libres* (most of which were, in fact, grazing lands) were to be considered national property.[11] In this context, a common assertion is that the 'nation' owns all the land and that therefore the nomads have to compensate the 'nation' for use of the grass. This compensation rule is then typically used to justify the imposition of a plethora of taxes on livestock ownership and marketing, ranging from a variety of sales taxes to taxes for 'use of the road'. On the other hand, one finds such reasoning conspicuously absent in the case of farmers' cultivation or fuelwood collection.

Reduced flexibility increased livestock losses during periods of extreme environmental variability, such as the prolonged drought period of 1968–76. At the height of the drought (1973) losses were estimated at 20 to 70 per cent [*Konczacki, 1978*]. Although some losses might have been exaggerated, it seemed that the capacity of the nomadic system to manage the effects of the drought had been greatly reduced, compared with earlier droughts such as the one in 1930 [*Grégoire, 1982a*].

At the same time, however, population growth in the wider West African region increased the price of meat relative to labour. Sahclian herds grew steadily – further adding to the tensions between nomads and farmers [*Konczacki, 1978; Crotty, 1980*].[12] Increased profitability of livestock ownership also led more and more farmers to invest in herds of their own. These herds were not always given in custody to the nomads following the traditional institutions. Thus emerged new contenders for water and grass with no linkage to the pastoralist regulatory mechanisms.

Development policies with respect to livestock production in the Sahel have generally not countered the above negative trends because they were often based on paradigms that did not stress the value of flexibility with respect to natural resource use in arid and semiarid environments. Examples of paradigms that underestimated the value of flexibility were sedentarisation, group ranching, and the promotion of on-farm integration of agriculture and livestock production. The majority of such well-intended development programmes have largely failed [*Hogg, 1987; Sandford, 1983*]. Sometimes nomads settle spontaneously and apparently voluntary.

However, as shown by the 'Cain and Abel' model, any increase in transaction costs necessary to uphold nomadic property rights reduces the value of flexibility and thereby induces the sedentarisation of nomads, *ceteris paribus*. Thus, an apparently 'spontaneous' transition from specialised herding to farming need not be interpreted as an optimal evolution but may represent a constrained, and impoverishing, response [*Smith, 1978; McCown, Haaland and de Haan, 1979*]. In general, sedentarisation – spontaneous or as part of a resettlement scheme – has produced negative economic, social and ecological effects, as the many attempts at sedentarisation of pastoralists in Africa show [*Konczacki, 1978: 59*].[13]

Other once-popular livestock sector projects included the establishment of ranches. The development of ranching assumes that the local ecosystem is capable of supporting herds year-round when these herds are confined to a specific territory. However, the limitations of the ecosystem to support cattle on a permanent basis caused many ranching projects to fail or to resort to additional feed inputs by importing grain or the by-products of certain agro-processing industries (for example, cotton mills, sugar cane processing factories, beer industries) from more southern regions at considerable cost [*Crotty 1980*].

The 'integration' of crop and livestock production has also been emphasised as a preferred agricultural policy. However, integration has nearly always been pursued at the farm level rather than from a wider regional perspective. For the semi-arid tropics, the importance of integration of livestock and crop production at the farm level – the key factor in the transformation of European agriculture – has been largely overstated [*Breman and de Wit, 1983*]. Such integration of farming and livestock production at the farm level is often constrained by unfavourable combinations of agro- climate, soil conditions, population density, and labour demands [*Delgado, 1979*]. The opportunity to keep livestock year-round on the farm – the potential for sedentary mixed farming – is severely limited by natural fodder supply per unit of land in the Sahelian and northern Sudanian regions.[14] Moreover, while potential feed supply per acre increases towards the south, opportunity costs of feed production also increase because of the increase in land scarcity. Consequently, the introduction of animal traction in the Sahel has not only suffered from very low adoption rates,[15] it has also often failed to produce the expected intensification effects. Rather, being a labour-saving technique, animal traction has led to area expansion [*Jaeger and Matlon, 1990*].

Given the agro-climatic conditions in the Sahel, increasing population pressure does not automatically induce the transition to agricultural intensification and an increase in output per unit of land as described by Boserup [*1965*]. Increases in population pressure, if not reduced by high out-migration rates, may result in an expansion of cultivation onto marginal lands, thereby raising the opportunity costs of grazing land. By increasing cultivation at the extensive margin, farmers encounter increased competition with nomads. This induces a phenomenon known as 'preventive' clearing. When the nomads are absent, farmers 'preventively' clear land in order to secure property rights, given that both nomads and farmers will normally respect the security of usufructuary property rights. Upon their return, the nomads are confronted with a *fait accompli*. Such encroachment by farmers is often backed by formal legislation. Niger's agrarian reform of 1977 specified that fields left fallow for more than nine years were considered 'free'. The tenure insecurity created by this legal reform led farmers to reduce fallow periods and embark upon strategies of 'preventive' clearing. We may think of this as farmers 'gathering' fields for possible future use. Accelerated environmental degradation and an intensification of conflicts between nomads and farmers were the results [*Thomson, 1982*].

Above the farm level, however, the wider regional environment offers several opportunities for crop-livestock integration – but integration based on economic exchange. Various traditional types of contracting attest to the benefits of such exchange opportunities [*Bromley and Chavas, 1989*]. The widespread phenomenon of farmers renting their cattle to nomads under a variant of the sharecropping contract is a good example of an economic exchange based on the comparative advantages of the two production systems. The nomad herds the farmer's cattle in exchange for a share of the outputs, usually specified in terms of calves and/or milk. Informational and incentive problems are reduced under such sharecropping contracts. Nomads profit from the increased access to capital, while farmers profit from a diversification of their assets across ecological zones. Such investment opportunities are also highly valued by urban investors [*Kintz, 1982*]. Another type of contract is known as the *contrat de fumure*, under which a farmer allows the nomad to graze cattle on the crop stubbles left after the harvest when the animals can no longer damage the crops, in exchange for the benefits of animal manure. Outside of the growing season, both farmer and nomad benefit from the establishment of a different set of property rights [*Dahlman, 1980; Wade, 1992*].

Some of the more recent pastoral policies attempt to restore indigenous common property regimes by creating exclusive pastoral zones. 'Territorialization' of pastoralists has been advocated by a number of observers [*Adams, 1975; Gallais, 1979*]. However, typical pastoral property regimes were not defined in terms of a specific territory. In fact, property regimes in line with the economic theory outlined above enabled continual mobility without restricting nomadic groups to a particular zone. The delimitation of pastoral zones, or the establishment of 'group ranches' under territorially exclusive property regimes, does not constitute an appropriate policy for resource use in the semiarid tropics. Empirically, such policies have often been associated with overuse of the resource base, amplification of negative effects of drought periods, and increased conflicts between nomads and farmers, among nomadic groups, and within nomadic groups [*de Haan, 1990; Little, 1987; Mortimore, 1989*]. Moreover, such policies sometimes end up merely allocating exclusive grazing rights to groups of sedentary farmers at the expense of pastoralists [*Grégoire, 1982a*].

The transfer of property rights over pastoral resources to the state – ostensibly to reduce conflicts over such resources – often results in even more ambiguity and insecurity. For instance, the installation of deep tubewells opened up areas previously too arid for grazing, but local pastoralists did not obtain property rights to the new wells. Rather, the wells became state property, and quickly turned into open access resources. New immigrants were attracted by the wells, and refused to abide by the old rules of the traditional common property regimes. The 'bore-hole paradox' was born: before the introduction of bore holes, shortage of water precluded degradation of the grasslands, while access to water was subject to social control. After the introduction of bore holes, grazing could continue for longer periods, while access to water was deregulated and became effectively 'open access'. At the same time, herd sizes increased through an increase in labour productivity: less labour was now necessary to water the animals. The combined effects resulted in serious overgrazing of the areas in the vicinity of these wells; see, for example, Crotty [*1980*] and Kintz [*1982*].

Equity, efficiency, and environmental sustainability strongly suggest that much can be gained from the restoration of non-exclusive property rights to pastoralists, and from the (re)creation of property regimes that allow for the exploitation of the comparative advantage of different production techniques in a regional context. In particular, measures should be taken to reduce transaction costs associated with herd movements within and across national boundaries.[16]

V. CONCLUSIONS

Nomads and farmers seem to have been in conflict throughout history and throughout the world. One Hebrew version of the Biblical story of Cain and Abel provides the first recorded clash between a nomad and a farmer. In some respects, conditions today are not much improved. Conflicts between nomads and farmers continually recur. However, next to conflict, complementarity is also a structural characteristic of the dual economy represented by Cain the farmer, and Abel the pastoralist. The two economic systems complement each other with respect to the exchange of outputs but seem to be continually at odds with one another over inputs, especially over the control of land use. Without a fundamental change in development policies for the Sahel, the gloomy scenario of Cain and Abel may be brought to its ultimate conclusion. Myth and reality have already become dangerously close in the recent history of the region.[17]

Abel's problem is seen to be one of explaining to Cain that if the latter would claim exclusive property rights, both would be worse off. In other words, Abel seeks to prevent a Pareto-inferior outcome. We have argued that the prevention of such an outcome should also be the focus of current development policies with respect to the agro-pastoral production systems of the West African Sahel. Policies should, first, acknowledge the structurally different techniques that underlie the agricultural and pastoral systems, respectively. Second, this recognition should then lead to the formulation of policies that further the establishment of an institutional setting within which both sectors can flourish. In particular, the acknowledgement of the structural differences in production techniques should have direct implications for the formulation of improved property regimes.

final version received January 1994

NOTES

1. On the concept of flexibility and the economic analysis of risk in an intertemporal setting, see Dreze and Modigliani [*1972*]; Epstein [*1980*].
2. Moreover, risk preferences have played a prominent role in economic studies that focused on ex ante risk reduction, notwithstanding the difficulty of the direct measurement of risk preferences. One advantage of the formulation of economic theory under temporal uncertainty is that it establishes the value of information or the value of an adaptive strategy under general risk preferences.
3. To simulate results, a computer model was developed using the matrix language Gauss. The graphs that accompany the main text are based on this model.
4. The rainfall regime described above was simulated using Gamma distributions. A random variable **e** has a gamma distribution with parameters $\boldsymbol{\alpha}$ and $\boldsymbol{\beta}$ ($\boldsymbol{\alpha} \geq 0$ and $\boldsymbol{\beta} \geq 0$) if **e** has a continuous distribution for which the probability density function

$$h(e \mid \boldsymbol{\alpha}, \boldsymbol{\beta}) = \{\boldsymbol{\beta}^{\alpha}/G(\boldsymbol{\alpha})\}\, e^{\alpha-1} \exp^{-\beta e} \qquad \text{for } e \geq)$$
$$0 \qquad \text{for } e \geq)$$

The first and second moments are:

$$E(e) = \boldsymbol{\alpha}/\boldsymbol{\beta}$$
$$Var(e) = \boldsymbol{\alpha}/\boldsymbol{\beta}^2$$

For the computer simulation (as presented in the graphs), a pattern which was linear in E(e) and Var(e) with respect to movements along the North–South axis was chosen.
5. The transactions costs associated with mobility are assumed to take the following form:

$$TC = \boldsymbol{\delta} \mid x_2 - x_1 \mid$$

TC = transactions costs

$\boldsymbol{\delta}$ = transactions cost parameter.

6. Given a certain period 1 location, the expected value of the ex post utility function was numerically calculated by an iterative simulation method. A logarithmic utility function was used. Many of the results presented below will hold *irrespective* of the nature of risk preferences.
7. For instance, nomads may sow some plots at the beginning of the rains and move north with their herds in search of pasture, leaving the sown plots unattended until their

return at the end of the season. Alternatively, a section of the nomadic population may cultivate some crops on valley-bottom lands during the short rainy season, while the other section accompanies the herds on their seasonal movements.

8. In Botswana, comparisons with ranching show that the production of protein per hectare under the traditional production system is significantly higher [*de Ridder and Wagenaar, 1984*].
9. At the same time, pastoralist mobility was the basis for the development of various long-range trading networks. This is particularly true for the caravan trade across the Sahara with the Mediterranean region, and the sub-Saharan trade with the southern savannah and forest zones of West Africa.
10. For instance, movements further south often led to increased taxation by the different farming populations along the way.
11. Even in the rare cases where legislation seemed to favour pastoralist property rights, the de facto enforcement usually favoured the farmers. Thus, in Niger, all lands north of the cultivation limit (approximate latitude 15° 10′ north) were officially declared pastoralist zones. However, this legal restriction did not prevent farmers from entering these areas in the 1960s. They were: '... effectively supported by government administrators apparently unwilling to carry out the legal restrictions on the northern limits to cultivation' [*Franke and Chasin, 1980: 98*].
12. Increases in herd size may have been a combined response to both relative prices and to the reduction of flexibility of the pastoralist system. Several authors have argued that a large herd size *per se* can function as a risk-reducing strategy. It constitutes an insurance in times of excessive mortality induced by drought [*Monod, 1975; Van Raay, 1974; Sandford, 1983*]. Others argue that state-sponsored vaccination campaigns have also significantly increased herd size, but that herds are now of a poorer quality, because of a decrease in natural selection and an increase in overgrazing.
13. For East Africa, Hogg [*1987*] shows that sedentarisation of nomads around an irrigation scheme had detrimental ecological effects. Moreover, the pastoralists who were settled closest to the center of an irrigation scheme eventually ended up the poorest, while the pastoralists on the fringes of the scheme were able to increase their wealth through a combination of access to the irrigation scheme and continued access to the grazing areas on the fringes and outside of the scheme.
14. It is here that the fundamental difference lies between the West African savannah and the high-altitude grasslands of East Africa, where population pressure often does induce a pattern of intensification based on an on-farm integration of agriculture and livestock production. In many regions of East Africa, such integration has far greater potential to be realised within the same farming system, mainly because of better soils. Consequently, the agroclimates of the East African high savannah and highlands have produced a whole series of societies whose economic strategies were based on the integration of crop cultivation and herding. Thus, typical 'pastoralist' peoples of this region may in reality be more cultivator than pastoralist [*Oliver, 1992*].
15. Many development programs in the Sahel have promoted animal traction by distributing subsidised packages consisting of animals (cattle and donkeys), ploughs and weeders. The subsidised access to animals has of course been very popular among the farmers of the region. However, the actual use of the equipment, as measured by acreage ploughed and weeded, is often very low, with the exception of certain cotton-growing areas.
16. For instance, West African states should consider the adoption of a uniform and simple taxation system. Even if the total tax load per animal remains unchanged, any reduction in the mere number of different taxes and bureaucratic requirements would significantly reduce transaction costs.
17. The recent 'wars between brethren' (namely the violent conflicts between Mauritania and Senegal and between Mali and Burkina Faso) were directly linked to the herder/farmer problem and may serve as ominous examples. Touareg rebellions in Algeria, Niger and Mali erupted shortly after we started work on this article.

REFERENCES

Adams, M.E. 1975, 'A Development Plan for Semi-Arid Areas in Western Sudan', *Experimental Agriculture*, Vol.2, pp.277–87.

Adamu, Mahdi and A.H.M. Kirk-Greene (eds.), 1986, *The Pastoralists of the West African Savannah*, Selected Studies presented and discussed at the Fifteenth International African Seminar Held at Ahmadu Bello University, Nigeria, July 1979, Manchester: Manchester University Press in association with the International African Institute.

Bah, Thierno Mouctar, 1986, 'Les Armées Peul de l'Adamawa au 19e Siècle', in *The Pastoralists of the West African Savannah*, Selected Studies presented and discussed at the Fifteenth International African Seminar Held at Ahmadu Bello University, Nigeria, July 1979, edited by Mahdi Adamu and A.H.M. Kirk-Greene, Manchester: Manchester University Press in association with the International African Institute.

Baier, Stephen, 1976, 'Economic History and Development: Drought and the Sahelian Economies of Niger', *African Economic History*, Vol.1, pp.1–16.

Baroin, Catherine, 1985, *Anarchie et cohésion sociale chez les Toubous: Les Daza Késerda (Niger)*, Cambridge: Cambridge University Press; Paris: Editions de la Maison des Sciences de l'Homme.

Behnke, R.H. and I. Scoones, 1991, *Rethinking Range Ecology: Implications for Rangeland Management in Africa*, Overview of paper presentations and discussions at the Technical Meeting on Savanna Development and Pasture Production, 19–21 Nov. 1990, Woburn, UK, London: Commonwealth Secretariat.

Boserup, Ester, 1965, *The Conditions of Agricultural Growth: The Economics of Agrarian Change Under Population Pressure*, New York: Aldine Publishing.

Breman, H. and C.T. de Wit, 1983, 'Rangeland Productivity and Exploitation in the Sahel', *Science*, 221 (4618), pp.1341–47.

Bromley, Daniel W., 1989, 'Property Relations and Economic Development: The Other Land Reform,' *World Development*, Vol.17, No.6, pp. 867–77.

Bromley, Daniel W., 1991, *Environment and Economy: Property Rights and Public Policy*, Oxford: Blackwell.

Bromley, Daniel W. (ed.), 1992, *Making the Commons Work: Theory, Practice, and Policy*, San Francisco, CA: ICS Press.

Bromley, Daniel W. and Michael M. Cernea, 1989, *The Management of Common Property Natural Resources: Some Conceptual and Operational Fallacies*, World Bank Discussion Paper 57, Washington, DC, 1989.

Bromley, Daniel W. and Jean-Paul Chavas, 1989, 'On Risk, Transactions, and Economic Development in the Semiarid Tropics', *Economic Development and Cultural Change*, Vol.37, No.4, pp.719–36.

Chavas, J.-P., Kristjanson, Patricia M. and Peter Matlon, 1991, 'On the Role of Information in Decision-Making: The Case of Sorghum Yield in Burkina Faso', *Journal of Development Economics*, Vol.35, No.2, pp.261–280.

Cissé, S., 1982, 'Les Leyde du Delta Central du Niger: tenure traditionnel ou exemple d'un aménagement de territoire classique', in Le Bris, Le Roy and Leimdorfer [*1982: 179–89*].

Clanet, Jean-Charles, 1975, 'Les Eleveurs de l'Ouest Tchadien', Doctorat de 3ème cycle, Rouen: Université de Rouen.

Cousins, Ben, 1992, 'Managing Communal Rangeland in Zimbabwe: Experiences and Lessons', Case Study prepared for Workshop on New Directions in African Range Management Policy, Matopos, Bulawayo, Zimbabwe, 13–17 Jan. 1992. London: Food Production and Rural Development Division, Commonwealth Secretariat.

Crotty, R, 1980, *Cattle, Economics and Development*, Slough, England: Commonwealth Agricultural Bureaux, pp.127–129.

Dahlman, Carl J, 1980, *The Open Field System and Beyond*, Cambridge: Cambridge University Press.

de Haan, C. 1990, 'Changing Trends in the World Bank's Lending Program for Rangeland Development', paper presented at the International Rangeland Symposium, Reno, Nevada, 15 Feb. 1990.

Delgado, Christopher F., 1979, 'The Southern Fulani Farming System in Upper-Volta: A Model for the Integration of Crop and Livestock Production in the West African Savannah', *African Rural Economy Paper No. 20*, East Lansing, MI: Department of Agricultural Economics, Michigan State University.

Demsetz, Harold, 1967, 'Toward a Theory of Property Rights', *American Economic Review*, 57 (May), pp.347–59.

de Ridder, N. and K.T. Wagenaar, 1984, 'A Comparison Between the Productivity of Traditional Livestock Systems and Ranching in Eastern Botswana', Proceedings of the 2nd International Rangeland Congress, Adelaide.

Dreze, J.H. and F. Modigliani, 1972, 'Consumption Decisions Under Uncertainty', *Journal of Economic Theory*, Vol.5, pp.308–35.

Epstein, L.G., 1980, 'Decision Making and the Temporal Resolution of Uncertainty', *International Economic Review*, Vol.21, No.2, pp.269–83.

Feder, Gershon and David Feeny, 1991, 'Land Tenure and Property Rights: Theory and Implications for Development Policy', *The World Bank Economic Review*, Vol.5, No.1, pp.135–53.

Feder, Gershon and Raymond Noronha, 1987, 'Land Rights Systems and Agricultural Development in Sub-Saharan Africa', *The World Bank Research Observer*, Vol.2, No.2, July 1987, pp.143–69.

Forde, Daryll, 1960, 'The Cultural Map of West Africa: Successive Adaptations to Tropical Forests and Grasslands', in Simon Ottenberg and Phoebe Ottenberg (eds.), *Cultures and Societies of Africa*, New York: Random House, pp.116–38.

Franke, Richard W. and Barbara H. Chasin, 1980, *Seeds of Famine: Ecological Destruction and the Development Dilemma in the West African Sahel*, Montclair, NJ: Allanheld, Osmun & Co.

Frantz, Charles, 1986, 'Fulani Continuity and Change Under Five Flags', in *The Pastoralists of the West African Savannah*, Selected Studies presented and discussed at the Fifteenth International African Seminar Held at Ahmadu Bello University, Nigeria, July 1979, edited by Mahdi Adamu and A.H.M. Kirk-Greene, Manchester: Manchester University Press in association with the International African Institute.

Gallais, Jean, 1979, 'La Situation de l'élevage bovin et le problème des éleveurs en Afrique occidentale et centrale', in *Les Cahiers d'Outre-Mer*, Vol.32, pp.113–44.

Graves, Robert and Raphael Patai, 1964, *Hebrew Myths: The Book of Genesis*, New York: Doubleday.

Grégoire, E. 1982a, 'Rapport des debats' and 'Synthese des debats', in Le Bris, Le Roy and Leimdorfer [*1982: 189–95*].

Grégoire, E. 1982b, 'Un Systeme de Production Agro-Pastoral in Crise: Le Terror de Gourjae (Niger)', in Le Bris, Le Roy and Leimdorfer [*1982: 202–11*].

Hardin, Garrett, 1968, 'The Tragedy of the Commons', *Science*, 162, Dec. pp.1243–48.

Hogg, R, 1987, 'Settlement, Pastoralism and the Commons', in David Anderson and Richard H. Grove (eds.), *Conservation in Africa: People, Policies and Practice*, Cambridge: Cambridge University Press, 293–306.

Jaeger, William K., and Peter Y. Matlon, 1990, 'Utilization, Profitability, and the Adoption of Animal Draft Power in West Africa.' *American Journal of Agricultural Economics*, 72 (Feb.), pp.35–48.

Kintz, D, 1982, 'Pastoralisme, Agro-Pastoralisme et Organisation Foncière: Le Cas des Peulhs', in Le Bris, Le Roy and Leimdorfer [*1982*].

Konczacki, Z.A., 1978, *The Economics of Pastoralism: A Case Study of Sub-Saharan Africa*, London: Frank Cass.

Lainé, Gilles, 1982, 'Évolution du régime foncier dans une société d'éleveurs nomades: le cas des Twareg Kel Dinnik dans la région de Tahoua (Niger)', in Le Bris, Le Roy and Leimdorfer [*1982: 195–202*].

Larson Bruce A. and Daniel W. Bromley, 1990, 'Property Rights, Externalities, and Resource Degradation: Locating the Tragedy', *Journal of Development Economics*, Vol.33, No.2, pp.235–62.

Le Bris, E., Le Roy, E. and F. Leimdorfer (eds.), 1982, *Enjeux fonciers en Afrique noire*, Paris: Karthala.

Little, Peter D, 1987, 'Land Use Conflicts in the Agricultural/Pastoral Borderlands: The Case of Kenya', in Peter D. Little and Michael M. Horowitz (eds.), *Lands at Risk in the Third World*, Boulder, CO: Westview Press, pp. 195–212.

Lovejoy, P.E., and S. Baier, 1976, 'The Desert-Side Economy of the Central Sudan', in Michael Glantz, (ed.), *The Politics of Natural Disaster*, New York: Praeger.

Lowe, R. G., 1986, *Agricultural Revolution in Africa? Impediments to Change and Implications for Farming, for Education and for Society*, London: Macmillan.

McCay, Bonnie and James M. Acheson, 1987, *The Question of the Commons: The Culture and Ecology of Communal Resources*, Tucson, AZ: University of Arizona Press.

McCown, R.L., Haaland, G. and C. de Haan, 1979, 'The Interaction Between Cultivation and Livestock Production in Semi-Arid Africa', in A.E. Hall, G.H. Cannell and H.W. Lawton (eds.), *Agriculture in Semi-Arid Environments*, Ecological Studies No.34, Heidelberg: Springer Verlag, pp.297–332.

Monod, T. (ed.), 1975, *Pastoralism in Tropical Africa*, Oxford: Oxford University Press.

Mortimore, Michael, 1989, *Adapting to Drought: Farmers, Famines and Desertification in West Africa*, Cambridge: Cambridge University Press.

National Academy of Sciences, Panel on Common Property Resource Management, 1986, *Common Property Resource Management*, Washington, DC: National Academy Press.

Neale, Walter C., 1969, 'Land is to Rule', in Robert Frykenberg (ed.), *Land Control and Social Structure in Indian History*, Madison, WI: University of Wisconsin Press.

Oliver, Roland, 1992, *The African Experience*, New York: Harper Collins.

Penning de Vries, F.W.T., 1983, 'The Productivity of Sahelian Rangelands: A Summary Report', *Pastoral Development Network Paper No. 15b*, London: Overseas Development Institute (Jan.).

Sandford, Stephen, 1983, *Management of Pastoral Development in the Third World*, Chichester: Wiley.

Sen, Amartya K., 1981, *Poverty and Famines: An Essay on Entitlement and Deprivation*, Oxford: Clarendon Press.

Shapiro, Kenneth H. (ed.), 1979, 'Livestock Production and Marketing in the Entente States of West Africa: Summary Report', Ann Arbor, MI: Center for Research on Economic Development, University of Michigan.

Sihm, Poul A., 1989, 'Pastoral Association in West Africa: Experience and Future Strategy', paper presented at the Professional Development Workshop on Dryland Management, World Bank, 10–11 May 1989.

Smith, Susan E., 1978, 'The Environmental Adaptation of Nomads in the West African Sahel: A Key to Understanding Prehistoric Pastoralists', in Wolfgang Weissleder, (ed.), *The Nomadic Alternative: Modes and Models of Interaction in the African–Asian Deserts and Steppes*, The Hague: Mouton Publishers.

Starr, Martha A., 1987, 'Risk, Environmental Variability and Drought-Induced Impoverishment: The Pastoral Economy of Central Niger', *Africa*, Vol.57, No.1, pp.29–50.

Swift, Jeremy, 1986, 'The Economics of Production and Exchange in West African Pastoral Societies', in *The Pastoralists of the West African Savannah*, Selected Studies presented and discussed at the Fifteenth International African Seminar Held at Ahmadu Bello University, Nigeria, July 1979, edited by Mahdi Adamu and A.H.M. Kirk-Greene, Manchester: Manchester University Press in association with the International African Institute, pp.175–90.

Thomson, J. T., 1982, 'Le Processus juridique, les droits fonciers et l'aménagement de l'environment dans un Canton Hausaphone du Niger', in Le Bris, Le Roy and Leimdorfer [*1982: 172*].

Van Raay, Hans G.T., 1974, 'Fulani Pastoralism and Cattle', Occasional Paper No.44, The Hague: Institute of Social Studies.

Wade, Robert, 1992, 'Common Property Resource Management in South Indian Villages', in Daniel W. Bromley (ed.) *Making the Commons Work: Theory, Practice, and Policy*, San Francisco, CA: ICS Press.

Warren, A., and J. K. Maizels, 1977, 'Ecological Change and Desertification', Background Document, United Nations Conference on Desertification, Nairobi: United Nations Environment Programme.

[16]

ELSEVIER

Agricultural Economics 10 (1994) 193–200

AGRICULTURAL ECONOMICS

Extensification of agriculture and deforestation: empirical evidence from Sudan

Abdelmoneim H. Elnagheeb

Department of Agricultural and Applied Economics, Georgia Experiment Station, University of Georgia, Griffin, GA 30223-1797, USA

Daniel W. Bromley *

Department of Agricultural Economics, University of Wisconsin-Madison, 427 Lorch Street, Madison, WI 53706, USA

(Accepted 29 June 1993)

Abstract

Extensification of agriculture is one of the major factors contributing to the destruction of forests in Africa. In Sudan, such horizontal expansion comes at the expense of land devoted to trees and other vegetation, thereby inducing conditions that are inimical to sustainable agricultural production. Different factors have contributed to extensification. Although high economic returns from crop (mainly sorghum) production was an important factor encouraging extensification of rainfed mechanized farming, other factors outside agriculture have also contributed to that expansion. This paper uses data from eastern Sudan and an acreage response model, to identify the most important factors influencing acreage expansion. Different measures and forms of risk were used in the acreage response model. The paper shows how policies in the energy sector can indirectly influence acreage expansion in the agricultural sector.

1. Introduction

Degradation of natural resources in the developing countries can be regarded as arising for three primary reasons: (1) explicit government policies to satisfy domestic needs or to increase exports to earn foreign exchange; (2) misguided management policies that have as their intent the actual protection of natural resources; and (3) the interrelations between other economic policies and the natural resource base of a country (Bromley, 1986). In this paper we report on empirical research highlighting the third of these phenomena – the interaction of various economic policies and events that may seem, on the surface, to be unrelated. Specifically, this research illustrates the linkage between energy supply and pricing policy and agricultural extensification – that is, the horizontal expansion of agriculture into forested areas – in eastern Sudan. [1] While

* Corresponding author.

[1] The impacts of agricultural extensification on forestry and agricultural production have been discussed elsewhere (e.g. Elnagheeb and Bromley, 1992; Ibrahim, 1987).

SSDI 0169-5150(93)E0036-M

the specific venue of the research is Sudan, similar phenomena exist throughout the Sahel.

When imported oil was a cheap source of energy in Sudan, there was scant incentive to clear land for charcoal production. The high cost of land clearing was one of the main factors that protected forested areas against horizontal expansion of rainfed agriculture (Affan, 1984). However, when oil prices began to rise in the 1970's, charcoal suddenly became a competitive energy source for urban dwellers deprived of affordable petroleum products. Moreover, the increase in the population of urban areas from in-migration has led to significant increases in the demand for charcoal. The subsequent increase in charcoal prices soon cast the forest in a new light to farmers and herders who then began to exploit forests to produce charcoal for urban markets. Consequently, the increased revenue potential from clearing land for agriculture has meant that land-clearing costs no longer act as an impediment to accelerated deforestation for creating arable land. Hence, the high returns from charcoal production were hypothesized to be another important factor contributing to the expansion of agriculture into marginal lands at the expense of forested areas. This continued expansion of rainfed agriculture in response to important but *unintended* incentives can be a serious policy problem facing many poor countries.

2. Setting

The rainfed mechanized farming schemes got their start in Sudan in 1944, in an area of about 12 000 feddans, [2] primarily to feed troops stationed in East Africa during World War II. The Government then began to encourage the private sector to participate in these schemes. The high economic returns of early settlers encouraged other participants and so resulted in a fairly rapid expansion of the area cleared for cultivation. By 1985 the total area under rainfed mechanized farming was about 7.4 million feddans (Earl, 1985). While called mechanized farming, in fact only land preparation and sowing are mechanized. Weeding (if any) and harvesting are manual operations. The grain is cut by hand and threshed by stationary harvesters (Ibnouf, 1985). Four crops are grown – dura (sorghum), sesame, millet and cotton. However, dura accounts for 80–90% of the land area (Affan, 1984). Sesame is the second most important crop, while millet and cotton are grown in very limited areas. This trend seems persistent over time.

On the rainfed mechanized schemes, land is leased by the Government to farmers in lots of 1000–2000 feddans for a renewable period of 25 years at a nominal land rent (LS0.05 per feddan per year [3] – approximately $0.13 per acre – in 1976). These farms are referred to as *demarcated farms*. In addition to the demarcated farms, there are large areas of land that have been cleared without authorization; these areas are referred to as *undemarcated farms*. Whether authorized (demarcated) or not, the typical farming practice is continuous cropping – defined here as putting cleared land under production of the same crop (dura) for successive years without fallowing (or with a very short fallow period). Shifting cultivation to new areas (which are sometimes marginal lands) occurs when yields decline below a profitable level. Although some ecological safeguards – such as shelterbelts and crop rotation – are required by the Mechanized Farming Corporation, these practices are rarely followed. In general, no fertilizers, insecticides or pesticides are applied to these cropped lands and so it comes as no surprise that, over time, productivity declines. [4]

3. Empirical model

An acreage response model was used to study the acreage expansion in the rainfed mechanized

[2] feddan = 1.04 acre ≈ 0.42 ha.

[3] LS, Sudanese pound = $2.70 in 1976.

[4] Fertilizers, insecticides and pesticides are imported and made available only to irrigated schemes. Following the rotation prescribed by the Mechanized Farming Corporation (MFC) would eliminate (or at least reduce) the need for these chemicals in the rainfed mechanized farms. However, easy access to land and lack of law enforcement discourage farmers to follow the MFC's recommendations.

sector of Sudan. In most of the econometric studies of acreage response it has been recognized that risk with respect to price, yield and income influences farmers' production decisions (Adesina and Brorsen, 1987; Behrman, 1968; Chavas and Holt, 1990; Just, 1974; Ryan, 1977; Trail, 1978; Wilson et al., 1980; Wolgin, 1975). In these studies, risk has been expressed in a 'symmetric' form which considers both very high and very low returns as undesirable (Markowitz, 1970). However, one expects producers to be more concerned about negative than positive deviations from a targeted price, yield or income. Therefore, an 'asymmetric' risk analysis that utilizes only the negative deviations may be preferred to a symmetric risk analysis (Tronstad and McNeill, 1989).

Models estimated in this paper utilize both symmetric and asymmetric forms of risk. Different variables were used to represent riskiness of price or production. These variables range from simple expressions such as a moving range or absolute difference between expected and actual price (Brennan, 1980) to more complicated expressions such as moving standard deviations (Behrman, 1968; Just, 1974).

Dura accounts for 80–90% of the land area under the rainfed mechanized sector (Affan, 1984). Hence, the focus here is on the acreage response for dura only. Millet and cotton are grown on very limited areas. Therefore, variation in prices of millet and cotton can be expected not to affect the acreage response for dura. Sesame is the second crop in rainfed agriculture and shares with millet and cotton the remaining 10–20% of the land area. Therefore, the initial models included sesame price, sesame price risk and the covariance between dura and sesame prices as explanatory variables. However, nested F-tests could not reject the null hypothesis that all coefficients on sesame variables were simultaneously equal to zero. Hence, these variables are not included in the empirical model. The price of charcoal is included because farmers can make use of cleared trees to produce charcoal. This is expected to be an added incentive for farmers to clear more land for cultivation. The revenue from charcoal can offset, or at least reduce, the cost of land clearance (Earl, 1985). The empirical model, based on Behrman (1968), is given by Eq. (1):

$$\ln(A_t) = \beta_0 + \beta_1\,\text{EDP}_t + \beta_2 C_t + \beta_3\,\text{CP}_t + \beta_4\,\text{EDY}_t + \beta_5\,\text{ERF}_t + \beta_6\,\text{DPR}_t + \beta_7\,\text{RFR}_t + e_t \tag{1}$$

where

$$e_t = \rho e_{t-1} + u_t$$

and

$$u_t = N(0, \sigma^2)$$

and, for time period t, $\ln(A_t)$ is the natural logarithm of dura-cultivated area in feddan; EDP_t is expected dura real price [5] in 0.01 Sudanese pounds (LS) per kilogram; C_t is cost of dura production in LS per feddan; CP_t is charcoal price in LS per 80-lb sack [6]; EDY_t is expected dura yield in kilogram per feddan; ERF_t is expected rainfall in millimeter; DPR_t is dura price risk; and RFR_t is rainfall risk. Economic theory provides little help in choosing the appropriate functional form and so different functional forms were tried. The form in Eq. (1) gives the best fit of the data.

The data used in this study are limited to the eastern region (Gedarif) which contains the largest area devoted to rainfed mechanized agriculture. The data do not distinguish between demarcated and undemarcated schemes. More complete data were available for the period 1969–1985 and were used for this study. Data sources include different publications. Data on areas cultivated, rainfall and yields are from the Mechanized Farming Corporation (MFC, 1984). The Department of Agricultural Economics and Statistics (1986, 1987, 1989) provided data on areas cultivated, yields and production costs, while the Department of Statistics (undated) is the source of data on prices. Data on consumer price index and charcoal prices are from the National Energy Administration (1987). Charcoal prices for the eastern region were not available. Hence,

[5] The consumer price index was used to deflate dura price and cost of production. While a price index for agricultural inputs would have been a better index for deflating costs of production, lack of data precluded this approach.

[6] lb. pound ≈ 0.454 kg.

we used charcoal prices for the province of Khartoum, a main market for the charcoal produced in Gedarif. Costs of production data are supplemented with data from Thimm (1979) and El Hadari and Suliman (1980). The data are estimates based on cross-section surveys conducted annually by the different government departments.

The expected real price (EDP_t) is assumed to be a linear function of last year's real price (DP_{t-1}) according to the maximum-likelihood-estimated equation: [7]

$$\text{EDP}_t = 0.0763468 + 0.566671\ \text{DP}_{t-1} \qquad R^2 = 0.46$$
$$(2.035) \qquad (3.446) \qquad (2)$$

where t-values are given in parentheses.

Farmers need not form expectations about charcoal price because charcoal making can proceed rapidly. Therefore, the price of charcoal at time t is the observed market price in that year. Land preparation and sowing costs are a major part of production costs and both are known to farmers before land allocation decisions are taken. Hence, production costs are treated as non-stochastic. The expected dura yield and expected rainfall are assumed to be last year's yield and rainfall, respectively. [8]

Two forms of risk analysis (symmetric and asymmetric) are used. Within each form two variables (simple and complex) are used to represent risk. Hereafter, X_t is dura real price or rainfall, while EX_t refers to the expected value. For both price and rainfall risk, the following risk variables are defined. The symmetric-simple measure of risk (SXR_t^s) is the absolute value of the difference between the actual and expected values for the previous year:

$$\text{SXR}_t^s = \text{abs}(X_{t-1} - \text{EX}_{t-1}) \qquad (3)$$

On the other hand, the symmetric-complex measure of risk (SXR_t^c) is a moving standard deviation of X_t over the previous three years (Behrman, 1968):

$$\text{SXR}_t^c = \left[\Sigma_k \left(X_{t-k} - X_{\text{BAR}_t}\right)^2/2\right]0.5 \qquad (4)$$

where

$$X_{\text{BAR}_t} = (1/3)\ \Sigma_k X_{t-k} \qquad k = 1, 2, 3$$

The asymmetric-simple measure of risk (ASXR_t^s) equals the absolute value of the difference between actual and expected values for the previous year if the expected value exceeds the actual corresponding value and zero otherwise:

$$\text{ASXR}_t^s = \begin{cases} \text{abs}(X_{t-1} - \text{EX}_{t-1}) & \text{if } \text{EX}_{t-1} > X_{t-1} \\ 0 & \text{otherwise} \end{cases} \qquad (5)$$

The asymmetric-complex measure of risk (ASXR_t^c) is given by:

$$\text{ASXR}_t^c = \left[\sum_k (\text{XR}_{t-k})^2/2\right]^{0.5} \qquad k = 1, 2, 3 \quad (6)$$

where

$$\text{XR}_{t-k} = \begin{cases} X_{t-k} - X_{\text{BAR}_t} & \text{if } X_{\text{BAR}_t} > X_{t-k} \\ X_{\text{BAR}_t} & \text{otherwise} \end{cases}$$

Economic theory suggests that the supply of a commodity increases as its (expected) price increases ($\beta_1 > 0$). An increase in production costs is expected to decrease the acreage for dura ($\beta_2 < 0$). By converting the cleared trees into charcoal the farmer can make some small profit, or at least reduce the net costs of land clearance. Therefore, we hypothesize that an increase in charcoal price will induce farmers to clear and cultivate more land ($\beta_3 > 0$). An increase in expected yield (EDY) will mean an increase in expected income and so β_4 is expected to be positive. Because we are concerned here with rainfed agriculture, the area cultivated is expected to increase as farmers expect higher rainfall ($\beta_5 > 0$). Assuming that farmers are risk-averse, an increase in perceptions of risk (DPR or RFR) is expected to shift the acreage curve to the left ($\beta_6 < 0$; $\beta_7 < 0$).

[7] A Durbin h-test indicated first-order autocorrelation. The equation was, therefore, estimated by maximum likelihood.

[8] Last year's rainfall gave better statistical results than the average rainfall over the last 2, 3 and 4 years. We also regressed yield on time and experimented with the expected values as a proxy for expected yield. However, yield from the previous year gave better statistical results.

4. Empirical results

Four versions of Eq. (1) were estimated by maximum likelihood procedures (Judge et al., 1982). The four versions differ only in the risk variables (DPR and RFR). Accordingly, these four versions are the symmetric-simple, symmetric-complex, asymmetric-simple and asymmetric-complex risk models. The symmetric form of risk is tested against the asymmetric form, and the simple measure of risk is tested against the complex measure using the non-nested *J*-test (Davidson and MacKinnon, 1981). The results of the pairwise *J*-test are presented in Table 1. Generally, Table 1 shows that the asymmetric-risk models were preferred to the symmetric-risk models and the simple measures of risk were preferred to complex measures (for more detail, see Elnagheeb and Bromley, 1991).

Table 2 presents the maximum likelihood estimates of the four risk models along with the estimates of the conventional non-risk model. In all models, the majority of coefficients (at least five out of seven) are significant at the 5% level of significance. The signs of all significant coefficients conform with a priori expectations. Dura acreage increases with dura's expected price and expected yield and decreases with increases in the cost of production. The insignificance of the expected rainfall coefficient might be due to

Table 1
Results of the non-nested *J*-test [a]

Tested hypotheses (H_0)	Alternative hypotheses (H_1)			
	SSRM	SCRM	ASRM	ACRM
SSRM		−0.197	1.489 *	
SCRM	2.007 ***			1.690 **
ASRM	0.624			0.900
ACRM		0.181	1.007	

[a] Entries are the values of the *t*-statistic for testing H_0.
SSRM, symmetric-simple risk model; SCRM, symmetric-complex risk model; ASRM, asymmetric-simple risk model; ACRM, asymmetric-complex risk model.
*, ** and *** indicate statistical significance at the 15%, 10% and 5% level, respectively. A significant *t* implies the rejection of H_0.

Table 2
Maximum likelihood estimates of dura acreage response function

Variable	Model				Non-risk model
	SSRM	SCRM	ASRM	ACRM	
Intercept	6.5383 ***	6.2612 ***	6.8429 ***	6.9837 ***	7.0525 ***
	(17.323)	(13.513)	(18.519)	(17.190)	(16.517)
Expected dura	4.8874 ***	3.9687 ***	1.7706 *	4.0139 ***	3.1177 **
price, EDP	(3.988)	(4.150)	(1.792)	(5.692)	(2.856)
Cost, *C*	−12.6588 **	−1.6545	−9.5532 **	−13.5655 **	−19.4478 ***
	(−3.230)	(−0.230)	(−1.983)	(−2.388)	(−5.086)
Charcoal	0.06443 ***	0.08236 ***	0.06667 ***	0.079977 ***	0.049006 ***
price, CP	(3.243)	(3.989)	(6.431)	(5.901)	(3.188)
Expected dura	0.001305 **	0.00271 ***	0.0023 ***	0.0030 ***	0.0018 **
yield, EDY	(2.043)	(4.219)	(4.599)	(5.225)	(2.381)
Expected	0.0006	0.0000169	0.0001508	−0.0002421	0.0001961
rainfall, ERF	(1.259)	(0.035)	(0.279)	(−0.582)	(0.334)
Dura price-	−2.51142 **	−2.55884 **	−3.81440 ***	−1.71877 **	
risk, DPR	(−2.235)	(−2.492)	(−3.493)	(−2.796)	
Rainfall	−0.0011524 *	−0.0023291 **	−0.0002945	−0.0004146 *	
risk, RFR	(−1.726)	(−1.982)	(−0.378)	(−1.455)	
Rho, ρ	−0.508720 **	−0.829008 ***	−0.911691 ***	−0.914384 ***	−0.497130 **
	(−2.289)	(−5.741)	(−8.594)	(−8.747)	(−2.219)
Chi-square	43.881 ***	41.284 ***	45.821 ***	45.301 ***	32.480 ***

Numbers in parentheses are the *t*-values.
*, ** and *** denote significance at the 10%, 5% and 1% level, respectively; one-sided test for all coefficients and two-sided test for chi-square and ρ.

collinearity between expected rainfall and expected yield.

An interesting result is that charcoal price has a positive coefficient which is significant at the 5% level of significance in all models. This finding supports the hypothesis that higher charcoal prices act as an added incentive for farmers to clear land for cultivation. The result may explain, at least partially, why farmers in the rainfed mechanized schemes do not leave a portion of their land in trees for shelterbelts as required by the Mechanized Farming Corporation. The result also illustrates the interrelationships between the energy and agricultural sectors. Policies such as import restrictions on oil products and distorted prices of energy resources, influence charcoal prices and indirectly influence land-clearing costs – and thus influence the total acreage under dura production.

If farmers are risk-responsive (presumably risk-averse), they should cultivate smaller areas as price and rainfall risk increase. This hypothesis is supported by all risk models in Table 2. The coefficients on the price and rainfall risk variables are negative in all models and significantly different from zero except for the asymmetric-simple measure of rainfall risk. Further, a nested F-test rejected, at the 10% level of significance, the null hypothesis that both coefficients on price and rainfall risk variables are simultaneously equal to zero. The hypothesis is rejected in all risk models. The $F(2, 8)$ values are 4.16, 3.72, 7.15 and 6.83 for the symmetric-simple, symmetric-complex, asymmetric-simple and asymmetric-complex risk models, respectively (the tabulated F-value is 3.11). Hence, our results suggest that both price and rainfall risks are important decision variables in the intended level of dura production in the rainfed farming schemes of Sudan.

Table 3
Acreage response elasticities [a] (at the means)

Variable	Model				Non-risk model
	SSRM	SCRM	ASRM	ACRM	
Dura price	0.528	0.429	0.191	0.434	0.337
Cost	−0.503	–	−0.380	−0.539	−0.773
Charcoal price	0.234	0.299	0.242	0.290	0.178
Expected yield	0.359	0.745	0.643	0.829	0.505
Price-risk	−0.130	−0.161	−0.099	−0.316	
Rainfall-risk	−0.164	−0.106	–	−0.195	

[a] Only significant (at the 10% or less level) elasticities are reported.

As expected, omission of the risk variables biased the estimates of the coefficients of the remaining variables and consequently biased the estimates of their respective elasticities. Since the expected dura price (EDP_t) is assumed to be a linear function of last year's price (DP_{t-1}), the elasticity of DP_{t-1} can be obtained from (see Eq. 2):

$$\epsilon = (\partial \ln(A_t)/\partial \text{DP}_{t-1})(\text{DP}^*)$$
$$= 0.566671(\partial \ln(A_t)/\partial \text{EDP})(\text{DP}^*) \quad (7)$$

where DP^* is the average of DP_{t-1}. The acreage response elasticities for the risk and non-risk models are reported in Table 3.

Table 3 shows that dura acreage response was price-inelastic; a 1% increase in real dura price resulted in about 0.4–0.5% increase in dura acreage. Omission of the risk variables has led to underestimated price elasticity – except for the asymmetric-simple risk model. This result is consistent with results from other research (Adesina and Brorsen, 1987; Hurt and Garcia, 1982; Ryan, 1977). Therefore, any policy decisions related to the price of dura in a non-risk model would likely result in underestimated dura acreage response. Both price-risk and rainfall-risk elasticities from the asymmetric-simple risk model are the least (in absolute value) when compared to those obtained from the other risk models. The acreage response elasticities from the symmetric-complex and asymmetric-complex risk models compare favorably except for the risk variables. The asymmetric-complex risk model gives the highest elasticities, in absolute value, with respect to the risk variables. These results imply that dura acreage seems more responsive to asymmetric than to symmetric price and rainfall risk.

Although price risk is found to be an important decision variable, its elasticity is smaller, in absolute value, than the price elasticity in all risk models. This result accords rather well with that found by Adesina and Brorsen (1987), Winter and Whittaker (1979) and Ryan (1977).

Table 3 also shows that dura acreage was as responsive to cost of production as it was to dura price. This result is important because a good part of the costs of production is the cost of gasoline which is subsidized by the government. Hence, the government can directly influence the dura acreage through controlling both the amount and price of gasoline.

5. Conclusions

Data from the rainfed mechanized farming sector of Sudan were used to estimate an acreage response model for dura (sorghum). Models that utilize symmetric and asymmetric forms of risk using different variables (simple and complex) to measure risk were estimated.

Dura acreage increased with dura's expected price, or expected yield and decreased with costs of production. Sesame prices were not found to influence dura acreage. An increase in charcoal price could be an added incentive for farmers to increase dura acreage. Therefore, policies that directly influence charcoal prices – e.g. oil import restrictions – should consider the impacts of charcoal pricing on acreage expansion. Although production of charcoal will save the country some badly needed foreign exchange, it will have an expansionary effect on the dura acreage. This process of deforestation will eventually have a negative effect on the production of charcoal itself as more trees are destroyed.

Farmers in the rainfed mechanized farming were found to be responsive to risk in prices and rainfall. Omission of risk from acreage response models would likely lead to underestimated price elasticities. Price and rainfall risk negatively influence dura acreage. Hence, policies to reduce dura price variability should consider the likely acreage-increasing effect of such policies. Hence, for any policy that leads to agricultural expansion, the benefits from such an expansion in total dura production should be compared to its costs in terms of the environmental degradation from accelerated deforestation (Simpson, 1978; El Tayeb and Lewandowski, 1983; El Taheir, 1987; Whitney, 1987).

Acknowledgements

This research was supported by the Government of Sudan, the U.S. Agency for International Development and the Graduate School and the College of Agricultural and Life Sciences at the University of Wisconsin-Madison. We acknowledge the valuable assistance of our colleagues Jean-Paul Chavas and Matt Holt.

References

Adesina, A.A. and Brorsen, W.B. (1987) A risk responsive acreage function for millet in Niger. Agric. Econ. 1: 229–239.

Affan, K. (1984) Towards an appraisal of tractorization experience in rainlands of Sudan. Monograph Series 19, Development Studies and Research Center, Faculty of Economic and Social Studies, Univ. Khartoum, Sudan.

Behrman, J.R. (1968) Supply Response in Underdeveloped Agriculture. North-Holland, Amsterdam.

Brennan, J.P. (1980) Some effects of risk on the supply of wheat in Victoria. MSc Agric. thesis, Univ. Melbourne, Vic., Australia.

Bromley, D.W. (1986) Natural resources and agricultural development in the tropics: Is conflict inevitable? In: A. Maunder and U. Renborg (Editors), Agriculture in a Turbulent World Economy. Gower, Oxford, pp. 319–327.

Chavas, J. and Holt, M.T. (1990) Acreage decisions under risk: the case of corn and soybeans. Am. J. Agric. Econ., 72: 529–538.

Davidson, R. and MacKinnon, J.G. (1981) Several tests for model specification in the presence of alternative hypotheses. Econometrica, 49: 781–793.

Department of Agricultural Economics and Statistics (1986 Input use and production costs in rainfed mechanize areas of Sudan: Results of 1984/85 Farm Survey. Khar toum, Sudan.

Department of Agricultural Economics and Statistics (1987 Input use and production costs in rainfed mechanize areas of Sudan: Results of 1985/86 Farm Survey. Kha toum, Sudan.

Department of Agricultural Economics and Statistics (198 Input use and production costs in rainfed mechanize areas of Sudan: Results of 1987/88 Farm Survey. Kha toum, Sudan.

Department of Statistics (undated). Internal Trade Statisti Khartoum, Sudan.

Earl, D.E. (1985) Sudan – the economics of wood ene production on mechanized farms. Report 008, Natio Energy Administration, Khartoum, Sudan.

El Hadari, A.M. and Suliman, A.A. (1980) Dura product under rainfed conditions in the Sudan with special re ence to the Gedarif area. Res. Bull. 25, Department of Rural Economy, Univ. Khartoum, Sudan.

Elnagheeb, A.H. and Bromley, D.W. (1991) Risk forms and measures in acreage response functions. Paper presented at the Annual Meeting of the American Agricultural Economics Association, 4–7 August 1991, Manhattan, KS.

Elnagheeb, A.H. and Bromley, D.W. (1992) Rainfed mechanized farming and deforestation in central Sudan. Environ. Resour. Econ., 2: 359–371.

El Taheir, B.A. (1987) Agroforestry in the Savanna zone of the Sudan: with reference to mechanized crop production schemes (MCPS) in the Gedaref region. Master's essay, Australian National University.

El Tayeb, G. and Lewandowski, A.M. (1983) Environmental degradation in Gedaref district. Sudan Environ. Newsl. Inst. Environ. Stud. 3, Univ. Khartoum, 7 pp.

Hurt, C.A. and Garcia, P. (1982) The impact of price risk on sow farrowings. Am. J. Agric. Econ., 64: 565–568.

Ibnouf, M.A.O. (1985) An economic analysis of mechanized food production schemes in the Central Plains of the Sudan. Ph.D. Dissertation, Michigan State University, East Lansing.

Judge, G.G., Hill, R.C., Griffiths, W.E., Lütkepohl, H. and Lee, T.C. (1982) Introduction to the Theory and Practice of Econometrics. Wiley, New York.

Just, R.E. (1974) An investigation of the importance of risk in farmer's decisions. Am. J. Agric. Econ., 56: 14–25.

Markowitz, H. (1970) Portfolio selection. Yale University Press, New Haven, CT.

MFC (1984) Agricultural Statistics Bulletin 3, Mechanized Farming Corporation, Khartoum, Sudan.

National Energy Administration (1987) Handbook of Sudan Energy. Khartoum, Sudan.

Ryan, T.J. (1977) Supply response to risk: the case of U.S. pinto beans. West. J. Agric. Econ., 4: 83–87.

Simpson, M.C. (1978) Alternative strategies for agricultural development in the central rainlands of the Sudan with special reference to Damazin area. Paper 3, Rural Development Studies, Univ. Leeds, England.

Thimm, H-U. (1979) Development projects in the Sudan: an analysis of their reports with implications for research and training in arid land management. United Nations University, Tokyo.

Trail, B. (1978) Risk variables in econometric supply response models. J. Agric. Econ., 29: 53–61.

Tronstad, R. and McNeill, T.J. (1989) Asymmetric price risk: an econometric analysis of aggregate sow farrowings, 1973–86. Am. J. Agric. Econ., 71: 630–637.

Whitney, J.B.R. (1987) Impact of fuelwood use on environmental degradation in the Sudan. In: P.D. Little, M.M. Horowitz and A.E. Nyerges (Editors), Lands at Risk in the Third World. Westview, Boulder, CO/London.

Wilson, W.R., Arther, L.M. and Whittaker, J.K. (1980) An attempt to account for risk in an aggregate wheat acreage response model. Can. J. Agric. Econ., 28: 63–71.

Winter, J.R. and Whittaker, J.K. (1979 Estimation of wheat acreage response functions for the northwest. West. J. Agric. Econ., 4: 83–87.

Wolgin, J.M. (1975) Resource allocation and risk: a case study of smallholder agriculture in Kenya. Am. J. Agric. Econ., 57: 622–630.

[17]

Rainfed Mechanized Farming and Deforestation in Central Sudan

ABDELMONEIM HASHIM ELNAGHEEB
Department of Agricultural Economics, University of Georgia, Georgia Experiment Station, Griffin, GA 30223–1797, U.S.A.

and

DANIEL W. BROMLEY
Department of Agricultural Economics, University of Wisconsin-Madison, Madison, WI 53706, U.S.A.

Abstract. Sudan is threatened by a serious deforestation problem. Total forested area decreased by about 20 percent over the last two decades, largely as a result of the expansion of rainfed mechanized farming (RMF). To safeguard against the problems of deforestation, the government's Mechanized Farming Corporation requires each farmer to leave at least ten percent of the total farm area under shelterbelts. Few farmers pay attention to this clause. This paper addresses the problem of RMF expansion and analyzes the effects of different factors on the preservation of shelterbelts. Results indicate that the following factors influence the decision to preserve shelterbelts: farmer's belief in the value of shelterbelts, the production of gum arabic, farm size, farmer's wealth, years a farm has been cultivated, and type of farm.

Key words. Deforestation, rainfed mechanized farming, shelterbelts, Sudan, logit model, probit model, random utility model.

1. The Problem

One of the perplexing and central issues in any program for agricultural development is whether or not production can be increased or maintained without decreasing the natural resource base (Whitney, 1987). Natural forests represent one natural resource that has traditionally been over-exploited in the developing countries. Deforestation has been occurring throughout the developing countries at rapid rates, primarily to clear land for agriculture and/or for production of wood fuel. This process of deforestation has been exacerbated by long spells of drought,[1] rapid rates of population growth, poor agricultural policies, overgrazing, and poor forest management practices and policies.

Among the African countries, Sudan has been threatened by a serious deforestation problem. Total forested area decreased by about 20 percent over the last two decades (Biswas *et al.*, 1987). While the Sudan Forest Department has set as its target 15 percent of the total land area to be reserved in forests (Musnad, 1983), less than one percent of the country's total area has actually been preserved in forests. Two activities are con-

Environmental and Resource Economics **2**: 359–371, 1992.

sidered the main causes of deforestation — woodcutting for production of fuelwood, and the expansion of agriculture.

Although Sudan is rich in arable land, farming is primarily concentrated in areas with access to drinking water. In such areas, farming has been expanding at the expense of neighboring forests. This is particularly true in the case of the rainfed mechanized farming (RMF) schemes under the management of the government. The Mechanized Farming Corporation (MFC) is the supervisory and administrative agency of the rainfed mechanized sector in Sudan. Because extensive removal of the vegetative cover will eventually lead to serious erosion problems, the MFC requires that at least ten percent of the area of each farm be left under shelterbelts to protect the soil. However, most farmers do not abide by this condition in their lease from the MFC. This paper addresses the problem of expansion of rainfed mechanized agriculture at the expense of forests. In particular, we are concerned with the virtual absence of shelterbelts on RMF farms in Central Sudan. In the paper we will analyze the influence of different factors expected to affect a farmer's decision on areas to be left under shelterbelts.

2. The Context

Rainfed mechanized farming in Sudan started in the early 1940s near Gedarif (the Eastern Region), initially covering an area of 12,000 feddans (1.0 feddan = 0.42 hectare). The goal of this new endeavor was to produce sorghum (dura) to feed the British troops stationed in East Africa during World War II. The high profits obtained from sorghum cultivation created considerable interest and participation in rainfed agriculture. By 1985, the total cultivated area was estimated at 7.4 million feddans (Earl, 1985).

Under the official rainfed mechanized schemes two types of farms exist. The first type includes farms that are leased by the Government — through the Mechanized Farming Corporation — to farmers for a period of 25 years. Farm sizes in this group vary from 1,000 to 2,000 feddans. The areas suitable for cultivation under rainfed mechanized conditions are demarcated by the government and hence farms under this system are referred to as the *demarcated farms*. The second type includes farms created by local people — as well as by outsiders (squatters) — without government permission. These are referred to as the *undemarcated farms*. At times, the total area of undemarcated farms has almost equaled the total area covered by the demarcated farms. The Mechanized Farming Corporation has claimed that the undemarcated farms are responsible for most of the deforestation and soil degradation in the rainfed sector (MFC, 1984).

The importance of RMF in Sudan's agriculture is obvious from the vast area it covers, and from its contribution to the total national production of sorghum (the primary staple crop), and sesame. In 1985, the RMF sector contributed about 61 percent of the total national production of sorghum, and 38 percent of total sesame production (Department of Agricultural Economics and Statistics, 1987).

3. Impacts of Rainfed Mechanized Farming Expansion

The rapid and extensive expansion of rainfed mechanized farming schemes in Sudan has meant that nomadic herders lost a large share of their traditional grazing areas and migration routes. More serious impacts also resulted. Namely, the expansion in large-scale mechanized farming came at the expense of traditional rainfed agriculture, with resulting conflicts between alternative land uses and users. Primary participants in these conflicts included traditional farmers, nomads, large-scale mechanized farmers holding leases from the government, forestry officials trying to protect forest reserves, fuelwood sellers, and charcoal-makers. These conflicts were — and remain — difficult to resolve because of the vast areas of the country now covered by mechanized agriculture. Of equal importance, ambiguities in the laws governing land tenure and use contribute to the tension. Specifically, the ways in which authority is exercised by local, regional, and central levels of government — and the various line ministries — leave much room for manipulation by those in a position to influence particular outcomes. The land-use conflicts are further exacerbated by growth in numbers of both people and livestock, and by recent increases in the movement of nomads and small farmers as a result of severe droughts.

Adding to the already-complex situation, one finds the government willing and often eager to convert the undemarcated farms to the demarcated category. This interest has created powerful incentives to clear more land for cultivation, resulting in yet greater conflict between local people and 'intruders'. The extensive removal of trees not only destroys shelterbelts, but threatens supplies of gum arabic, charcoal, and other forestry products (Larson and Bromley, 1991). Gum arabic is an important cash product, of which Sudan is the World's major producer. Production of gum arabic has declined significantly — especially during the 1980s. The decline in gum production then brought about a serious shortage of foreign exchange, which has, in turn, precipitated a serious shortage of imported oil. This situation has encouraged charcoal-making which puts yet further pressure on the forests.

The expansion of large-scale mechanization into marginal and fragile lands contributes to the degradation of the forest, and to the disturbance of the ecological balance. Consequently, crop yields have been declining as a result of soil erosion and other factors (Affan, 1984). Furthermore, as farmers have moved further into the interior of the country, lines of communication have been lengthened, and transportation costs have increased.

4. The Conceptual Model

An increase in the value of services flowing from a standing forest, other factors held constant, is expected to lengthen the optimal rotation and hence discourage early deforestation (Hartman, 1976; Ehui *et al.*, 1987, 1989). There are two types of services flowing from standing trees in the mechanized farms: (1) the conservation of soil fertility and protection of soil against erosion; and (2) the production of gum arabic. An increase in the value of either of these services is likely to encourage farmers to leave shelterbelts in the farming schemes.

The decision on retention of shelterbelts within the mechanized farms is driven by a comparison of the opportunity cost of keeping that part out of agricultural production — this is the foregone agricultural income. The farmer will, in theory, compare the present value of net returns with and without shelterbelts. In the short run, it may be in the farmer's interest to clear the entire farm areas and use it for agriculture (Simpson, 1978). The rainfed mechanized farms are considered long-run investment because the purchase of expensive equipment is part of the anticipated farming operation. Under this assumption, we expect a farmer to care more about long-run profit as the amount being invested in agricultural equipment increases. However, some RMF farmers are quite wealthy and treat the scheme as an investment which should yield a quick return. Consequently, there seems to be little regard for the deforestation implications of their practices (Affan, 1984; Hamoudi, 1983).

The prevailing economic incentives are such that rich farmers can afford to buy and clear a large number of farms and move to new areas when productivity on existing parcels declines below profitable levels. Although it is illegal to sell a farm within the demarcated schemes, a number of farmers do sell their allotted farms. This is easy to arrange for the original owner who will sign a contract with the buyer stating that the latter is a representative of — or manager for — the original owner.

One expects farm size to influence the decision to leaving shelterbelts. That is, when farm size is quite small, remaining shelterbelts occupy a relatively larger proportion of the total cultivated area. Leaving part of the farm under shelterbelts therefore reduces the area which can be used for agriculture, and thus reduces the potential revenue from the farm plot (Atta Elmoula, 1985).

The length of the planning horizon will have an important impact on the decision to undertake soil conservation — by shelterbelts or otherwise. A longer planning horizon is thought to encourage conservation decisions (Lee, 1980). The *demarcated farms* in the rainfed mechanized schemes are leased by the Government to farmers for a period of 25 years. This lease period is claimed by the MFC to be 'too short' and is used to explain why farmers feel unattached to their land and thus unconcerned about long-run conservation measures such as shelterbelts (MFC, 1984). Because the lease period is standardized, it is difficult empirically to determine its effect on a farmer's decision on shelterbelts. Instead, we used the number of years the farmer has been cultivating the farm.

Security of tenure can create incentives for producers to make long-run improvements and use techniques that allow sustainable production (Lutz and Daly, 1991). By definition, the undemarcated farmers face some greater degree of tenure insecurity than those on demarcated farms. With the passage of time, however, it is not unreasonable to postulate that the perception of security on undemarcated farms increases. Hence, the number of years an undemarcated farmer has been cultivating the land may be expected to have a positive effect on his willingness to leave shelterbelts.

5. The Empirical Model

The empirical model used in this study is a random utility model (McFadden, 1981). Simply put, a farmer will leave shelterbelts only if benefits from leaving shelterbelts exceed costs. Perception of (future) benefits and costs from shelterbelts will vary among farmers. The farmer is assumed to maximize the utility of (perceived) net benefit. If the farmer leaves shelterbelts, his utility is $u_1 = u(1, X)$ and if he does not, his utility is $u_0 = u(0, X)$, where X is a vector of variables assumed to influence net benefit.

Although the farmer is assumed to know his utility function with certainty, this function contains some elements that are unobservable to the analyst and they are treated as stochastic. Hence, we treat u_0 and u_1 as random variables with some given parametric probability distribution. Letting $v(0, X)$ and $v(1, X)$ denote the means of u_0 and u_1, respectively, we can write u_0 and u_1 as:

$$u(j, X) = v(j, X) + e_j; \quad j = 0, 1, \tag{1}$$

where e_0 and e_1 are independently, identically distributed random variables with zero means. Further, $j = 0$ when the farmer does not leave shelterbelts and $j = 1$ when he does.

The farmer's decision on shelterbelts will depend on which is greater; u_0 or u_1. The farmer will be willing to leave shelterbelts only if $u_1 \geqslant u_0$:

$$v(1, X) + e_1 \geqslant v(0, X) + e_0 \tag{2}$$

The farmer knows which is greater; u_0 or u_1. However, from the analyst's viewpoint, the farmer's decision is a random variable whose probability distribution is given by

$$\begin{aligned} P_0 &= \Pr(\text{farmer will not leave shelterbelts}) \\ &= \Pr(v(1, X) + e_1 < v(0, X) + e_0), \\ P_1 &= \Pr(\text{farmer will leave shelterbelts}) \\ &= \Pr(v(1, X) + e_1 \geqslant v(0, X) + e_0) = 1 - P_0, \end{aligned} \tag{3}$$

where Pr stands for probability.

Now define $\varepsilon = e_1 - e_0$ and let $F_\varepsilon(\cdot)$ denote the cumulative distribution function (CDF) of ε. Equations (3) can now be written as:

$$P_0 = F_\varepsilon(-\Delta v),$$
$$P_1 = 1 - F_\varepsilon(-\Delta v), \tag{4}$$

where

$$\Delta v = v(1, X) - v(0, X). \tag{5}$$

If $F_\varepsilon(\cdot)$ is the standard normal CDF, the model in equations (4) represents the conventional probit model. If, however, $F_\varepsilon(\cdot)$ is the CDF of a standard logistic variate, equations (4) represent the conventional logit model. Both models can be estimated by maximum likelihood techniques (Maddala, 1983).

For comparison purposes, we estimated both a logit and a probit model. Let $y = \Delta v$ as defined in equation (5). In the logit model, P_1 from equations (4) is given by:

$$P_{1i} = \Pr(\text{WTSB}_i = 1) = \exp(y_i)/(1 + \exp(y_i)), \tag{6}$$

while in the probit model:

$$P_{1i} = \Pr(\text{WTSB}_\text{i} = 1) = \Phi(y_i), \tag{7}$$

where $\Phi(\cdot)$ is the standard normal CDF and WTSB is explained below.

Based on the discussion in Section 4, y_i is given by:

$$y_i = \alpha_0 + \Sigma_j \alpha_j X_{ij} + \alpha_{11} X_{i1}^2 + \alpha_{22} X_{i2}^2 + \beta D_i + \Sigma_j \psi_j D_i X_{ij} + \delta_1 S_{i1} + \delta_2 S_{i2} \quad j = 1 \ldots 3; \quad i = 1, \ldots, n, \tag{8}$$

where for the ith farmer

WTSB_i = 1 if the farmer is willing to leave shelterbelts, zero otherwise.

X_{i1} = farm size in feddans.

X_{i2} = wealth in thousand Sudanese pounds.[2]

X_{i3} = The number of years since the farmer has received the farm.

D_i = 1 if the farmer is a demarcated farmer, zero otherwise.

S_{i1} = 1 if the farmer believes in the value of shelterbelts, zero otherwise.

S_{i2} = 1 if the farmer produces gum arabic from his trees, zero otherwise.

The functional form in equation (8) was based on a choice from a broader quadratic form that included quadratic forms for all continuous variables and interaction terms between the demarcated variable '*D*' and all other variables. The *t*-statistic was then used to drop insignificant variables one at a time. We notice that the coefficient estimates were stable.

6. Data, Survey Design, and Results

The data used in this study were collected through an interview of farmers in the Damazin Region of Central Sudan in 1988. The Damazin region is divided into administrative units (villages). A stratified random sampling method was employed to obtain a random sample of farmers from both demarcated and undemarcated farms using villages as strata. The total sample size is 130—57 for the demarcated farmers, and 73 for the undemarcated farmers. Each subsample represented ten percent of the farmers listed with the MFC in 1988. The survey was designed to obtain, among other things, information about factors expected to influence a farmer's decision on shelterbelts. To assess the belief of farmers in the value of shelterbelts, each selected farmer was asked whether he believes that shelterbelts help increase, or at least maintain, the productivity of his farm. Table I gives some descriptive statistics on variables used in the analysis for both the demarcated and undemarcated farms.

The maximum likelihood estimates of the logit and probit models (equations 6 and 7) are presented in Table II. For comparison, the slope coeffi-

Table I. Descriptive statistics. Demarcated vs undemarcated farms

Variable definition[a]	Mean	
	Demar.	Undem.
Sample size	57	73
Willing to leave SB[b] [WTSB] (= 1 if willing, 0 otherwise)	0.07018	0.09589
Believe in value of SB [BELIEVE] (= 1 if believes, 0 otherwise)	0.61404	0.50725
Produce gum arabic [GUM] (= 1 if produces, 0 otherwise)	0.14035	0.04110
Farm size in feddans [FARM SIZE]	1251.80	338.21
Area under trees in feddans	135.25	67.06
Wealth in thousands LS[c] [WEALTH]	76.614	16.352
Years has been cultivating [YEARS]	8.3	10.2

[a] Variable names are in brackets.
[b] SB = Shelterbelts.
[c] LS = Sudanese pound.

Table II. The maximum-likelihood estimates of the logit and probit models

Variable[b]	LOGIT Coef.	LOGIT *t*-value	PROBIT[a] Coef.	PROBIT[a] *t*-value
CONSTANT	−9.482480	−3.172**	−4.689860	−3.652**
BELIEVE	3.385780	2.222**	1.880040	2.235**
GUM	3.816450	2.517**	1.981220	2.525**
FARM SIZE	0.017268	1.968**	0.008218	1.894*
WEALTH (LS000)	0.205024	2.023**	0.09751	1.991**
YEARS	0.070524	1.389	0.028479	1.134
$(\text{FARM SIZE})^2$	−0.000017	−1.921*	−0.000008	−1.842*
$(\text{WEALTH})^2$	−0.002596	−1.718*	−0.001241	−1.606*
DEMARCATED (D)	−74.1518	−2.117*	−36.7961	−2.102**
D × FARM SIZE	0.052168	1.955*	0.026511	1.889*
D × WEALTH	0.20143	1.223	0.094245	1.065
D × YEARS	−0.438848	−1.497	−0.242331	−1.420
χ^2	40.084**		39.308**	
McFadden's R^2	0.53		0.52	
CORRECT PRED.[c]	0.96		0.95	

[a] For comparison we present both the logit and probit estimates. The slope coefficient from probit ≈ $(1.732/\pi) \times$ slope coefficient from logit (Maddala, 1983).
[b] See Table I for variable definitions.
[c] Correct predictions = proportion of respondents correctly predicted by the model.
*, ** = Significant at 10 percent and 5 percent, respectively.

cients from the logit model should be multiplied by $1.732/\pi$, where π = 3.14159 (Maddala, 1983). The comparison was reasonable.

Both models have a good overall explanatory power. Two measures of goodness-of-fit were used and are presented in Table II. First, McFadden's R^2 is reasonably high for this type of cross-section data.[3] The second measure of goodness-of-fit is the proportion of correct predictions. This measure is calculated based on the predicted index y_i (see equation 8). The predicted y_i is given by $\hat{y}_i = X'_i\beta$, where X_i is the vector of explanatory variables for the ith respondent and β is the estimated coefficient vector. Using the logistic distribution (the normal distribution in case of probit model), and $\hat{y}_i$, the probability, $\hat{P}_i$, of a farmer's willingness to leave shelterbelts (WTSB) is estimated. If this probability is greater than 0.5, the individual is classified as WTSB, otherwise as not WTSB. If the predicted and actual outcomes match, the individual is correctly predicted. On this basis, 100 percent of those who were not WTSB were classified as such by the logit model, and 99 percent were so classified by the probit model. As for those who stated that they were WTSB, 55 percent were predicted correctly by both the logit and probit models. The overall proportion of correctly predicted individuals is 96 and 95 percent for the logit and probit model, respectively. In both models, the likelihood ratio test rejected the hypothesis that all slope coefficients are simultaneously equal to zero as indicated by the chi-square statistic, significant at the one percent level. The following discussion is based on the logit model.

Table II shows that a farmer who believed in the value of shelterbelts was more willing to leave shelterbelts than a one who did not. The result was expected because lack of knowledge or non- acceptance of conservation principles can lead to unfavorable conservation decisions (Lee, 1980). This result indicates the importance of extension education programs in including the preservation of shelterbelts. Perhaps pilot farms that demonstrate to farmers the economic value of shelterbelts would play a valuable role in the arid tropics.

Although researchers recognize the value of gum trees, particularly acacia senegal (hashab), in maintaining the agro- ecological balance and improving soil fertility, farmers may require direct benefits from these trees. Results from this study indicate that production of gum arabic was a factor encouraging farmers to leave shelterbelts. A farmer who produced gum arabic was more willing to leave shelterbelts than a one who did not. As intimated earlier, this result conforms well with theory where an increase in the value of services flowing from a forest is expected to prolong optimal rotation and discourage early deforestation (Hartman, 1976; Ehui *et al.*, 1987, 1989). An important implication of this result is that a policy that introduces gum trees in the rainfed mechanized farms may be useful in encouraging farmers to leave shelterbelts. Such a policy will not be effective without making this alternative land use attractive to farmers. Getting the gum prices right, and providing marketing outlets, are equally important. This is particularly important in the case of the mechanized farms where alternative income-generating activities exist. Wrong pricing policies in the past contributed significantly to the decline in gum production (Larson and Bromley, 1991).

An increase in farm size was found to encourage both demarcated and undemarcated farmers to leave shelterbelts.[4] However, the negative coefficient on the quadratic term indicates that their willingness to leave shelterbelts (WTSB) decreases beyond a certain farm size. This farm size was found to be about 2042 feddans for the demarcated farms, and 508 feddans for the undemarcated farms.[5] The average *demarcated* farm was about 1252 feddans, while the average *undemarcated* farm was about 338 feddans. Thus, the ratio of the average size of an undemarcated farm to a demarcated farm is about 0.27 which is almost equal to the respective ratio of the sizes that maximize farmers' willingness to preserve shelterbelts (508/2042 = 0.25). Although the average size for both the demarcated and undemarcated farms is less than what will maximize a farmer's willingness to retain shelterbelts, an argument for an increase in farm size cannot be made in isolation of other factors.

Table II also shows that an increase in wealth increased a farmer's willingness to retain shelterbelts. As indicated previously, very wealthy farmers often buy farms from others and engage in shifting cultivation — a practice which tends to discourage the maintenance of shelterbelts (Affan, 1984; Hamoudi, 1983). This argument is supported in our research by the negative coefficient on the quadratic wealth term. A farmer's willingness to retain shelterbelts decreases beyond 78,285 Sudanese pounds for the demarcated farms, and drops off at 38,488 Sudanese pounds for the undemarcated farmer. This level of wealth is close to the average wealth for the demarcated farmer (LS76, 614), but about twice the average wealth of the undemarcated farmer (LS16, 352). It has been argued elsewhere that providing income support to farmers in times of stress should slow down rapid deforestation and encourage local people to participate in protecting the environment (Teklu *et al.*, 1991). Our results suggest that this may be helpful for the undemarcated farmers.

Table II shows that the demarcated farmer's willingness to retain shelterbelts decreased as the number of years he had been cultivating land increased. An opposite result holds in the case of undemarcated farmer. Recall that for demarcated farms the lease period is twenty five years and perhaps as years pass, and as the remaining lease period diminishes, the demarcated farmer may become less concerned about the effects of his practices on the farm. While expired leases may be renewed annually on an ad hoc basis, there is enough uncertainty to act as a possible impediment to long-term investments in trees (Ministry of Finance and Economic Planning, 1988).

On the other hand, as time passes the undemarcated farmer tends to feel more secure. Not having been evicted to date seems to reassure farmers that, perhaps, they will not be. It would be ironic if the 'illegal' farms were more conducive to conservation of trees and shelterbelts than the 'legal' ones. An obvious remedy would be to allow the lease on demarcated farms to be renewed for a rolling horizon to allow some incentive to long-range planning and investment.

An important result in Table II is that the coefficient on the demarcated variable '*D*' is negative and statistically significant. Since this variable enters the model in the interaction terms as well as individually, the effect of demarcation on a farmer's willingness to retain shelterbelts will depend on farm size, wealth, and years of farming. Evaluated at the average of these variables, the effect of demarcation is positive. What makes this effect positive is the high level of wealth and large farm size enjoyed by the demarcated farmers. However, when we hold other factors fixed, and when farm size and wealth are held at their averages (1251.8 feddans and LS76,614), the demarcated farmer becomes less willing to retain shelterbelts than the undemarcated farmer after about 15 years of farming. That is, after the lease period has run approximately sixty percent of its life, the legal demarcated farmers become less inclined than the illegal undemarcated farmers to engage in conservation behavior by retaining shelterbelts.

7. Summary and Conclusions

The Sudanese Mechanized Farming Corporation requires each farmer on its rainfed mechanized farms to leave at least 10% of the total area under shelterbelts as a defense against erosion. This requirement is ignored by most farmers. In this study we used data from the Damazin Region of Central Sudan to explore why farmers fail to retain shelterbelts. Our results suggest that a farmer's belief in the value of shelterbelts in conserving soil and producing gum arabic are important in encouraging the retention of shelterbelts. From this one could conclude that the Sudanese government could have an important impact on forestry and land-use practices if it would undertake targeted extension programs to increase awareness about the benefits of shelterbelts. Such programs would certainly include the prospects for growing gum-producing trees in shelterbelts. Government pricing policy for gum arabic, which until recently emphasized holding down the producer price of gum, could also play an important role in stimulating the retention of shelterbelts.

Although our research suggests that an increase in farm size will increase the likelihood that a farmer will leave shelterbelts, this likelihood decreases beyond a certain farm size. Similar results hold for an increase in a farmer's wealth. These results can be explained by the fact that some farmers practice shift-cultivation. Wealthy farmers can afford to buy many farms and move among them as productivity decreases. Since control of the farm does not lapse with non-use, abandoned farms can be returned to after a period of time sufficient to allow for restoration of soil fertility.

While the interest in retaining shelterbelts seems to diminish with the duration of the cultivation period on demarcated farms, it is difficult to conclude that the lease period alone is important in this respect. More important perhaps is the amount of time *remaining* on a lease. This suggests a role for rolling-horizon leases. This modification must be coupled with an increased attention to enforcement of the existing conditions of the lease.

Interestingly enough, our results suggest that the illegal undemarcated farmer became more secure as time passes. This increased security serves as an important factor encouraging undemarcated farmers to leave shelterbelts. On the other hand, the ready conversion of the undemarcated farms to regular (demarcated) farms has created incentives to clear more land to put under cultivation. This process has resulted in conflicts between local people and 'intruding' land users. An effective land-use policy must make clear the criteria for resolving conflicts and uncertainties over rights of land use. Some of these criteria may not be welcomed by the powerful large-scale mechanized farmers. The areas in undemarcated farms should also be surveyed so that legitimate property rights might be established. Since the total area covered by this type of farms is about equal to the area under demarcated farms, the production potential from such areas is substantial.

Notes

[1] Drought may be related to deforestation because the latter might have led to declining rainfall (O'Brien, 1978).

[2] A farmer's wealth is here measured as the total value of all equipment, farm buildings (huts), water reservoirs, and the per-year total salaries of permanent workers.

[3] McFadden's $R^2 = 1 - [L(\beta)/L(0)]$, where $L(0)$ is the value of the log-likelihood function subject to the constraints that all regression coefficients — except the constant term — are zero, and $L(\beta)$ is the value of the log-likelihood function without constraints (Amemiya, 1981).

[4] In a survey of RMF farmers in the Eastern Region of Sudan, Atta Elmoula (1985) found that about 30 percent of the farmers did not want to leave shelterbelts because they thought the trees would materially reduce the area available for crops.

[5] The change in probability, P, with respect to an explanatory variable X_j, is given by $\partial P/\partial X_j = (\partial F/\partial y)(\partial y/\partial X_j)$, where $F(y)$ is the logistic (or standard normal distribution) function and y is given by equation (8). Since y is quadratic in farm size and wealth, setting this change in probability equal to zero allows us to solve for farm size and wealth which maximizes the probability.

References

Affan, K. (1984), 'Towards an Appraisal of Tractorization Experience in Rainlands of Sudan', Development Studies and Research Center, Faculty of Economic and Social Studies, Univ. of Khartoum, Sudan, *Monograph Series* No. 19.

Amemiya, T. (1981), 'Qualitative Response Models: A Survey', *J. of Econ. Literature* **19**, 1483—1536.

Atta Elmoula, M. E. (1985), 'On the Problem of Resource Management in the Sudan', Institute of Environmental Studies, University of Khartoum-Sudan, *Environmental Monograph Series*, No. 4.

Biswas, A. K., Masakhalia, Y. F. O., Odero-Ogwel, L. A., and Pallangyo, E. P. (1987), 'Land Use and Farming Systems in the Horn of Africa', *Land Use Policy* **4**, 419—443.

Department of Agricultural Economics and Statistics (1987), *Input Use and Production Costs in Rainfed Mechanized Areas of Sudan: Results of 1985/86 Farm survey*, Khartoum, Sudan: Ministry of Agriculture.

Earl, D. E. (1985), Sudan — The Economics of Wood Energy Production on Mechanized Farms. Report No. 8, Khartoum, Sudan: National Energy Administration.

Ehui, S. K., Hertel, T. W., and Preckel, P. V. (1987), Forest Resource Depletion, Soil Dynamics and Agricultural Productivity in the Tropics. Staff paper No. 87—22, Purdue University, Department of Agricultural Economics.

Ehui, S. K. and Hertel, T. W. (1989), 'Deforestation and Agricultural Productivity in Cote d'Ivoire', *American J. of Agricultural Economics* **71**, 703—711.

Hamoudi, A. B. (1983), 'Soil Degradation Resulting from Mechanized Agriculture in Rainfed Areas', in El Tom, M. A., ed., *Preassessment of Natural Resource Issues in Sudan*, Khartoum, Sudan: The Institute of Environmental Studies, University of Khartoum.

Hartman, R. (1976), 'The Harvesting Decision When a Standing Forest Has Value', *Economic Inquiry* **14**, 52—58.

Larson, B. A. and Bromley, D. W. (1991), 'Natural Resource Prices, Export Policies, and Deforestation: The Case of Sudan', *World Development* **19**, 1289—1297.

Lee, L. K. (1980), 'The Impact of Landownership Factors on Soil Conservation', *American J. of Agricultural Economics* **62**, 1070—1075.

Lutz, E. and Daly, H. (1991), 'Incentives, Regulations, and Sustainable Land Use in Costa Rica', *Environmental and Resource Economics* **1**, 179—194.

Maddala, G. S. (1983), *Limited Dependent and Qualitative Variables in Econometrics.* New York: Cambridge University Press.

McFadden, D. (1981), 'Econometric Models of Probabilistic Choice', in C. F. Manski and D. McFadden, eds., *Structural Analysis of Discrete Data with Econometric Applications*, Cambridge, MA: The MIT Press.

Mechanized Farming Corporation (1984), *Task Force Report on Revised Role of MFC and Other Issues Relating to an Improved Performance of the Corporation*, Khartoum, Sudan: MFC.

Ministry of Finance and Economic Planning-Sudan (1988), Environmental and Economic Aspects of Land Use Policy in Sudan with Particular Focus on Mechanized Farming, Working paper, Ministry of Finance and Economic Planning, Sudan.

Musnad, H. A. (1983), 'Deforestation Resulting from Clearing Land for Agriculture, Grazing Pastures, and Charcoal Production', in El Tom, M. A., ed., *Preassessment of Natural Resource Issues in Sudan*, Khartoum, Sudan: The Institute of Environmental Studies, University of Khartoum.

O'Brien, J. (1978), 'How Traditional is Traditional Agriculture' in Mirghani, H. M. and Gad Karim, H. A., eds., *Essays on the Economy and Society of Sudan*, Khartoum, Sudan: Economic and Social Research Council.

Simpson, M. C. (1978), Alternative Strategies for Agricultural Development in Central Rainlands of Sudan with Special Reference to the Damazin Area. Rural Development Studies No. 3, University of Leeds, England.

Teklu, T., von Braun, J., and Zaki, E. (1991), Drought and Famine Relationships in Sudan: Policy Implications. Research Report 88, International Food Policy Research Institute.

Whitney, J. B. R. (1987), 'Impact of Fuelwood Use on Environmental Degradation in Sudan', in P. D. Little, M. M. Horowitz, and A. E. Nyerges, eds., *Lands at Risk in the Third World*, Boulder and London: Westview Press.

[18]

World Development, Vol. 19, No. 10, pp. 1289–1297, 1991.
Printed in Great Britain.

0305–750X/91 $3.00 + 0.00

Natural Resource Prices, Export Policies, and Deforestation: The Case of Sudan

BRUCE A. LARSON
US Department of Agriculture, Economic Research Service, Washington, DC

and

DANIEL W. BROMLEY*
University of Wisconsin, Madison

Summary. — Environmental destruction is often the result of price policies for primary commodities that determine how individuals will use — and abuse — natural resources. In this paper, we analyze how domestic policies under colonial and independent governments in Sudan contributed to *Acacia senegal* deforestation and the demise of the international gum arabic trade. When primary commodities are produced from environmentally beneficial species, such as *Acacia senegal* trees, the impact of a declining market for the primary commodity will have economic and ecological repercussions on other sectors in the economy. Poverty and risk are central to this process.

1. INTRODUCTION

In this paper, we analyze how domestic policies under colonial and independent governments in Sudan contributed to *Acacia senegal* deforestation and the demise of the gum arabic trade. This relationship between domestic policy and resource degradation, however, is not unique to Sudan or gum arabic. In developed countries, which are the main importers of primary commodities from the developing areas, technical change and input substitution place a bound on acceptable qualities, prices, and fluctuations over time. In terms of the induced-innovation hypothesis (Hayami and Ruttan, 1985), a backstop technology always exists whose availability is a function of the primary commodity price history. Supply uncertainties, quality problems, or attempts by governments to increase prices to earn much needed foreign exchange — all characteristics of the gum market and Sudanese policy — hasten the introduction of new technologies and the development of substitutes, increase the price elasticity of import demand, and lead to an overall reduction in import demand.

When the primary commodity is produced from an environmentally beneficial species, such as *Acacia senegal* trees, the impact of a declining market for the primary commodity will have economic and ecological repercussions on other sectors in the economy — crop production and animal husbandry. Poverty and risk are central to this process. Due to the structure of demand in the international market, primary commodity prices cannot reflect local scarcities or values (Perrings, 1989). With a shift in the terms of trade due to a disappearing export market, there may be no alternative for poor farm households but to increase agricultural production, reduce fallow periods, and cut trees for fuelwood to maintain income and a minimum level of consumption (Larson and Bromley, 1990).

2. AN HISTORICAL PERSPECTIVE ON THE GUM ARABIC TRADE

Gum arabic, the exudate from the *Acacia senegal* tree, is a water soluble gum that has been used as an emulsifier, thickener, and stabilizer in

*The views expressed in this paper are the authors' and do not necessarily represent the views or policies of the Economic Research Service. The authors wish to thank, without implicating, two anonymous reviewers whose comments were appreciated and improved the final product.

food and medicinal products for over 2,000 years.[1] Sudan has been the major producing and exporting country, accounting for about 80–90% of world gum arabic supplies. Like many primary commodities, most of Sudan's gum over the last hundred years has been exported to developed countries, such as the European Community, other northern European countries, the United States, and Japan. Gum arabic was Sudan's most important export until the 1920s, and remained one of the country's main exports through the 1960s, accounting for about $50 million annually or about 7–10% of total foreign exchange earnings each year.

Ancient Egyptian writings refer to gum arabic imported from Sudan, called *kami*, that was used as an adhesive for mineral pigments and for mummifying (Beshai, 1984). Eventually, the gum was exported to Europe through various Arabian ports and acquired the name "gum arabic." It became known as Turkey gum when trade routes were controlled by the Turkish empire. The gum subsequently became known as East India gum when a reexport trade developed in India where gum imported from Africa and Arabia was then sold to Europe and the United States. Trieste was known as the "great gum sorting center" until the end of the 19th century (Beshai, 1984).

Gum arabic was one of the few agricultural commodities exported from the southwestern corner of the Sahara during the era of the Atlantic slave trade. Mauritanian gum exports grew from about 500–600 metric tons in the early 17th century to nearly 2,000 tons by the 1830s, although exports fluctuated widely (Webb, 1985). After the collapse of the slave trade in the late 1700s, gum arabic became the most important product traded by the Europeans in southern Mauritania and along the mouth of the Senegal river until the 1870s.

The gum trade in Sudan has existed since at least ancient Egyptian times, when nomadic groups gathered gum arabic during yearly migrations. Gum trade routes linked the remote production areas in Sudan to larger Sudanese markets such as Omdurman and to Egypt, which was the main intermediate destination for Sudanese gum (Blunt, 1926). As new uses in industrial and food products began to grow, the gum trade in Sudan began to flourish in the latter part of the 19th century (Hill, 1959).

After the Anglo-Egyptian agreement of 1899 laid the foundations for the joint administration of Sudan, the value and significance of the gum trade in Sudan quickly increased during the colonial era.[2] Railroads, built primarily for security reasons, played a large role in developing the gum trade. Until the early 20th century, Sudanese gum was mainly exported to Egypt from where it was reexported. After 1906, when the Nile-to-Red Sea Railway was completed (from Khartoum to Port Sudan), gum began to be exported directly from Sudan, and the trade through Egypt gradually diminished. Gum was brought to market in Omdurman by steamer from Kordofan cities on the White Nile. After the opening of the El Obeid-Kosti branch of the railroad in 1912, which allowed a more direct route from Kordofan to Port Sudan, gum production began to increase and El Obeid in Kordofan Province became (and remains) the major gum center in Sudan. During 1906–19 gum arabic accounted for 16–43% of the value of exports from Sudan (Blunt, 1926).

While transportation technology facilitated large-scale movements of gum, the British also instituted changes in the domestic marketing of gum in an attempt to standardize measures and improve tax collection. During the 19th century, the domestic marketing of gum in Sudan involved a system in which brokers, acting on behalf of private exporting firms, bought the gum from desert suppliers or other small merchants. Blunt (1926, p. 23) writes that:

> after 1899, traders went out into the country with scales to buy the gum from Arabs. The trader would put his leg on one side of the scales, the gum being placed on the other scales. A leg was considered to weigh 10 rottles (about 10 pounds), and with pressure could be made to equal 100 rottles or more.

By 1924, the government had created an auction system where buyers would bid for the gum of a single producer. The producer, however, was under no obligation to sell if the highest bid price was unacceptable.

Beyond setting up a more structured gum arabic marketing system to facilitate tax collection, the colonial administration focused its attention, and its financial and human resources, on large-scale farming to supply needed products for Britain. Cotton became the dominant crop in the 1920s when the British developed the Gezira irrigation scheme to supply the Lancashire cotton mills. Large-scale farming schemes in nonirrigated areas began during 1944–45 in Kassala Province under a sharecropping arrangement with the colonial government to supply food to British troops stationed nearby.

In 1954, the government began encouraging private-sector investments in large-scale farming, a policy continued at independence. The government originally demarcated 1,000-acre rectangular plots, later raised to 1,500 acres, that could be leased by the private sector. Half of the plot was leased to the farmer for four years, while the other half was kept in fallow, and then a new lease to the fallow land would be granted at the end of the four years. The four-year lease was generally unpopular because new investment in land clearing was required every four years. This led to a situation in which much of the land was continually cropped, including land designated for fallow, until the soil was exhausted and the farmer was forced to move to a new area. Through this shifting of land, large amounts of forest were cleared (US Department of State, 1986).

The potentially lucrative gum trade continually induced merchants and governments to try to extract a surplus from the market. "Gum wars" were fought along the Mauritanian coast to control the lucrative trade in the early 1800s. Webb (1985) notes the wide disparity between prices paid to desert suppliers in Mauritania and Senegal, and the prices on the European markets, after deducting freight costs. Gum production in Sudan almost ceased during the rebellion of the Mahdi in the later decades of the 19th century. This trend was not reversed until after the chiefs of the market in Omdurman convinced the Khalifa that his private treasury would improve by allowing the collection of the gum (Blunt, 1926). In 1898, a 20% royalty was established in cash or kind at government weighing stations, which was later changed to a cash-only system in 1901.

Following independence in 1959, Sudan was dependent on cotton exports and continued to follow an agricultural policy dominated by the irrigated sector and large-scale farming schemes. Through the development of large-scale mechanized farming, Sudan was said to be the "bread basket" of the Arab world. Public investment, technological developments, and infrastructure improvements were directed to irrigated and mechanized farming. Even though the traditional sector employed about 70–80% of the population and produced a significant amount of food and cash crops, it was basically ignored in national development plans.

3. THE BEGINNING OF THE END OF THE GUM TRADE

In 1969, the Gum Arabic Company (GAC) was established by the Sudanese government to control all export marketing of gum. The GAC was authorized to announce an export price at the beginning of the gum season and also to supervise a minimum floor price at local auction markets. With the creation of the GAC, the structure of the international market became one of Sudan dominating on the export side and selling to very few buyers in the United States, the European Community, and Japan. Other minor suppliers in the world market, such as Niger and Senegâl, followed Sudan's price-setting lead. In the domestic market, the GAC became a monopsony buyer of Sudanese gum, while the gum continued to be produced by sedentary farmers, primarily in Kordofan province.

Through its ability to determine both the producer floor price in domestic auction markets and the export price, the GAC was able to manipulate directly producer incentives to supply gum arabic and aggregate demand on the international market. Unfortunately for Sudan, the Sahel drought of the early 1970s — along with flawed pricing policies of the GAC — brought fundamental changes to the domestic and international gum market. To understand these changes, it is necessary to analyze: (a) the producer incentives to supply gum during the 1960s and early 1970s; and then (b) the international demand for Sudanese gum as an input for food-processing industries in developed countries.

(a) *Producer incentives to supply gum*

After the railroad connection to El-Obeid was completed in 1912, and gum collection became an important source of revenue in Kordofan Province, a bush-fallow agricultural system developed that integrated acacia trees on fallow lands to maintain soil productivity over time. This system also permitted the capture of the proceeds from the acacia trees — gum arabic, fuelwood, building materials, and fodder. The system of customary land tenure also evolved at this time to accommodate a bush-fallow system. The right to the continued control of land in fallow, and to any resulting gum trees, emerged as a result of the many land disputes which followed a rush to claim control over acacia trees (Seif el Din, 1985).

Bush-fallow agriculture involved a 10–25 year rotation cycle on each plot of land wherein crops were grown for 6–10 years, and then the land was left in fallow for 3–15 years (UNSO, 1983). Each family would control two to four plots of land, which on average totaled about 30–40 acres (Reeves and Frankenberger, 1982; Seif el Din, 1985). Changes in soil productivity, which improves during acacia fallow and declines during tillage, motivated the need for the land-rotation cycle in the bush-fallow system. The basic system can be described as follows. Crops are grown on a plot of land for four to six years, after which the soil is exhausted and the land is left fallow. During the fallow period, natural acacia regeneration and sowing takes place. Initial gum arabic harvests begin on four to five year old acacia trees (UNSO, 1983, pp. 79, 103), although seven to 12-year old trees are the most productive (UNSO, 1983, p. 80). Gum harvests could continue on trees up to about 15 years old, at which time the land was returned to crop production.

Recent data on the quantity and distribution of trees on fallow land are not available. Blunt (1926, p. 19), however, wrote that "a so-called gum garden may consist of 15 trees spread out over 15 acres or 200 trees on 1 acre."[3] While acacia trees on fallow lands were tapped for gum arabic after four to six years, the trees also had many important local uses, such as fuelwood, building materials for huts, wells, and fences, and animal fodder.

By the early 1960s, bush-fallow agriculture was not subsistence oriented. The farm household's production decisions — land allocation between tillage and fallow, crops to produce, gum arabic to harvest, trees to cut — were driven by the relative benefits of the production activities, both in terms of current income and consumption possibilities as well as in the future environmental impacts of current decisions. Households purchased consumption goods, inputs, and short-term credit from village merchants. Credit was necessary during harvests when hired labor was needed and had to be paid before crops were sold. The *Shail* system — in which crops were sold prior to harvest — was the major form of credit.

Millet and sorghum were the main staple crops produced while groundnuts for export, and sesame for the domestic oil market, were produced as cash crops. Two or more crops were often grown in one field so as to spread risks and to adjust labor demands during peak periods. Goats, cattle and sheep were also owned by farm families. The animals provided needed products to the household, and acted as a form of insurance against poor crops. The agricultural cycle was separated into three parts: from January to the first rains in June the fields were cleared of the previous year's weeds; June to August was planting and weeding (first millet, then groundnuts and sesame); and the harvest began in August. The clearing of new land took place well in advance of sowing. Labor and simple weeding tools were the main variable inputs, although seed, water, and sacks for storage would be purchased during the year. The majority of labor demands were met with family labor, although some labor was also hired.

Throughout this century, most gum harvesting in Sudan occurred on tapped trees. Tapping began generally in November, when the hot and dry season followed the rainy season of June to August. The first harvest took place 30–40 days after tapping, which could then take place every week or two until the next rains. An average tree would yield about 100–300 grams of gum per year. On a sparsely wooded stand it was possible to collect 12–16 kg per acre, while on a densely wooded stand the yield could increase to about 40 kg per acre (UNSO, 1983, p. 80). During 1960–67, the minimum producer price at the El Obeid auction market remained at about 64 Sudanese pounds per metric ton, which was about 45–55% of the export price (f.o.b.). During 1969–71, the minimum producer price rose to 100 Sudanese pounds per metric ton. Throughout the 1960s, total gum production in Sudan remained about 50,000 metric tons per year (UNSO, 1983; Beshai, 1984).[4]

During this same period, however, the area devoted to crops continued to increase. Table 1 shows the area devoted to the main crops grown in Kordofan Province, where most of Sudan's gum is produced. Total area in millet, sorghum, sesame, and groundnuts expanded from 482,620 ha in 1961 to 1,324,890 ha by 1970. The area devoted to millet production expanded from 126,740 ha in 1961 to about 315,000 ha in 1970. Over the same period, the area allocated to groundnuts remained between 88,550–153,600 ha, before exploding to 376,440 ha in 1971. The area in sorghum expanded from about 175,000 ha in 1961 to about 392,810 ha in 1970. The area in

Table 1. *Land in major crops in Kordofan Province**

Year	Millet	Sorghum	Sesame	Groundnuts
1961	126.74	175.42	91.91	88.55
1962	73.44	201.86	117.09	97.36
1963	188.43	222.00	180.46	103.24
1964	189.27	203.96	95.26	101.98
1965	190.11	210.67	169.55	131.36
1966	181.72	163.25	188.43	104.92
1967	213.61	203.96	232.50	95.68
1968	213.19	203.12	195.57	89.81
1969	279.50	387.35	233.76	153.60
1970	315.17	392.81	495.21	121.70
1971	498.99	406.24	468.77	376.44
1972	668.11	439.81	793.59	360.08
1973	728.54	505.28	431.42	413.37

Source: Various issues of Sudan, *Yearbook of Agricultural Statistics* and Sudan, *Bulletin of Agricultural Statistics of the Sudan.*

**Data are in 1,000s of hectares.*

sesame production expanded from 91,910 ha in 1961 to about 495,000 ha in 1970. The animal and human population of Kordofan province was also greatly expanding over this period (Ibrahim, 1978).

The expansion of area in these four crops, which occurred predominantly in areas that intersected the gum belt, was due to increasing population pressure and attempts by farmers to maintain output in the presence of declining yields. Table 2 shows outputs yields in Kordofan province during the 1960s of millet, sorghum, sesame, and groundnuts. The years 1966–69 were also a period of consistently below-average rainfall in El-Obeid.[5] While yields were surely related to rainfall, however, yields also declined during this period because the horizontal expansion of crop land and reduced fallow periods exposed larger amounts of land to erosion, which in turn reduced soil productivity for future years.

During the 1960s, the pressure on the acacia stock for local uses, such as fuelwood, fodder, and charcoal production, when combined with an expansion of land in crops, led to a decline in the acacia stock, although exact data on the extent of the deforestation are lacking. It seems likely that the production of gum arabic could remain relatively constant over the 1960s (about 50,000 metric tons) in the face of diminishing tree stocks because a large fraction of trees were not tapped due to the low producer price of gum. By the end of the 1960s, however, the quality of the resource base had diminished and had become less resilient to periods of drought.

The growth in animal and human populations in Sudan during the 1960s also increased pressure on the resource base. For example, Ibrahim (1978, p. 8) provides rough estimates from animal taxation registers. During 1956–66, cattle increased from 8.9 million to 12.5 million, camels increased from 2.3 million to 2.5 million, sheep increased from 8.0 to 10.6 million, and goats increased from 6.9 to 9.5 million.[6] Actual animal populations, however, may be 10 times larger than official estimates. Over the same period, the Sudanese population grew from 11.6 to 15.4 million.

A large number of boreholes were also dug in the first two decades of independence, which turned seasonal pastures into permanent grazing lands. As a result, overgrazing occurred around water holes and main cattle routes. Ibrahim (1978, p. 2) writes, however, that: "compared with the damages caused by the expansion of rain-fed cultivation in areas of poor precipitation the damages caused by nomadic pastoralism and partial overgrazing are relatively small."

In the early 1970s, when the rain-fed agricultural sector was at its most vulnerable due to declining productivity, deforestation, and increasing population, a severe drought hit the Sahel. In an attempt to maintain output, the area devoted to crops continued to increase. For example, Table 1 shows that by 1973 the area in sorghum was 505,280 ha, the area in groundnuts was 413,370 ha, the area in millet was 728,540 ha, and the area in sesame was 793,590 in 1972, before dropping to 431,420 ha in 1973. Thus, in just three years during 1970–73, the area in the main crops expanded from 1,324,890 ha to

Table 2. *Output and yields of major crops in Kordofan Province**

Year	Millet		Sorghum		Sesame		Groundnuts	
	Output	Yield	Output	Yield	Output	Yield	Output	Yield
1961	121	0.955	158	0.901	57	0.620	64	0.723
1962	41	0.558	171	0.847	42	0.359	83	0.852
1963	81	0.430	184	0.829	58	0.321	79	0.765
1964	115	0.608	153	0.750	37	0.388	81	0.794
1965	93	0.489	153	0.726	52	0.307	70	0.533
1966	81	0.446	82	0.502	42	0.223	59	0.562
1967	93	0.435	145	0.711	59	0.254	65	0.679
1968	70	0.328	113	0.556	33	0.169	46	0.512
1969	128	0.458	310	0.800	60	0.257	90	0.586
1970	148	0.470	234	0.596	175	0.353	50	0.411
1971	195	0.391	244	0.601	99	0.211	93	0.247
1972	113	0.169	200	0.455	180	0.227	87	0.242
1973	116	0.159	240	0.475	77	0.178	135	0.327

Source: Various issues of Sudan, *Yearbook of Agricultural Statistics* and Sudan, *Bulletin of Agricultural Statistics of the Sudan*.
*Total output is in 1,000s of metric tons; yield is in metric tons per hectare.

2,078,610 — a 57% increase. This increase in land allocated to crop production had to come at the expense of forests and pastures.

Due to the low (nominal) producer price of gum arabic over the previous few decades (declining in real terms), households were better off cutting trees to sell as firewood and for livestock feed than maintaining the trees for gum production. In other words, the discounted value of the trees was such that the optimal time to harvest had been reached. Deforestation during this time thus was not necessarily due to irrational behavior or land tenure problems. Instead, at a time when the need to maintain a minimum level of consumption was dominant, deforestation was the "optimal" choice for the farm households of the gum belt.

In the middle of the drought (during the early 1970s), the GAC drastically changed its pricing of gum arabic at both the producer and international levels. In 1973, the producer price was raised from 102.52 Sudanese pounds per metric ton, approximately where it had remained since 1968, to 184.65 pounds per ton. This price was further increased to 340.02 pounds per metric ton for the 1974 season. The producer price thus rose by more than 300% in nominal terms in just over two years.[7] The rise in the producer price was designed to increase the incentives to collect gum arabic and, implicitly at least, to slow deforestation and maintain the productive capabilities of the agricultural sector.

The jump in the producer price of gum did indeed provide a strong incentive to increase gum production. In fact, trees were overtapped and killed in the process (UNSO, 1983). Under these circumstances, a high price of gum may have led to deforestation for two reasons. The first reason is poverty. Given the desperate situation of the farming population during the drought, the need to maintain consumption in the short run may have overwhelmed any future environmental costs from overtapping and killing trees. As Larson and Bromley (1990) show in a dynamic household model, these environmental costs — future productivity costs — are strongly influenced by the marginal utility of income in the present. If it is assumed that the marginal utility of income is large at low income/consumption levels, future environmental costs to the household are small and resources are used intensively in the short run.

The second reason is expectations. Did the farmers believe that the price increase was transitory or permanent? In an asset-pricing model, the value of the asset (trees) to its owner is derived from current and future income created with the asset (such as gum arabic revenues) as well as the asset's scrap value. With a permanent price increase, all future returns from the trees are higher, and the value of the standing forest increases. Thus, the incentives are created to protect the standing forest as well as delay the time of harvest (Hartman, 1976). With a transitory price increase, however, the value of the standing forest does not fundamentally change, but the incentive is created to intensify use to earn higher short-run returns. Since the price of gum had been kept low for many years, the farmers in the gum belt may very well have expected that the price jumps in 1973 and 1974 were only transitory. In effect, a temporarily high price is not capitalized into the value of the resource (living and in the ground), and the gum only had a high value if it was actually harvested in that period.

By the middle 1970s, the acacia stock was greatly depleted. UNSO (1983) reports that as much as 80% of all natural stands were destroyed in West Africa. While data on the extent of deforestation in Sudan are not available, a 500,000 km^2 band across central Sudan was estimated to be directly affected by desertification by 1978 (Ibrahim, 1978).[8] While 1960–75 brought severe change to the farm households in Sudan, the international market during the same period witnessed similar change.

(b) *Export pricing and international demand*

During the 20th century, the demand for gum arabic has been derived from food processing industries in the developed western countries. Gum has been used extensively in confectionery products (jujubes, pastilles, gum drops, lozenges) to retard and prevent the crystallization of sugar, and for its thickening power. Gum arabic has also been used in the dairy industry as a stabilizer in ice creams and sherbets. The gum's viscosity and adhesive properties are widely used in bakery products such as glazes and toppings. The introduction of spray-dried flavors created a demand for the gum as a fixative. The gum has also been used in pharmaceuticals, medicines, cosmetics, adhesives, inks, lithography, and textiles.

During the 1960s the export price of Sudanese gum remained about $500–600 c.i.f. per metric ton, with about 55–60,000 metric tons traded on the international market per year (UNSO, 1983). In 1970, with the export price of gum remaining at $500–600 c.i.f. per metric ton, the main importing areas were the European Community with 32,385 metric tons, the United States with 12,300 metric tons, northern European countries with 3,300 metric tons, and Japan with 3,200 metric tons (UNSO, 1983). Together, these four areas accounted for approximately 83% of the world market (UNSO, 1983). In the international market, with Sudan accounting for about 80–85% of the total, the GAC initially assumed that Sudan held a monopoly position. Under pressure from the central government to earn much-needed foreign exchange, and at a time when the Sahel drought had greatly reduced agricultural production and agricultural exports from Sudan, the GAC-administered export price of gum arabic rose from $600 c.i.f. per metric ton in 1972, to $4,000 c.i.f. by 1974.

The effect on the market is clear. Gum arabic exports fell from over 43,000 metric tons in 1971 to 16,160 metric tons in 1975, although Sudanese production remained at about 43,000 metric tons in 1975 due to the relatively high producer prices offered in that year. Even though prices had increased 370% (to $2,400 per metric ton during the 1973 season), international demand initially remained strong, and Sudanese exports only dropped 20% from 1972 to 36,000 metric tons. Thus, in the very short run, international demand was inelastic, which the GAC took as a sign of monopoly power in the international gum market.

As the induced innovation hypothesis would predict, however, the price elasticity of demand for gum arabic on the international market rapidly increased. High prices for gum arabic induced firms to switch to existing substitutes and to develop new technological improvements in food processing. Substitutes soon began to capture a major part of virtually every use of gum arabic. As UNSO (1983, p. 45) reports, "formulas were reshuffled, technologies were changed, the balance tipped in the direction of substitute products or lines or products containing gum arabic (confectioneries) were dropped altogether." For example, in the United States, where modified starches displaced the use of gum arabic in flavoring products, imports dropped from 12,00 metric tons per year in the 1960s to 2,700 metric tons in 1975 (UNSO, 1983). Other gum substitutes include gelatins, dextrins, cellulose gum, xanthan gum, locust bean gum, and synthetic polymers.

By the end of 1974 the export price had fallen to $2,100 per metric ton, and in 1975 the Gum Arabic Company set the export price at $1,200 (f.o.b.), which it maintained until 1978. Nevertheless, the world market bottomed out in 1975 to about 21,000 metric tons, with Sudan exports dropping to about 16,000 metric tons, or only about 34% of 1970 exports. Because there are costs involved in switching between gum arabic and other substitutes, producers were initially cautious about switching back to gum arabic too quickly even though prices stabilized in the mid-1970s. With the steady f.o.b. price, Sudanese exports gradually climbed to 35,000 metric tons by 1978. During this same period, however, gum production continually declined from about 46,000 metric tons in 1974 (when the producer price was about 340 Sudanese pounds per metric ton) to about 28,500 metric tons in 1978 (when the producer price was 250 Sudanese pounds per metric ton) (UNSO, 1983). In effect, the large short-run supply response during 1973–74, which occurred due to overtapping of trees, resulted in a smaller long-run supply response.

Through the late 1970s and into the early 1980s, the GAC export price slowly increased, and gum arabic exports slowly grew to about 43,500 metric tons in 1979, before returning to 35,000 in 1981. At the same time, the producer price of gum gradually increased to 422 Sudanese pounds per metric ton, and gum production climbed to about 40,000 metric tons. Thus, even though gum arabic began to regain some of its previous market share, the structure of the international market had changed. Substitute products, which had quickly gained market share, continued to improve and retained a portion of the market even after prices declined.

Although gum production began to recover in the late 1970s, the 1982–84 drought, combined with continued political unrest, again greatly reduced gum production and export supplies. While gum arabic exports were about 38,000 metric tons and accounted for about $57 million in foreign exchange in 1983 (about 8% of total export earnings of Sudan), production during the 1984–85 season dropped to a record low of 10,000 metric tons.

In 1986, a mission report from a United Nations project to restock the gum belt for desertification control summarized the situation in Sudan:

> Hashab cultivation [acacia trees used to produce gum arabic] used to be a key component of the production systems within the project area. However, the drought which struck the area during the last decade affected to a large extent the ecological balance leading to the disintegration of these production systems and increased desertification affecting the regenerative capacity of the land (UNSO, 1986, p. 29).

UNSO (1986) reported optimistically that the project was beginning to restock farmers' lands with acacias, both through direct sowing and planting seedlings. Regardless of current acacia restocking efforts, the structure of the international market has been irreversibly changed.

Aggregate demand for gum has fallen, is more price elastic, and more quality conscious. It thus remains to be seen if UNSO's restocking effort will actually reforest significant amounts of land in the longer term and if the agricultural and gum arabic production systems can be rehabilitated.

Due to erratic supplies of gum from Sudan during the 1982–84 drought, and the development of other water-soluble gums and new starch-based substitutes, the international market in gum arabic is moving towards a collapse. A report prepared for the US Agency for International Development (Flowerman, 1985) concluded that, with continued supply problems in Sudan, gum arabic may become a specialty ingredient only purchased in very small quantities. If that trend should persist, Sudan may be on the verge of losing a major export crop that is also vital to the ecology of the gum belt. The demise of the international gum arabic trade would decrease the value of acacia trees (in the ground) to the inhabitants of the gum belt and, therefore, increase the rate of deforestation.

4. CONCLUSION

Concern for the environment has become one of the overriding issues in the economic development process. Deforestation, desertification, species extinction, and rainforest destruction have attracted widespread attention throughout the developing world, and among the development community in general. Whether in the form of road building, subsidized or taxed input and output prices, or resource management programs, development policies to increase agricultural output and the extraction of primary commodities have also been implicated in the degradation process. Much of the criticism directed to development policies has implicated the international donor community. It is important to recognize, however, that environmental destruction is also the result of domestic pricing policies that determine how individuals will use — and abuse — natural resources.

The analysis of *Acacia senegal* deforestation and gum arabic in Sudan emphasizes the crucial role of domestic policy formulation, as opposed to the general concern for projects and for rates of natural resource use over time. Through control of both producer and export prices, public-sector pricing policies had a direct impact on production incentives over a vast area of land in Sudan, as well as on demand in the international market. When this policy history was combined with a poor farming population that had alternative income generating activities, the process of resource degradation was put in motion. In the international market, such policies induced technological innovation that permanently altered the structure of international demand for gum arabic.

There is much to learn from an historical perspective on environmental problems in developing countries. At a time when environmental problems are forefront in the development policy dialogue, we suggest that an historical perspective of existing resource problems can provide a useful understanding of the relationship between economic development policy and resource degradation.

While hindsight may be easy, the current status of natural resources in the developing countries makes it imperative to learn from previous events. The gum arabic example emphasizes this fact. For example, under British rule, Nigeria also had a brief period where a concerted effort was made to expand the returns for the government from the gum trade (Egboh, 1978). Throughout most of the 19th century gum collected in Nigeria was taken by caravan to Tripoli where it was sold as Senegalese gum. The British colonial administration was very interested in the gum producing capacities of Bornu Province since the British had to buy gum at market prices in Trieste and Bordeaux. Rather than selling the gum to British merchants at very low prices, however, the Nigerian producers switched to other income-generating activities. As a result, acacia trees were cut for fuel, and land was cleared for agricultural production. The British experience in Nigeria thus foretold developments in the gum trade after independence in Sudan.

NOTES

1. In Africa, *Acacia senegal* forests have been found across the Sahel from Somalia to Senegal. This area in Africa, extending eastward to the Indian desert, has become known as the gum belt. In Sudan, *Acacia senegal* forests extend to about 14–16 degrees north latitude, although the main producing areas are centered around 10 degrees north latitude (UNSO, 1983, p. 68). By stabilizing soils and reducing erosion, the acacia forests have acted as a buffer between deserts to the north and agricultural lands and pastures to the south. Being a member of the legume family, acacia trees also improve soil productivity by fixing nitrogen in the soil.

2. The British decided that Sudan should be brought under British rule to protect their interests in Egypt from the Italians, Belgians, and French. Not wishing to confront directly the other European powers, however, the British made the conquest in the name of the Khedive and Egypt.

3. Gum produced in gum gardens has been known as garden gum or "geneina," while gum tapped and harvested from trees on village lands known as forest gum or "wadi." While the distribution of production between garden gum and forest gum is not known, the basic economic incentives for using the trees remain similar, with modifications to account for alternative tree and land use rights.

4. It should be noted that some Sudanese gum may be sold directly to Chad through informal channels and, thus, not counted in official production figures, and vice-versa. The importance of such trade in terms of total Sudanese production, however, is small.

5. For example, the annual mean rainfall in El-Obeid was 325 mm per year during 1931–60 (Ibrahim, 1978), and remained about 325 mm per year during the 1960s, even though the yearly average was about 415 mm per year during 1960–65, but then fell to 220 mm per year during 1966–70.

6. These numbers are rough calculations from Ibrahim (1978, p. 8, Diagram 1).

7. Nominal prices are reported in this section because it is difficult to assess the rate of inflation in western Sudan during this period. As one guide, however, Sudan's Consumer Price Index reported in World Bank (various years) can be used to give a rough estimate of real prices. Using 1970 as a base year equal to 100, the nominal price of 102.5 pounds in 1972 translates into a real price of 89 pounds; the nominal price of 184.7 translates into a real price of 139 pounds; and the nominal price of 340 translates into a real price of 203. Real prices over the three years increased by approximately 130%. As noted in the text, up to this time the nominal price of gum had remained flat, which implies that the real price of gum had been falling.

8. By 1982, this area had spread to 680,000 km^2 (Reeves and Frankenberger, 1982).

REFERENCES

Beshai, A. A., "The Economics of a primary commodity: Gum arabic," *Oxford Bulletin of Economics and Statistics*, Vol. 46, No. 4 (November 1984), pp. 371–381.

Blunt, H. S., *Gum Arabic with Special Reference to its Production in the Sudan* (London: Oxford Univeristy Press, 1926).

Egboh, E. O., "The Nigerian gum arabic industry, 1897–1940: A study in rural economic development under colonial regime," *Cahiers d'Etudes Africaines*, Vol. 18, No. 69–70 (1978), pp. 215–221.

Flowerman, P. M., "Marketing Sudanese gum in the U.S.A.: Facts and options," Mimeo (Khartoum, Sudan: Checchi and Company Consulting, Prepared for the United States Agency for International Development, Bureau for Africa, October, 1985).

Hartman, R., "The harvesting decision when a standing forest has value," *Economic Inquiry*, Vol. 14, No. 1 (March 1976), pp. 52–58.

Hayami, H., and V. W. Ruttan, *Agricultural Development: An International Perspective* (Baltimore: The Johns Hopkins University Press, 1985).

Hill, R., *Egypt in the Sudan* (London: Oxford University Press, 1959).

Ibrahim, F. N., "The problem of desertification in the Republic of Sudan with special reference to Northern Darfur Province," Monograph Series No. 8 (Khartoum, Sudan: Development Studies and Research Centre, Khartoum University Press, 1978).

Larson, B. A., and D. W. Bromley, "Property rights, externalities, and resource degradation: Locating the tragedy," *Journal of Development Economics*, Vol. 33 (1990), pp. 235–262.

Perrings, C. P., "Optimal path to extinction? Poverty and resource degradation in the open agrarian economy," *Journal of Development Economics*, Vol. 30, No. 1 (January 1989), pp. 1–24.

Reeves, E. B., and T. Frankenberger, "Farming systems research in north Kordofan, Sudan No. 2," Mimeo (Lincoln, NB: Intersormil, Institute of Agricultural and Natural Resources, University of Nebraska, 1982).

Seif el Din, A. G., "The gum hashab and land tenure in Western Sudan," Mimeo (Madison, WI: Land Tenure Center and The International Council for Research in Agroforestry, 1985).

Sudan, Government of, Ministry of Agriculture, Food and Natural Resources, Department of Agricultural Economics, Statistics Division, *Bulletin of Agricultural Statistics of the Sudan* (Khartoum: Government of Sudan, various issues).

Sudan, Government of, Ministry of Agriculture, Food and Natural Resources, Department of Agricultural Economics, Statistics Division, *Yearbook of Agricultural Statistics* (Khartoum: Government of Sudan, various years).

United Nations Sudano-Sahelian Office (UNSO), *The Gum Market and the Development of Production* (Geneva and New York: UNSO, 1983).

United Nations Sudano-Sahelian Office (UNSO), *Restocking of Gum Belt For Desertification Control Phase II Mission Report* (Geneva and New York: UNSO, 1986).

United States Department of State, *Sudan — A Case Study* (Washington, DC: American University, 1986).

Webb, J. A. L., Jr., "The trade in gum arabic: Prelude to French conquest in Senegal," *Journal of African History*, Vol. 26, No. 2–3 (1985), pp. 149–168.

World Bank, *World Tables* (Washington, DC: The World Bank, various years).

[19]

Deforestation: institutional causes and solutions

1 The problem of deforestation

I propose to explore here the institutional dimensions of what is generally regarded as 'deforestation'. Before proceeding, the concept of deforestation requires some clarification. I will employ the limiting definition of deforestation and regard it as the *wilful and permanent* transition in vegetative cover *from* that which is clearly 'forest' (regardless of the commercial or aesthetic value of the trees) *to* that which is clearly devoted to other uses – with trees seen as undesirable invaders. On this definition, the clear-cutting of portions of a forest with the intention of allowing regeneration of trees does not qualify as deforestation – even though all the trees are removed at a certain time. In other words, the central idea here is the *intended permanence of a change in land use* from the growing of trees to some other purpose. In that sense, deforestation is a land-use issue more than it is a 'forestry' issue – though the implication for the practice of forestry on the parcels under consideration is profound. This definition removes us from concern for timber management practices (clear-cutting versus selective harvesting) and places our focus on the conversion of land cover and land use.

The matter of deforestation is of concern around the world, but the major issues these days seem to focus on the developing countries, which tend to be situated in the tropics. The issues of concern for deforestation are slash and burn agriculture, the spread of roads into remote areas, rapid population growth, the lack of viable economic opportunities in non-forested areas, cattle ranching, fuelwood gathering, the 'frontier' and its weak or incoherent property institutions, the need for export earnings to service foreign debt, powerful logging interests, and often weak or corrupt governments.

We see increased attention to deforestation in the rather large literature over the recent past, with much of the attention devoted to the circumstances listed immediately above (Allen and Barnes, 1985; Barbier et al. 1991; Deacon, 1994, 1995; Deacon and Murphy, 1997; Sandler, 1993; Southgate et al. 1991; Vincent, 1990). The institutional dimension enters most of these studies through the claimed weakness of government laws, widespread corruption, and the incoherence of property regimes in the forest. My purpose is not to review this literature but rather to offer a somewhat different perspective on the matter of the institutional 'causes and solutions' to deforestation. Because we are interested in the institutional causes of deforestation, the first task is to address the matter of 'causation'.

2 The problem of causation

The definition of deforestation used here shall be that it is the *wilful and permanent transformation of land cover from that which is forested to that which is not*. Notice that this definition precludes the practice of swidden agriculture common in many areas. While swidden agriculture annoys a number of writers, and is often blamed for accelerated soil erosion, it seems best to regard swidden as simply a form of land management in which different kinds of crops (including trees) are used in serial rotation. We see, therefore, that swidden agriculture does not constitute deforestation any more than managed (plantation) forestry constitutes deforestation.

Notice also in my definition of deforestation the emphasis on the *wilful transformation* of land cover and land use. Many 'explanations' of deforestation will focus on population growth, or the building of roads, or incompetent government policies, or the political power of timber concessionaires as the *cause(s)* of deforestation. The problem with such analyses is that they tend to focus too quickly on what seem to be the obvious precursor to deforestation rather than seeking, with greater care, other possible causes. This is to confuse the *first cause* (origin) of an occurrence with the *final cause* (purpose) of an occurrence. It is my contention here that the cause(s) of deforestation can only be determined by giving explicit recognition to the idea of intent. Put somewhat differently, deforestation does not happen by accident or by neglect. It happens because there are purposes to be served by deforestation. Our task is to search for those purposes.

We can see this most clearly if we consider population growth – often cited as a cause of deforestation. Obviously population growth is not *intended to* bring about deforestation. That is, population growth, or migration into forested areas, does not come about *for the purpose of* causing deforestation. Population pressure may be the *origin* (first cause) of deforestation, but it cannot be the *final cause* of deforestation. The idea of final cause requires the establishment of a connection between events and the purpose or intent behind those events. In that sense, final cause can be understood as follows:

> the 'final cause' of an occurrence is an event in the future for the sake of which the occurrence takes place...things are explained by the purposes they serve. When we ask 'why?' concerning an event, we may mean either of two things. We may mean: 'What purpose did this event serve?' or we may mean: 'What earlier circumstances caused this event?' The answer to the former question is a teleological explanation or an explanation by final causes; the answer to the latter question is a mechanistic explanation (Russell, 1945: 67).

This distinction between teleological and mechanistic explanations, I suggest, will be helpful in understanding the causes of deforestation and will, therefore, be essential in formulating meaningful institutional responses to the problem. The search for final cause – the teleological explanation – allows us to go beyond any particular event and to inquire what purpose it is intended to serve in the future. The more common search for cause, on the other hand, tends to look for antecedent conditions, or circumstances that are mechanically related to the event. Consider road building into remote forested regions – an activity that will, in many instances, be followed by deforestation. Can we therefore say that roads 'cause' deforestation? Assume that the roads are pushed into remote areas precisely to gain access to timber. In this case, the desire for access to timber is the *final cause* of the new roads; roads are not the *final cause* of timber being harvested (though roads facilitate timber harvesting). The quest for timber causes roads to be built, so roads are the mechanistic explanation for deforestation – but the quest for timber is the teleological explanation for the construction of roads. Roads are merely the means to the easier acquisition of timber.

Now assume that roads are developed in remote areas for the purpose of allowing sedentary agriculture to flourish where trees now grow; this is the process of land conversion that is of concern to many. Here sedentary agriculture is the *final cause* of the roads and the subsequent deforestation. We now see that when it is said that roads cause deforestation it is analogous to an assertion that roads cause sedentary agriculture. But does it make sense to say that roads *cause* sedentary agriculture? It is rarely expressed that way. Roads allow settlements in the forest, but the issue of final cause must be more carefully considered. Usually it will be said that population growth and poor peasants cause deforestation by creating a demand for agricultural land whose access is denied by thick forests. Roads open up new territory, timber is cut off, and then sedentary agriculture can be established. But these 'explanations' confuse the mechanistic explanation with the teleological explanation. Coherent policy analysis of deforestation can only arise from attention to teleological explanations.

Consider the usual explanation of powerful timber concessionaires as the cause of deforestation. It seems more correct to argue that the quest for timber is the *final cause* of the powerful timber concessionaires, who then become the mechanistic explanation (*the proximate cause*) for deforestation. But, as above, if the activities of the timber companies do not result in a permanent change in land use, then the timber concessionaires are merely the mechanistic explanation for harvesting, but they are not the mechanistic explanation for deforestation (since deforestation is not the same as timber harvesting). We then must decide whether the problem is the harvesting activity or the environmental implications of harvesting, even in the absence of a permanent change in land use.

This emphasis on final cause reminds us that coherent land-use policy in the developing countries requires that we pay attention not just to proximate cause (the mechanistic explanation), but to the purposes for land conversion. That is, we must investigate whose interests are served by such conversion in land cover and land use, and how those interests manage to manipulate the political system so that their purposes can be achieved. These are the core institutional explanations for deforestation to which I now turn.

3 The institutional dimension of deforestation

The foregoing discussion suggests that careful analysis of the institutional dimensions of deforestation has been plagued by the failure to distinguish between mechanistic and teleological explanations. We seem much better at identifying the former than the latter. In an assessment of deforestation and the 'rule of law' – the quintessential institutional explanation – Deacon writes that:

> consistent associations were found between deforestation and political variables reflecting insecure ownership...The explanatory power of the model is fairly low, however, so firm conclusions would be premature...the task of developing analytical models that better illuminate the fundamental causes of deforestation remains. Any such model must recognize that many, possibly most, of the factors taken as causes in popular accounts of deforestation are really determined endogenously...the political indicators of insecure property rights examined here should not be regarded as truly exogenous either...Unraveling this chain of

causation is centrally important to any policy intended to control deforestation or the use of other natural resources. Absent an understanding of these causes, and a firm basis for separating causation from correlation, policy in this area will mistakenly treat symptoms rather than causes (Deacon, 1994: 429).

In a related paper, one year later, Deacon observes that:

> While knowledge of ownership issues is important for understanding the process of deforestation, this knowledge does not point to a straightforward fix. The sheer size, multiplicity of access points, and communal service flows of tropical forests make monitoring and enforcement very costly in some situations and virtually unimaginable in others. Redefining nominal rights in ways that appear to correct inefficiencies in the written law may yield gains in some instances, but an approach to environmental protection that leans heavily on this approach seems directed more at symptoms than causes. Similarly, policy approaches based on the use of Pigovian taxes or marketable permits can be expected to encounter the same monitoring and enforcement problems that keep the market from providing forest services efficiently (Deacon, 1995: 16–17).

Finally, Sandler writes that:

> Tropical deforestation is a complex problem stemming from a host of activities including forest farming, logging, cattle ranching, and large-scale infrastructure projects. The driving forces behind these activities are population pressures, highly skewed land ownership, and/or misdirected government policies (Sandler, 1993: 232).

We see here the results of three careful assessments of the alleged causes of deforestation in the tropics. Do the authors seem confident that they have found the unique causal factors? Not really, unless the catch-all category 'bad policies' is regarded as a cause. But, do *bad policies* constitute a final cause? Does it seem useful to regard 'bad policies' as the *purposes* for which deforestation is the antecedent event? This seems unlikely. Rather, 'bad policies' are the proximate cause which then allow a range of human behaviours to occur whose ultimate impact is deforestation. But what is the final cause – the teleological explanation?

The problem with conventional studies of deforestation, it would seem, is that they have regarded deforestation as the end state requiring explanation and have therefore focused analytical attention upon the antecedent circumstances that appear, at first glance, to 'cause' deforestation – population pressure, road building into remote areas, land-hungry peasants, insecure property rights, and so on. But if we see deforestation not as the end of the causal chain but as an intermediate step along the way, then I believe it allows us to find some much needed clarity in the quest for an explanation for deforestation. That is, the search for a teleological explanation would ask: *what event or circumstance in the future is served by deforestation*? When we locate that event or circumstance, we will have discovered the final cause of deforestation. Lacking this, many of the conventional explanations are seen to be merely mechanistic explanations that focus on antecedent circumstances.

When we understand that deforestation as an event serving some subsequent purpose, it becomes logically necessary to conclude that there are only two possible explanations for deforestation that can satisfy the conditions of final cause: (1) to earn resource rents (revenues) from harvesting trees; and (2) to provide land for other uses. The first of these regards trees as a source of income for the state,[1] while the second of these regards forested land as having an unacceptably high opportunity cost for the state if it remains forested. Indeed, the two 'causes' really collapse into one – the high social opportunity cost of forested land, the conversion of which will provide access to scarce land, with the costs of conversion being partially (or fully) covered by the selling off of the forest cover.[2]

The obvious conclusion from this sequence, it might be thought, takes us back to population growth as the real cause of the high social opportunity cost of land remaining under forest cover. But this would be too simple – and incorrect. Perhaps the final cause is the unwillingness of governments to undertake actions that might relieve the shortage of land for other uses. That is, perhaps forested land has a high social opportunity cost in its current use because of the failure of the government to address the issue of land scarcity elsewhere in the economy. If non-forested land is controlled by a few large landowners, and if the government is unwilling to address the land scarcity brought on by this ownership structure, then the social opportunity cost of forested land is artificially inflated and provides part of the 'justification' for government support of deforestation activities. This brings us back to wilful intent (purpose) and illustrates that population pressing up against scarce land cannot be the *final cause* of deforestation, it only looks that way because governments allow that perception to persist.

We see here the very serious difficulty of building coherent econometric models that offer some hope of actually *explaining* economic phenomena. In other words, we see the difficulty in building sound conceptual models that have empirical content. The usual pattern is to build causal models from the data we have available – miles of road built, population growth, income, security of ownership, and so on. But such models are driven by data availability, not by a conceptual approach that seeks final cause as opposed to mechanistic cause. The empirical problem is obvious: it is difficult to get governments to admit that they are unwilling – or unable – to take actions that will solve the problems associated with landless people. It is equally difficult to get some governments to admit that they need (or want) the revenue from the widespread harvesting and land conversion activities that deforestation entails. That is, the intentions of government policies are difficult to include in an econometric model. Yet the quest for final cause is impossible without reference to intent.

All other alleged explanations are merely mechanistic; as such they provide no insights about policy reform. As long as a particular nation-state is driven by a desire to earn rents from harvesting trees, and as long as land hunger (itself often the result of other policy failures) drives governments to open up remote areas, then very little is to be gained by suggesting that nations stop building roads, or that property rights be made more secure, or that population control be implemented, or that government corruption be rectified, or that the powerful logging interests be reined in. The only way to confront deforestation is to focus on its *final cause*. This causal chain is summarized in Figure 1.

The separation of mechanistic from teleological explanations allows us to focus analytical attention – and policy formulation – on wilful intent by policy-makers. It is no longer adequate to discuss 'bad' policies, or weak governments, or the insecurity of property rights. Indeed, the identification of final causes allows us to see that

Mechanistic Causes	→	*Deforestation*	→	*Final Causes*
Insecure property rights Road building Population pressure Weak/corrupt government Powerful logging interests Bad policies				Earn resource rents Solve land hunger

Figure 1 Mechanistic and final causes of deforestation

governments must *intend* that deforestation occurs – otherwise they would stop it. In other words, deforestation serves the purposes of the government. It is not a matter of bad policy, or of innocence as to why deforestation occurs, or even of incapacity to change deforestation practices. Rather, deforestation serves the purposes of the state and its government. This conclusion is, I suggest, the inevitable conclusion of a careful assessment of the teleological explanation of deforestation.

For social scientists this is not a welcome conclusion. We usually operate with two maintained hypotheses: (1) that most governments generally seek to do what is right by their citizens; and (2) that the only impediment to improved policy is careful analysis and the provision of new information upon which improved policies can be based. This implies that, in the case of deforestation, governments surely wish to know that deforestation is caused by insecure property rights, road building, population pressure, powerful logging interests, and other bad policies. We can then help governments to correct all of these circumstances that 'cause' deforestation.

However, this approach is misguided since it ignores the real *causes* of deforestation. Careful assessment of deforestation in the developing world would reveal that most governments know precisely what they are doing and why they are doing it. If this is the case, then it is a very different challenge to tell governments that they should stop seeking to earn revenue from their forests or that they should not try to solve the land hunger problem. On the other hand, this realization opens up other avenues for assisting governments to deal with deforestation. Perhaps land hunger can be addressed by other policy reforms? Perhaps we need to be more sensitive in our discussions with policy-makers about the costs of deforestation? It is not very helpful to plead with such individuals that deforestation is contributing to global warming; nor is it useful to ask them to save those assets (forests) while failing to help with the very real problem of land hunger. In other words, as I suggested at the outset, deforestation is less about 'forestry' than it is about economic policy in general, and land-use policy in particular.

4 Getting institutions right

If we start from the realization that deforestation happens not by accident or neglect but because governments intend for it to happen, then we gain a certain clarity on a problem that has been blamed on a number of disparate causes and circumstances. As above, it certainly brings a different perspective to discussions with government officials who may be understandably reluctant to admit the obvious. If we assume that some governments genuinely seek to reverse decades of deforestation, then it will be necessary to insist that these new intentions must be accompanied by a serious change in *de facto* and *de jure* circumstances. That is, we may well find that governments have, in the past, expressed concern about deforestation but have been unwilling or unable to do much to stop it. This disjuncture between words and deeds is not lost on most observers and generates, in time, a level of cynicism that must be rectified.

In simple terms, if the government is serious about change then a necessary condition is the introduction of the rule of law and judicial oversight on government action. It is safe to generalize by saying that environmental progress is largely limited to those countries that have a judicial branch that stands independent of the government of the day. Of course an enlightened and well-intentioned government can make good progress, but when a different government comes in all of the earlier progress might easily be overturned. Unless there is an institutionalized anchoring of environmental policy, real progress is certain to be elusive. Part of this institutionalized anchoring must be in terms of the rules of land use – property regimes. That is, we must start with the legal arrangements that define land-use practices in general, and forested land use in particular. These legal arrangements indicate who may exercise decision control over the way the land is managed, and hence such legal arrangements are the essence of what we mean by the terms *ownership* of land.

Consider the private ownership of a forested plot. We say that the owner has the *right* to exercise managerial control over that land and all others (non-owners) have a *duty* to respect the integrity of the ownership interest of the individual with rights. All rights require correlated duties; the essence of a right for one party is a duty for all other parties. Under this legal arrangement, if the private owner chooses to exercise the right of ownership by undertaking widespread deforestation, others who may be offended at this have no legitimate basis to object. Should a political movement arise to protest this action the owner would be able to claim that his actions were protected by his right of ownership. In the absence of a change in the law, those who found this action unacceptable would have no recourse.

While the institutional dimension of private ownership seems clear, things are not always as clear as they may seem. The Endangered Species Act in the United States can prevent the cutting of trees essential to habitat preservation for certain endangered species on private land. Thus, the presumptive rights of private landowners to undertake actions that may constitute deforestation are now restricted; deforestation is against the law in some places. And by 'being against the law' we mean that a judicial structure stands ready to enforce legal relations. While trite in some respects, it is not uncommon – especially in the developing world – to have laws that no one expects to be enforced. To *have* laws is not necessarily to *live* by laws; laws are only meaningful if they are enforced. That is what I mean by the 'rule of law'. The point is not one of merely having laws, but having institutional structures in place to force the unwilling to follow the law.

Of course it is one thing to force a private landowner to follow the law; it is a very different matter to force a government agency to follow the law. But in the US, government agencies are constantly being sued to force them to follow the law. The US Forest Service is sued by some environmental groups to force it to manage the national forests in keeping with certain multiple-use laws; the Environmental Protection

Agency is sued by another environmental group to force it to reconsider its standards for 'clean' water; the US Department of Agriculture is sued by yet another group to force it to monitor pesticide applications more closely; and the Corps of Engineers is sued by yet another group to prevent it from violating wetlands being protected by some state department of natural resources. Finally, the US Fish and Wildlife Service (in the Department of the Interior) may go to court to prevent the Bureau of Reclamation (also in the Department of the Interior) from doing something to a river that will destroy some endangered species. All of these are illustrations of what it means to have an institutional structure based on judicial oversight.

Returning to the problem of deforestation, we need to focus very briefly on the rule of law as it pertains to property relations. The majority of the world's forested areas are on common-property land or on government land (state property). By state property I mean land where ownership and control over natural resource use and management rest in the hands of the state and the management responsibility is assigned to government agencies. National forests and national parks are examples of state-property regimes. The state may either directly manage and control the use of state-owned natural resources through government agencies, or it may lease the natural resource to groups or individuals who are given usufruct rights for a specified period of time. State-property regimes remove managerial discretion from the user and situate it, instead, in government agencies.

When enforcement is present – when there is the rule of law – national parks and forest preserves ensure that the natural resources under such management regimes will be conserved for future generations. To be successful, such regimes require governmental structures and functions that can match policy pronouncements with meaningful administrative capacity. The more frequent situation, unfortunately, tends to be that of grand policy pronouncements about protecting forests and then a lack of serious enforcement consistent with the declared intentions. This can happen because of an absence of knowledge about proper use, or it can arise because of inadequate funding to make timely enforcement decisions. More seriously, deforestation occurs in such property regimes when those with political connections manage to regard the national forests as their own private domain, despite the official declarations of an intent to protect forested areas under a state-property regime. As indicated previously, it is not the pronouncements of government that matter in the domain of deforestation; rather, it is the real *intentions* that give meaning to the search for final causes.

When we leave state property, much of deforestation occurs on land that is under common-property regimes. Here intentions matter as well. First, we find many common-property regimes in which there has been a breakdown in compliance with the accepted management rules by those who are legitimate co-owners of the regime. If economic opportunities elsewhere in the local economy are limited then there will be insufficient capacity to absorb the increased population of those who are legitimate users of the forest resources under the regime of common property. Moreover, if spreading privatization in the land base of the surrounding area precludes seasonal adaptation to fluctuating resource conditions – a problem of particular importance in semi-arid grazing regimes – then excessive harvesting of a local forest resource may be necessary for survival by members of the group. This problem represents a form of disintegration of the *internal authority* of the property regime.

The pressure on common-property regimes arises for the same reason that state-property regimes are under pressure – the inability of the government to solve the fundamental problem of economic opportunity beyond the forest. This is exacerbated by the fact that governments often hold common property in low esteem. Many governments disregard the interests of those segments of the population dependent upon common-property regimes and so external threats to forested areas in common-property regimes will not receive the same governmental response as would a threat to private property. This problem is really no different from the situation in which the government is unable – or unwilling – to enforce the management rules on its own forested areas. With common-property regimes the willingness of the government to protect forest resources in common property is partly explained by the government's perception of the political and economic importance of those dependent upon the common areas. If those threatening village forests enjoy political favour from the state then the protection of common forests will be indifferent at best. This pressure represents a disintegration of the *external legitimacy* of the property regime.

When that happens, a common-property regime becomes a *de facto* open access regime, with the logical implication that aspiring users are free to behave as they wish without regard for the interests of those dependent upon the natural resources (Bromley, 1989). In essence, when governments fail to take actions that may stop deforestation, they are sanctioning the idea that a nation's forested area is simply an open access regime, available to whoever desires its bounty. This is precisely how much deforestation proceeds and persists.

5 Conclusions

The fundamental problem in land-use policy in the world is that, in many settings, forest cover is seen as an impediment to economic development. Indeed, forest cover is at the extensive margin as that concept is normally applied. Because of this, many governments imagine – or are pressured to imagine – that forests stand in the way of economic development. At the same time, the past two decades have seen extraordinary attention to land use and land cover in the poorer nations as the extent of the world's forest cover has become an international issue. No one was paying attention when, in the early history of the US, large tracts of land were denuded of forest cover in the most savage and wasteful manner.[3] As the European immigrants moved west across the new nation, magnificent trees fell in their wake. This was, at the time, regarded as 'progress'.

Today, inhabitants of nations seeking 'progress' are told, instead, that the trees must be left standing. When they are told that by representatives of the developed world – places where old-growth timber is the rarest of natural assets – they are not amused. And who can blame them? Global climate change and the press for biodiversity have combined to bring extraordinary public scrutiny to land-use matters that are properly issues of national sovereignty. But then traditional ideas of national sovereignty in the face of global implications are outdated.

The clear identification of the final causes of deforestation adds, I believe, clarity and promise to the struggle over sovereignty with respect to natural resource use in the developing world. The cause of deforestation is no longer a mystery, and it is no longer a problem that arises because of the uncontrollable acts of millions of poor and scattered peasants and loggers throughout the tropics. When we realize that deforestation occurs because governments wish for it to happen, we can begin a policy dialogue with a much more focused set of participants. If those in the developed world wish for tropical deforestation to cease, then it is clear to whom the necessary economic incentives must be directed for that to happen. And it is no longer credible for the governments in the tropics to wring their hands in frustration – protesting that they know not what to do about the problem.

Notes

1. A second way that some governments undervalue the forest is by failing to extract much of the rents that accrue to those given the opportunity to harvest timber.
2. This is the approach taken by Deacon (1995). He assumed that the agricultural good produced from the newly liberated lands was exported and the revenues were then used to import a manufactured good. The net effect on deforestation was indeterminate. When deforestation occurred to earn revenues for the state, the results also depended on the assumptions employed. Deacon did not undertake empirical work in this paper but surveyed other works for insights about the effects. He notes that '...the empirical basis for identifying sources of deforestation and linking them to governmental policies is very meager at present. Hence, the conclusions reached and policies recommended in the deforestation literature lean heavily on logical reasoning. The lack of empirical evidence magnifies the importance of using an explicit analytical framework when drawing conclusions about this important policy issue. More importantly, perhaps, it strongly suggests that it is now time for those interested in deforestation to shift the direction of research away from the descriptive accounts and *a priori* reasoning and toward the careful empirical analysis needed to document the relationships involved and to measure their magnitudes' (Deacon, 1995: 17).
3. Parts of the upper Midwest are still referred to as the 'cut-over' region.

References

Allen, Julia C. and Douglas F. Barnes (1985), 'The causes of deforestation in developing countries', *Annals of the Association of American Geographers*, **75** (2), 163–84.

Barbier, E.T., J.C. Burgess and A. Markandya (1991), 'The economics of tropical deforestation', *Ambio*, **20** (2), 55–8.

Bromley, Daniel W. (1989), 'Property relations and economic development: the other land reform', *World Development*, **17** (6), 867–77.

Deacon, Robert T. (1994), 'Deforestation and the rule of law in a cross-section of countries', *Land Economics*, **70** (4), 414–30.

Deacon, Robert T. (1995), 'Assessing the relationship between government policy and deforestation', *Journal of Environmental Economics and Management*, **28** (1), 1–18.

Deacon, Robert T. and Paul Murphy (1997), 'The structure of an environmental transaction: the debt-for-nature swap', *Land Economics*, **73** (1), 1–24.

Russell, Bertrand (1945), *A History of Western Philosophy*, New York: Simon and Schuster.

Sandler, Todd (1993), 'Tropical deforestation: markets and market failures', *Land Economics*, **69** (3), 225–33.

Southgate, Douglas, Rodrigo Sierra and Lawrence Brown (1991), 'The causes of tropical deforestation in Ecuador: a statistical analysis', *World Development*, **19** (9), 1145–51.

Vincent, J.R. (1990), 'Rent capture and the feasibility of tropical forest management', *Land Economics*, **66** (2), 212–23.

Name index